KT-462-965

Cézanne

This is the second volume in a
series by Henri Perruchot entitled
ART AND DESTINY
Further titles will include the
biography of
MANET

Portrait of Cézanne, 1874. By Camille Pissarro.

HENRI PERRUCHOT

Cézanne

TRANSLATED BY HUMPHREY HARE

PERPETUA BOOKS

First published by
PERPETUA LIMITED
32 Newton Road
London W.2
and distributed for them by
Michael Joseph Ltd
26 Bloomsbury Street
London W.C.1
1961

Set and printed in Great Britain by Tonbridge Printers Ltd, Peach Hall Works, Tonbridge, Kent, in Bembo eleven on thirteen point, on paper made by Henry Bruce at Currie, Midlothian, and bound by James Burn at Esher, Surrey

Foreword & Acknowledgements

CÉZANNE was a secret man. Those who knew him have left behind contradictory portraits which are not the least of the biographer's difficulties. I have, however, tried to assemble in this book everything that is known about him today; I have read and compared all the known documents concerning him; I have visited the places where he lived and seen the landscapes and the things he knew. I have written nothing I cannot justify.

I wish to acknowledge a particular debt to Mr John Rewald's brilliant and scholarly works on Cézanne and the History of Impressionism; also to the valuable studies of MM. Lionello Venturi, Gerstle Mack, Bernard Dorival and Jean de Beucken. I would also like to express my gratitude to Mme Émile Bernard, who kindly placed her family archives at my disposal and furnished me with important unpublished information, and to Mme É. Blondel-Flory, MM. R. Avezou, Michel-Ange Bernard, Jules Joëts, Hubert Juin, Émile Lombard, Henry de Madaillan, Victor Nicollas and Lucien Noël, who have supplied me with documents, helped me to authenticate various details or drawn my attention to useful sources of information.

H. P.

Contents

FOREWORD & ACKNOWLEDGEMENTS 7

ILLUSTRATIONS 11

PROLOGUE 19

PART ONE

A Vocation (1839–1862)

I The Little Box of Water Colours 27

II School and Friendships 31

III 'I, Too, am a Painter' 47

IV The Attics of Paris 67

V The Bank 74

PART TWO

Impatience (1862–1872)

I Le Déjeuner sur l'Herbe 81
II Experiments 91
III Battles 100
IV 'He Dreams of Huge Pictures' 110
V The Peace of the Sea 129

PART THREE

The Painter Abused (1872–1882)

I The Banks of the Oise 139
II The Public 152
III The Shouting and the Silence 160
IV Storms 180
V Resignation 187

PART FOUR

Mont Sainte-Victoire (1882–1895)

I Isolation 203
II The Bell-Tower of Gardanne 211
III Claude Lantier 217
IV The Big Pine 228

PART FIVE

The Lyricism of Evening (1895–1906)

I Ambroise Vollard 255
II The Springtime of the World 263
III The Bonfire at the Jas 279
IV The Old Man of the Rue Boulegon 289
V The Last Season 300

CHRONOLOGY 321
BIBLIOGRAPHY 329
INDEX 341

Illustrations

In the knowledge that there are several fine albums of colour reproductions of Cézanne's paintings available, the publishers have not attempted to reproduce his work in this biography. Instead, all the known photographs of Cézanne have been gathered together for the first time. Unfortunately, Cézanne was rarely photographed and the pictorial gaps in his life are considerable. Several of the prints were badly damaged or out of focus, but their rarity justifies their inclusion.

The publishers extend their thanks to the many people who have made this material available, but in particular to the grandson of the artist, M. Jean-Pierre Cézanne, who placed the family archives at our disposal; M. Louis Malbos, Director of the Musée Granet, Aix-en-Provence, for his close co-operation; the Atelier Cézanne; the Bibliothèque Méjanes, Aix; and the Galerie Bernheim-Jeune, Paris. Wherever possible the source of each picture is given in the list of illustrations.

1. *Back of frontispiece*

   Memorial plaque to Cézanne at the corner of Rue des Chapeliers, Aix-en-Provence. By Renoir.
   Photo: Henry Ely-Aix

2. *Frontispiece*

   Portrait of Cézanne, 1874. By Camille Pissarro.
   Collection: R. von Hirsch, Basle
   Photo: Bulloz

BETWEEN PAGES 48 AND 49.

3. Louis-Auguste Cézanne, the artist's father.
Collection: Jean-Pierre Cézanne

4. Rose Cézanne, the artist's sister, *c.* 1880.
Collection: G. Mack

5. Marie Cézanne, the artist's sister, *c.* 1870.
Collection: G. Mack

6. Paul Cézanne: Self-portrait from a photograph, *c.* 1861.
Photo: Bulloz

7. Paul Cézanne, 1861. The earliest known photograph (aged 22).
Collection: Jean-Pierre Cézanne

8. Book of manuscript music copied out by Cézanne at the age of 16, when second Cornet player in the school band at Aix.
Collection: Jean-Pierre Cézanne

9. Émile Zola, aged 25 (1865).
Collection: Famille Zola

10. Drawing by Cézanne illustrating a letter to Zola, 20 June, 1859 (aged 20).
Collection: Unknown

11. Paul Cézanne, aged about 32 (*c.* 1871).
Photo: Léo Larguier

12. Le Jas de Bouffan, Aix-en-Provence.
Photo: Crespi

BETWEEN PAGES 112 AND 113.

13. Paul Cézanne on the way to his 'Motif,' near Auvers-sur-Oise, 1873.
Collection: Atelier Cézanne, Aix-en-Provence

14. 'Sur le Motif,' 1875. (Standing, left to right) Lucien Pissarro, Cézanne, Camille Pissarro.
Collection: Jean-Pierre Cézanne

15. Pissarro and Cézanne, *c.* 1873.
Photo: Roger-Viollet

16. Portrait of Cézanne, *c.* 1873. Drawing by Camille Pissarro.
Collection: Louvre, Paris. Photo: Louvre

17. Paul Cézanne (seated) in Camille Pissarro's garden at Pontoise, *c.* 1873. (Standing, left to right) Lucien Pissarro, Rodo Pissarro, Paul-Émile Pissarro and Camille Pissarro.
Collection: Jean-Pierre Cézanne

18. Paul Cézanne on the road near Auvers-sur-Oise, 1873.
Collection: Jean-Pierre Cézanne

19. Paul Cézanne, *c.* 1875. Photograph given by Cézanne to Achille Emperaire.
Collection: Atelier Cézanne, Aix-en-Provence

20. Paul Cézanne: Self-portrait, *c.* 1875.
Collection: Louvre, Paris

21. Cézanne: a contemporary caricature by 'Stock', referring to the incident at the Palais de l'Industrie, 20 March, 1870.
Collection: Musée Granet, Aix-en-Provence. Photo: Henry Ely-Aix

BETWEEN PAGES 176 AND 177.

22. Paul Cézanne, aged about 36 (*c.* 1875).
Collection: Jean-Pierre Cézanne

23. Portrait of Cézanne, *c.* 1880. Lithograph by Renoir.
Collection: Musée Granet, Aix-en-Provence. Photo: Henry Ely-Aix

24. Renoir at the Château des Brouillards, Montmartre, in the early 1890s.
Collection: Jean-Pierre Cézanne

25. Père Tanguy: Bill for paints supplied to Cézanne (undated).
Collection: Jean-Pierre Cézanne

26. Émile Zola, *c.* 1877.
Collection: Hachette. Photo: Pierre Petit

27. Père Tanguy: Account for the sale of paintings by Cézanne between 1873–1885.
Collection: Jean-Pierre Cézanne

28. Paul Cézanne in his Paris studio, 1894.
Collection: Jean-Pierre Cézanne

29. Paul Cézanne at Barbizon, Fontainebleau Forest, 1894.
Collection: Jean-Pierre Cézanne

BETWEEN PAGES 240 AND 241.

30. Paul Cézanne, 1889. Photograph for his card of admission as exhibitor in the International Exhibition, 1900.
Collection: Jean-Pierre Cézanne

31. Victor Chocquet.
Collection: Jean-Pierre Cézanne

32. Portrait of Victor Chocquet. Drawing by Cézanne. (*c.* 1877–82)
Private Collection: Basle

33. Paul Cézanne, fils. Drawing by Cézanne.
Collection: Jean-Pierre Cézanne

34. Paul Cézanne, fils.
Collection: Jean-Pierre Cézanne

35. Hortense Cézanne, the artist's wife, *c.* 1900.
Collection: Jean-Pierre Cézanne

36. Hortense Cézanne towards the end of her life, with her niece, Mademoiselle Conil, and grand-daughter.
Collection: Jean-Pierre Cézanne

37. Paul Cézanne in his studio at Aix, seated in front of the small version of his painting, 'Bathers.' A photograph taken by Émile Bernard (1904).
Courtesy Michel-Ange Bernard. Collection: Jean-Pierre Cézanne

38. Cézanne's studio in the Chemin des Lauves, Aix-en-Provence, (*c.* 1906).
Photo: Jouven

39. Paul Cézanne in the garden of his studio at Aix, with Gaston and Madame Bernheim de Villers (*c.* 1904).
Collection: Bernheim-Jeune Photo: Josse Bernheim-Jeune.

40.–42. Cézanne at Les Lauves, Aix, *c.* 1904. Photographs by Gaston Bernheim de Villers and Josse Bernheim-Jeune.

43. Paul Cézanne and Gaston Bernheim de Villers at Les Lauves, Aix, *c.* 1904.
Collection: Bernheim-Jeune Photo: Josse Bernheim-Jeune.

44. 'Hommage à Cézanne,' 1904. By Émile Bernard.
Collection: Musée Granet, Aix-en-Provence. Photo: Henry Ely-Aix

BETWEEN PAGES 304 AND 305.

45. Paul Cézanne in the countryside near Aix. A photograph taken by Émile Bernard (1904).
Courtesy: Michel-Ange Bernard. Collection: Atelier Cézanne, Aix-en-Provence

46.–48. Cézanne 'Sur le Motif' in the last year of his life. Photographs by the painter K. X. Roussel at Les Lauves, Aix, 1906.
Collection: Bernheim-Jeune

49. Paul Cézanne and Maurice Denis, Les Lauves, Aix, 1906.
Photo: K. X. Roussel

50. 'Cézanne working at Les Lauves, 1906.' Painting by Maurice Denis (seated, right).
Courtesy: Madame Boulet, Clermont de l'Oise. Photo: Henry Ely-Aix

51. 'Cézanne at Work.' Painting by Hermann Paul, the caricaturist, after a sketch from life, 1906.
Collection: Musée Granet, Aix-en-Provence. Photo: Henry Ely-Aix

52. 'Un Cézanne rêveur.' Terracotta bust by Philippe Solari, *c.* 1904.
Collection: Musée Granet, Aix-en-Provence. Photo: Henry Ely-Aix

53. Posthumous bronze of Cézanne by the Fauve painter, Louis Valtat (1869–1952).
Bibliothèque Méjanes, Aix-en-Provence. Photo: Henry Ely-Aix

54. Le Château Noir, Aix-en-Provence.
Photo: Henry Ely-Aix

55. Monument to Cézanne at the Château Noir, Aix, by Edith Vieil-Noë (1873–1935), born at Le Château Noir in which her mother, Madame Jules Vieil, rented a room to Cézanne in 1899. The clay sketch was made during the life of Cézanne and the bust completed *c.* 1925–1927.
Courtesy: Musée Granet, Aix-en-Provence. Photo: Henry Ely-Aix

56. Bust of Cézanne (*c.* 1921) by Henri Pontier (1842–1926), Director of the École des Beaux Arts, Aix, and Director of the Musée Granet at the time of Cézanne's death.
Collection: Madame Giraud, Aix-en-Provence. Photo: Henry Ely-Aix

57. Cézanne's studio in the Chemin des Lauves, Aix. A photograph taken after the death of Cézanne at the time of Marcel Provence.
Collection: Atelier Cézanne, Aix-en-Provence

IN TEXT

Page 270 Cézanne: Letter to Joachim Gasquet.
Collection: Bibliothèque Méjanes, Aix-en-Provence

Page 311 Cézanne: Letter written to his son during the last months of his life.
Collection: Jean-Pierre Cézanne

Page 317 Funeral announcement of Paul Cézanne. The date of death is incorrect. Cézanne died on 22 October, 1906. The 'error' was intentional so that the interment might be postponed, without violation of the letter of the law, long enough to permit Cézanne's wife and son to reach Aix in time for the ceremony (G. Mack).
Collection: Jean-Pierre Cézanne

Illustrations 1, 21, 23, 44, 50, 51, 52, 53, 54, 55, and 56 supplied by the Photo Service of the Musée Granet, Aix-en-Provence, by courtesy of the Director M. Louis Malbos.

Cézanne

PROLOGUE

PROLOGUE

My father was a man of genius; he left me an income of twenty-five thousand francs.—CÉZANNE

IT was the year 1850. For more than half a century Aix-en-Provence had been asleep. It had once been a capital, but was now only a sub-prefecture. It had reached its apogee during the seventeenth and eighteenth centuries, when the great families of the district, the Vauvenargues, the Estienne d'Orves, the Raousset-Boulbon, the Forbin, the Saint-Marc and many others, built their fine town houses on the Cours. But those days were over. 'Aix is Pompeii,' Louise Colet said.

In 1850, aristocratic Aix still numbered seven hundred names, but it had outlived itself and was no more than an echo from the past. Its survivors lived parsimonious lives immured in their old town houses among their period furniture, and formed a sad, narrow and invisible society, jealous of its past and of its lost wealth. On Sundays, a solitary sedan chair was to be seen; it belonged to the Marquise de la Garde, and she passed by like a vision from another age. Indeed this was what she was, for she remembered being presented to Marie Antoinette at Versailles. But the only chairmen she could now obtain were the undertaker's men whom she dressed in her livery. Even for 1850, Mme de la Garde was a surprising anachronism; and so was the imaginary frontier that separated the two sides of the Cours, the southern alley being reserved for people of quality, and the northern for plebeians.*

The Aix-en-Provence of 1850 was becoming bourgeois and commercial. The Cours, the heart of the town, where only cafés had been allowed before the Revolution, now harboured stage-coach and carriers' offices. Under Louis Philippe, a Faculty of Letters, a School of Arts and Crafts as well as secondary schools had been founded. The first gas lamps were being erected and a cattle market had been opened. For the last four years, an engineer named François Zola, had been building a canal to improve the water supply, though the town already

* This separation continued until 1918.

possessed thirty fountains. A railway between Aix and Rognac was also under construction. Yet, Aix stood apart from the stir of the real industrial revolution. Aix preferred dreaming of what she had once been rather than of what she might become. Except for hats and sweets, there were no industries. Noisy, populous, industrial Marseilles had already ousted her supremacy. Now Aix wished merely to retain certain prerogatives as an academic town and the seat of both the Court of Appeal and the Archbishop. Priests and canons, professors and magistrates strolled under the plane trees of the Cours, which now replaced the old elms from which a handful of nobles had been hanged during the Revolution. Aix was devout; and though the dowagers and elderly aristocrats were to some extent characteristic of the old capital of Provence, the soutane was far from lacking in importance. The town was crowded with Franciscans and Jesuits; and they lent a special atmosphere to the languid, melancholy charm of its silent streets in which the fountains splashed.

* * *

Among the twenty-seven thousand inhabitants of Aix, there was one man who was a constant subject of conversation. He was not popular; the nobility ignored him; the middle-classes held aloof from him, and secretly envied him; and the lower classes either admired him or were jealous of him.

His name was Louis Auguste Cézanne. He was fifty-two years old. A rather tall man with a heavy clean-shaven face, he had a high forehead, retreating hair, and two deeply incised lines between his thick eyebrows. He seemed a typical Louis Philippe bourgeois: stout of body and innocent of intellectual aspirations. There was a hardness, but also a certain irony, in his expression. No one doubted that he was a shrewd man; and he was to give abundant proof of it.

Some two hundred years earlier, at the very time of Aix's splendour, a poor family who had been living at Cézanne, a little village in the Alps, emigrated to Briançon. They had not travelled very far, a mere twenty-four kilometres over the Mont Genèvre Pass which had in its day given passage to Hannibal, Caesar and Charles VIII. Nor can they have felt very much out of their element, since Cézanne, a village of

French traditions and language, was, and had been for a long time, part of the Briançonnais.* On changing districts, the family adopted the name of their village of origin. They became known as Cézanne, Cézane or Césane; the spelling was to vary for some time to come.

The Cézannes made no fortune in Briançon. One of them, Blaise, became a cobbler and was richer in progeny than he was in money. Some of his ten children took to the road again, and at least one of them arrived in Aix before 1700. His name was Denis, and though his family too proliferated, it did not grow rich. They were wig-makers and tailors and seemed unlikely to rise above their modest circumstances until Thomas François Xavier, a grandson of Denis Cézanne, who was born in 1756, again sought to better his luck elsewhere. He left Aix and set himself up as a tailor some twenty kilometres to the south-east, beyond Mont Regaignas, in the little town of Saint-Zacharie. In 1818 he died, having fared neither better nor worse than his relatives. But he left a son, the Louis Auguste Cézanne with whom we are at present concerned.

Born at Saint-Zacharie during the Directoire, on 10 Messidor in the Year VI (28 June, 1798), Louis Auguste had been a sickly child. But as he grew older, his health improved and, by the time his father died, he was a strong young man possessed of considerable vitality. He was also very ambitious and, realising that Saint-Zacharie was unlikely to afford him any opportunity of rising above his family's lowly estate, he moved to Aix, where he found employment with a family of wool merchants named Dethès.

At the beginning of the nineteenth century, hat-making, one of the small, traditional Aix industries, was prospering. The neighbouring farmers raised rabbits and factories in the town processed the hair into felt. In 1821, when he was twenty-three, Louis Auguste decided to make himself an expert in the hat-making trade and went off to Paris for instruction.

* The names of the families living in Cézanne at that period were entirely French: Blanchet, Bouvier, Roux, Martin, Faure, Tisserand, Poncet, Manson, etc. In 1713, by the Treaty of Utrecht, Cézanne was involved in the fate of the Briançonnais valleys on the eastern slopes, which were exchanged by France for the valley of Barcelonnette. Later, when the names were Italianised, Cézanne became Césana.

He remained in the capital for four years, working hard and becoming in turn apprentice, skilled workman and clerk in the office. His employer thought highly of him; so, it was said, did his employer's wife, though doubtless for other reasons. To a less ambitious young man, his position might well have seemed ideal; but not to Louis Auguste. In 1825, he returned to Aix, determined to make a position for himself. He was then twenty-seven.

He must have managed to save a certain amount of money in Paris for, on his return to Aix, he took a man named Martin into partnership and opened a hat-shop, wholesale and retail, at 55, Le Cours, on the corner of the Rue des Grands-Carmes.* It is probable that the two partners soon found they had insufficient capital, for they took in a third, a certain Coupin, who was as shrewd as Louis Auguste, and the house of Martin, Coupin and Cézanne was founded. The people of Aix thought they were mad. In the cafés on the Cours, there was a current joke which made play of the name of Cézanne (seize ânes – sixteen donkeys), and they said: 'Martin, Coupin and Cézanne add up to eighteen asses.'†

The joke was not, however, a very pertinent one since the 'eighteen asses' soon made it plain to the people of Aix that their business was expanding rapidly. Louis Auguste had taken the first step towards making his fortune.

Indeed, nothing mattered to Louis Auguste but money; it was the one indubitable sign of success. He was shrewd, intelligent and inventive, prudent, though he could be daring on occasion, clever, hard and meticulous; he spared neither himself nor others. He was tyrannical and hot-tempered, sober by temperament and parsimonious by necessity. Utterly single-minded in his determination to make a fortune, he accumulated *louis* upon *louis*. Ardent though his temperament might have been, it was not until he was forty, and his hatter's business soundly established, that he took a girl of twenty-four as his mistress. Her name

* The Rue des Grands-Carmes is today the Rue Fabrot.

† There is still a faded sign on the front of the shop announcing: 'Chapellerie du Cours Mirabeau, Gros et Détail.' But, contrary to the opinion of a local scholar, Marcel Provence, this certainly cannot be the sign of the house of Martin, Coupin and Cézanne, since the Cours only became the Cours Mirabeau half a century later, in 1876.

was Anne Élisabeth Honorine Aubert, the daughter of a chair-maker and the sister of one of his employees.* From this liaison was born a son, Paul, on 19 January, 1839, and two years later a daughter, Marie, on 4 July, 1841, both of whom Louis Auguste acknowledged at their birth. He nevertheless waited nearly three years more before making up his mind to regularise the liaison. He eventually married Élisabeth Aubert on 29 January, 1844, when he was forty-five years of age.

There can be no doubt that his capital assets at this time were already considerable for, in the following year the three partners separated, and Louis Auguste not only remained as sole proprietor but also extended his activities in other directions.

The breeders who supplied the rabbit-skins to the Aix industry were frequently short of cash. Louis Auguste had from time to time advanced them money, on interest, so that his business should not suffer from a lack of raw materials. He quickly realised how profitable these operations might be. He expanded them and soon became money-lender to a great number of people both in Aix and the neighbourhood. He gradually gave up hat-making, and money-lending became his major interest. There were, however, certain difficulties in expanding this interest, for at that time the Bargès Bank, in the Rue de l'Ancienne-Madeleine, largely monopolised the business. Cézanne père realised he must found another bank to compete with it. It was undoubtedly taking a risk but events played into his hands. In 1848, the Bargès Bank failed. Determined to replace it, he approached the cashier of the late bank, whose name was Cabassol. This man had no money, but an extensive experience of local banking. They came to terms at once and signed a renewable contract of partnership for five years and three months. Cabassol was to contribute his 'industry' and his expert knowledge while Louis Auguste put up the capital.† Profits were to be shared equally. The Cézanne and Cabassol Bank opened on 1 June with a capital of one hundred thousand gold francs.‡

* * *

By 1850, the Cézanne and Cabassol Bank had been in business for

* She was born in Aix on 24 September, 1814.

† From archives in the Aix-en-Provence Registry Office.

‡ Approximately £17,000 today.

two years and was flourishing. Each as shrewd as the other, and equally in love with money, the two partners allowed themselves no single luxury. They drew no more than four thousand francs a year between them for personal expenditure;* though Louis Auguste enjoyed five per cent interest on his capital, which gave him a supplementary income of five thousand francs.† He had, however, never been in the habit of spending money and success did not change him. When disposing of his hatter's business, he had put aside some top hats for important occasions, as well as a number of caps with flaps and long peaks for daily wear, thus providing himself with headgear for the rest of his life. '*As vi lou liché daou pero Cézanne* (have you seen old Cézanne's spade)?' people said of Louis Auguste's cap. But he pretended not to hear. He was contemptuous of the old dowagers in their silk dresses and the elderly aristocrats in their starched shirts. He well knew their financial circumstances were deplorable and that he could buy up most of them despite his untidy clothes and the heavy boots of untanned leather he had adopted because they required no polishing. Louis Auguste knew the precise financial circumstances of every inhabitant of Aix.

He was soon to show Aix just how successful he was by buying a fine country house, the Jas de Bouffan, which had been built by M. de Villars, when Governor of Provence. For this he paid eighty thousand gold francs.‡

Now that he had made a fortune and assured the future of his family, what more could he want? Yet, having satisfied his own ambitions, he did want something more – he wanted his children to continue his work and increase the family power. And for Louis Auguste Cézanne power was synonymous with money. To make and multiply money were the only reasonable human activities.

His son, Paul, must one day succeed him; and the bank of Cézanne and Cabassol become the Paul Cézanne bank.

When he eventually died at the age of eighty-eight, he left one million two hundred thousand gold francs.§

* Approximately £350 today.
† About £875 today.
‡ Approximately £14,000 today.
§ Approximately £210,000 today.

A Vocation

PART ONE

[1839-1862]

CHAPTER ONE

The Little Box of Water-colours

> The other day, I saw the young daughter of a friend of mine with a box of colours. To think of putting such tools into a child's hands!—DEGAS

THE old house which contained the shop of Martin, Coupin and Cézanne, was separated from the other houses on the Cours by the Rue des Grands-Carmes on the west and by a narrow alley, the Passage Agard, on the east. This was a short cut between the Cours and the Palais de Justice. The door to the flat above the shop was under the arch over the entrance to the alley.

Louis Auguste's son, Paul, had not been born in the house on the Cours. For her lying-in his mother had gone to 28, Rue de l'Opéra, which was a prolongation of the Cours. This may well have been an attempt to avoid gossip. But she was apparently not so concerned twenty-nine months later, when Marie, Paul's sister, was born, since on that occasion she remained at home.

In front of the shop, under the trees, Paul played amid the light and colour of the busy life of the Cours. On this, the plebeian side, which was also the side of life and sunshine, the coaches arrived from Avignon, Marseilles and the Var. On market days the big wagons, painted yellow, red and green, came in from the country and drovers in blue smocks brought in herds of cows and flocks of sheep. The terraces of the cafés were full of men smoking clay pipes and playing cards over a bottle of Palette wine; the sun patterned their brown coats and sky-blue smocks with green reflections and violet shadows. This was the Provence of the peasants and there was much gaiety and laughter.

Paul's mother – a tall, dark handsome woman still under thirty – had difficulty in keeping him under control. The moment she took her eyes off him, he wandered off among the crowd and the animals, sniffing the rich odours of the Aix countryside, garlic, olive, pepper, tomato and aubergine, which mingled with the acrid smell of sheep come down from the heights of the Trévaresse.

At four years old, Paul Cézanne was an odd child, and not always a very agreeable one. He already had his father's temper and obstinacy and, when he was thwarted, stamped his feet in almost hysterical rage, which would cease as suddenly as it had begun. On the other hand, he was very affectionate; he was devoted to his sister Marie, adored his mother, and was fond of his father, though he feared him. One stern word from that authoritative voice and Paul became silent and still. But, indeed, no one in the house dared murmur when Louis Auguste had spoken.

Business continuing to prosper, the Cézannes moved to a larger house in a quiet, though dark and tortuous street, the Rue de la Glacière, and on 29 January, 1844, when Paul was just five years old, his parents regularised their relationship by marriage.

Paul was, of course, still too young to understand the significance of this ceremony which made him and his sister legitimate. He had, however, recently discovered a new game, which pleased his mother, since it was a quiet one: he had begun making drawings on the walls with pieces of coal. One day, a friend of Louis Auguste, M. Perron, seeing one of Paul's drawings, exclaimed: 'But it's the Mirabeau bridge!' And, indeed, it was the bridge over the Durance that Paul had drawn.

Mme Cézanne was delighted. Unlike Louis Auguste, she was imaginative, romantic and something of a dreamer. No doubt she inherited these qualities from her mother, the chair-maker's wife, who came from a family of humble Marseilles artisans called Girard. The Girards had adorned their history with some remarkably imaginative details. One of their ancestors, so they asserted, had been a general in Napoleon's armies and had married a native wife in St Domingo whereby they had Negro blood in their veins. There was no truth in this story whatever, but the Girard family derived great satisfaction from it.

At the primary school in the Rue des Épinaux, Paul became a quiet and attentive pupil, who satisfied his masters. As the months went by, he made friends among his school-fellows, in particular with Philippe, the son of Solari, the stone-mason. Philippe was a gentle boy with an equable temper, an ideal companion. Paul and he played endlessly together, or, much to his mother's anxiety, wandered off through the old quiet streets of the town which Paul loved.

When his father came home to the Rue de la Glacière, his mind full of his business affairs, and raised his voice or was sharp with his family, Paul's one desire was to be forgotten. His father's authoritative presence paralysed him and he retired within himself or, if he could, disappeared. He found moral support, however, in his sister, Marie; she was quite fearless and even prepared to stand up to Louis Auguste himself. And there was no doubt which of his two children Louis Auguste preferred. He thought Paul silly and awkward, and too inclined to give up when faced with the slightest difficulty; he would have to pull himself together if he were ever to be a worthy successor to his father.

The school in the Rue des Épinaux was a mixed one; Marie was now attending it too. The children walked there together, and it was Paul's duty to look after his young sister. But the little girl soon discovered how incompetent he was: and it was she who helped him out of the difficulties in which he was continually becoming involved. From protectiveness to tyranny was but a step. Paul admired her cleverness and good sense, and generally followed her lead, but when her solicitude became too imperious, he would turn on her. 'Shut up,' he would say, 'if I touched you, I might hurt you.'

The revolution of 1848, which took place when Paul was nine, swept Louis Philippe from his throne. The Second Republic began amid unrest which was followed by an economic crisis. Bad harvests in 1846 and 1847 had created serious shortages and the people were growling in Paris. But Louis Auguste continued on his successful way. On 1 June, he opened his bank at 24, Rue des Cordeliers (it was transferred a little later to 13, Rue Boulegon). He was so relentless in his pursuit of money that he refused his wife not only luxuries but many necessities. And it may well have been to lighten the burden of Mme Cézanne's housekeeping that the decision was taken to make Paul a day-boarder at the Saint-Joseph School, near the church of Sainte-Marie-Madeleine.

Paul went to Saint-Joseph's in 1849 and he adapted himself to his new life as he adapted himself to everything. He was not a fighter; he yielded, and took refuge in an inaccessible private world. His behaviour often seemed contradictory, or at the very least unexpected. He was too unstable, and almost unhealthily sensitive, to be understood easily: he could be shy or noisy, indifferent or enthusiastic, rude or friendly, entirely according to the circumstance. He seemed to be too much affected by external influences and his masters at Saint-Joseph's reproached him with weakness of character. Yet, from time to time, he would become unaccountably stubborn and intransigent and give way to an inexplicable anger. On the other hand, there was no pupil who worked harder than he, though his success at his lessons was due more to patient and methodical hard work than to startling gifts. He was in no sense a brilliant pupil.

After school was over Paul, with Philippe Solari or Henri Gasquet, the son of the baker in the Rue de Lacépède, would wander about for a while in the streets of Aix with their speaking names – the Rue Rifle-Rafle, the Rue Esquicho-Coudé* – and linger round the fountains.

At Saint-Joseph's there was a Spanish monk who gave the pupils drawing lessons. Paul worked particularly hard in this class. Drawing – that game he had discovered for himself when he was five years old – undoubtedly had a special attraction. His mother, in a flight of fancy, even went so far as to assert that he would one day be a great artist. She had never entered a picture gallery in her life, but her reasoning was typically her own and seemed to her irrefutable: was not her darling son, she said, called Paul like Rembrandt and Rubens?

Louis Auguste paid no attention to such nonsense; he was busy making money and no opportunity passed him by. Though he had now become a banker, he was still interested in even the smallest deal.

From time to time, he bought lots of second-hand goods, which he sorted and resold. He discovered in one of these lots a little box of water-colours for which it was hardly worth the trouble of finding a purchaser. He took it home and gave it to Paul. Let him amuse himself with daubing!

The Cézannes subscribed to the *Magasin Pittoresque*, a popular periodical of the time. Paul, who was delighted with his present, began to colour the magazine's illustrations.

* The street in which 'the elbows are constricted' – because of its narrowness – in Provençal.

CHAPTER TWO

School and Friendships

> The acacias were weeping over the walls, the moon shone blue on the porch of Saint-Jean, and we were fifteen . . .
>
> CÉZANNE (*recorded by Joachim Gasquet*)

SAINT-JOSEPH'S SCHOOL was clearly not good enough for a banker's son; the only establishment in Aix worthy of his predestined future was the Collège Bourbon, to which the sons of all the best families went. In October 1852, at the age of thirteen, Paul entered the sixth class as a boarder.

He was not much upset by the change. Unlike most boys, he did not mind being a boarder and he donned the uniform which symbolised the end of his freedom with apparent indifference. It was a blue uniform with red piping, the collar embroidered with gold palms.

The long, grey, stone façade of the Collège Bourbon gave on to the Rue Cardinale.* It was a huge, dilapidated and rather sombre building that had once been a convent. Dark, damp and melancholy, the plaster of the classrooms on the ground floor sweated. In the dim chapel, built by Puget it was said, the odours of mould and incense mingled. The refectory smelt of fat and dishwater. But none of this worried Paul. He took pleasure in the two courtyards and their shady plane trees, and in the big moss-grown swimming-pool; and he liked the nuns, who supervised the linen and the sanatorium, and glided so silently through the long corridors. From the windows of the first floor, where the classrooms were lighter, you could look out on to neighbouring gardens and at night-time sometimes hear the frogs singing to the moon.

Paul worked as he had always done, with a quiet and studious application, though he showed no preference for any particular subject. He appeared to give as much care to an arithmetical problem as to a

* It is now the Lycée Mignet.

history lesson or a Latin prose. If he had a favourite subject, it was probably Latin, which embodied the past that was still such a living thing in Provence. Nor, apparently, had he altogether escaped his heredity: his arithmetic reports were always excellent.

Paul's close attention to his lessons might suggest that the contradictions so apparent in his behaviour in the past had now decreased. He had been bullied and snubbed so often at home by his father and had acquired such a habit of silence when Louis Auguste was there that it might be supposed he would blossom out in the companionship of school. But this was not so. The contradictions in his character tended to increase. He was paralysed by shyness and found it difficult to be natural with his schoolfellows. He hated being touched; any sort of physical contact was morbidly abhorrent to him and was apt to make him lose his temper. One day, when on the stairs, he had been accidentally kicked by a boy sliding down the banisters. From that moment, he had developed this phobia, which was accompanied by a frightened distrust of others. There was no doubt that he was unduly sensitive, very far indeed from possessing his father's robust and ironical contempt for the world.

Louis Auguste was well aware that the Aix bourgeoisie would not accept him, for it was both jealous and snobbish; but, with money behind him, he was merely contemptuous of it. Paul, whose personality and whose every attempt at independence had been crushed by his overbearing father, could summon up no such indifference. He was shy, proud, sensitive and easily hurt. Though he never admitted it, he suffered from the ostracism to which his family was subjected. The school comprised a cross-section of Aix society. The sons of the presiding judge and of the rector of the university were there; and there also was Paul, the son of the banker Cézanne, who had formerly been a dealer in rabbit-skins and had married his mistress.

* * *

That same year, another boy had come to the Collège Bourbon as a boarder and, though the same age as Paul, he had been placed two grades lower, in the eighth class and even there had some difficulty in keeping up with the others. His name was Émile, the only child of

François Zola, the engineer, to whom Aix was shortly to be grateful for its increased supply of water.*

From the moment he arrived, Émile was the object of vindictive hostility from the other boys; both seniors and juniors bullied him. He suffered from a number of disadvantages: he was in the eighth class at the age of twelve and, though small for his age, was a head taller than most of his class-mates. Nor was his appearance prepossessing: he was short-sighted, blushed like a girl when spoken to, and had clearly left his mother's apron strings for the first time. Indeed, his mother and grandmother came to see him in the school parlour every day. Moreover, he was not a native of Aix, but a foreigner, a 'Franciot,' a 'Parisian,' who talked not only with a ridiculous accent but with a lisp. Worst of all, he was poor. He lived in an impossible district, somewhere near the Pont-de-Béraud, which was inhabited by gipsies and tramps. Since he had entered the school, Émile's family had moved to the Rue Bellegard – not that this was any improvement. Besides, everyone knew why the Zolas so constantly changed their address. Each time they moved, it was to have a room less and save a little more on the rent; in the end, no doubt, they would be living in a cave. It was common knowledge that creditors had been ringing at the Zolas' door for the last five years, ever since the father, who had engineered the canal, had died. And since young Zola had no father, you could bully him to your heart's content.

Émile did his best to stand up to the other boys, but what could he do against so many? Till now, his life had been comparatively easy; he had been spoilt by his family, had run wild and played truant through the streets or along the banks of the Torse, the little river that wound through Pont-de-Béraud. He was gentle, peaceable, generous, kindly, and inclined to be a dreamer; he loved animals and flowers. Imprisoned in this gloomy school, he was pained and surprised that these young louts should wish to attack him. There was nothing he could do but try to escape and hope to be forgotten; find some solitary corner in which to cry. His happiest moments were when he was banished to the end of the farther courtyard and, by general edict, sent to Coventry.

Paul, however, took a different view from his school-fellows.

* Émile Zola was born in Paris on 2 April, 1840.

Though not in the same class as Émile, he was able to talk to him from time to time. He thought Émile a 'dreamy weakling' but a 'nice chap'; and, unexpected though it might be in so shy a boy, Paul reinforced his opinion by taking action. One day, when Émile had again been sent to Coventry, Paul flouted the interdict and went to talk to him. The other boys at once set on Paul. But their usual victim was at least no longer entirely alone.

Émile was very grateful and the next day brought Paul a large basket of apples. This sign of gratitude sealed their friendship.*

* * *

Though they were not yet aware of it, Cézanne's and Zola's friendship began a new chapter in their lives.

Cézanne had rescued him and Zola no longer felt quite alone in the hated school. Cézanne's friendship gave him courage; and he began to adapt himself to the life of a boarder. Moreover, encouraged by his friend's success at his lessons, Zola began to work too. He made up for lost time and was soon top of his class. Ambition dawned in him and he began to write. Though he had scarcely known his alphabet at seven and a half, he now began an historical novel based on his reading of Michaud's *Histoire des Croisades*. He recovered his enthusiasms and his zest for life.

Moreover, he communicated these enthusiasms to his friend. It was through Zola that a whole new universe was revealed to Cézanne; with Zola, he could escape from the atmosphere of his home. But Zola offered him more than the refuge of his friendship: he drew him into a realm of enchantment. The two boys talked endlessly during the breaks: of literature, for they had both begun to read everything they could lay their hands on – 'stories that were a waking dream, the great romances of adventure' that held them enthralled for weeks on end – and also of their own lives. Zola had lived in Paris. He talked to Cézanne about his father, whose romantic and adventurous career thrilled their young imaginations.

Before coming to Provence, where he died at the age of fifty-two,

* 'You know, Cézanne's apples have their origins in a very distant past!' the painter was to say much later with a wink, as he recounted this incident.

François Zola, the son of a Venetian father and a Corfiote Greek mother, had travelled all over Europe and North Africa. He had been an army cadet at Pavia and Modana, and had become a second-lieutenant of artillery in the army of Prince Eugène. In 1823, he had worked as a surveyor in Austria on one of the earliest railways in Europe, the line between Linz and Biedweiss. In 1830, he had gone to Algiers, where he had helped fight the cholera epidemic; and a year later had joined the Foreign Legion as a lieutenant.

Returning to France, he had conceived the idea for a new harbour at Marseilles in the Anse des Catalans; invented in Paris a machine for moving earth; and through the years had fought hard to get his plan for a dam and a canal at Aix accepted. For this purpose he had eventually succeeded in founding a company with a capital of 600,000 francs.* He had also fallen in love with a girl of nineteen, whom he had seen one Sunday when coming out of church, and had married her. In his passionate impetuosity and his taste for wild adventure, François Zola was a typical romantic of 1830. To Cézanne, his own father's life, with its steady, methodical rise to a success that could be measured only by figures in a ledger, seemed remarkably dull compared to this highly coloured tale. The romantic movement had scarcely touched Aix, had awakened no more than a distant murmur in the lethargic town. But now, in this school yard, Cézanne was suddenly made free of it in all its wild vitality.

For Zola, on the other hand, romanticism was an everyday matter; adventure lay just round the corner. His life had nothing of the rather torpid calm which surrounded the Cézannes, nor had he their security. He had been only seven years old when his father died. The work on the canal had been going on for only three months, when François Zola, who had had to go to Marseilles for two days, developed pleurisy. All his life, Zola was to remember the hotel room in the Rue de l'Arbre, in Marseilles, and his father's pale, dead face. The very word death still oppressed him, and reminded him of his terror of five years before.

Since that time, his mother and his grandparents, constantly engaged in law suits which they invariably lost, and hounded by a horde of

* Approximately £100,000 today.

creditors, had been struggling against the increasing poverty which was the logical consequence of his father's adventures. On half holidays, Zola took Cézanne to see the places where he had played as a child. They sometimes had stones thrown at them, the usual welcome given to the children of the town by those of the suburbs. Thirty years later Cézanne and Zola still remembered this.

Cézanne and Zola were soon joined by a third friend: Baptistin Baille. Though in the sixth class with Cézanne, he was two years his junior and a year younger than Zola.* A pleasant, sensible boy, Baille was better balanced and far less sensitive than the other two; he suffered neither from Cézanne's alternations of depression and exuberance, nor from the anxiety latent beneath Zola's ardours.† Nevertheless, under the stimulus of their example, Baille did his best to share in his friends' enthusiasms, their reading and their dreams. The three boys, who were soon known at school as the 'inseparables,' swore eternal loyalty. They were determined to remain friends all their lives, conquer the future and make their mark on their times. Zola, in particular, was sure that fame awaited them.

The three friends joined in all the silly jokes with which schoolboys relieve the monotony of their lives; they jeered at the vice-principal, who had a long nose and was nicknamed 'Pifard,' at 'Rhadamante,' who had never been seen to laugh, at 'You've deceived-me-Adèle,' a notorious cuckold, at Spontini, a Corsican usher who was always prepared to show them his dagger stained with the blood of three of his cousins killed in a vendetta, at 'Paraboulomenos,' the scullion, and at 'Paralleluca,' who washed up the dishes.

They were nevertheless somewhat isolated among their schoolfellows. The other boys lived very much from day to day and could not share in their dreams. The inseparables' enthusiasms and aspirations seemed odd to them.

Their work, however, far from suffering from their friendship,

* Baille was born in 1841.

† Zola's anxiety neurosis, which was not dissimilar from Cézanne's phobia of being touched, was no doubt partly due to the profound impression made on him by his father's death, but there may also have been another reason: in 1845 (when he was five), his parents had dismissed a servant, an Arab boy aged twelve, for indecently assaulting him.

seemed to have profited from their mutual rivalry. At the prize-giving, on 10 August, they all did well. Zola, in particular, won several prizes and received the first honourable mention for general excellence; and though he had been the despair of his masters at the beginning of the year, he now moved straight up into the sixth class.*

When summer came and the sun baked the Aix countryside, the friends developed a passion for swimming which they had learned in the somewhat murky pool at school. Now that the holidays were here, they would hurry off to the Arc, the little river that wound through the fields in the valley to the south of the town, there to spend many hours splashing naked in the pools, catching frogs, looking for eels, drying themselves on the warm earth or merely lying in the cool water.

Sometimes, too, they went for rambles in the neighbouring countryside. Zola had always loved the outline of its hills, its pines loud with cicadas, its olives and cypresses. A 'Franciot,' a foreigner though he might be, it was he who imbued his friends with the love of this serene yet passionate land.

These were enchanted holidays; but now the flat at 14, Rue Matheron, quite close to the bank, to which Cézanne's parents had moved for greater convenience, seemed intolerably dull to him. On 1 September, Louis Auguste had renewed his contract with Cabassol. As enterprising and hard-fisted as ever, though they were capable on occasion of some carefully calculated gesture of generosity, the two partners were doing well. Their business was constantly expanding. They had no failures; a customer would have had to be very clever indeed to get the better of them. There was a story told in Aix of how a customer from Marseilles, to whom the bank had advanced a large sum, was on the point of bankruptcy. Determined not to lose his money, Louis Auguste had gone to Marseilles and taken over the management of his debtor's business. As a result, the financial circumstances had improved, the debtor was able to resume his business, and presumably to refund the Cézanne and Cabassol bank with interest.

Coming home saturated with sunlight, Paul Cézanne, in spite of his

* Cézanne obtained the first honourable mention for Latin prose, the second for history and geography and – which must have pleased his father – the first prize for arithmetic.

first prize for arithmetic, could muster no interest for Louis Auguste's continual talk of figures, loans, contracts, interest and money.

When the new term began, Cézanne and Baille were consistently at the top of the fifth class; and Zola, even though he had been awarded a double remove, continued to be successful. However, he took a dislike to the classics master and lost interest in the dead languages, preferring the sciences. Nevertheless, the friends excelled in every subject, even in religious instruction, for which Zola showed considerable enthusiasm at this time, surpassing Cézanne, whose faith was sincere if somewhat ingenuous. His First Communion, made at Saint-Joseph's, before entering the Collège Bourbon, had remained one of the most vivid impressions of his childhood. Curiously enough, there was one subject in which Cézanne never did particularly well. In the fifth class, there were lessons in object drawing and painting, but he seemed to take little interest in them.

Though older now – he was nearly fifteen – Cézanne had not changed much: he was as moody and unstable as ever, alternating between enthusiasm and depression. 'For me, the sky of the future is very overcast!' From time to time, owing to his difficult temperament, the friendship of the inseparables was in imminent danger of being destroyed because of some absurd and minor disagreement. And no doubt it would have been but for Zola's diplomacy. Friendship, for Zola, was a cult and a profound necessity.

Though they had many tastes in common, the three friends were very different. It was evident in the different ways in which they worked: Baille was a plodder, a pupil who would clearly succeed in all his examinations. Cézanne, though he worked as hard as Baille, was less reliable though certainly as clever. He attacked his subjects 'almost painfully,'* made them his own and, endowed as he was with an extraordinary memory, mastered them for ever. As for Zola, he applied himself methodically, but never spent more time on his work than was absolutely necessary. He felt a certain need, however, to fulfil a task conscientiously before turning happily to something else.

In March 1854, the quiet of Aix was disturbed by international events. A little more than two years before, during the night of

* Joachim Gasquet.

1 December, 1851, Louis Napoleon Bonaparte had carried out his *coup d'état;* and now the Crimean War was beginning. On their way to take ship for the east, the regiments passed through Aix; for week after week they were marching through the town. Aix was in a state of chaos and billeted the troops with considerable reluctance. The authorities had to coerce the townspeople into doing so. The schoolboys, on the other hand, were more welcoming. They neglected their lessons and became difficult to control, for they could think of nothing but the long procession of cuirassiers, lancers, dragoons and hussars, the gay uniforms and the trumpets that gave the town so festal an air. It was a period of considerable disorganisation and quite time for the holidays to begin.

Baille won the first prize for excellence, Cézanne the second.* Zola was awarded the second honourable mention for excellence in his own class. He had also recently been given a bursary, which was a great help to his mother whose difficulties were growing no less. She had now left the Rue Bellegarde and had moved to the Rue Roux-Alphéran.

Bearing his prize volumes bound in blue cloth, Cézanne returned for the holidays to the Rue Matheron, where a few weeks before, on 30 June, his sister Rose had been born. But now Cézanne was rarely at home during the day. The three friends were always either swimming in the Arc or rambling over the countryside. The dam, which Zola's father had designed, had been finished this year, and it naturally became one of their favourite objectives. For Zola it was a form of pilgrimage and they often took the dusty road that ran east from Aix towards Le Tholonet. The village consisted of a few cottages and a church that looked like 'an abandoned farm'; but the bright sunshine and the huge, old plane trees gave the place a certain picturesque charm. To the south lay the red lands, still bloody, so legend had it, from the slaughter of a hundred thousand barbarians who had come down from the Baltic two thousand years before and been massacred by Marius' legions. To

* Cézanne also won the first prize for Latin prose and the second for Greek, the second honourable mention for history, the second honourable mention for arithmetic and the first honourable mention for painting (for object drawing, he received no mention).

the north was the Infernets Gorge and the dam lying among wild, stony hills, a waste of thorny scrub and sweet scented herbs.

The three boys often climbed the wooded slope, where the cicadas sang among the pines, and where beside the path stood a curious, gothic-windowed building called the Château Noir, or the Château du Diable, because, so it was said, an alchemist had once lived there and conducted sinister experiments; and from there, they went on to the Bibémus quarry, which overlooked the dam.

For centuries the Bibémus quarry had supplied the fine yellow stone of which many of the houses in Aix were built. From the hillside in which it lay there was an immense view over the vineyards of the red lands, the meadows beside the Arc, and the four-hundred-acre lake, the 'little sea' as it was called, the stony hills, the far grey line of the Sainte-Baume and Étoile chains, and in the foreground, quite close, rising clear in the limpid air, the blue cone of Mont Sainte-Victoire.

They returned day after day to this seminal landscape. In comparison the town seemed dull and its preoccupations banal. In the solitude of this countryside, they felt different, alive with vague dreams and still undefined ambitions. They intoxicated themselves with poetry and rivalled each other in declaiming verses to the echoing hills.

Sometimes, on their return to Aix, they went to Baille's third-floor attic, which was lit by a big window and crowded with broken chairs, old newspapers, damaged furniture and discarded pictures. But they transformed it into a world of their own; while they ate the raisins that hung drying from the roof, they read endlessly, wrote verse, and performed curious chemical experiments.

At night, they wandered through the quiet and unfrequented streets, where grass grew between the cobbles. The façades of the houses were silent and beautiful in the light of the paraffin lamps. There was no sound but the lisp of a distant fountain. Yet the very walls seemed to speak to them through the darkness.

* * *

Cézanne was now sixteen, Zola fifteen and Baille fourteen. Though they had now entered the ungrateful age, there was little difference apparent in the basic continuity of their lives. The alternation of school and holidays continued. They were merely somewhat noisier in their search for self-expression, and Cézanne and Zola joined one of their schoolfellows, Marguery, in forming a band. Marguery was rather a dull boy, but so ingenuously self-satisfied that his very naïvety disarmed the friends. Moreover, he wrote verses.

Marguery played first cornet, Cézanne second cornet and Zola the clarinet. Cézanne was not averse to music, though he had no serious desire to become an executant. His parents, for whom music was presumably a desirable social asset – Marie was being taught the piano – had insisted that he take lessons with Poncet, organist and precentor of the cathedral of Saint-Sauveur, which afforded him many a rap over his reluctant knuckles. The band, however, seemed a good idea and, indeed, the boys derived many advantages from it. They were allowed to take part in 'all ceremonious occasions.' Should a civil servant return from Paris with the Legion of Honour, they greeted him with appropriate music; when 'the saints who brought rain, or the Virgin who cured cholera' were carried in procession through the town, they were called on to accompany the prayers of the populace with suitable harmonies. They were regaled with cakes for their trouble.

Corpus Christi was their particular delight. For a whole week the festival continued in the town: ceaseless processions moved through the cobbled streets between rows of chairs ranged on the pavements; every window sported bright hangings; monks and nuns escorted the red velvet canopy, followed by young girls dressed in white and a crowd of penitents in blue, hooded robes, with slits for eyeholes. For eight days, Cézanne, Zola and Marguery blew their instruments in mutual rivalry as they trod the broom blossom and rose petals the children strewed before them.

The noisy part they played in the Aix festival was not, however, enough for Zola and Cézanne. Though far too shy as yet to accost the girls on the Cours, as many of their schoolfellows did, they went one night to serenade a pretty girl of their acquaintance with cornet and clarinet under her window. A parrot in the house was panic-stricken by the din and the neighbours shouted angrily at them from the windows.

But, for all this, they still continued to be excellent pupils; though, whenever they could, they went off on their long excursions in the countryside. They read widely and wrote innumerable verses. They pitied their friends who spent their time in cafés playing cards for drinks. They swore that they would never sink into sloth and mediocrity. They were intoxicated by their triune friendship, dreamed of the future, and were passionately devoted to poetry which seemed to them the path not only to beauty but to fame. They learned by heart whole acts of *Hernani* and *Ruy Blas*, and declaimed them to each other by the river bank on summer days.

* * *

On 13 August, 1856, there was the usual prize-giving, attended this year by the Archbishop of Aix and the Bishop of Dijon, and with it Cézanne's and Zola's time as boarders came to an end. From now on they were to be day boys. Baille was to remain a boarder. Cézanne and Zola were each awarded the prize for excellence in their respective classes. Cézanne, who had a remarkable facility for the composition of Latin verses, won the prize for classics; but he had no success in drawing, whereas Baille won the first prize and Zola the second.

Cézanne and Zola were delighted to have finished with the imprisonment of school. From now on, there was much less difference between holidays and term-time. Every day during the summer, and every Sunday during the term, they explored the countryside; climbing the slopes of Mont Sainte-Victoire, or taking the road to Roquefavour as far as the Château de Galice, where the garden was a paradise of flowers, or to Gardanne, whose picturesque houses stood on a mound surmounted by an old church.

They would set off at four in the morning (the first to awaken would summon the other by throwing pebbles at his shutters), and each time they would try to go a little farther until, intoxicated by their long walk, they returned to Aix in the evening, exhausted but happy, having whipped up their flagging energy with some Hugo poem as they strode along to the rhythm of the verse.

Baille joined them in the summer; and sometimes they took others with them, Philippe Solari, or Marius Roux, whom Zola had known before the Collège Bourbon, or again the younger Baille, Isidore, who was ten years old, and on whom they conferred the great honour of carrying their haversack. But they really preferred to be alone. Climbing hills was not merely an opportunity for physical exertion, but also a flight from humanity, a symbolic renouncement of towns and civilisation. 'Due to their hatred of cities,' they would 'declaim verses in the driving rain, without seeking shelter.' They decided to go to the banks of the Arc and there live the life of savages, swimming all day long, and taking with them five or six books, no more.

One night as darkness was falling, they decided not to return to Aix but to spend the night in a cave on beds of grass, thyme and lavender. Soon after they had gone to sleep, a great wind rose, whistling into the cave and waking them up again. By the pale light of the moon, they saw frightened bats wheeling about their heads and they began to regret the comfort of their rooms at home. By two o'clock in the morning, they could bear it no longer and returned to Aix.

When autumn came, shooting became a pretext for further wanderings. Not that there was much in the way of game in that countryside, apart from an occasional rabbit. They had to content themselves with thrushes, fig eaters and finches. But for all their guns and game-bags their hearts were not in it. They walked for miles without firing a shot. They often fired at a post, however, for the mere pleasure of making a noise. And when they found a shady spring, they left the birds in peace and talked of poetry.

For their loves were the poets; though they were now eighteen, seventeen and sixteen, they had banished women from their ideal city. They were afraid of women and sublimated their paralysing shyness into a 'superior austerity,' contenting themselves with imagining 'women met on journeys, beautiful girls appearing to them suddenly in some mysterious wood, who would remain all day with them, and then disappear like shadows into the dusk.' Though the game-bag might be empty of game, their heads were full of dreams.

One day, one of them pulled out from among the powder-flasks and boxes of caps a book by an author who was new to them and whose name their schoolmasters had never even mentioned: Alfred de Musset. Hugo's glory was extinguished for them on the spot. Musset became an enduring enthusiasm. They read and re-read his poems aloud. His satirical romanticism, his scepticism and his defiance – and perhaps even more his tears – spoke to them with the voice of a brother. Musset became a 'religion' to them. Had he not uttered 'the despairing cry of the century?'

The friends were writing more verse than ever. Zola was considering a vast history of man in three cantos, to be called *La Chaîne des Êtres*, embracing his past, his present and his future. They were all three determined to be poets. Their lives would be spent on a plane different from that of ordinary men, far removed from petty ambition, folly and wickedness. They would write, grow famous and know love. One day they would go to Paris and conquer it.

* * *

Thirty years earlier, in 1825, the town of Aix had acquired the ancient priory of the Knights of St John of Malta. The municipality had turned it into a museum and transferred to it the Drawing School which, thanks to the generosity of a Duc de Villars, had been in existence elsewhere since 1766.

The Drawing School was free. The classes were given by the Director of the museum, Joseph Gibert, who, born in Aix on 23 April, 1808, was an artist in the strictest academic tradition, and specialised in portraits of prelates, generals, ministers and Spanish infantas. A number of young men attended his classes and among them was Philippe Solari, who wanted to become a sculptor. Cézanne began to attend in the evenings.

Louis Auguste apparently placed no difficulties in his son's way. Drawing and painting, like music, were polite accomplishments which the children of well-to-do families had the right to practise in their leisure moments. Marie Cézanne was already painting little water-colours and it was clearly more desirable that Paul should attend Gibert's classes after school than lounge about the cafés and run after women.

At the Drawing School, Cézanne entered an environment that was new to him. Most of the young men he met there were intending to become professional artists, such as Auguste Truphème, brother of the sculptor François Truphème, and Numa Coste, son of a poor cobbler, who was three and a half years younger than Cézanne. Coste was working at the free school of the Brothers of the Christian Doctrine and doing his best to educate himself. Cézanne quickly made friends with him, and also with a man ten years older than himself, Joseph Villevieille, a hard working painter with practical bourgeois sense, who had been a pupil of Ingres' friend, Granet, in his early youth. Cézanne also made friends with a boy of seventeen, Joseph Huot, whose father had started life as a cameo engraver and had eventually become architect to the town of Aix. Joseph Huot had many gifts; he was as attracted by the theatre as much as he was by drawing and architecture; and everyone prophesied a great future for him.

From time to time, Cézanne went to look at the pictures and sculptures in the museum. The Aix Museum, opened in 1838, had enriched itself through the years. In Cézanne's time it contained a number of seventeenth-century baroque pictures, the work of minor French and Italian masters. He was particularly impressed by the *Joueurs de Cartes*, which the catalogue attributed to Louis Le Nain.

As the illustrations of the *Magasin pittoresque* had once done, these paintings aroused Cézanne's imagination and occasionally he tried to reproduce some canvas in the museum from memory.

* * *

In October 1857, both his friends having been moved up into the first class, Zola was promoted to the second. He had completed his year in the third with considerable distinction, winning the first prize for excellence, and the first prizes for religious instruction and drawing (in which Cézanne, who had also won the first prize for excellence, had as before completely failed to distinguish himself). In French composition, Zola had outstripped all his schoolfellows. His new master in the second class, impressed by one of his exercises, which Zola wrote in verse, was to say: 'You'll be a writer, Zola.'

In the meantime, the Zolas had been moving from lodging to lodging; for a while they had been in the Cours des Minimes, on the outskirts of Aix, and were now in a slum in the Rue Mazarine, inhabiting two small rooms opening on to an alley of which one end abutted on to the ruins of the old ramparts of the town. They had nothing left but debts; even their furniture had gone. Moreover,

Émile's grandmother had died in November; with inexhaustible activity and unimpaired gaiety, she had shown all the robust strength of a woman from the Beauce (there had not been a single white hair on her head) and had been wonderfully clever at making the most of the family's scanty resources. After her death, their situation became precarious to the point of desperation and Madame Zola determined to go to Paris to seek help from her husband's old friends.

For a time Zola remained in Aix alone with his grandfather. Despite his circumstances, he had not lost confidence. He was courageous, and poverty did not frighten him; he had made up his mind that his life would be devoted to 'work and struggle.' Then, suddenly, in February 1858, came a letter from his mother: 'Life in Aix is no longer possible. Sell the four pieces of furniture we still possess. With the money, you will have enough to buy third-class tickets for yourself and your grandfather. Hurry. I am waiting for you.'

Zola must have been much moved when he told Cézanne and Baille of this summons. Their wonderful life together was at an end. Yet, there was always the future. Zola was going to Paris and the other two would one day follow him. They would meet again in the capital and struggle side by side, united in loyalty to the days of their youth.

After a last excursion to Le Tholonet and the dam, Zola left his friends and, like a scout on reconnaissance for the main party, set out for the capital.

CHAPTER THREE

'I, Too, am a Painter'

That unpunished vice: painting.—A CRITIC

CÉZANNE was very distressed by Zola's departure. No doubt Baille was sorry too, but it did not interfere with his preparation for a double *baccalauréat*, in science and letters, for which he intended sitting at the end of the school year. His regret was perhaps a little superficial.

This was not at all the case with Cézanne. In the long letters he wrote to Zola, strange farragos of prose and doggerel, the jokes were often rather forced and hardly concealed his dismay: 'Since you left Aix, my dear chap, a sombre sorrow assails me and by God, I'm not lying. I hardly recognise myself, so dull, stupid and slow have I become.' Indeed, he was showing much less enthusiasm for his studies and there was little spirit in his work. He was always thinking of the next holidays, when his friend was due to come back to Aix.

There were, however, other distractions from his lessons. He was beginning to make considerable progress in drawing under Gibert; and he had fallen in love,

> 'D'une gentille femme.
> Brun est son teint, gracieux est son port,
> Bien mignon est son pied, la peau de sa main fine
> Blanche est sans doute . . .'

'For she was wearing gloves,' Cézanne added, turning his love to derision. But the idea of making advances to her paralysed him with shyness. He contented himself with watching his love from afar. He was awkward, unsure of himself, a prey to a self-doubt that was always breaking through the often wild humour. He would never, he confessed, succeed in love unless he had 'an unhoped-for piece of luck.' As for the *baccalauréat*, Baille would pass, but he would not: 'Sunk, submerged, drowned, petrified, liquidated and annihilated, that's what I shall be.'

He gave Zola all the local gossip, including a lively and mocking description of the bad weather at Aix in the month of May, when there were fifteen degrees of frost followed by pouring rain; prayers were said and psalms sung in the streets. 'I'm fed up with it,' wrote Cézanne. 'I hear nothing but *ora pro nobis* on every side.' But now and then there was a phrase revealing his loneliness. 'I feel a certain innate sadness,' he wrote between a couple of jokes.

Zola, in Paris, felt very much as Cézanne did. Thanks to an old friend of his father's, called Labot, an advocate of the Conseil d'État, he had succeeded in obtaining a bursary at the Lycée Saint-Louis, which he had entered on 1 March. No doubt, the separation was worse for Zola than it was for Cézanne. After all, Cézanne was still in Aix amid familiar surroundings. In this grey, dull, hostile Paris, Zola felt an exile. Loneliness depressed him and he felt sure he would make no friends in the Lycée Saint-Louis. As once before in Aix, he was now a stranger again. By an absurd paradox, he was known in Paris as the 'Marseillais,' whereas in Aix he had been called the 'Parisian.' The boys mocked his accent; and his poverty was more of a disability than ever. His bursary made him an intruder among these sons of bourgeois. The boys at Saint-Louis were sharper-witted and more alert than those of the Collège Bourbon. Precocious young Parisians, they aped the speech and manners of grown men. They pitied Zola and teased him. At eighteen, he was only in the second class, was a provincial and a foreigner.

Not only had Zola lost his friends and the sunshine of Provence, but he was appalled by the apparent superiority of the boys among whom he lived. He withdrew into himself, did no work and omitted to prepare his lessons; having so often won the prize for excellence, he was now always at the bottom of the class. Literature was his only refuge. Occasionally his schoolmaster would read aloud one of his French compositions; but this was his only success. He spent his time in class reading Hugo and Musset, concealed behind the back of the boy in front; he had also just discovered Rabelais and Montaigne. He wrote verses and a play: *Enfoncé le Pion.* And he sent a constant stream

3. Louis Auguste Cézanne, the artist's father

4.

5.

4. Rose Cézanne, the artist's sister [*c.* 1880]

5. Marie Cézanne, the artist's sister [*c.* 1870]

6. Cézanne: Self-portrait from a photograph [*c.* 1861]

7. Paul Cézanne, 1861. The earliest known photograph [aged 22]

8. Book of manuscript music copied out by Cézanne at the age of 16, when second Cornet player in the school band at Aix

9. Émile Zola aged 25 [1865]

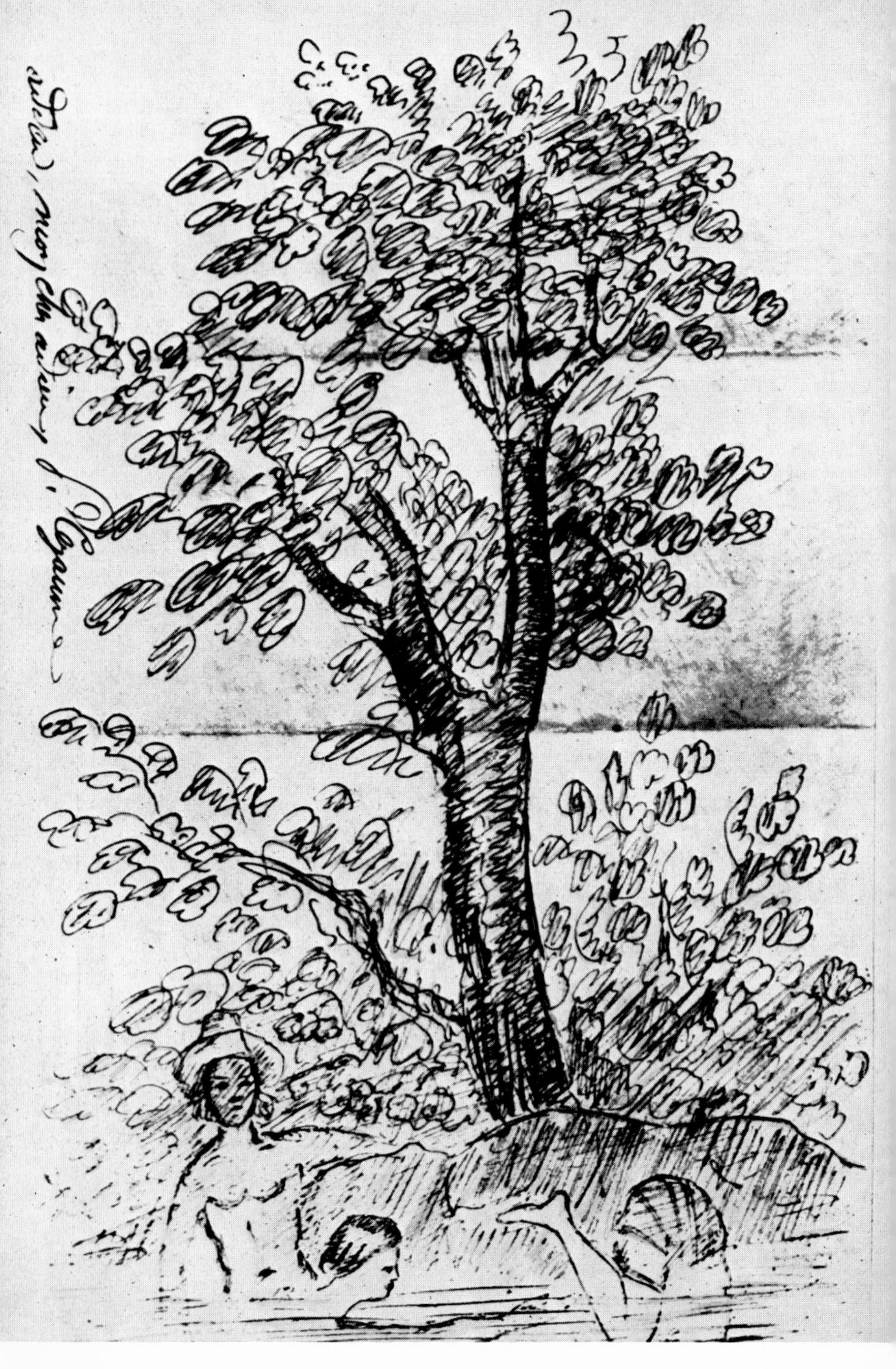

10. Cézanne: Drawing illustrating a letter to Zola, 20 June 1859

11. Paul Cézanne, aged about 32 [*c.* 1871]

12. Le Jas de Bouffan, Aix-en-Provence

of letters to Cézanne and Baille, telling them of his unhappiness, asking them to write more often and at greater length, complaining what bad correspondents they were, particularly Baille.

And when he went home to 63, Rue Monsieur-le-Prince, he was oppressed with the family's poverty, for they had found no relief from their distress in Paris.

The friends were longing for the holidays. Cézanne had conceived the idea of collaborating with Zola on a monumental drama in five acts about Henry VIII of England. But before he could engage on this project, there was the appalling obstacle of the *baccalauréat*. As the time drew near he became more and more frightened of the examination. He foresaw his 'early failure.'

In fact, the scholastic year ended somewhat pathetically for Cézanne. He had an honourable mention for excellence and another for Latin composition but, as he had foreseen, these were his only successes. On the other hand, at Gibert's he had won second prize for drawing, his first success in this direction. Baille passed his *baccalauréat* in the sciences at the end of July, and was to take the examination in letters on 14 August, ten days after Cézanne. As he had feared, Cézanne failed. He would have to sit again in November; his holidays would be spoiled.

When Zola returned to Aix, the three friends began their rambles again. Yet, after the first joy of being reunited, there seemed to be a shadow over their gaiety. Zola's departure the previous February had not only interrupted the course of their friendship but, though they were unaware of it, had put an end to the carefree period of their youth. They were now on the verge of manhood and life was becoming serious. No doubt things seemed outwardly unchanged as they walked through the sunny, dusty countryside, and declaimed verses beneath the olive trees and the pines. Cézanne and Zola teased Baille about his greediness as they used to do; and Cézanne was still as much of a spendthrift as ever. To Zola, who expressed astonishment at seeing him spend all his money the day he received it, he said: 'Damn it, suppose I died tonight, do you want my parents to inherit it?'

When the holidays were over the three friends were separated again. On the first of October Zola returned to Paris to the Lycée Saint-

Louis; Baille went to Marseilles to prepare for the entrance examination to the École Polytechnique; while Cézanne remained alone in Aix, where his father intended sending him to the Law School.

* * *

In November, Cézanne passed his *baccalauréat*, which temporarily delighted him; but he had now to join the Law School and law profoundly bored him.

> Hélas! j'ai pris du Droit la route tortueuse.
> –J'ai pris n'est pas le mot, de prendre on m'a forcé!
> Le Droit, l'horrible Droit d'ambages enlacé
> Rendra pendant trois ans mon existence affreuse!

What he wanted to do, though the desire had matured curiously slowly, was to draw and paint. It seems likely that he may have mentioned this to his mother. But, if his father knew of it, he was certainly unimpressed; he felt that it was time his son began to take life a little more seriously.

In Paris Zola had fallen gravely ill. For six weeks he was feverish and delirious. When he left his bed, his mouth was ulcerated and his teeth loose; he was unable to talk and had to communicate by writing on a slate. When he looked at the advertisements on the wall opposite his window, he realised that he could no longer make out the letters.

Meanwhile, Cézanne's life was divided between the law, which he loathed more every day, and the classes at the Drawing School, where he was now working from life. He began to form a plan which would certainly have infuriated his father had he known of it: he wrote to Zola asking him to find out about the competitive examination for the Académie des Beaux-Arts in Paris.

At Gibert's, Cézanne had once again joined Numa Coste, Huot, Truphème, Solari, Villevieille and a few others. And there was also a new and rather picturesque recruit called Jean Baptiste Mathieu Chaillan.

Chaillan, who was twenty-seven, was the son of a Trets peasant. His origins were apparent in his 'slow movements and his tanned, bull neck, hard as leather.'* That autumn, he had left his village, dressed in

* Zola.

yellow nankeen jacket and trousers, and had set off on foot for Aix to become an artist. When he reached the Cours, he asked a policeman 'where the artists of Aix met.' 'The artists?' said the policeman. 'I don't know of any; but go and look in the Café des Deux Garçons, there are people in the back room there who always make a lot of noise.' The advice was sound. The artists welcomed the ingenuous young man kindly if a little mockingly. 'Have you been studying painting at the Trets École des Beaux-Arts?' Numa Coste asked him. 'No, I haven't studied,' replied Chaillan proudly. 'One has no need to study. What one man has done, another can do. Why shouldn't I be able to do what Rembrandt and Van Dyck did?'* Nevertheless, he condescended to accompany the artists of Aix to Gibert's.

Cézanne judged Chaillan with a kindly eye. He thought he was a good chap 'with a certain innate sense of poetry' who had merely 'lacked guidance.' What did Cézanne mean by 'guidance?' Probably Gibert's teaching. For though he criticised Gibert on occasion, in general he accepted the academic standards of his master with docility.

Outside the stability of his classes life was frightening in more ways than one for Cézanne. Women, for instance, were part of a strange and mysterious world, as sinful as it was fascinating. Was not love as Zola idealised it an absurd chimera, a fantasy of the mind? 'The love of Michelet,' Cézanne wrote to Zola, 'that pure and noble love, can exist; but, you must admit, it is very rare.' For his part, Cézanne was always in love, but he never seemed able to make any progress. When Baille returned to Aix for the Christmas holidays, he tried to convert him to the view of 'realism in love.' Cézanne discussed it with him at length; and he was certainly more adept at discussion than action. Then Zola, from Paris, called his friends to order. Realism in love, he proclaimed, was 'unworthy of our youth!' Michelet was right. Idealism alone could save the world; it was one of the necessary conditions for progress.

Such a profession of faith at this time was very much to Zola's credit, for he was in a state of profound depression. So disgusted was he with life, and so incapable did he feel of facing the future, that he was seriously considering – and this was obviously a form of suicide – giving up his studies and taking a job in an office. It was only at the

* Recorded by Maurice Raimbault.

very last moment that he hesitated, suddenly aware of the 'abyss' at his feet. Panic-stricken at the thought of the dull life that might await him, his ambition was aroused once more to 'desperate and absurd revolt.' 'Life is a struggle, I thought; we must accept the struggle and not retreat in the face of fatigue and difficulty.' He determined to pass his *baccalauréat*, then to study law and become a barrister. It would be his second profession, for he knew that he was born to be a writer.

Zola was naturally influenced by his family's poverty. But no such considerations haunted Cézanne. He was often exasperated by his father's autocratic attitude, and there is no doubt that he sometimes rebelled against it; nevertheless, thanks to his father's fortune, which was ever increasing, he was protected against the material difficulties of life. He had no need to worry about money; and since he had no expensive tastes, no vanity, fundamentally few needs and derived his only real pleasures from his thoughts, he was completely indifferent to it.

In this year, 1859, Louis Auguste bought for the sum of 85,000 francs,* a country house about a kilometre and a half from Aix on the Roquefavour road. It had once been the country house of the governor of Provence, M. de Villars, and was called Le Jas de Bouffan.† It was a fine eighteenth-century building with a magnificent avenue of old chestnut trees, a long façade, tall windows and a red-tiled roof. It stood in a big garden containing a pond adorned with a stone dolphin and lions. There were forty acres of fields and vineyards, and the farm buildings lay to one side of the house, behind a screen of mulberry trees. Louis Auguste had already had the estate on lease for some time and had sub-let the fields on market days to herdsmen requiring pasturage for their beasts. He now intended to make the house a summer residence. All the well-to-do Aix families had a town house for winter and a country house for summer, when the little town became stiflingly hot.

The news of the purchase created some resentment in Aix. This, surely, was the vanity of a parvenu! But in fact, proud of his achieve-

* Approximately £14,000 today.

† Provençal for The House of the Winds.

ments though he might be, Louis Auguste had no greater taste for the overt vanities of life than his son had. His peasant ancestry was strong in him. He was contemptuous of display and cared only for the solid realities. Indeed, he was more inclined to conceal his success than to make a show of it. The purchase of the Jas de Bouffan estate, though it aroused so much jealousy and comment, was a comparative trifle to Louis Auguste as the 85,000 francs he paid for it was probably no more than a tenth or twelfth part of his fortune at this time. Nor had he any intention of making a parade of the house. The previous owner had left it in poor condition, the garden had run wild and many of the rooms were in a state of dilapidation. Louis Auguste was not prepared to spend a great deal of money on extensive repairs so he simply shut up the uninhabitable rooms and let the garden go.

Cézanne appeared to be even less impressed by the purchase of the house than was his father; he did not even bother to tell Zola about it. The one advantage the Jas de Bouffan had for him was that he could go there and work in complete peace and solitude. From the upper rooms, the countryside could be seen in all its splendour. The light carved the slopes of the distant hills into innumerable facets; the pines and cypresses, the laurels and evergreen oaks took on a marmoreal quality in the clear air; and the Provençal landscape was luminous, serene and lyrical.

But Cézanne was bored with Aix. He longed for Paris; all his dreams of love and painting were centred on his vision of the capital. He had recently fallen in love with a seamstress, Justine, whom he declared to be very pretty. The only trouble was that Justine always, as he said, 'looked the other way.' 'When I gazed at her, she dropped her eyes and blushed. And recently, I've noticed that when we're in the same street, she's inclined to turn about and make off without looking back.' And worst of all, the adventure, which had hardly begun, came to an abrupt end. 'One day,' Cézanne told Zola, 'a young man, a first-year student like myself – in fact, Seymard, whom you know – came up to me. "My dear chap," he said, first shaking my hand, and then taking me by the arm as we walked towards the Rue d'Italie: "I'm going to point out to you a charming girl whom I love and who loves me." I must admit that I straightaway saw a sort of black cloud before my eyes; I felt somehow that I was out of luck; and I was quite right for, as noon struck, Justine came out of her seamstress's workroom and, far away though she was, Seymard pointed to her and said: "That's the girl." I could see no more, my head was swimming, but Seymard dragged me along with him – and I touched the girl's dress . . .' And Cézanne lamented: 'Oh, what castles in the air I had been building! And how silly they were! But, you see, that's how it is: I kept thinking that, if she didn't dislike me, we might go to Paris, where I would become a painter and we should be together. I thought we might be happy. I dreamed of painting pictures, of a studio on the fourth floor, and of seeing you and of our laughing together. I didn't want to be rich – you know what I'm like – and I thought we could live happily on a few hundred francs. God knows, it was a wild dream!'

Cézanne could laugh about it; nevertheless, there was an underlying bitterness. But now the holidays were drawing near. Zola would be in Aix, and so would Baille, who was working very hard and had little time to write to his friends. Cézanne was delighted when he heard that Zola was due to arrive at the end of July. 'You know, if I were a good jumper, I would have hit the ceiling with joy, so much did I jump,' he wrote.

Though working hard for his *baccalauréat*, Zola had continued to write verses. He was beginning to feel more at home at the Lycée Saint-Louis, where he had made friends with a schoolfellow, Georges Pajot, who seemed to him to possess both intelligence and imagination. Emboldened by his innate need for the esteem of others, he risked reading a poem he had dedicated to the Empress to his schoolfellows. He did not, however, achieve the success for which he had hoped. It was harshly criticised. When Cézanne heard of this he thundered in his heroic-comic way against the 'myrmidons,' who had been incapable of appreciating his friend's genius.

At the beginning of August, Zola passed the written part of the *baccalauréat*, but success in the oral eluded him. He could not remember the date of Charlemagne's death; and his opinions on La Fontaine were thought to be heretical by the examiner in French literature. He decided to spend the holidays in Aix and try again in Marseilles in November.

Together again, the friends made the most of their time. Painting, poetry and love were discussed inexhaustibly. Cézanne was continually drawing and painting. Zola fell in love with a young woman of Aix, whom he nicknamed 'l'Aerienne,' but he could no more declare his passion than could Cézanne; however, he wrote a long love poem entitled *Rodolpho*. He also drew. At Villevieille's, he drew two women bathing in the manner of Jean Goujon and, at the Jas de Bouffan, he helped Cézanne paint a screen, some fifteen feet by nine, for Louis Auguste's study. On one side, there were country scenes and, on the other, garlands of leaves and flowers. Cézanne now always took a sketch-book or a canvas on their rambles. When he wanted to paint a picture of brigands, Zola, Baptistin and Isidore Baille disguised themselves in multi-coloured rags and posed for him at the Infernets. Then Cézanne himself sat to Chaillan, who wanted to paint his portrait. Alas, the portrait was no masterpiece. Chaillan had more assurance than talent. As for Baille, the future student of the Polytechnique, he determined to take lessons in literature so as not to be left behind and 'to approach mathematics as a poet and philosopher.' Nevertheless, he found it increasingly difficult to keep up with his friends in their wilder dreams and ambitions.

Zola's second year in Paris had been more successful than the first. He insisted that, if Cézanne wanted to become a painter, he must at all costs persuade his father of the necessity of his going to study in Paris. Aix could teach him nothing. The townspeople of Aix were philistines; Gibert was a pedant; and the Louvre was a necessity. In Paris, moreover, they would derive mutual encouragement from their friendship in their struggle for fame. Had Cézanne, Zola asked, spoken to his father of his vocation and ambitions as a painter?

Cézanne had spoken to his father, even though he was afraid of him, and well knew how annoyed Louis Auguste was whenever he surprised him with a paint-brush in his hand. Louis Auguste had at first been incredulous; the boy must be mad to want to do any such thing. It was not a question of whether or not he had talent: as far as Louis Auguste was concerned, to want to paint was merely absurd. It was no profession for a sensible man. He found it difficult to believe that his son, who should in the nature of things succeed him one day in the management of the bank, could be thinking seriously of anything so silly. It was high time that young Zola went back to Paris, for there was no doubt that he was influencing Paul and corrupting him with these absurd ideas. And since he was merely the son of a bankrupt engineer, it was more than likely that he was seeking some personal advantage. Nor was there any doubt that Paul's mother was partly to blame; her vanity would be flattered if Paul became a painter. Louis Auguste often found them whispering and plotting together. Surely, now that Paul was twenty, he would soon realise how utterly ridiculous the idea was.

Though Cézanne was angrily ordered back to his law studies, he was nevertheless tentatively planning, with the encouragement of his mother and Zola, to go to Paris in the following March.

* * *

In November Baille left Aix for Marseilles, where Zola was soon to follow him to sit for his *baccalauréat* again. This time he failed in the written examination and returned rather sadly to Paris. Cézanne, however, passed his first law examination with success on 28 November.

Alone again, Cézanne was immeasurably bored by Aix. 'So far,' he wrote to Zola, 'the usual and customary eventlessness has folded our dull town in its tedious wings.' He had returned to his law studies without enthusiasm. But his devotion to painting was continually increasing. He often went to the museum to copy some academic canvas, Dubufe's *Prisonnier de Chillon* or Frillie's *Baiser de la Muse*, which he interpreted with a personal impetuosity. For his mother, who was his sympathetic ally in his struggle against his father, he painted the *Fillette au Perroquet*. Madame Cézanne was delighted with the *Baiser de la Muse* which he also gave her, and hung it on the wall of her room. But Louis Auguste was far from pleased. 'My boy,' he said, 'you must think of the future. One starves with genius, but eats with money!' Yet, in spite of his testiness, Louis Auguste was concerned to see his son so unhappy. But, as Zola wrote to Cézanne at this time, 'life is a ball that does not always roll in the direction in which the hand tries to propel it.'

No one could have been in a better position to realise this fact than

Zola at this time. His failure in the *baccalauréat* had brought his bursary to an end and he had been forced to interrupt his studies. It was clear that he must find a job. But he was completely demoralised, felt himself incapable of earning his living, and could not bring himself to take any active steps towards it. He continued writing, but without much enthusiasm. He spent his time reading and smoking, longing for his friends and dreaming of inaccessible loves. 'I have very little to tell you,' he wrote to Baille in the last days of December. 'I hardly go out, and live in Paris as if I were in the country. I am in a back room, can hardly hear the noise of the traffic and, if it were not for the spire of Val-de-Grâce in the distance, could easily believe myself to be still in Aix.'

Villevieille had recently come to live in Paris, but Zola had no particular desire to see him: Villevieille was not Cézanne. Nevertheless, there was one event at this time which roused him a little from his lethargy: Marguery, who had played first cornet in the Collège Bourbon band, had recently joined the staff of the Aix newspaper, *La Provence*, and a novel of his was being serialised in it. Zola thought he would try his luck there too, and sent off *La Fée amoureuse*.

Thanks to Labot, at the beginning of 1860 Zola was expecting to get a job in the office at the docks. He could not go on being an expense to his mother, 'who can barely support herself.' He would divide his life into two halves. 'This is my position,' he wrote to Baille, 'to earn my living no matter how and, if I don't want to bid good-bye to my dreams, busy myself at night with my future. It'll be a long struggle, but it doesn't frighten me; I feel something latent within me and, if that something really exists, it will sooner or later see the light of day. So, no castles in Spain; a logical caution, first to make sure of enough to eat, and then to find out what there is in me, which may be much or little, and if I'm wrong, at least I'll be able to eat in my obscure employment and, like so many other people have to do, go through this wretched world with my tears and my dreams.' At least, this was what Zola intended in his better moments. But most of the time he was utterly despairing. His mother had changed her address once again and the lodgings she had taken were so small that Zola had to live out in a furnished room. His life seemed to be falling to pieces around him. He had lost his faith in himself and thought everything he had written 'puerile and detestable.' Paris was a desert of cold stones from which he could raise no echo. If only Cézanne could persuade his father to let him come to Paris in March as they had planned! Zola lived in that hope. 'I am utterly dejected, incapable of writing a word, incapable even of walking. I think of the future and it seems so appallingly black that I recoil in horror. No money, no job, nothing but discouragement. No one to lean on, no wife, no friend near me. Indifference and contempt on every side. These are all I see when I raise my eyes to the horizon . . .'

During February, it looked as if Cézanne was about to get his way. Louis Auguste seemed to be on the point of yielding at last to his son's pleas, which were supported by the rest of the family. Nevertheless before coming to a final decision, he determined to consult Gibert. Whether this was true fatherly concern or merely the tactics of a clever man well aware of his adversary's weak point, it is difficult to say. In the event, Gibert strongly disapproved; he would, of course, be losing a pupil.

This postponement seemed to Zola to augur very badly, particularly since Cézanne, always prone to lapse so promptly from enthusiasm to hesitation, now wrote asking him a most singular question: was it really possible to work well in Paris? Zola, who was well aware how easily his friend became discouraged and how incompetent he was at coping with everyday life, at once sent him a precise programme for his Paris days; its austerity was no doubt calculated to disarm Louis Auguste. 'This is how you will be able to divide your time. From six o'clock till eleven, you will go to a studio to paint from the life; then you'll have luncheon; then, from noon till four, you'll copy, either in the Louvre or in the Luxembourg, whatever masterpiece you please. This makes nine hours' work; I think it sufficient and that you will soon be doing good work with such a programme. We shall have all our evenings free and we can employ them as we like without prejudice to our studies. Then, on Sundays, we'll take flight and go a few miles out of Paris; there are delightful spots and, if you feel like it, you can record on canvas the trees under which we eat our luncheons.' Nor did Zola neglect the question of money. With the 125 francs monthly allowance* his father had agreed to give him, Cézanne should just be able to manage. 'I want to give you an outline of your expenses. A room at 20 francs a month; luncheon at 18 sous and dinner at 22 sous, which makes two francs a day, or 60 francs a month; add the 20 francs for your room and it makes 80 francs a month. Then you'll have to pay for the studio; that of Suisse, one of the least expensive, is, I think, 10 francs; over and above this, I add another 10 francs for canvases, paints and brushes, which makes 100 francs. You'll have 25 francs left for washing, light, and all the little expenses one has, such as tobacco and small pleasures. So you see you'll have just enough to manage on, and I assure you I'm not underestimating, indeed rather the contrary. Besides, it'll be very good training for you; you'll learn the value of money and how a clever man can always make do.' This last sentence was clearly written for Louis Auguste's eye. Moreover, Zola added: 'I advise you to show your father this calculation; perhaps the sad reality of the figures will persuade him to open his purse-strings a little wider. Besides, you'll be able to make a little money here yourself. Studies made in the studios and particularly copies made in the Louvre sell very well; and even if you only sell one a month, it will be a decent addition to your margin for the little pleasures of life. It all depends on finding a dealer, which is merely a matter of looking around. Come bravely; once bread and wine are assured, one can devote oneself safely to the arts.'

Unfortunately, Gibert, who was in any case probably rather sceptical about Cézanne's talent, maintained his opinion that it was no more difficult to become a painter in Aix than it was in Paris. Louis Auguste had no inclination to contradict him and it was therefore decided that Paul must first finish his law studies; meanwhile he might continue to work at drawing and painting in his spare time. After all, he had here in Aix an excellent master, as well as access to a museum full of masterpieces. Everything was clearly for the best. Besides, his little sister Rose had fallen seriously ill. Surely this was no time to leave home?

Cézanne's destiny was at stake, and he knew it. Paris lay waiting for him beyond the hills, the great centre of all success in the arts. His

* Approximately £20 today. The rich banker was clearly not being very generous. Perhaps he hoped to discourage his son.

disappointment was cruel and he became increasingly depressed, spending all his time out of the house, returning only to eat and sleep. Life in the Cézanne household was becoming ever more difficult.

But Cézanne continued to paint despite his dejection. He was inclined to be carried away by gusts of fury in which he hurled himself on his canvas and scraped out everything he had just painted. He had begun to doubt himself, and felt powerless to render what he wanted to express. Again and again he would abandon his palette in disgust.

'The painting I love though I cannot succeed in it . . .' Cézanne wrote in one of his letters to Zola. They had become rare now: Cézanne confessed that he no longer had the courage to write to his friend. But the phrase shocked Zola. 'You, not succeed!' he wrote. 'I think you're mistaken about yourself.' Zola was unhappy too. He had been hurt by his friend's failure to come to Paris in March. At the beginning of April, he had started work in the Docks Napoléon, in the Rue de la Douane, where he was earning sixty francs a month. He was intolerably bored. From nine in the morning till four in the afternoon, he filled in customs declarations and copied correspondence. The sun shining on the dirty windows of the office was a nostalgic reminder of his lost freedom. He was surrounded by dusty files and clerks 'who were for the most part stupid.' In spite of his own unhappiness, he nevertheless tried to summon up a little enthusiasm to communicate to Cézanne. 'The great painter of the future' must not give in. Things had not gone as they had hoped; but it would be absurd to think all was lost. He must behave sensibly. Zola outlined the conduct Cézanne must pursue: 'You must please your father by attending to the law as assiduously as possible. But you must also work hard and with determination at drawing – *unguibus et rostro*.'

Realising that they always discussed poetry in their letters and hardly ever painting, Zola – probably thinking he was being egoistic – decided to write to Cézanne about his passion and to give him advice. Cézanne – who very likely had his own reasons for not discussing painting with Zola – must have read his friend's interminable dissertations with some amazement. Zola was a dear, kind, affectionate fellow, but really very ignorant about painting. Indeed, Zola admitted it: in painting, he said, he could 'at the most distinguish between black and white.' This did not, however, prevent his holding positive opinions. He took a literary view of painting and could see nothing in a picture but its story. He warned Cézanne, in the name of poetry, against realism; and he declared his admiration for Greuze and for Ary Scheffer, 'that painter of genius,' who had died the previous year, and had been 'a passionate lover of the ideal.'

Zola also adjured Cézanne to resist the temptations of commercial art. 'The realists do create art – in their own way – and they work conscientiously. But commercial artists, who paint in the morning for their evening's supper, are merely grovellers.' Zola also told his friend of a dream: 'I had written a beautiful book, a sublime book for which you had designed sublime and beautiful illustrations. Our two names shone in letters of gold on the title page and went down to posterity inseparably linked in fraternal genius. Alas, it is still only a dream.'

Towards the end of April, Louis Auguste seemed less adamant. Cézanne informed Zola of it, who replied: 'Be firm, but not lacking in respect. Remember that it is your future which is being decided and that all your happiness depends on it.' But was the sky really clearing? One day Louis Auguste seemed to be giving in; but the next he was as intransigent as ever. These prevarications sapped Cézanne's will-power. After Villevieille, whom Zola had at last gone to visit on Easter Monday, Chaillan had now succeeded in getting to Paris. He was working in Père Suisse's studio, copying in the Louvre, and was very sure of himself. Truphème was shortly due to leave for Paris too. Cézanne's temper became increasingly uncertain. During the Easter holidays, Baille went out to the Jas de Bouffan; Cézanne would scarcely speak to him, and Baille came away very distressed. He had recently written to Zola, saying: 'When you realise that I am incapable of giving expression to art either in painting or poetry, don't you feel that I am unworthy of you?' To which Zola replied: 'When you see us, the art student and the scribbler, incapable of making a position for ourselves in life, don't you think us unworthy of you, poor bohemians that we are?' And now, on being rebuffed by Cézanne, Baille complained to Zola who, in his anxiety to preserve their friendship, hastened to calm him down and also to persuade Cézanne to be kinder. 'I have the impression,' he wrote to Cézanne, 'that the link between you and

Baille has weakened, that one of the links in our chain is on the point of breaking. It distresses me and I pray you to remember our happy times together, the oath we made, glass in hand, to march through life, arm in arm, along the same path.' No doubt Baille was not exactly as they were, no doubt his 'mind was not made in the same mould' but he nevertheless had a right to their kindness and deserved their affection. To Baille he wrote: 'As for poor old Cézanne,' he must be forgiven, for he 'does not always know what he is doing, as he is prepared to admit himself . . . When he upsets you, you mustn't take it to heart, but put it down to the bad demon who clouds his thoughts.' Very careful himself in his remonstrances to Cézanne, he counselled Baille to be tactful: 'Write to him regularly, and don't complain too much of his delays in answering you; let your letters be affectionate, as in the past, and free from all mention, all reminder of your little quarrel; in a word, let your relationship continue as if nothing had happened. He's a convalescent we're treating, and if we don't want him to have a relapse, we must avoid all imprudence.'

Zola was persuasive, for the only thing he possessed in life was the friendship of Cézanne and Baille. His job was becoming increasingly depressing. Sometimes, for a change of air, he went out to Saint-Cloud, Saint-Mandé or Versailles. Soon he found he could bear it no longer and resigned. He preferred poverty to stagnation. His decision was greeted with letters of dismay from Baille.

Baille, still very upset by Cézanne's behaviour to him (Cézanne had not renewed their correspondence), was finding it more and more difficult to understand why his friends acted as they did. Their behaviour distressed him. Placid, reliable and commonsensical, he blamed Zola 'for not facing reality bravely, for not trying to achieve a position in life of which you could be proud.' To which Zola replied: 'My poor dear chap, you talk like a child. Reality seems to be nothing but a word to you! Where did you encounter it? . . . I want a position in life merely so as to be able to dream at my ease. Sooner or later I shall return to poetry . . . You talk of the false fame of poets; you call them mad, you declare you won't be so foolish as to go and die in an attic merely for applause as they do . . .' Though Baille's attitude was 'blasphemy' and betrayed a profound misunderstanding, Zola did not care. Against all reason, he clung to their friendship, though every vicissitude in the lives of all three of them undermined it a little more. 'Of course, our different points of view in no way weaken our friendship!' he wrote.

Nevertheless, their relationship did not improve. In June, Zola admitted that Baille's letters made him lose patience. 'The word *position*,' he wrote, 'appears several times in your letter, and it makes me very angry. Those eight letters have something of the enriched grocer about them and they irritate me.' He added bitterly: 'This letter you've written to me is not that of a young man of twenty, not that of the Baille I knew . . . Are you really being sincere? Do you really no longer dream of liberty? . . . Are all your aspirations limited by material success? If it is so, my poor chap, I'm sorry for you; for, in that case, everything I've written to you will seem to you, as you say, lacking in reason, composure and commonsense.'

This quarrel naturally tended to make Zola think about his friendship with Cézanne. Was he right continually to try and whip up Cézanne's feeble energies, detach him from his family and the lethargy of Aix, and push him into the career of a painter? During this month of June, Cézanne was more discouraged than ever. His struggle with his father was still continuing. And also his struggle with painting. In a moment of exasperation, he talked of throwing away his paint brushes and giving it all up. But the fit passed; and he went back to his easel to torture himself afresh; for he could no more derive satisfaction from his painting than he could break himself of his desperate passion for it.

'God help me if I am your bad genius,' Zola wrote to him, 'if I am leading you to disaster by vaunting dreams and art. But I cannot believe it; the Devil cannot be concealed behind our friendship, leading us both to disaster. Take your courage in both hands, pick up your brushes again, and give your imagination free play. I have faith in you; and, if I am encouraging you in the path of misfortune, let it recoil on my own head.'

Zola, though his circumstances were of the greatest difficulty (he was making every effort to find employment but without success), had nevertheless recovered his fighting spirit. 'All or nothing,' was his motto. He was determined to live his life as he wished and, though it might mean failure, he would not give up his idea. Whatever happened, he was going to be a writer. 'I do not want,' he wrote to Baille, 'to follow anybody else's way of thought; not that I am ambitious to be the originator of a school – in general, such a man is always systematic – but I would like to find some unexplored approach, and achieve something more than the crowd of contemporary scribblers.' Much to Zola's regret, Cézanne appeared to have no such ambitions. Indeed he seemed less self-assured than ever and enthusiasm continued to alternate with depression. 'Illusion is my wet-nurse,' he wrote.

On the walls of the drawing-room at the Jas de Bouffan, he had painted four panels representing the Seasons; when finished, he signed them ironically, 'Ingres.' In the meantime, Zola was continually being informed either that Cézanne was coming to Paris in the near future or, alternatively, that he was going to give up painting for ever. 'I am writing to you to no purpose, since my actions contradict my words,' Cézanne wrote to Zola in July.

Zola was vexed and accused his friend of lacking strength of character. Cézanne's own irresolution was probably more responsible for his continual indecisiveness than his father's opposition. Zola scented apathy. Was Cézanne still urging his views on his father? Had he still any ambition? 'Is painting only a whim that caught you by the hair one day when you were bored? Is it merely a hobby, a subject for conversation, a pretext for not working at the Law? If so, I can understand your behaviour; you're quite right not to push things to extremes and create new difficulties for yourself with your family. But if painting is your vocation – as I have always thought it was – and if you think you can succeed when you have studied properly, then, as far as I am concerned, you're an enigma, a sphinx, an impenetrable mystery.'

Things were going from bad to worse for the friends. Their ship was leaking at every seam. In spite of all Zola could say, Baille was still offended and thought Zola had treated him as a 'fool.' Not at all, Zola replied. Nevertheless, he had to admit that the Baille who wrote him letters 'of such commonsense, of such hopeless reality' was no longer the gay companion of the past. He longed to go to Aix. Once there, he believed he could soon calm Baille and galvanise Cézanne into action.

But his life was very difficult. He had no money. His meals consisted only of bread and cheese, or even merely of bread dipped in oil. He could live only by gradually pawning his few possessions. Poverty was undermining his health and he was becoming nervous, anxious and unstable. The best remedy, he thought, would be a holiday in Aix, but he had to postpone it continually throughout the summer. However, there was one event that pleased him: Cézanne and Baille met in Aix during the summer and seemed to have forgotten their differences.

By the middle of October, Zola had given up all hope of being able to go to the Midi. There was no chance of seeing his friends this year. Weakened by lack of food, he succumbed to lethargy, 'despaired and thought of nothing.' Baille had told Zola that Cézanne would go to Paris the following March but Zola had been disappointed so often that he no longer believed in these plans and could not bring himself to write to Cézanne about their chances of meeting.

Contrary to Zola's belief, Cézanne had not given up the idea. In his own tortuous way, which so irritated his friend, he was aiming for his goal. His father had not given in; but nor had he. He had almost ceased going to the Law School now, and spent all his time this winter painting. He painted in the Drawing School, in the Museum, and at the Jas de Bouffan. He painted out of doors, sitting 'on the frozen earth, taking no thought for the cold.' He copied engravings, Cuyps and Lancrets, and he painted a dramatised self-portrait from a photograph. He even painted his father, sitting with his legs crossed, wearing a cap and reading a newspaper. The fact that Louis Auguste had consented to sit seemed almost an admission of defeat.

Nevertheless, realising his son was about to escape him, Louis Auguste, in a last flash of anger, overtly accused Zola of having 'by a base calculation' influenced Paul to go to Paris for his own personal advantage. But it was the last show of resistance. Zola, furious at the accusation, spent the last days of April preparing his defence and writing a letter of justification to Baille. But he never had time to send it. Very early one morning, he was awakened by hearing his name shouted on the stairs. He hurried to the door. Cézanne was on the landing.

Louis Auguste had capitulated. Only two days previously, nothing had been decided. And then, quite suddenly, Louis Auguste had said 'yes.' He determined to accompany his son to Paris and take Marie with them. Since Paul was set on sampling bohemian life, let him do so. Perhaps a few months of short commons would succeed better than any argument in instilling a little sense into the boy. The decision taken, Louis Auguste went to the cupboard for his polished shoes and his top hat. He would take the opportunity of visiting his Paris correspondents.

CHAPTER FOUR

The Attics of Paris

One night, I sat Beauty on my knee. – And I found her bitter. – And I insulted her.—RIMBAUD: *Une Saison en Enfer*

LOUIS AUGUSTE did not stay long in Paris. Having spent two or three days in a hotel in the Rue Coquillière, near the Halles, he returned with his daughter to Aix. Paul was to have an allowance of 150 francs a month* (twenty-five more than was originally intended), which would be paid to him by MM. Lehideux, the Paris correspondents of the Cézanne and Cabassol Bank.

At last Cézanne and Zola were together again. Their dream had come true. Cézanne took a furnished room in the Rue des Feuillantines, not far from the Panthéon district in which Zola lived.

It was with surprise and delight, and even with a certain awe that Cézanne discovered the Paris of 1861. The young provincial of twenty-two, with a broad Midi accent, was plunged suddenly into a completely unfamiliar world. The Second Empire was at its height. Beautiful *demi-mondaines* were ruining the sons of rich families and living in preposterous luxury, the fashionable met at Tortoni's and the Café Anglais, while Baron Haussmann had turned Paris into a building lot. On the Left Bank, where Cézanne and Zola lived, the Boulevard de Sébastopol† had just been pierced; the Rue de Rennes, the Rue des Écoles and the Rue Monge were being laid out; and the Palais des Thermes was in process of construction.

For Cézanne, who loved silence and solitude, Paris seemed a strangely noisy place. Zola, who had been moving from lodging to lodging, had ended up in the Rue Soufflot, in a house frequented by prostitutes, and often raided by the police. In spite of his letters, Cézanne had never really grasped the reality of Zola's wretched circumstances. Despite

* Approximately £25 today.
† Today the Boulevard Saint-Michel.

ill-health due to undernourishment, his inability to find a job, and the faded old overcoat and disreputable trousers that were his whole wardrobe, Zola had not lost confidence. He was continuing to be what he had always wanted to be: a poet; what was more, he had just finished a composition of some twelve hundred lines.

Zola hastened to take Cézanne to the Louvre, the Luxembourg and Versailles. In particular, the Salon of 1861 filled Cézanne with admiration. He extolled the canvases of Cabanel, Gérome, Meissonier and other official 'Masters' who were exhibiting there.

Cézanne set to work without delay. He intended entering for the examination for the École des Beaux-Arts, and to prepare himself for it he joined the Académie Suisse, to which he went every morning at six o'clock.

The Académie Suisse was established on the second floor of an old house in the Île de la Cité, at the corner of the Boulevard du Palais and the Quai des Orfèvres.* It had been founded by the Père Suisse, who had been a model in his youth. Many famous artists – Delacroix, Courbet and Bonington among them – had climbed the dirty and dilapidated wooden stairs that led to a large smoky studio, sparsely furnished with benches. There was no teaching at the Suisse; for a monthly fee, the students were simply provided with a model: a man during the first three weeks of the month, and a woman during the last.

In the same house there worked a dentist well-known for his low charges (he would extract a tooth for a franc) and his rough but effective methods. His huge sign was visible from far down the quay: 'Sabra, the dentist of the people.' From time to time, his patients would lose their way, walk into the studio, and at sight of the nude model retreat hastily, much to the amusement of the students. The future was very much in ferment at the Académie Suisse. The students scoffed at the Empire, criticised the famous painters of the day and were continually extolling new ideas, new principles of faith or revolt.

Only five or six years ago, a young bourgeois, Édouard Manet, had worked there; and this year, when he was approaching thirty, he was

* The house has been pulled down. The Préfecture de Police stands on its site.

exhibiting at the Salon for the first time. Up to a few months before a certain Claude Monet had also been working there but at the moment he was doing his military service in Algiers. It was at the Académie Suisse that this young man of twenty had made friends with another young painter, Camille Pissarro, who had been born in the Danish island of St Thomas in the Virgin Islands, and had come to France in 1855 to devote himself to painting. Pissarro had never been a student at the Académie Suisse, but he had often gone there to meet his friends when he was in Paris.

In this milieu, so new to him and so different from the School of Drawing at Aix, Cézanne was bound to feel strange. Fortunately, he met at the Suisse a man to whom his accent did not seem ridiculous: a compatriot called Achille Emperaire. He made friends with him at once.

Emperaire was a strange man. Physically, he was a hunch-backed dwarf with a huge head, bushy hair, and puny limbs. But he was possessed by an overbearing pride, and haunted by the beauty of women of whom he painted endless obsessional nudes. In an obstinate determination to increase his stature, he exercised every morning for an hour on the trapeze. He was ten years older than Cézanne, having been born in Aix in 1829, and was the son of an inspector of Weights and Measures at the Sous-Préfecture of Aix. All his life he had been ambitious for fame. Like Cézanne, he had attended Gibert's classes in Aix, and in 1857, when Cézanne was still at the Collège Bourbon, he had left for Paris. He lived, no one quite knew how, spending no more than ten sous* a day, but he was convinced of his genius and never abandoned his ambitions.

Cézanne and Emperaire had endless discussions about art. Emperaire took Cézanne to see the Rubens, the Titians, the Giorgiones and the Veroneses in the Louvre. Throwing back his mane of hair and wagging his little beard, he proclaimed his admiration for these princes of colour and of the splendours of the flesh, encouraging still further Cézanne's romantic imagination. In some ways they were very alike, as was proved by their immediate sympathy for each other. It was only over Delacroix that Emperaire and Cézanne disagreed. For Cézanne,

* Rather less than 2/– today.

Delacroix was a Master among Masters; but for Emperaire he was a mere dauber beside Tintoretto.

Cézanne gradually made more friends at the Académie; amongst them Antoine Guillemet, a charming young man with lively eyes and a handsome face and presence; and Francisco Oller y Cestero, a Spaniard born in Puerto Rico, who introduced him to Pissarro.

Pissarro, who was kindness itself, soon became very interested in Cézanne; he thought he showed talent and encouraged him to persevere. And this must have helped Cézanne for, if Paris had taught him anything, it was that to become a real artist he had everything to learn. He realised sadly that he knew nothing at all. How rash he had been to abandon the path in life that had been traced out for him. Cézanne had hardly been a month in Paris when, in moments of depression, of which there were many, he was already talking of returning to Aix and going into business. 'I don't want to strike a funeral note in these few lines,' he wrote on 4 June to Joseph Huot, 'but, *I must admit*, I am not feeling very gay. I seem to be jogging my little life from side to side . . . I thought, when I left Aix, that I was leaving boredom far behind me. I've merely changed locality, and boredom has followed me.'

Zola was distressed that his friend had become discouraged so soon. He tried to remonstrate with him but without success. 'Alas,' he wrote to Baille, 'it's no longer as it was in Aix, when we were eighteen, free and careless of the future.' Zola's own circumstances were far from satisfactory. Yet nothing – his poverty, his ill-health and his frightening uncertainty about the future – could impair his joy at being with Cézanne again. He would have liked to help him with advice and counsel. Unfortunately Cézanne showed little inclination to listen to him. Depressed and discontented, Cézanne was easily offended and became impatient with Zola's interminable discourses. He was annoyed by his protective attitude. Was Zola by any chance trying to put the 'grapnel' on him? Interrupting his friend, he would tell him that he understood nothing about it.

Zola wanted to publish three of his poems in a single volume; it was not that he was satisfied with them, but he was, as he said, 'tired of silence.' He longed to succeed in the most material sense of the word.

But Cézanne's preoccupations were quite different; his concern was with the eternal problems of his art, and he had become quite suddenly aware of their appalling difficulties; the realisation of this made him febrile and irascible, which Zola found disconcerting. He was unable to understand the reason for Cézanne's attitude and felt rebuffed. He thought his friend stubborn, ridiculous and unreasonable; and complained in long letters to Baille.

'To prove something to Cézanne,' he wrote, 'is like persuading the towers of Notre Dame to dance a quadrille. He may say "yes," but in fact won't budge an inch . . . He's all of a piece, stiff and hard under one's hand; nothing can bend him or drag a concession from him. He will not discuss his thoughts; he has a horror of argument, in the first place because talking is tiring, and secondly because he might have to change his mind if his opponent were right . . . All the same, he's the best chap in the world.' Zola concluded resentfully: 'I had hoped he might change a little as he grew older. But he's exactly as he used to be. My attitude towards him is therefore quite simple: I never try to talk him out of his moods; at the most, I give him only indirect advice; I rely on his good nature for the continuation of our friendship and never try to force him into an intimacy he does not want; in a word, I efface myself completely, always greet him with good humour, and seek him out without importuning him, leaving him to decide how much or how little intimacy he desires . . . Don't think there is any sort of cloud between us; we're still very united.'

Cézanne's and Zola's friendship was in no way broken but their meetings had become fewer. Zola had dreamed of expeditions into the countryside round Paris and along the banks of the Seine, as they had rambled in Provence; he had hoped for a life of the closest companionship; but these plans had dissipated like smoke. Cézanne, it was true, had started to paint a portrait of Zola, but work on it had been interrupted, and it only progressed when Zola plucked up courage to knock at Cézanne's door after luncheon. It was the one hour of the day, it seemed, when there was time for their friendship. In the morning, till eleven, Cézanne was at the Académie Suisse; he then had a fifteen sous luncheon by himself; in the afternoon, he went to work with Villevieille, who was now doing well and who helped him with advice; he then had dinner and went to bed. 'Was this what I had hoped for?' Zola sighed.

But there was nothing Zola could do about it. Cézanne sometimes disappeared for whole days at a time. The friends he had made at the Académie Suisse, his dear Zola, who was so touching in his importunate affection, Villevieille and his charming wife, who always welcomed him so cordially to their comfortable house, and Chaillan, whom he liked seeing occasionally, could none of them cheer him. Throughout the months of June and July, his distress was increasing. He drew and painted at the Académie Suisse and with Villevieille, but with even greater irritation and disgust, both with himself and with his work.

Worried and unhappy, Cézanne had left the Rue des Feuillantines for the Rue d'Enfer near by. He was hiding from his friends. Zola heard that he was considering leaving Paris for Marcoussis in the Seine-et-Oise. This seemed to Zola an absurd admission of failure. But there was nothing he could do about it.

Zola himself was in great need of encouragement. His health still far from good, he had taken a minor job correcting the works of an economist, who had promised to introduce him to writers and perhaps find him a publisher. It would be a long, hard struggle; and to whom could he turn for encouragement in moments of depression? Baille, like Cézanne, was also complaining; he hated the career for which he was preparing himself. Were all three of them to be failures? 'You can't believe,' wrote Zola to Baille, 'how much I resent your weakness in the struggle . . . When I see you doubting your intelligence and believing us incompetent, I tend to wonder whether it is only pride that enables me still to have confidence in my own and to attempt to do what you despair of. What is this ill wind that is blowing over us? . . . Have we already struggled so much that we must despair of victory, must we retreat before we have even advanced? I tell you, you're lacking in courage and you discourage me too; unlike you, I have not denied my youth; I have not said good-bye to my dreams of fame; I'm still staunch, and yet I'm the poorest and the most trammelled . . .'

In August, much to Zola's surprise, Cézanne returned from Marcoussis, fell into his arms and spent six hours a day with him.

Zola was delighted though anxious. Cézanne seemed more unstable than ever. Sometimes for a whole afternoon he would sing the same absurd little song; and then, in a sudden fit of depression, talk of returning to Aix at once. This idea was still firmly fixed in his mind; and Zola was well aware of it. Cézanne would gaze in consternation at his canvas or his drawing, and give way to the desire to throw down his palette and easel and become a shopkeeper, a clerk, no matter what, so long as he could rid himself of his obsession to paint. Zola did his best to convince him that returning to Aix would be sheer folly.

'If you write to him,' he advised Baille, who was on the point of taking the entrance examination to the École Polytechnique, 'try to mention the fact that we shall all soon meet again – and paint it in the brightest colours; it is the only way of holding him.' But, even with Baille's help, Zola was doubtful of success. Twice already Cézanne had been on the point of packing his bags.

On the second occasion, in an attempt to prevent Cézanne leaving Paris, Zola had suggested that he should go on with his portrait. Cézanne had agreed and at first had seemed delighted; but, alas, the portrait would not come right. Cézanne painted it over and over again, in a fury of discontent. Zola sat with infinite patience, as still and silent 'as an Egyptian sphinx.' But nothing would go right. Cézanne became increasingly discouraged.

One morning, when Zola arrived to sit, he found Cézanne busy packing his trunk. 'I'm leaving tomorrow,' he said. 'What about my portrait?' Zola asked. 'I've destroyed it,' said Cézanne, 'and I'm leaving.'

They went out to lunch together. Cézanne grew calmer and promised to stay. But Zola had lost all confidence in him. If Cézanne did not leave this week, he would leave next. 'He may even be doing the right thing,' Zola wrote to Baille. 'Paul,' he went on sadly, 'may have the genius of a great painter, but he will never have the genius to become one.'

Shortly afterwards, Louis Auguste welcomed the prodigal back to Aix. He seemed to have won.

CHAPTER FIVE

The Bank

If I exist, I am not another.—LAUTRÉAMONT: *Les Chants de Maldoror*

LOUIS AUGUSTE congratulated himself on having allowed his son to make the Paris experiment. It had ended as he had hoped. There was nothing like a good dose of reality to purge over-imaginative minds of their dreams. It seemed unlikely that Paul would now relapse into these puerile absurdities.

Cézanne showed no bitterness at his failure. Disgusted with Paris and painting, he felt relieved at having done with it and was delighted to be back in Provence. He was touched by the welcome he received from his mother and sisters, and even by his father's satisfaction, though it was perhaps a trifle too obvious. With no apparent regrets he began his apprenticeship in the family bank.

* * *

The general satisfaction was short-lived; despite his good intentions, Cézanne found it impossible to concentrate on the ledgers. He was bored and depressed; insidious memories of Paris diverted his attention: the Académie Suisse, the hours spent working with Villevieille, Zola and their dreams of fame. What was Zola doing now? They had parted coldly, and had not written to each other since. Baille, who had passed into the Polytechnique, was now in Paris. No doubt, on holidays, he and Zola made expeditions together.

On the slightest pretext, or none at all, the returned prodigal played truant from the office, wandering about the countryside and gazing at those landscapes he knew so well but which he seemed to discover each time anew. With every sense alert, he drank in the shapes and colours of the land, of the pines and olives in the autumn wind, of the red earth of Le Tholonet and, far off, dominating the whole landscape, the pyramid of Mont Saint-Victoire, now blue, now rose.

When he returned to the bank (where his father watched his comings and goings in silence), the narrow Rue Boulegon seemed to him a melancholy place. Life there consisted merely of monotony and routine.

It did not take long for Louis Auguste to realise that his son was going to escape him for good and all. He had been seen lying in the grass at the Jas de Bouffan, drawing. He had bought paints and canvases again; and he had returned to the Drawing School. It was becoming increasingly obvious that argument was useless. Paul had shown no interest in the business and had learned nothing. Moreover, in the Bank's big ledger, he had recently written:

> Cézanne le banquier ne voit pas sans frémir
> Derrière son comptoir naître un peintre à venir.

Louis Auguste was now sixty-three and, had things gone as he wished, he would have been in a position to think of retiring and handing the business over to his heir. But it was now clear to him that he would have no successor at the Bank. His son's passion for painting had proved the stronger. There was no alternative to allowing Paul to do what he wanted. After all, as his mother said: 'The boy can afford it.'

Back at the Drawing School, Cézanne was working with his old friends, Solari, Numa Coste, who was now a clerk in a solicitor's office, and the brilliant Joseph Huot who, not content with his successes at Gibert's, had founded an amateur theatrical company, the Théâtre Impérial du Pont de l'Arc, for which he wrote the plays himself. Cézanne painted out of doors with Numa Coste and worked also at the Jas de Bouffan where he had organised a studio for himself in the attic. The best proof that Louis Auguste had now yielded once and for all to his son's vocation was that he made no objection to a big window being pierced in the wall of the house to light the studio, though the exterior effect was not altogether happy.

And now Cézanne had to become reconciled with Zola. They had still not written to each other. Baille, however, had sent Cézanne a word at the end of the autumn. Through him, Cézanne had learned that Zola, who still had no proper job, was hoping to get one soon with Hachette; but he had no idea of the appalling circumstances to which his friend was now reduced.

In that glacial Paris winter of 1861, the idealistic young poet of twenty-one, who was still turning out hundreds of alexandrines so as 'to conquer the form,' had nothing left at all: no money, no food and no fuel with which to keep warm. He often had to pawn his last few clothes and had nothing to wear. To keep warm, he wrapped himself in the blankets off his bed (which he called 'going Arab') and sometimes had to endure this condition for three or four days at a time. He was becoming increasingly weak and ill, though his ill-health was perhaps even more psychological than physical. It made him ill to realise that he was 'losing not only the present, but the future too.' Yet, his determination to conquer Paris was still alive.

'My mind is awake and functioning marvellously,' he wrote. 'I believe that I am even growing through suffering. I see and understand better. New senses, which I lacked for certain things, have been vouchsafed me.'

A friend from Aix had put him in touch with a group of students in the Quartier Latin who were publishing a satirical review, *Le Travail*, which was critical of the Empire. They were in search of a poet. Zola submitted some verse. His contribution was accepted and published, though its idealism, tinged with religion, was not altogether to the taste of the editor, a twenty-year-old student from the Vendée called Georges Clemenceau. 'If the review continues publication,' Zola wrote, 'I may begin to make something of a name.' But the police had their eye on *Le Travail*, and were awaiting the opportunity to prosecute.

Day after day, Zola waited for a letter from Hachette. An old friend of his father's, M. Boudet, a member of the Académie de Médecine, had given him an introduction to these publishers but the firm delayed writing to him. On 1 January, 1862, M. Boudet asked Zola to deliver his New Year cards round Paris for him. It was disguised charity; Zola was rewarded with a *louis*. With Baille, whom he saw regularly on Sundays and Wednesdays ('we don't laugh much'), Zola talked of the past, the future, and no doubt often of Cézanne. Zola could not have believed that Cézanne would be discouraged so quickly, that he would prefer the line of least resistance to the struggle for fame.

Then suddenly, in January, he received a letter from Cézanne, who said he was painting again and contemplating a return to Paris in March. 'My dear Paul,' Zola replied immediately, 'I haven't written to you for a long time, I don't really know why. Paris did our friendship no good; perhaps to exist happily it needs the sun of Provence? No doubt it was some unfortunate misunderstanding that cooled our relationship . . . No matter, I believe you are still my friend; I hope you think I'm incapable of behaving basely and that you still have the same esteem for me as in the past . . . But I don't want to write a letter of explanations to you. I want merely to answer your letter as a friend, and talk to you a little, just as if your stay in Paris had never happened.'

Cézanne felt reborn now that he had taken up his brushes again. Like Zola, he could say that he had grown as a result of his difficulties and that his understanding was greater. He was becoming aware of his true character, realising his essential instability and his need of continuous change. The thought of Paris was beginning to haunt him again; but he knew very well that as soon as he found himself there, he would be obsessed by thoughts of Aix. He needed them both. As he learned from experience, he was able to turn this weakness of his into a strength.

Nevertheless, Cézanne hesitated and did not set off for Paris in March after all. Meanwhile Zola had at last got the job in Hachette. He began by doing up parcels, but it was not long before he was moved to the advertising department. Despite the promotion, he still sighed for his lost freedom. But things were better. He was writing with greater fury than ever; spending all his evenings, Sundays and free days at his desk.

The weeks went by, summer came, and for a while the three friends were reunited in Aix. Cézanne painted a view of the Infernets dam. Zola was writing the first pages of a novel, *La Confession de Claude*, a bitter love story, set against a background of the kind of poverty that he himself had suffered. But now the future was smiling with promise. 'Faith has returned. I believe and hope,' Zola was able to declare.

Back in Paris in September, he began making plans. He approved of

Cézanne's wish to divide his time between Paris and Aix. He thought it a 'way of avoiding the influences of the schools so as to develop any originality one may have . . . We shall organise our lives, spending two evenings together a week and working the others.' And, he added, 'The hours we spend together will not be wasted.'

Cézanne, however, did not arrive in Paris until the beginning of November. Once again, he had had to convince his parents of the necessity, combating not only his father's stubbornness but his mother's affectionate solicitude. He wanted, he said, to complete his studies and enter for the examination to the École des Beaux-Arts.

Impatience

PART TWO

[1862 - 1872]

CHAPTER ONE

Le Déjeuner sur l'Herbe

> The great penguin people had no traditions, no intellectual culture, no arts . . . An immense ugliness lay over everything.—ANATOLE FRANCE

CÉZANNE'S mood when he returned to Paris was very different from that in which he had left the capital more than a year previously. He had no doubt now of where his vocation lay and at once set about organising his life. Faithful to the Left Bank, he went to live in the Rue de l'Est,* a quiet street by the Luxembourg Gardens, which he could see from his window. He rejoined the Académie Suisse, where he worked regularly every day from eight till one, and again in the evening from seven till ten. Since Villevieille was out of Paris, he asked a friend named Chautard to correct his studies.

So for the first time the three inseparables were together in Paris. Between work they met frequently and gave each other mutual encouragement. Zola wrote in his room every evening till midnight, abandoning poetry for the time being to produce a stream of novels in the hope that he might find a publisher. His job with Hachette bored him. It could only be a temporary solution. However, it had put him in touch with a number of famous writers, and others less so but equally important in Zola's eyes, such as Duranty, the unrecognised apostle of realism in literature, a sad, rather bitter man, to whom Zola listened with passionate interest.

Occasionally the friends saw other young men from Aix: Chaillan, still disarmingly ingenuous and imperturbably daubing away and, less enthusiastically, Truphème, who had won the first prize for painting in Aix the previous year, and was now working at the École des Beaux-Arts. A friend of Truphème's had said that he 'dethroned Delacroix'; and this irritated Cézanne, who idolised that painter.

* This street no longer exists.

Delacroix was sixty-three at this time. He was ill and his life was drawing to a close. Nevertheless, his work was still accepted if with reluctance. His critics compared him to his disadvantage with Ingres; in fact, Ingres was the object of more lip service than true appreciation.

The painting that found real favour during this period was that taught at the École des Beaux-Arts: pastiche and the sentimental anecdote. Though Cézanne had received his first artistic education from the conformist Gibert, and sought advice from Villevieille and Chautard, both of whom were entirely academic, this approach to painting embarrassed and irritated him. There was a curious and illogical streak in Cézanne. Only eighteen months ago he had been admiring the paintings in the Salon; and now he wanted to join the École des Beaux-Arts, although he was already instinctively reacting against the teaching given there.

At this time painting for Cézanne was almost an opportunity for confession, a means of freeing himself from his obsessions. He was trying to express his own dark universe in macabre inventions that were implicit with a feverish and frustrated sexuality. Jokingly he said: 'I don't need women, they put me off. I don't even know what they're good for; I've always been too frightened to try.' But his joking merely revealed his underlying anxiety. His painting was violent in composition, dark and sombre in tone, with here and there a strident patch of colour. He was maddened by his incompetence for, having more temperament than technique, he could not give expression to his vision. He distorted forms and tortured anatomy in an absurdly awkward attempt at realism.

He laboured painfully at his canvases, applying layer upon layer of paint with the palette knife, accentuating and exaggerating with a curious brutality, the result manifesting an impetuous, chaotic and uncontrolled energy. It was as if he were trying to live his emotions in his painting, rather than to translate them. Intellectually a realist, romantic by temperament, he was clumsily endeavouring to fuse irreconcilable tendencies.

However, he was never discouraged for long, and in January 1863, two months after his arrival in Paris, he was writing to Numa Coste and Villevieille: 'I am working calmly, and eating and sleeping calmly too.' He had renewed his friendships with his companions of the Académie Suisse, Emperaire and Oller, with whom he sometimes went to paint in the neighbourhood of Saint-Germain, and also with Pissarro and Guillemet.

Pissarro helped Cézanne a great deal. There was no one more loyal, sensitive yet sensible, modest yet assured, and Cézanne was happy in his company. Cézanne's liking for Guillemet was of a different order: four years Cézanne's junior, Guillemet had the great merit of being amusing; he was handsome, good-tempered, superficial and Rabelaisian. He enjoyed the good things of life and had no financial anxieties, since his father, a wholesale wine-merchant, made him a substantial allowance. He was one of Cézanne's favourite companions.

When spring came, Cézanne and Zola made expeditions into the surrounding countryside almost every Sunday. They would leave by an early train, get out at Fontenay-aux-Roses, and walk through the strawberry fields to the woods of Verrières. They sometimes lost their way, and on one occasion discovered a lake 'full of reeds and weedy water,' which they christened the 'Green Lake.' It became the goal of many of their expeditions. While Cézanne tried to paint the lake, Zola lay in the shade of a tree, reading, dreaming and gazing up at the sky through the leaves. In the evening, on their way home, they often went by Le Plessis-Robinson to enjoy for a while its noisy, holiday atmosphere. There the tavern was overhung by the branches of an old chestnut tree; the air was mild; barrel-organs poured out interminable waltzes; the women's dresses seemed to float under the lamps; and laughter sounded 'like shivers' in the night.

* * *

Cézanne failed the entrance examination to the École des Beaux-Arts. 'He paints riotously,' declared one of the examiners. Cézanne was annoyed by the decision, which seemed to him unjust. But Pissarro consoled him, assuring him that the teaching at the Beaux-Arts was sterile, and that living art, the painting of tomorrow, would never come out of that school.

'Living art' had for years past been struggling against the officialdom of painting, as well as against the taste of a conventional bourgeois public entirely preoccupied with material matters and totally lacking in artistic sensibility. This public no more recognised the talent of Corot than it did that of Delacroix, Millet or Courbet. Vitality was suspect, originality intolerable. The views of the Hanging Committee of the Salon, accepted as law by amateurs of art, were at once a reflection – and a condemnation – of the opinion of the majority. To be hung on the line in the Salon was the one chance a painter had to sell his work. But the Hanging Committee in general was far from exercising judicial detachment. Its members put forward the claims of their pupils or friends. Votes were bartered. Acceptances and rejections were often decided without the works even being seen. And the number of pictures submitted, amounting to several thousands, in no way diminished the confusion resulting from these intrigues. Indeed, on one occasion the Hanging Committee had inadvertently rejected works by its own members, having failed to take note of the signatures. This danger was now prevented by a rule that entitled the work of artists who were members of the Academy, or had won medals at previous Salons, to be hung automatically without examination.

In 1863 the Hanging Committee, influenced by certain of its members, was exceptionally intransigent. It refused to accept work that was not narrowly and conventionally academic. Four thousand paintings were rejected, including a canvas by Pissarro, who had had a landscape accepted in 1859.

The discontent aroused among painters by this decision was so fierce that news of it eventually reached the Tuileries. As a result, on 22 April, the Emperor went to the Palais de l'Industrie,* where the Salon was then held, and after a rapid glance at the rejected works, he decreed that they should also be shown to the public, but in another part of the Palais. Everyone would then be able to judge for himself. This 'Exhibition of Rejected Works' was to open a fortnight after the Salon, on 15 May. The Imperial Decree was published in the *Moniteur* on 24 April.

* Erected for the Universal Exhibition of 1855, the Palais de l'Industrie no longer exists. It was pulled down in 1900, when the Avenue Alexandre III was laid out across its site.

This decision caused considerable excitement and gave rise to very diverse views. Some praised the Emperor for his liberalism, others criticised him for contesting the Hanging Committee's selections. Others, who had no doubts concerning the soundness of the selections made, were delighted that the bad artists should be held up to ridicule by a public exhibition of their works. The painters were allowed, however, if they so wished, to withdraw from the exhibition, and some did. But for the painters in conflict with the supporters of academic art there could be no dilemma: this was too good an opportunity to appeal directly to the public. Pissarro was naturally among them, and three of his landscapes were among the six hundred pictures and sculptures on view to the public on 15 May. The works on show were a very mixed lot; the Hanging Committee of the Salon, in its annoyance, had deliberately hung the poorest pictures in the best places. The exhibition attracted an enormous crowd; there were seven thousand visitors the first day; and since the Salon itself was almost empty, the wits said that next year the members of the Hanging Committee would take care to be among the rejected. But in actual fact, most members of the public came to mock; and in this they were encouraged by the press. The exhibition became known as the Salon des Refusés and Cézanne, like every other young artist, naturally went to see it. Many of the works displayed were grossly incompetent; on the other hand, never had so many paintings revealing the most daring tendencies of the period been shown before. The public laughed indiscriminately at them all; but its sarcasms were mostly reserved for the more remarkable works. Édouard Manet, who had received an 'honourable mention' for his *Espagnol Jouant de la Guitare* two years before, was among the rejected. He exhibited three pictures and three etchings. One of these pictures, *Le Bain*, aroused more scandal than any other work in the exhibition. It showed two fully-dressed men and a nude woman sitting by a stream, together with another woman paddling half undressed, and was considered thoroughly immoral. The canvas was also technically provocative in its contempt for academic canons. Its simplicity and clear colouring were considered vulgar and outrageous. The Emperor himself characterised the picture as 'indecent'; and it was soon derisively given a new title: *Le Déjeuner sur l'Herbe*.

Cézanne realised at once how far removed this painting was from the ineptness of the official allegories and sentimental anecdotes. It was, no doubt, very different from what he himself was searching for at that time. But its colour, audacity and precision delighted him. He recognised in Manet a master, and his picture as 'a kick in the backside' for the gentlemen of the Institute and the École des Beaux-Arts.

Zola accompanied Cézanne to the Salon des Refusés. They agreed about the paintings. Zola also admired *Le Déjeuner sur l'Herbe;* but it was the revolutionary modernism of the subject that attracted him, rather than the virtuosity of its technique, to which Cézanne endeavoured to draw his attention. Zola's remained a literary approach.

The Salon des Refusés, by emphasising the profound differences that separated the hide-bound official art from the 'unofficial,' gave this new generation of artists an awareness of their own existence. They began to meet and talk more than they had done in the past, and to form groups and friendships. At this time Guillemet introduced Cézanne to Frédéric Bazille from Montpellier, a young giant of twenty-one – a head taller than any of his friends – with a blond beard and long moustaches. He belonged to a Protestant family of rich wine-growers and had come to Paris to study medicine, in deference to his family's wishes, and to paint, in deference to his own.

Bazille attended the studio of a teacher at the École des Beaux-Arts named Gleyre; but soon found the teaching too dull for his taste. He preferred the painting of Delacroix and Courbet; while Manet, in the Salon des Refusés, was a revelation to him. In their common enthusiasm, Cézanne and Bazille made friends at once.

At this time Bazille shared a studio in the Rue de La Condamine, in the Batignolles, with a friend who also worked at Gleyre's, a slender young man of about the same age as himself, Auguste Renoir.* One day Bazille took both Cézanne and Pissarro to his studio. 'I'm bringing you two capital recruits,' he said to Renoir.

The son of a poor tailor, Renoir had earned his own living from the age of thirteen; he had decorated porcelain, fans, venetian blinds and

* Renoir was born at Limoges on 25 February, 1841.

even cafés; and was generally poorly paid. His ambition was to become a 'real painter,' and he had managed to save enough money to attend regular classes for a year. In April 1862, he had entered the École des Beaux-Arts and worked with Gleyre. But he did not get on well with his teachers. He was reproached for being unable to understand that 'the big toe of Germanicus must have greater majesty than the big toe of the coal-merchant on the corner.' His use of colour was also thought to show dangerous tendencies. 'Take care not to become another Delacroix!' one of his masters had said angrily. On another occasion, Gleyre had remarked with asperity: 'I suppose you paint simply for fun?' To which Renoir retorted with candour: 'Of course, and if it wasn't fun, I assure you I wouldn't do it!'

At Gleyre's, Renoir and Bazille formed part of a small, undisciplined group, which worked independently of the other students in the studio. Claude Monet, who had known Pissarro at the Académie Suisse, and whose military service in Algiers had been interrupted by illness, became the leader of this group. Compelled to submit to academic teaching by his family, Monet barely concealed his hostility to Gleyre, and incited Renoir and Bazille to rebellion, as well as another member of the studio, a young Englishman called Alfred Sisley.*

In the discovery of a common bond these young men, who had till now been more or less isolated in their struggles, gained assurance. Zola, whom Cézanne took to the studios, enjoyed the atmosphere of battle, and delighted in the passionate discussions. The young men swore by Delacroix, Courbet and Manet, and mocked the teaching of their masters, and of Gleyre in particular, who had said, when correcting a study by Monet: 'Not bad, not bad at all, but it's too much like the model. You've got a squat model; and you paint him squat. He's got huge feet; and you paint them as they are. It's all very ugly. You must remember, young man, when you're painting the figure, always to think of the antique.' Cézanne, who was becoming much less unsociable in this atmosphere, raged against 'teachers who have no sand in the belly!' As a declaration of rebellion he began to wear a red waistcoat and, to Zola's despair, went to sleep on public benches, using his shoes as a pillow. He was making a cult of the provocative.

* Sisley was born in Paris on 30 October, 1839, in the same year as Cézanne.

Cézanne often ate in a little restaurant much frequented by students. The *patronne's* husband was a scavenger and Cézanne asked him to sit for his portrait. The scavenger refused. 'But you work at night,' said Cézanne. 'You do nothing during the day.' The man said he rested during the day. 'Very well, I'll paint you in bed!' said Cézanne. The scavenger got into bed and put on a cotton nightcap, but was persuaded to remove it, throw off the sheets and pose naked. Cézanne painted a picture of pure realism, in which he depicted the *patronne* bringing her husband a bowl of hot wine. It was a sardonic work, nicely calculated to make 'the Institute blush with rage and despair.' Guillemet found a title for it: *Un Après-Midi à Naples* or *Le Grog au Vin*.

Stimulated by the general excitement, Zola was emboldened one Saturday evening to place the manuscript of a volume of verse on Louis Hachette's desk. Hachette, now a man of sixty-three, had had a difficult boyhood under the First Empire. His father had been ruined, and his mother had become a linen maid at the Lycée Impérial* so that he might be admitted as a boarder. He had passed into the Normale Supérieur in 1819, and had won the gold medal for the best pupil. He had founded the business in the Rue Pierre-Sarrazin in 1826, since when it had continuously expanded. Louis Hachette read Zola's work and sent for him on the Monday. He talked to him kindly about his poems, refused to publish them, but encouraged him to persevere and advised him to write prose; as an additional encouragement he increased Zola's salary to two hundred francs a month.

It was some time now since Zola had left the Rue Soufflot. Since then he had changed lodgings more than once. In July, he took a three-roomed flat at 7, Rue des Feuillantines. In his need for friendship, and the warmth of a group with aims and ambitions similar to his own, he made a habit of providing dinner on Thursday nights for his friends. Any who cared to come were welcome: Cézanne, Baille, Chaillan, Guillemet, Pissarro and friends from Aix who might visit the capital, such as Antony Valbrègue, a young man of nineteen from a comfortably-off Aix family, who wrote verse. Cézanne and Baille, who had known him in Aix, introduced him to Zola, and they at once became friends. No doubt, the dinners were sparse and the wine

* Now the Lycée Louis-le-Grand.

watered, but the diners, as Zola declared, hungered for success and fame more than for material nourishment.

* * *

1863 was coming to an end. Cézanne continued to work hard. He went to the Louvre frequently: it was almost his school. At that time, there were many copyists in the Louvre and the grand gallery was often crowded with their easels. Cézanne sometimes took his own to join them, but more often he went to meditate in front of the great masterpieces, and make rapid notes in his sketchbook. He was as much attracted by the sculpture as by the painting, particularly that of Michelangelo and Puget. Puget was 'one of those who smell of garlic. There is *mistral* in Puget; he can make marble live.' During the winter, Cézanne copied Delacroix' *La Barque du Dante:* and in doing so he was perhaps rendering a private homage to the old master who had died that August, at the age of sixty-five, in the loneliness of his genius. Delacroix remained always an unforgettable example to Cézanne.

In 1864, Cézanne wrote to Numa Coste: 'My hair and beard are more abundant than my talent. Nevertheless, I am not discouraged about my painting.' Numa Coste had had the misfortune to draw an unlucky number in the conscription lottery: he would have to do seven years' military service. Cézanne, for whom his father had bought a substitute, advised his friend to anticipate his calling up so that he might be able to select his regiment and be garrisoned in Paris. Baille, who now knew a number of officers, might be able to help him and Coste would still be able to devote some time to painting.

Cézanne did not intend returning to Aix till July. In the meantime, he hoped to send a canvas to the Salon. It was said that this year's Hanging Committee would be much less intransigent, and that a room would be allotted to exhibitors 'judged too weak to take part in the competition for prizes' but who nevertheless wished to exhibit. Pissarro and Renoir, like Cézanne, intended submitting their work, but Monet, Bazille and Sisley proposed to abstain, as did a new friend Cézanne had made at the Académie Suisse, Armand Guillaumin who, though very poor, had left his job on the Orléans Railway to devote himself to painting.

In the event, the Hanging Committee showed a certain spirit of conciliation. They accepted two of Manet's works, which aroused an uproar among the critics and the public; they also accepted two landscapes by Pissarro and a canvas by Renoir, which was not, it was true, very good (immediately after the Salon, Renoir destroyed it in a fit of remorse), but they rejected Cézanne.

Cézanne did not apparently take this much to heart. The fact was that he had fallen in love. He even cut off his beard in honour of his beloved, or as Zola told Valabrègue, he sacrificed its 'tufts on the altar of victorious Venus.'

At this time he was painting the portrait of a young woman. Her name was Gabrielle Éléonore Alexandrine Meley, and she was the same age as Cézanne. Her mother was dead and she helped an aunt in her flower shop in the Place Clichy.

Whether or not this was the girl Cézanne was in love with we may never know, but it is certain that Zola was in love with her. Though fundamentally as shy as Cézanne, Zola was more aggressive. His need to assert himself compensated for his self-doubt. Success and fame were desirable because he felt a need for tangible certainties, the protective barrier they afforded and the peace they brought or should bring. His was a constant effort towards reassurance. Had Zola, at this time, ever 'known' a woman in the Biblical sense of that word? We do not know. But, like Cézanne, he had the same 'passion of the chaste for a woman's body, an overwhelming longing for the nakedness of the flesh, so much desired and never possessed.'* Gabrielle became Zola's mistress.†

In July Cézanne and Baille went to Aix, leaving Zola in Paris. After three rejections, the publishers Hetzel et Lacroix had accepted a volume of Zola's short stories, *Contes à Nanon*, based on his memories of Provence. It was published in October 1863.

* Zola: *L'Oeuvre*.

† My placing of the rather obscure start of Zola's relationship with Gabrielle Meley, who was eventually to become his wife, in 1864 may be questioned. My authority is a photograph of Madame Zola, taken by Zola himself in 1901, and now in the collection of the Assistance Publique at Médan. It is inscribed 'to the companion of thirty-seven years.'

CHAPTER TWO

Experiments

> 'It is only his initial force, *id est* his temperament, that can carry a man forward to the goal he should attain.'—CÉZANNE: *Lettre à Charles Camoin*, 22 February, 1903

ALTHOUGH Aix was very dear to him, Cézanne did not intend to stay there long. He wanted only time to draw breath and assimilate what he had learnt, and then to return to Paris. But his family saw to it that he had much less freedom than he enjoyed in Paris.

Though Louis Auguste had given in, he was still inclined to be sullen about the situation. Paul's incomprehensible vocation was not only a disappointment to him, he was irritated by the comment it aroused. Having made a success of his own life, it was infuriating to have a son of twenty-five who was a failure, not only in his own eyes, but in the eyes of others. It made him irritable and bitter, and this created an intolerable atmosphere for Cézanne. His comings and goings were watched and remarked on; he had to account for his actions. Moreover, whether from malevolence, or mere love of gossip, the little town kept its eye on him and reported everything he did.

His peculiar behaviour, his temper and his silences, even the clothes he wore, tended to arouse either amusement or disapproval. It was lucky for young Cézanne that he had his father behind him. But Cézanne was fundamentally indifferent to his father's fortune. He was not like Zola, for whom fame meant also wealth. To have a hundred and fifty or two hundred francs a month to live on and buy paints and canvases was all Cézanne required to be able to work in peace. But it was impossible to achieve the peace he desired in Aix. He felt oppressed even by his mother's love, which made the struggle to get away again all the more difficult.

His sister Marie also tried to prevent his going and to keep him within the narrow world of the family. She had recently had an offer of marriage from a naval officer; but her parents had not approved and she had resigned herself to their wishes. This was the more unfortunate, since she had few pretensions to beauty. Indeed, she was rapidly developing into the traditional old maid and turning to religion for consolation. Lacking a husband, her natural authority weighed heavily on her brother, and on her sister Rose, who was only ten. In a moment of anger Cézanne said his family were 'the most horrible people in the world, and bores into the bargain.' They could neither understand him nor, indeed, his painting, which they considered the whim of a spoilt child.

Cézanne escaped from them as much as he could. He went to the museum to see the pictures he admired, *Les Joueurs de Cartes*, attributed to Louis Le Nain, the Granets, and Puget's self-portrait. Or he went out into the Aix countryside, sometimes even as far as l'Estaque, where his mother had leased a little fisherman's cottage on the Place de l'Église.* The village was characteristically Provençal and had great charm. Cézanne loved its peace. But most often he would shut himself up in the Jas de Bouffan. He made it his own domain, and annexed the big salon, in which he continued his mural decorations, occasionally drawing his inspiration from the engravings in one of his art books.

He allowed no one to enter his studio. It was indescribably untidy, littered with empty tubes, old brushes and unfinished canvases. Cézanne spent day after day there, trying to give form to the visions that haunted him. He worked a certain amount from nature, but at this time it interested him less than the endeavour to express himself. But in this he was scarcely successful. As a painter, Cézanne was like a pioneer seeking to discover a new world, none of whose secrets had been transmitted to him. Except for Gibert, he had had no master. He had to explore alone and teach himself. It was a desperate apprenticeship. Infuriated by his failures, he tore canvases to pieces or kicked them into a corner of the studio; only to begin again and work harder than ever at the next picture.

Cézanne saw only a few friends at this time; Solari, Marguery, who had become a barrister, Henri Gasquet, now a baker, and Valabrègue.

He had also made friends with a young naturalist, Fortuné Marion.

* Place Maleterre today.

Intelligent and passionately devoted to the natural sciences, Marion had made discoveries in the Aix region which had brought him to the attention of Gaston de Saporta, the Aix expert, and of the professors of the Faculté des Sciences of Marseilles, who had been so struck by his talents that, two years before, in 1862, they had appointed him laboratory assistant in Natural History. At that time he was barely seventeen.

Since then, Marion had passed his *baccalauréat* and was now working for his degree and assembling information for two theses, one of which was on Early Man in the Bouches-du-Rhône. He was also intensely interested in music and painting; and painted in his spare time. He developed a great admiration for Cézanne, both as a man and as a painter. He was aware of Cézanne's latent power, and felt sure from the first that when he had disciplined it he would be on the road to becoming one of the greatest painters of the period. Whenever he could, Marion went with Cézanne on his painting expeditions. He set up his easel next to Cézanne's, listened to his views on painting with respect, and in return instructed him in the geology of Provence.

At the end of October, Cézanne received a copy of the newly published *Contes à Ninon*. Zola, in Paris, was busy turning to good use such contacts as he had made and whose number, as he had recently written to Valabrègue, he was continually trying to increase. His old friend of the Pension Notre-Dame, Marius Roux, now a journalist in Paris, wrote an article about the book in *Le Mémorial d'Aix*, and on the whole the critics received it favourably. The young men in Aix who either knew Zola or had heard tell of him, and were also longing to make their way in the capital, read it with enthusiasm. At last, a boy from Aix was beginning to make a name for himself. The conquest of Paris had begun.

* * *

Cézanne returned to Paris at the beginning of 1865, after six months' stay in Provence.

He did not go back to the Left Bank, but went to live in the Marais, at 22, Rue Beautreillis, in a seventeenth-century house, the Hôtel de Charny. Though it was inhabited mostly by clerks and people of modest means, it still had an air about it: an elegant façade, and a handsome dark green door opening into an arched vault where there were still *boiseries*. Cézanne leased an attic on the fourth floor, which was reached by a staircase at the farther end of the courtyard. It is not recorded whether he knew that some six or seven years earlier Baudelaire had lived in the house, but it seems probable. For Baudelaire was one of Cézanne's favourite poets. He could recite the whole of the *Fleurs du Mal* thanks to his extraordinary memory. (He also knew by heart the contents of most of the picture galleries in Europe, though he had never visited them.)

It was probably through Oller, who lived in the house, that Cézanne found his attic. The two friends no doubt often walked together along the quay to the Académie Suisse, where Cézanne had begun to work again.

He soon renewed contact with all his friends, and in particular with Zola, who had left the Rue des Feuillantines in July, and was now living in a sixth-floor flat with a balcony, at 278, Rue Saint-Jacques, where he continued his 'Thursday evenings.' But Zola was terribly overworked at this time, for he was determined not to let slip the modicum of renown he had acquired with *Contes à Ninon*, and was branching out in every possible direction.

Louis Hachette had unfortunately died the preceding year; but Zola was still employed in the business for ten hours a day. Nevertheless, he managed to write an article of one hundred to one hundred and fifty lines each week for *Le Petit Journal* and, every fortnight, another, of five or six hundred lines, for *Le Salut Public* of Lyons. He was also trying to find time to finish the novel he had begun two or three years before, *La Confession de Claude*. Zola had suffered too much poverty not to want to exploit his success. 'You must realise that I don't write all this stuff simply for love of the public,' he wrote to Valabrègue . . . 'The question of money has had a good deal to do with it, but I also think journalism has a powerful effect and I am not at all sorry to be able to appear on fixed days before a considerable number of readers.' By journalism Zola was able at least to double his income, and was probably earning altogether about five hundred francs a month.*

There were also other advantages: by writing critical articles, he

* Rather more than £20 a week today.

was able to praise the writers he admired and thereby make allies of them. 'At the moment, I must simply go on and on whatever happens. Whether I write a good or a bad article, it must appear . . . Every day, my position is improving; every day, I take another step forward.'

This aggressive attitude to life was typical of all Cézanne's friends. Gleyre, whose eyes were failing, had closed his studio the previous year. Monet, Renoir, Bazille and Sisley no longer had a master. Monet, who had been spending some time in Normandy with Bazille, had brought back two seascapes which he intended to submit to the Salon. In the meantime he was sharing a studio with Bazille in the Rue de Furstemberg, close to that once occupied by Delacroix. Cézanne and Pissarro frequently went there. Bazille was now perfectly happy, for he had persuaded his family to allow him to give up medicine and devote himself entirely to painting. Cézanne also sometimes went with Renoir to the Pasdeloup Concerts to applaud Wagner's music, which at this time was disapproved of as much as Manet's painting. In 1861 *Tannhäuser* had been taken off after three performances before hostile audiences.

Cézanne was instinctively a supporter of Wagner. Indeed, he was a supporter of every form of revolt. But he rarely had time to bother with anything but painting. At the Académie Suisse he painted one of the studio models, a Negro who answered to the name of Scipio. Clearly influenced by Delacroix, the picture had great solidity and a remarkable architectural quality. Was Cézanne pleased with the result? He should have been, for he had succeeded in mastering his innate impetuosity for the first time; but he was always indifferent to his own works. Unlike Zola, who wanted every page he wrote, whether good or bad, to be published, Cézanne was never satisfied, and completely casual about the fate of his canvases. He was inclined to leave them where they fell; as far as he was concerned, they were no more than exercises. He gave the *Nègre Scipion* to Monet, as casually as he had given Zola so many of his works, including of course the portrait of Gabrielle.

Submission time for the Salon was drawing near. It was said that the Hanging Committee would be prepared once again to show a certain indulgence. But this did not worry Cézanne. As far as he was concerned, there were only two kinds of painting: his own, painting that had 'guts,' and which he hoped one day to 'realise' (I'm one of the intense ones,' he said), and the painting of the *others*, the men who lacked 'temperament.' He considered his own originality far too outrageous for the members of the Hanging Committee. They were sure to reject him. Nevertheless, he felt bound to submit something to them, if it were only 'to put them in the wrong.'

Cézanne's picture was rejected. Nevertheless, the Hanging Committee had shown considerable moderation. They had accepted the entries of Renoir and Pissarro, as well as those of Monet and Guillemet, who were hung in the Salon for the first time. They also accepted two canvases from Manet, *Ecce Homo* and a nude, *Olympia*, which raised yet another storm of protest. 'What is this odalisque with a yellow stomach, this disgusting model picked up Heaven knows where, doing as Olympia?' wrote Jules Claretie. 'As if in the morgue, the crowd presses round the putrefying *Olympia* and the horrible *Ecce Homo* by M. Manet,' wrote Paul de Saint-Victor, critic of *La Presse*. Monet, on the other hand, had a considerable success. His two seascapes were much praised. Some of this praise was, however, due to the fact that certain of Manet's admirers had failed to distinguish between the names of the two artists.

For Cézanne, *Olympia* was far and away the most important picture in the Salon. He admired it even more than he had admired *Le Déjeuner sur l'Herbe* two years before. For him, *Olympia* 'was a new state of painting,' the beginning of a 'Renaissance.' 'There is a pictorial truth of things. That rose and white lead us to it by a path of which our sensibility has been unaware till now . . .'

Manet observed and painted with an objective eye. He might have little 'temperament'; but he succeeded, thanks to this submission, in 'getting the tone.' Cézanne accepted the lesson. He realised he must submit to reality too, and control his natural romanticism, which his long friendship with Zola had only tended to increase. Obscurely, he understood that the road to greatness lay through humility. He set to work on a few simple paintings of still life using the brush more often than the palette knife, and paying particular attention to transitions and relationships of tone. Manet's painting, so carefully studied, taught him a few tricks of technique: for instance, that it sufficed to paint a knife at an oblique angle in relation to the canvas, and against a background of falling drapery, to suggest space and depth in a picture.

Nevertheless, Cézanne could not easily discard his romanticism. Though he painted a picture such as *Pain et des Oeufs*, a concise study from which man was completely excluded, he was at the same time engaged on still lifes with skulls.

For better or worse, under the pressure of circumstance and the influence of his painter friends, Zola was also yielding to realism.

Only yesterday, Hugo and Musset had been their gods. Today, they were totally under the influence of Manet and Baudelaire. They had caught up with their period.

* * *

In September Cézanne was back in Aix. His friends were astonished at the change in him. 'That dumb nigger of yours talks,' Valabrègue wrote to Zola. 'He produces theories and develops doctrines. Worst crime of all, he even allows you to discuss politics with him (theoretically, of course), and he says the most terrible things about the Tyrant.'

During the autumn, Cézanne was busy painting portraits. Valabrègue sat for him when he could. But Cézanne had discovered the most patient of models in his uncle, Dominique Aubert, who had a coarse and rather ugly face, thick eyebrows, a heavy moustache and beard, high cheekbones and deep-set eyes. Cézanne painted him many times, sometimes depicting him bareheaded, sometimes in a cap or a cotton nightcap, or even in a monk's habit or a barrister's gown. Cézanne looked on these works mainly as exercises. With minor modifications of detail, he returned unwearyingly to the same theme; it was the picture that demanded his attention, not the model. It seemed that he was beginning to realise that a picture existed in its own right and, no matter what its subject, had its own laws, and that these were concerned with line, colour and significant form. The individual character of his model was of no interest to him, except in so far as it excited his sensibility and stimulated him to an act of creation.

The publication, in October, of *La Confession de Claude* seemed to the Aix group something of a manifesto. Zola, who was as concerned about his friends' publicity as his own, asked Marius Roux, who was to write the review of it in *Le Mémorial d'Aix*, to take the opportunity of bringing the talents of Cézanne and Baille, to whom he had dedicated the book, before the public. It would, he said, 'please their families.' On 3 December, Marius Roux, writing from Paris, published the following article:

'We are a group here of natives of Aix, all old schoolfellows, all linked by true bonds of friendship; we do not know precisely what the future holds in store for us, but in the meantime we work and struggle . . .

'M. Cézanne is one of the best pupils from our school that Aix has sent to Paris. We remember him as a hard worker and a conscientious student. Here, thanks to his perseverance, he will become a good painter. Though a great admirer of Ribera and Zurbaran, our painter is, however, no copyist, and his work has an originality which is all his own. I have seen him at work in his studio, and if I cannot as yet predict for him the brilliant success of the painters he admires, I am sure of one thing, which is that his work will never be second-rate. The second-rate in art is the most disastrous thing of all. It is better to be a stonemason, if that is your trade; but if you are a painter, you must be a good one or die in the attempt.

'M. Cézanne will not die; he has acquired sound principles in the Aix School, has found much good example here, and he has too much courage and perseverance not to reach his goal.

'Were I not afraid of committing an indiscretion, I would give you my views on some of his canvases. But, in his modesty, he refuses to believe that what he is doing is good enough, and I do not want to hurt his feelings as a painter. I am waiting for him to show his work to the public. I shall not be the only one to speak out on that day. He belongs to a school that has the privilege of provoking criticism.'

Similar orders had no doubt gone out to Marguery, who combined writing with the law. '*La Confession de Claude*,' he wrote in *L'Écho des Bouches-du-Rhône*, 'is dedicated to MM. Paul Cézanne and J. B. Baille, both of whom we know; they are making names for themselves respectively in the arts and the sciences.'

Unfortunately, however, Zola did not receive so good a press as he had the previous year for *Contes à Ninon*. The critics considered the realism of *La Confession de Claude* 'hideous.' Furthermore, the novel was denounced as immoral and dangerous. The authorities took notes. Zola's lodgings (he had now moved to 142, Boulevard Montparnasse) were ordered to be searched. His record was examined and enquiries were made at Hachette. Nevertheless the Procureur Général of the Seine, in a report to the Garde des Sceaux, stated that there were no grounds on which to prosecute the novel as being against public morality.

The case was allowed to drop; but it had created difficulties for Zola at Hachette and he courageously sent in his resignation at the end of January. Literature and journalism were to be his only sources of livelihood from now on.

Cézanne, no doubt, heard only echoes of all this. Nor, presumably, did he pay much attention to the articles of Roux and Marguery. From the purely material point of view, Zola's feverish ambition awakened little response in him. Thanks to his father, he had no need to make his living as Zola had. He could afford to be indifferent to the financial hazards of life, and concentrate all his energies on his interior struggle, while envisaging a more distant future. 'The day will come,' he said, 'when a single original carrot will be pregnant with revolution.'

His friend, Marion, had made the acquaintance of a young German of twenty, who was passionately devoted to music and a great admirer of Wagner. His name was Heinrich Morstatt, and his father had sent him to Marseilles to learn business. At the end of December, Cézanne and Marion invited him to come to Aix for Christmas so that he might play them some of the works of the misunderstood musician.

In homage to Wagner, Cézanne hoped one day soon to paint a picture entitled *L'Ouverture de Tannhäuser*.

CHAPTER THREE

Battles

> We now know how unpopular our most cherished thoughts are.—ZOLA: *Mon Salon*, dedicated to Cézanne

WHEN Cézanne returned to Paris in February, he found that Zola had joined Hippolyte de Villemessant's popular newspaper, *L'Événement*.

Zola had already made overtures to Villemessant the preceding year: 'I want to succeed as soon as possible,' he wrote candidly to one of Villemessant's closest collaborators. 'In my haste, I have thought of your paper, which can make me known more quickly than any other. I am therefore speaking frankly . . . I know that you like trying people out, making the names of new contributors. Try me. Make my name. You will always have the pick of the litter.' The letter remained unanswered. But Zola returned to the charge; he asked Ludovic Halévy to intervene on his behalf.* Villemessant was surprised and amused and suddenly yielded.

Villemessant had the proportions of a giant, the red face of a gourmandiser and the inexhaustible loquacity of a commercial traveller. He was jovial, exuberant, vulgar, and enjoyed his notoriety. He had launched newspaper after newspaper and his latest, *L'Événement*, was a daily evening paper.

He made a cult of the indiscreet story; his readers' curiosity must be aroused in every edition; and he was prepared to go to almost any lengths to achieve this. He paid his contributors well but sacked them immediately if they lost the public's interest. He was as ruthless as he was generous. He took to Zola. Zola suggested the idea, which was then new, of a column of literary gossip. Villemessant took him on, and on 31 January he introduced Zola to the readers of *L'Événement* with one of his usual fanfares, an article which was calculated either to

* Letter from Zola to Ludovic Halévy, 22 January, 1866. Bibliothéque de l'Institut de France, MS. 4490, pièces 352, 352 *bis*.

launch a man or crush him: 'If my new star succeeds, so much the better. If he fails, the answer is quite simple. He has himself told me that, should he fail, he will resign his engagement and cease to be a member of my team. I have spoken.'

At Hachette, Zola had been earning two hundred francs a month; Villemessant, who was pleased with him, gave him five hundred. Zola was delighted. The critical attacks on *La Confession de Claude*, far from depressing him, had excited him. 'Today, I'm known,' he wrote to Valabrègue, 'people fear me and insult me . . . I have faith in myself, and I'm going boldly forward.' The idealistic poet of the past was now dead. The period of apprenticeship was over. The decisive battles were at hand.

Indeed, they were at hand for them all. Cézanne had brought a number of canvases back from Aix. He intended submitting two of them to the Salon, one of which was a portrait of Valabrègue. Not that he had any desire that they should be accepted; on the contrary, the approval of the Hanging Committee would have vexed him. Unlike some painters, who submitted their most conventional works in the hope of conciliating, Cézanne deliberately selected those most likely to arouse the Committee's opposition. In recognition of his daring, his painter friends, sure of his rejection, 'organised an ovation for him.'*

It was also thought that the Hanging Committee for the Salon of 1866 would be particularly intransigent. The reception the critics and the public had given *Olympia* the previous year had shown concessions to be not only useless but dangerous. The Hanging Committee would clearly make itself ridiculous by exhibiting too great a tolerance. The young painters, on the other hand, were tired of being at the mercy of this tribunal whose competence they contested. They wanted to revive the Salon des Refusés, and were talking of organising a petition to this effect. They were not all as bold as Cézanne, who was deliberately carrying the war into the enemy camp. Zola, made confident by his success with Villemessant, was delighted by the prospect of a battle. He wanted to measure himself against the public; moreover, he liked a fight for its own sake. In battle, uncertainties were resolved and one could become oneself at last, the man one wished to be.

* Marion: letter to Morstatt, 28 March, 1866.

Cézanne was not the most subdued of the noisy diners at Zola's on Thursdays. He had changed much in appearance. Bearded and long-haired, he had deliberately adopted an attitude of coarseness and slovenliness. The violence of his opinions, his southern tendency to boast, and his natural timidity formed a somewhat surprising mixture. The pious child of the past had disappeared, and he would mutter imprecations whenever he passed a priest in the street.

At this time, he wore a 'black, shapeless, rusty' felt hat, a 'huge overcoat that had once been pale brown,' but which the rain had faded and stained with 'large green patches,' and trousers that were too short, revealing 'blue socks.'* He was continually thundering imprecations against official art: 'Is not a bunch of carrots, yes, a bunch of carrots, studied directly and painted candidly, precisely as one sees it, worth all the dull productions of the schools that are confected with tobacco juice and disgracefully cooked up from given recipes?'

In his studio in the Rue Beautreillis, he lived in indescribable disorder. A dressing-table, a divan bed, a broken-down old cupboard, and a few chairs that had lost their straw were all the furniture he had, together with a stove, round which was heaped the accumulated ashes of months. He refused to allow the room to be swept 'for fear the dust should adhere to his freshly painted canvases.' Paint brushes, tubes of colour, dirty plates and saucepans lay about everywhere. 'A torrent of sketches' covered the walls from ceiling to floor, and under them 'were stacked a heap of canvases thrown down pell mell.' Here and there, on the empty spaces of the walls, models had left their addresses, 'written in chalk' in childish hands, 'and straggling in all directions.'†

The unfortunate models required a great deal of patience in their dealings with Cézanne; he was often boorish, brutal and obscene. Sometimes he would stare at them while they were undressing and then, no longer able to bear the sight, would throw them out half naked on to the landing. Returning to his easel he would 'lay them on the bed of his pictures.'‡

He was also as unstable as ever, 'gay in the morning and melancholy

* Zola: *Le Ventre de Paris*.
† Zola: *L'Oeuvre*.
‡ Jochim Gasquet.

in the evening.' Nevertheless, at the moment, he was painting with an almost ferocious vitality, and declaring his artistic beliefs with an intransigence no less fierce. Ingres had 'no red blood.' The primitives had 'the colouring of a missal.' The École des Beaux-Arts should be burnt down, the Salon too, and even the Louvre, so that everything could be begun again from scratch. 'Life must be apprehended and rendered in its reality; it must be loved for itself, as the only true beauty, eternal yet changing; the stupid idea that it can be ennobled by being castrated must be dismissed, for its so-called uglinesses are what give it character . . .'

In the meantime, Zola had moved house again; leaving the Boulevard Montparnasse (the proximity of a shooting-gallery interrupted his work), he had taken a five-roomed flat with a balcony, 'a veritable palace,' where he lived with his mother at 10, Rue de Vaugirard, quite close to the Odéon and opposite the Luxembourg Gardens. The Thursday diners had been increased by a few friends from Aix: Valabrègue, who had not yet made up his mind to live permanently in Paris, and had been staying since March in a hotel in the Rue Vavin; and Philippe Solari, winner of the Granet Prize, which was awarded to its young artists by the town of Aix.

Solari was thin, sallow and rather ugly, but had bright eyes that held an expression of childish charm. With heedless prodigality, he was busily spending the twelve hundred francs of his prize money, and had sent a bust of Zola to the Salon.

At the moment, the sole topic of conversation was the Salon. News was beginning to leak out. Daubigny, the landscape painter, who was a member of the Hanging Committee this year, had tried to defend Cézanne's portrait of Valabrègue. There had been a furious argument. Daubigny had angrily declared that he preferred 'pictures that had boldness about them to the worthless paintings that were accepted for every Salon.' But he had been out-voted, and Cézanne's picture was rejected.

Cézanne was unconcerned; particularly since he had recently had the satisfaction of praise from a quarter which made the approval of the Hanging Committee a matter of small account to him. He had been introduced to Manet; and Manet, having seen some of his 'still lifes' in Guillemet's studio, had said they were 'vigorous in treatment.' Cézanne was delighted.

Manet himself, however, rather surprised him. He was an elegant man-about-town and something of a dandy, who never went out without a top hat, gloves and a stick, and was an *habitué* of the Café Tortoni. Witty, courteous, upper-class, and a man of the world, he seemed to be a revolutionary in spite of himself. He was upset by his repeated rejections for the Salon, and by the scandal he involuntarily aroused. He would have far preferred an official career, rising from honour to honour in regular progression. It seemed to Cézanne that Manet was lacking in 'temperament.'

Early in April, the Hanging Committee made its selections public. It had shown the expected intransigence. Though it had accepted Monet and Sisley, as well as one of the two canvases sent in by Bazille, who was submitting his work for the first time, and also a Pissarro landscape (Daubigny had had to fight hard for it), it had rejected not only Cézanne but Renoir, Guillemet, Solari and Manet, who had submitted his *Joueur de Fifre*.

There was a good deal of anger at this result, and also much canvassing for the re-establishment of the Salon des Refusés. Daubigny himself had advised Renoir to organise a petition to this end. Renoir, fearing the verdict on his work, had gone to the Palais de l'Industrie before the results had even been announced to wait for the members of the Hanging Committee to come out. He had accosted Daubigny, representing himself, since he was too shy to reveal his identity, as a friend of Renoir. His picture had been refused. 'What else can you expect?' said Daubigny. 'There were only six of us in favour of it against all the others. Tell your friend not to lose heart, for his picture has great qualities.' And Daubigny added: 'He should organise a petition to ask for an *exposition des refusés*.'

The young painters got busy; and Cézanne, no doubt with the approval of his friends, and probably with Zola's help, took the initiative by writing to the Comte de Nieuwerkerke, the superintendent of the Beaux-Arts. But there was no reply. The Comte de Nieuwerkerke doubtless had no intention of engaging in an argument with the daubers whom the Hanging Committee, over which he presided, had rejected. In his view they were so many Millets, whose work he confessed 'disgusted him,' that is to say 'democrats' – 'men who did not change their linen.'

Contemptuous silence was the surest way of exasperating the discontented and of stimulating Zola's aggressive instincts. It occurred to Zola that Villemessant might permit him to write the paper's report on the Salon. He could then attack the Hanging Committee, denounce the institution's vices, defend his friends, and undoubtedly be able to create a considerable stir. Cézanne, Guillemet and Pissarro would all provide him with copy. Guillemet, in particular, who was annoyed at being rejected this year, undertook to give him all the facts about the Hanging Committee, how it was elected and how it worked. Villemessant agreed.

On 19 April, Zola, who had adopted for the occasion the pseudonym of Claude, the hero of his *Confession*, announced in trenchant terms that he was about to begin 'a ruthless investigation 'of the Hanging Committee. He was well aware that he would anger a great many people since he was 'determined to make public great and terrible truths', but, he admitted, 'I shall take a particular delight in discharging my heart of its accumulated anger.' The same day – the coincidence was certainly not fortuitous – Cézanne sent the Comte de Nieuwerkerke a second letter in a style curiously resembling that of the contributor to *L'Événement:*

'Monsieur,

'I have recently had the honour of writing to you on the subject of two canvases which the Hanging Committee has rejected.

'Since you have not yet answered, I think I should emphasise the reasons that induced me to write to you. Since, however, you must have received my letter, I need not repeat the arguments I thought proper to place before you. I shall content myself with saying once again that I cannot accept the spurious verdict of colleagues to whom I have given no right to judge me.

'I am therefore writing to you to insist further on my previous demand. I wish to appeal to the public and to be exhibited in spite of the verdict. I can see nothing exorbitant about my demand, and if you ask other painters who are in the same position as myself, they will reply that they repudiate the Hanging Committee and that they wish to take part in one way or another in an exhibition that will be completely open to all serious workers.

'The Salon des Refusés should be re-established. Even if I were to appear in it alone, I earnestly desire that the public should at least realise that I have no more wish to be identified with the gentlemen of the Hanging Committee, than they have to be identified with me.

'I trust, Monsieur, that you will answer this letter. It seems to me that every courteous letter deserves a reply.'

We do not know whether, on this occasion, the Comte de Nieuwerkerke replied or not. There is a note in the margin of the preserved original of Cézanne's letter, saying: 'What he demands is impossible. It was recognised that the *exposition des refusés* detracted from the dignity of art, and it will not be re-established.'

Zola began his attack on 27 and 30 April, immediately before the Salon opened. He published a long and violent diatribe against the Hanging Committee, that strange tribunal presiding over the destinies of French art, so largely composed of the jealous, the die-hards and the second-rate, 'whose minor productions have a minor success and who cling to that success, scolding and threatening any colleague who dares to draw near.' They 'amputate art, and present the public with no more than its mutilated body.' 'I beg all my colleagues,' Zola concluded, 'to support me in this. I want to increase the effectiveness of my protest, and achieve the power to insist on the re-opening of those galleries in which the public was able to decide for itself, both with regard to the judges and to the condemned.'

On 4 May, Zola returned to the attack and, making a synthesis of his own ideas and those of his friends, in particular those of Cézanne, proclaimed his artistic convictions. He developed them at some length, saying: 'This is a time of struggle and excitement, we have our men of talent and our geniuses.' But what did the pontiffs of the Salon care? The Salon was 'an accumulation of mediocrity.' 'It contains two thousand paintings, but not ten men.'

Zola's articles certainly created a sensation. They were discussed in every studio, and on the boulevards. Cézanne was delighted with them.

'God knows,' he said, 'he puts those bastards in their place all right!' Manet, whom Zola had recently become acquainted with, gave him a long interview; he showed him his works and obliged him with his aesthetic opinions. Zola came away full of enthusiasm. He set about attacking the Salon in an article which was largely devoted to praising the painter of whom the Salon most disapproved. He expressed his admiration for *Olympia*, asserted that Manet's place 'was reserved in the Louvre,' as was Courbet's, and that of every other artist who 'had a powerful and original genius.' The article appeared on 7 May.

This, however, was going too far. Letters of protest streamed in to Villemessant's office. 'A few more articles on these lines,' wrote an anonymous correspondent, 'and I have no doubt that a great number of your intelligent readers (and whatever M. Claude may think, there still are a few) will give up reading a paper which treats them as fools and cretins.' 'M. Claude politely calls those who laugh at M. Manet's pictures fools,' said another, who signed himself 'a bourgeois subscriber, though an artist.' 'Why does not M. Manet remain content with being second-rate? Why does he have to be vulgar and grotesque? Why do his spotty figures appear to have come out of a coal-sack? One looks with a certain pity at involuntary ugliness; how can one help laughing at pretentious ugliness?' Many readers threatened to give up the paper. Villemessant was advised 'to raise the standard of criticism by confiding it to cleaner hands.'

Seeing that the scandal was getting out of hand, Villemessant prudently beat a retreat. Zola had intended writing twelve articles; but now he was to write only three more. Moreover, a certain Théodore Pelloquet, who was a supporter of the Hanging Committee and official art, would also write three. Their articles would appear alternately, and *L'Événement* would thus content everyone.

Zola's impetus was destroyed. Pelloquet countered everything he said. On 20 May, after the second article, he abandoned the struggle; not, however, without firing some parting shots. 'I have committed blasphemy by asserting that the whole of artistic history proves that only geniuses dominate their age . . . I have committed the horrible sacrilege of being disrespectful to the little reputations of the day . . .

I have been heretical in demolishing the narrow religions of the coteries and in stating firmly the great religion of art, which says to every painter: "Open your eyes, here is nature; open your heart, here is life . . ." I have been guilty of sacrilege and heresy because, tired of lies and mediocrity, I have sought for men among the crowd of eunuchs . . . And this is why I have been condemned.'

Though Zola was obliged to abandon the field, he did so with a challenge: 'I have defended M. Manet, as I shall defend throughout my life any honest individual who is attacked. I shall always be on the side of the vanquished. There is an evident struggle between men of indomitable temperament and the crowd. I am on the side of the men of temperament and I shall attack the crowd . . .'

Apart from Manet, Zola had also mentioned Pissarro – the 'artist I love' – in his articles, as well as Monet, of whom he said: 'There is genius, there is a man among the crowd of eunuchs!' But he did not mention Cézanne. Nevertheless, when he published the collected articles under the title of *Mon Salon*, he dedicated the book to his friend. 'Do you realise,' he wrote in his dedication, 'that we were revolutionaries without knowing it? I have had the opportunity of saying out loud what we have been whispering these ten years past . . . Nothing in the world would induce me to allow these articles to be lost; they are of no great value in themselves, but they have been, so to speak, the touchstone against which I have tried out the public. We now know how unpopular our most cherished thoughts are . . .'

* * *

If Zola's battle, which was of course Cézanne's too, had not ended in triumph, it seemed at least to give their group a greater cohesion. During the months of June and July, Cézanne, Zola, Baille, Solari, Valabrègue, Chaillan, Marius Roux and the rest of the Aix group, spent as much time as their respective occupations would allow at Bennecourt-sur-Seine, above Rouen.

Bennecourt consisted of a few yellow-washed houses, lying along some two kilometres of the river behind a screen of poplars. There were fields and wooded hills. In the Seine were islands covered with reeds. An old ferry clanked on its chains. It was a quiet place, unfrequented by Parisians. The party swam, boated and fished, enjoying themselves like schoolboys.

Zola brought Gabrielle, whom he now looked on as his wife; but this made no difference, she was merely 'a friend the more.' In the evenings, after dinner, they would go out into the yard of Mère Gigoux's inn and lie on bales of straw to smoke their pipes and discuss art and literature till midnight. They indulged in furious arguments, criticised the celebrities of the day, and were 'intoxicated by the hope of soon being able to overthrow everything that exists.'*

Zola, who had just published *Mon Salon*, and immediately afterwards a collection of his literary articles, *Mes Haines* (its contents were a great deal milder than its title suggested), had just begun a new novel, and was planning to write during the next few weeks a book entitled *L'Oeuvre d'Art devant la Critique*. He was indefatigable. 'I'm impatient, and would like to go forward even more quickly,' he declared. As for Cézanne, he was working hard. Zola wrote to Numa Coste: 'He is becoming increasingly confirmed in his natural and original bent. I have great hopes of him. We expect, too, that he will be rejected for the next ten years. At the moment he wants to paint big pictures, canvases of twelve or fifteen feet.'

Zola might have 'great hopes' of Cézanne, but he was surprised, disquieted and not in the least moved by his friend's work; for, though he had set himself up as an art critic, Zola understood nothing whatever about painting.

* Zola: *Une Farce ou Bohèmes en Villégiature.*

CHAPTER FOUR

'He Dreams of Huge Pictures'

> I love you as one should love: in despair.—MLLE DE LESPINASSE

THE party at Bennecourt broke up. Zola went back to Paris and Baille left for Aix, where he was to spend the rest of the holidays. At the beginning of August, Cézanne and Valabrègue followed him there.

Still elated by the battle they had fought in the spring, and by their discussions at Bennecourt, Cézanne and his friends made a clamorous return to Aix in the summer of 1866. Cézanne, who was in splendid health, walked about the Cours with a 'revolutionary beard' and 'immensely long'* hair, though he was beginning to show signs of going bald. He had by now acquired a certain prestige. Marion for one gave him a triumphant welcome. In Marion's eyes, Cézanne 'was increasing in stature all the time.' A friend of Valabrègue, Paul Alexis, was also an admirer of Cézanne. Alexis was the son of a rich solicitor and was studying law with no greater enthusiasm than Cézanne had shown for it in the past. He was nineteen, and longing for the day when he could leave Aix for Paris and become a writer. He envied Cézanne; and was doing his best to persuade his father that poetry alone made life worth living.

The group of gay and noisy rebels attracted a good deal of attention in the little town. 'People are really beginning to accept us. They wish us good morning,' wrote Marion to Morstatt, and a local poet went so far as to dedicate some verses to Cézanne in *L'Écho des Bouches-du-Rhône*. Cézanne especially aroused curiosity and people wanted to see his work. But having already experienced the disparagement of various fellow-citizens to whom he had given pictures, he adopted an intransigent attitude. To those people who asked to see his canvases, he shouted, 'To hell with you!' which struck panic into the importunate.

* Marion: letter to Morstatt, 28 August, 1866.

The people of Aix 'got on his nerves,'* and he made no attempt to conceal his contempt for them. But in spite of this, or possibly because of it, he was becoming a character in the town. Local painters who had seen his work began to imitate his manner, abandoning the brush for the palette knife and vying with each other in thickness of impasto. Gossip went so far as to suggest that he might be offered the directorship of the Museum. 'What a lot of fools!' Marion exclaimed.

In the meantime Cézanne had begun work on his *Ouverture de Tannhäuser*, in memory of his meetings with Morstatt and in homage to Wagner. He made a sketch for it in a single morning and Marion thought the picture 'superb.' 'It is as much of the future as is Wagner's music,' he wrote to Morstatt. But Cézanne was less easily satisfied. Though he was to return to the theme he abandoned it now and began working on portraits again. He painted his father, who was now sixty-nine, sitting in a high armchair, and reading *L'Événement;* no doubt a friendly gesture to Zola. It was a big canvas, 78″ × 46″, in which Cézanne achieved a certain objectivity by immobilising his model in an almost hieratic attitude. He was putting Manet's example to good use.

On a canvas of similar dimensions, Cézanne painted his friend Emperaire; but the dwarf's appearance was so much a caricature in itself, that Cézanne could not help lapsing into romanticism. He painted Emperaire with his ridiculous little legs on a foot-warmer and wearing a blue dressing-gown, a red jersey, and violet drawers. Above the disproportionately large head, he wrote in huge letters: ACHILLE EMPERAIRE, PEINTRE.

These ambitious works undoubtedly showed self-confidence. But audacity was succeeded by weariness. His family irritated him, as did the people of Aix. Since his financial future was assured, he made no concessions and there were no pressures to ameliorate his often ungrateful nature. In the meantime, however, his father often left him without money, which tended to aggravate his innate incompetence to organise his budget; and this was not calculated to improve his temper. 'I'm still more depressed when I haven't a penny,' he wrote to Zola, thanking him for a loan. Fortunately his mother, whose affection

* Guillemet: letter to Zola, 2 November, 1866.

remained constant, would occasionally slip him a bank note in secret.

Apart from a few excursions into the hills, Cézanne and his friends spent their days in a regular and monotonous routine. After the day's work, Cézanne at his painting, Marion at his geology, and Valabrègue at his poetry, they used to meet at the Jas de Bouffan. They would dine and then go for a stroll before going to bed.

At the end of September, the Aix Museum having acquired the Bourguignon de Fabregoules collection, Gibert invited Cézanne, Baille, Marion and Valabrègue to come to see it. 'I thought it all bad,' said Cézanne, 'which is very consoling!' How lucky Zola was to be able to throw himself with such impetuosity into the literary struggle, with the single-minded ambition, vulgar though it might be, to succeed merely for the sake of success! But where would the path lead which he himself had chosen? When he saw the pictures in the Bourguignon de Fabregoules collection he compared them with those experiments in painting out of doors which Monet, for example, was making. These canvases by old masters undoubtedly lacked the 'true and above all original aspect of nature' and he felt increasingly certain that pictures painted in the studio would never be equal to those painted in the open air. 'In painting scenes out of doors, the contrast of figures against the earth is astonishing, and the countryside is magnificent. I see superb things . . .' wrote Cézanne. But, as Pissarro maintained, grey was the dominant colour in nature, and it was 'terrifyingly hard to capture.'

Cézanne was not displeased with his latest portrait, which was of his sister Rose, now twelve years old, reading to her doll. Encouraged by this, he attempted a more difficult composition, a picture of Marion and Valabrègue out of doors. But it was beyond his ability and his models were not very enthusiastic; at least Valabrègue was not. 'We look hideous,' he wrote to Zola on 2 October.

The weather was breaking up and Cézanne 'felt rather depressed.' There was no particular reason for it. 'It comes over me every evening when the sun sets, and besides, it's raining. I feel a black depression,' and, 'between ourselves,' he wrote to Zola, 'art for art's sake is all nonsense.'

Fortunately, Guillemet, the gayest of companions, arrived in Aix, with his wife Alphonsine, during the first fortnight of October. He had already spent a month in Aix at the beginning of the year, and had

13 (opposite). Cézanne on the way to his 'Motif', near Auvers-sur-Oise [1873]

14. 'Sur le Motif' [1875]
(Standing left to right) Lucien Pissarro, Cézanne, Camille Pissarro

15. Pissarro and Cézanne [*c.* 1873]

C. Pissarro Cézanne

17. Paul Cézanne (seated) in Camille Pissarro's garden at Pontoise [*c.* 1873]
(Standing left to right) Lucien Pissarro, Rodo Pissarro, Paul-Émile Pissarro and Camille Pissarro

6. Portrait of Cézanne by Camille Pissarro [*c.* 1873]

19.

20.

18. (left) Paul Cézanne on the road near Auvers-sur-Oise [1873]

19. Paul Cézanne [*c.* 1875]. Photograph given by Cézanne to Achille Emperaire

20. Cézanne: Self-portrait [*c.* 1875]

21. Cézanne's '*pot de merde*'. A contemporary caricature by 'Stock', referring to the incident at the Palais de l'Industrie, 20 March 1870

liked the town. His was a happy nature, the weather was magnificent, the people charming, Cézanne's canvases excellent. Guillemet even went so far as to remonstrate with Louis Auguste and tell him that he should be more generous to his son; after all, his own father, the wine-merchant of Bercy, did not treat him so parsimoniously.

Guillemet did his best to cheer Cézanne and they and Marion often went out to paint together in the hills near the dam. But in spite of Guillemet's praise, Cézanne continued to be dissatisfied with his work. On 2 November he admitted to Zola that he had failed with the painting of Marion and Valabrègue, and that he had had no greater success with his *Soirée de Famille*. 'However, I shall persevere, and perhaps another time it will come right.' He began painting portraits again, making the docile Uncle Dominique sit for him every day, while Guillemet 'made appalling jokes at his expense.'* Every afternoon Cézanne sketched out a new portrait of his uncle. But Valabrègue also had to submit to the torture of sitting. The result was 'so brightly coloured' that the canvas reminded Valabrègue 'of the statue of the Curé de Champfleury, when it was covered with squashed mulberries.' Guillemet had been a pupil of Corot, and he often told Cézanne stories about the great landscape painter. But Cézanne had no greater admiration for Corot than he had for Ingres. 'Don't you think your Corot is somewhat lacking in temperament?' he said.

* * *

In January 1867, Cézanne – probably in company with the Guillemets – returned to Paris. Before leaving Provence he had sent a picture to a dealer in Marseilles, who was organising an exhibition. Valabrègue, who had remained in Aix, wrote to Zola that 'there has been a great deal of fuss; crowds gathered in the street outside; they were astounded. People wanted to know who Paul was; from that point of view there has undoubtedly been a certain excitement and success due to curiosity. However,' he added, 'I think that if the picture had been exhibited any longer, in the end the window would have been broken and the canvas destroyed.'

For all his bold front, Cézanne took these things to heart. It was clear

* Valabrègue: letter to Zola, November, 1866.

that Valabrègue did not think much of his work; and he guessed that Zola was disappointed in him, too. Though he could not help being affected, he concealed his feelings behind a jeering attitude which, like his swearing and fury over the work on which he was engaged, was a defensive reaction. 'I have never finished, never, never.' He was never satisfied, and though his dissatisfaction was real, he was inclined to exaggerate it and parade it. 'How black the skies of the future are for me!'

Zola was concerned about his friend. Was it simply a lack of talent which paralysed him?

During these last months, Zola had seen a great deal more of Manet. He liked the man as much as he respected the artist. He admired his distinction, his intelligence, his vitality, and his easy manners. During the past year, Manet and his friends had formed the habit of meeting almost every evening, but particularly on Thursdays, in the Café Guerbois at 11, Grande-Rue des Batignolles, near the famous restaurant of Père Lathuile.* They had two tables reserved for them on the left of the entrance. And here came Guillemet, Bazille and, on occasion, Pissarro, Fantin-Latour and Degas – a bitter man with a cruel wit. Writers and critics, such as Duranty, Théodore Duret and the novelist Léon Cladel often joined them, and Zola was assiduous in his attendance. But Guillemet had difficulty in persuading Cézanne to come to these meetings. The Provençal was still shy at heart and awkward in company and he looked on the *habitués* of Le Guerbois with suspicion. 'They're a lot of bastards; they dress as smartly as solicitors!' he said distrustfully to Guillemet. Moreover the conversation of the 'Batignolles Group,' as Manet's friends were called, seemed to him both superficial and over-subtle.

There was indeed much witty and amusing conversation, particularly on the part of Manet and Degas, and Cézanne had no aptitude for it. 'To hell with wit!' he said. Manet's raillery, his elegance and upper-class manner, his beard, so carefully trimmed into two points, his wash-leather gloves, light trousers and short coats, all annoyed Cézanne. Moreover, Manet, whom Zola admired so much, was not, in Cézanne's opinion, so original after all. Manet had no imagination; he required

* Le Guerbois is today the Brasserie Muller, 9, Avenue de Clichy.

to be inspired by his sitter before he could paint a portrait. 'They're a lot of eunuchs!' said Cézanne. When he did go to Le Guerbois he deliberately behaved like a peasant, unbuttoning his coat, shaking himself, pulling up his trousers and ostentatiously tightening his wide, red belt. On one occasion, when shaking hands all round, he reached Manet, took his hat off and said, in his broadest southern accent: 'I shan't shake your hand, Monsieur Manet, because I haven't washed for a week.'*

Cézanne would sit apart, silent, frowning and apparently lost in his thoughts. But if anyone had the temerity to express an opinion of which he disapproved, he would suddenly lose his temper and violently contradict the heretic; or, alternatively, get to his feet and walk out without bidding anyone good night. He succeeded in making himself far from popular and was looked on as an ill-bred boor.

Zola was much concerned at this behaviour. He felt Cézanne was making things unnecessarily difficult for himself; by behaving as he did he made success all the more difficult to achieve. Talent did not suffice by itself. You had to organise your life and pay continuous attention to your career. Bohemianism led nowhere. Zola was so convinced of it that he directed all his efforts towards achieving bourgeois security. At the moment, he was living with his mother and Gabrielle: a former admirer of Michelet, he had at least remained faithful to one of his ideals: his conception of monogamy in love. The first woman one fell in love with must be the woman one would love for ever. Gabrielle was and would remain that woman. Zola was as shy of women as was Cézanne. His idealism in love arose out of his latent fears: Zola was 'of those who have not the courage to break off an affair . . . from hatred of change and terror of the unknown.'† Nevertheless, though he sublimated his fears into an ideal, he was not above justifying that ideal by its practicality; he considered monogamy to be the guarantee of a quiet life, 'the basic condition for good work, for regular and solid effort for the great modern creators.' It may well have been that Zola's and Gabrielle's love was in fact a great deal less

* Reminiscences of Monet, recorded by Marc Elder in *Â Giverny, chez Claude Monet*.

† The quotations in this passage are from Zola (*Madeleine Férat* and *L'Oeuvre*).

profound than might be supposed from their enduring liaison – 'less love than calm satisfaction' – but they were undoubtedly in agreement on what they wanted from life.

Gabrielle had the same longing for success as had Zola. Coldly, austerely ambitious, she would support him, as he well knew, in all his struggles. She wanted to forget her working class origins. She never spoke of them and had broken off relations with all her family, including her father, who was still alive at this time. She concentrated entirely on being the companion of a writer who was struggling towards popularity and perhaps fame, ease and even wealth. She seemed to have been born for the part she was playing; she protected Zola from ordinary cares, arranged 'a tender home' for him, a cloistered life in which he could devote all his strength to his work. It was now Gabrielle who organised the 'Thursdays,' and assured their success. And she no doubt objected to Cézanne's bohemian behaviour even more than Zola did.

Despite this disapproval, Cézanne continued to go his own way. The Salon was to be of particular importance this year. A Universal Exhibition was to be held at the same time, and it was expected that huge crowds would come to Paris for it. All the young painters – except, apparently, Cézanne – were wondering whether the articles Zola had written the previous year would make the Hanging Committee more indulgent.

More defiant than ever, Cézanne chose two of his most displeasing canvases, of which one was the *Après-Midi à Naples ou Le Grog au Vin*, to submit to the Hanging Committee. But this in itself was not enough. To emphasise the aggressive nature of his entry, he waited till the last hour of the last day on which pictures were received, loaded his canvases on to a hand-cart and, together with a few friends, pushed it to the Palais de l'Industrie. On reaching the doors, he took his paintings from the hand-cart and triumphantly exhibited them to the crowd of painters and students, who received them with shouting and laughter.

It is improbable that Cézanne's demonstration, which gained a certain notoriety, influenced the Hanging Committee one way or the other. Daubigny was not this time a member, and in the event the Committee proved to be even more intolerant than it had ever been in the past. Zola's campaign, far from encouraging compromise, had made its attitude inflexible. Cézanne was rejected; but so were Pissarro, Renoir, Sisley, Bazille and Guillemet. Even Monet was turned down, though he had submitted a masterly work, *Femmes au Jardin*, which he had painted entirely in the open air. Cézanne was furious that the Hanging Committee had dared to reject Monet's canvas. And he was not alone in his fury. All the young painters of the group were raging against their dependence on the 'caprices of authority.'* For form's sake, and with little hope, they signed a petition demanding once again the re-establishment of the Salon des Refusés. But why should they not organise an exhibition of their own? Some of their elders, among them Courbet, Daubigny and Corot, approved the plan, and even promised to support the exhibition by sending work of their own. However, the project had to be abandoned for lack of money.

Cézanne and his rejected works now became an object of mockery to two journalists in particular, one in *L'Europe* and the other in *Le Figaro*. There was no doubt that if he continued to make himself conspicuous, he would acquire an unwelcome notoriety. Though Zola had not mentioned Cézanne in *Mon Salon*, and was in fact somewhat disquieted by Cézanne's painting, he nevertheless came to the rescue; probably all the more willingly since he had been unable this year to write articles on the *Salon*. *Le Figaro* published his reply on 12 April.

'This concerns,' Zola wrote, 'one of my childhood friends, a young painter whose vigorous and individual talent I must admire.

'You have quoted from *L'Europe* a paragraph in which mention is made of a M. Sésame who exhibited, in 1863, in the Salon des Refusés "two pig's trotters in the form of a cross" and who, this year, had another canvas called *Le Grog au Vin* refused.

'I must admit that I had some difficulty in recognising in this disguise one of my old school-friends, M. Paul Cézanne, who has had no pig's trotters in his artistic baggage, at least till now. I make this qualification, because I can see no reason why one should not paint pig's trotters as one paints melons or carrots.

'M. Paul Cézanne has, indeed, together with a numerous and distinguished company, had two canvases rejected this year: *Le Grog*

* Bazille: letter to his family, spring 1867.

au Vin and *Ivresse*. It has pleased M. Arnold Mortier to make fun of these pictures and to describe them with an imagination that does him credit. I am well aware that this is all a joke and that one should not take it to heart. Nevertheless, I have never been able to understand the singular method of criticism which consists in mocking, condemning and so confidently casting ridicule on what one has not even seen. I wish merely to point out, therefore, that the descriptions given by M. Arnold Mortier are inaccurate.'

When Gabrielle went to live with him, Zola's expenses increased. Leaving the Rue de Vaugirard, he had moved to the Batignolles, where Manet lived. In spite of the aggressive face he showed the world, Zola was often discouraged. 'You would not believe,' he confessed one day to Numa Coste, 'to what extent one suffers from sudden fits of depression in the hard trade I pursue.' At his 'Thursdays,' there was much complaint about the difficulties of the times. 'Nothing's going well,'* he wrote. The royalties from his books were still insignificant: only 1,500 copies had been printed of *La Confession de Claude*. In order to live, he had to increase his output for the newspapers. While working on his novel, *Un Mariage d'Amour*, he was writing a serial at two *sous* a line, *Les Mystères de Marseille*, for a provincial paper, *Le Messager de Provence*. Though it bored and even disgusted him, it at least helped to make ends meet. He was also hoping to adapt the *Mystères* for the stage with the collaboration of Marius Roux.

Valabrègue reproached him with prostituting his talent; to which Zola replied: 'At the moment, I need two things above all else, publicity and money. Of course, *Les Mystères de Marseille* means nothing to me. But I know what I'm doing.' On the other hand, Valabrègue congratulated Zola on his energetic defence of Cézanne: 'Paul is a child and ignorant of life; you are his guardian and his guide,' he wrote. 'You watch over him, he walks beside you and is always sure of being defended by you . . . His destiny is to paint pictures, as it is yours to organise his life!'

Was it because this was really so, and because Cézanne himself realised it, that he sometimes went to work at his friend's house in the Batignolles? In particular, he painted there a big canvas, *L'Enlèvement*,

* Letter to Valabrègue, 10 December, 1866.

depicting a dark man embracing a pale, swooning woman. Cézanne gave this savagely sensual canvas to Zola. He signed it and dated it, which is probably proof that he was not too displeased with it. The picture shows, however, that he was still far from having discarded his romanticism. 'Paul is working hard,' Zola wrote to Valabrègue, 'he dreams of huge pictures.'

As he walked through the streets of Paris, Cézanne looked longingly at the walls of churches, stations and markets, the bare walls he longed to cover with giant frescoes. 'What a position to make for oneself in the world! Conquer the crowd, open a new century, create an art!' And yet full expression in painting still escaped him: 'When I think of this damned business of painting, I could kill my father and mother!' It drove him frantic with its excitements and its disappointments, and he would give way to a passion of anger when a picture would not come out as he wished. His days were full of swearing, broken brushes and slit canvas. He was becoming increasingly violent and morose as he painted frantically, exhausting himself with the effort, and exhausting his models too by the interminable sittings he demanded of them, 'letting them go only when they were fainting and dead with fatigue.' And when he himself stopped painting, it was only 'to fall, his legs failing, his stomach empty.' Nevertheless, on occasion, he was able to feel a wild joy. 'When I accept one of my pictures,' he said in a moment of pride, 'it's a far more serious matter than if it had been accepted by all the Hanging Committees on earth . . .'*

Towards the end of May, Cézanne's mother came to Paris. He went home with her in June, at the very time that Valabrègue, having left Provence for good, was arriving in the capital. Thanks to a recommendation from Zola, Valabrègue was to work for Arsène Houssaye's *L'Artiste*.

* * *

As Zola had recently written to Valabrègue, Cézanne had 'great need to work and to take courage'; and he intended spending three months in Aix 'in complete solitude.' Indeed, almost as soon as he arrived there he went to ground in the Jas de Bouffan. During this summer of 1867, he saw no one but Marion, and sometimes Alexis. All his friends were

* The quotations in this passage are from Zola's *L'Oeuvre*.

in Paris. He worked without respite; and had started painting a few portraits again. They were 'really very fine,' Marion wrote; 'no longer done with the palette knife, but just as vigorous, and with a more deft and pleasing technique.' Marion's admiration for Cézanne was continually on the increase. When Cézanne began experimenting with water-colours, Marion was astonished by the remarkable results he achieved. They were, he wrote to Morstatt, 'extraordinary in colouring, and produce a strange effect of which I believed water-colour incapable.' But Marion's admiration for Cézanne at this time was even more extraordinary. Except for Pissarro, who was as interested as ever in the evolution of Cézanne's art, the only person in the world to understand the profound significance of his efforts was this young geologist of twenty-one.

Cézanne had often felt lonely and a stranger in Paris, even when among his friends. Sometimes, when depressed, he felt tempted to leave Paris for good. What was the use of pursuing so sterile a struggle there, when here, at the Jas de Bouffan, in the long, quiet sunlit days of the Provençal summer, he felt at peace with himself, and could be alone with his dreams and his canvas. Would it not be wiser to give up the struggle, stay here, and lead a quiet and happy life? As his mother said, 'he had the means.' He was free; and he could paint merely for his own pleasure.

By mid-August, Zola had had no news of Cézanne for a month. Since Marius Roux was in Marseilles – he was negotiating with the management of the Gymnase, the local theatre, which was to produce the play based on the *Mystères* – Zola asked him to go to see Cézanne. As far as Roux was concerned the meeting was a disappointment. Cézanne received him amicably enough, seemed glad to see him, but was disconcertingly reserved about his thoughts and plans. His conversation consisted of small talk mingled with such Sibylline utterances that Roux admitted he was unable to interpret them, supposing they had any meaning at all. 'As far as I am concerned, Paul is a veritable sphinx,' he wrote.

Cézanne was undoubtedly much more forthcoming with Marion, who considered that his friend was making progress day by day. At the moment, Cézanne was working on a second version of *L'Ouverture de*

Tannhäuser, which he was this time painting in clear colours. Marion wrote to Morstatt that 'a single canvas such as this is sufficient to make a reputation.'

Zola was due in Marseilles to attend the first few performances of the *Mystères* and Cézanne arranged to return to Paris with him. On 6 September Cézanne and Marion accompanied Zola to the first night. Zola thought the play 'foul,' and the public agreed with him. Boos and whistles greeted the final curtain. On 11 September, Cézanne and Zola returned together to Paris.

* * *

Cézanne did not, on this occasion, go back to the Rue Beautreillis. He seemed to have become even more restless than usual. Grumbling unhappily, he was constantly changing his lodgings, moving from the Rue de Chevreuse to the Rue de Vaugirard, and from the Rue de Vaugirard to the Rue Notre-Dame-des-Champs. He was for ever moaning about the difficulties he found in 'realising' himself and deploring his 'impotence.' Zola felt his friend's difficulties as if they were his own and watched him with concern. Failure moved him to tears, for could one ever tell in art who was mad and who was not?* Zola himself was a prey to considerable anxiety, much less sure of his powers than his ostentatious aggressiveness might lead the observer to suppose. But he concealed his worry. He no doubt risked giving Cézanne advice, but you could not argue with a man who was convinced that everyone wanted to imperil his integrity, and 'put the grapnel on him,' as he said.

Somehow Cézanne must be made to realise how hard the struggle for success was bound to be. But he would make no attempt to alter either his behaviour or his work. Instead, he seemed to be behaving as if he had no wish to achieve a career and success. At this moment, Zola himself was being roughly used by the critics over his novel *Thérèse Raquin* (the new title of *Un Mariage d'Amour*), which had been published in December. 'A morass of mud and blood,' wrote *Le Figaro*. 'M. Zola . . . sees women as M. Manet paints them, mud-coloured with pink make-up.'

* Zola: *L'Oeuvre*.

Cézanne was seeing a great deal of Solari at this time. They were both inclined to be eccentric in their behaviour and got on well together, since Solari, who was both a dreamer and naturally kindly, invariably gave in to Cézanne's caprices. Indeed, no one could have been more conciliating. They pooled their resources, and generally managed to spend them in the first few days of the month. When they had no money left, they lived as best they could. Cézanne had been sent a big jar of olive oil from Aix; in times of scarcity, during this winter of 1867 to 1868, it was often their only resource and they dipped pieces of bread into it, declaring the result to be 'sumptuous,' as they 'licked themselves from fingers to elbow.'*

Solari was working on a large statue of the Negro Scipio struggling with dogs for the next Salon. He had baptised his work *La Guerre de l'Indépendence*. Zola brought Manet to Solari's studio to see it. The weather was very cold and Solari had lit a fire. The statue was supported by a casual framework of broom-handles and chair-bars which warped in the heat, and the figure collapsed. No matter; instead of representing a standing Negro, symbolising the War of Independence, the statue would simply be that of a recumbent Negro being bitten by dogs.

'This,' said Cézanne mockingly, 'is typical of the realists.'

In spite of this mishap, Solari's statue was accepted for the Salon. This year, the Hanging Committee were in fact more tolerant: Solari, Manet, Pissarro, Bazille, Renoir, Monet and Sisley were all accepted, but Cézanne was rejected once again.

'Very well,' he said, referring to the members of the Hanging Committee, 'they'll be even more roundly committed to eternity!' And to his painter friends, who complimented him on the picture he had sent in – the second version of *L'Ouverture de Tannhäuser* – he asserted that his later canvases were very much better.

But though Zola was prepared to set his own opinions about his friend's work on one side and had a certain contempt for the Hanging Committee, he nevertheless felt that Cézanne's constant rejections were becoming disquieting. Despite the Hanging Committee's hostility to the innovators, they had all managed to get some of their work

* Joachim Gasquet.

accepted (Daubigny's influence had helped), and this year they were all to appear before the public; all, that is, except Cézanne.

There were 1,378 more pictures hung in the Salon than in the previous year; and the proportion of rejections was comparatively small. As the critic Castagnary, an habitué of the Guerbois, said: 'The doors have been opened to nearly everyone who presented himself.'* The Comte de Nieuwerkerke, however, was extremely angry, and called the Salon of 1868 a 'Salon of upstarts.'* But it was a triumph for Manet and the 'new painting'; and also a triumph for Zola, who could congratulate himself on having helped towards the victory. He was present at the opening: Manet was exhibiting his portrait. On the strength of this success, a new paper, *L'Événement Illustré*, asked Zola to write an account of the Salon.

Unfortunately the articles proved somewhat disappointing to the painters. Whether of his own accord, or on the orders of the editor, Zola made no mention of the artists whose work he disliked. His main preoccupation was to emphasise the triumph of his friends. 'Édouard Manet's success is complete,' he wrote, 'I did not dare to hope that it would be so rapid and so worthy.' But the articles lacked impact and had none of the sensational interest of the previous series.

Zola's articles began to appear on 2 May, and by the time the series came to an end on 16 June, with an eulogy of Solari, Cézanne had already been three weeks in Aix.

* * *

Surrounded by mauve hills, the plain was bright with sunlight. There was rarely a soul to be seen, only an occasional, distant figure moving slowly along the roads or among the vines. There was not a sound except the continuous noise of the cicadas and, at moments, a light breeze murmuring among the silver leaves of the olive trees. In the sunlit solitude of the Jas de Bouffan, Cézanne worked in total oblivion to the passing of time. When he happened to write to one of his friends, he dated his letter vaguely 'about the first days of July.' He was living in a vacuum. Except for Marion and, more rarely, Alexis (who was thinking of taking flight for Paris in spite of his father's

* *Le Salon de* 1868, in *Salons*, Vol. I.

disapproval), he saw no one. Occasionally, in the evening, he would go to the Cours, though he did not wish to see anyone he knew. In spite of his rejection by the Salon – and it was most improbable that Aix was not informed of it – he had nothing but contempt for the local artists, including Gibert. 'They're all goitrous,' he remarked. He was always 'so hard on bad painters.'* When he was not working in his studio at the Jas, he wandered off alone into the countryside, to dream by the Infernets dam, or at the foot of Mont Sainte-Victoire. Sometimes, by nightfall, he would find himself far from Aix, and would ask hospitality from a peasant for the night and sleep on the straw.

He was now painting in the open air, sometimes in the garden of the Jas de Bouffan, sometimes on the banks of the Arc. But he continued work on his big canvases in the studio. He wanted to use the various portraits he had made of his friends during these last years and place them in a landscape. He even intended, if the canvas was as successful as he hoped, to offer it, suitably framed, to the museum in Marseilles.

In the autumn, Marion, who was the only witness of the stubborn resolution with which Cézanne worked, wrote to Morstatt: 'Cézanne is working with all his might to control his temperament, to impose the rules of a cool technique on it. If he succeeds, my dear chap, we shall soon have powerful works of great achievement to admire.'

The year was coming to an end, and Cézanne began to think of returning to Paris. But the problems he had been trying to resolve had absorbed him to such an extent that he had become almost bemused. 'I shall write on a piece of paper everything I must do and everyone I must see, and I shall cross them out as I go along; thus I shall forget nothing.'

* * *

He arrived in Paris about the middle of December, and found Zola very busy and somewhat anxious, for he was still finding it difficult to earn enough money. He had published a new novel, *Madeleine Férat*, a curious work on the theme of 'impregnation' – in other words the permanent imprint made on a woman by her first lover† – and in

* Zola: *L'Oeuvre*.

† This thesis has been completely refuted.

which the three characters bore a certain resemblance, even though an indirect one to Cézanne, Gabrielle and Zola himself. The novel aroused considerable indignation and the Parquet had stopped its serialisation. But, in spite of the scandal, the book was not selling and Zola was beginning to wonder whether he would get anywhere by merely adding one book to another year after year. He was preoccupied and nervous. The memory of Balzac and the *Comédie Humaine* haunted him. It seemed to him that it was 'only by a quantity of volumes, by prolific creation that one can reach the public.' For months past he had been contemplating a vast fresco in which he would tell the 'natural and social' history of a family under the Second Empire. This was to be *Les Rougon-Macquart*. Into it he would pour all his memories and observations. He would describe Aix under the name of Plassans, and use the characteristics of his friends and acquaintances past and present for his characters. Cézanne would, of course, appear in the book. He would be the artist, while Louis Auguste would be a bourgeois, 'jeering, republican, cold, precise, avaricious.' A whole volume would be devoted to Cézanne; with him as his model he would create one of the most vigorously drawn characters in the fresco, depict the tragedy of a 'great painter who failed,' an 'incomplete genius,' a 'soldier of the uncreated,'* the 'terrible tragedy of a mind that destroyed itself.'†

During these days of 1869, Cézanne was still furiously pursuing his researches. He realised that he was beginning to cure himself of 'the romantic gangrene.'‡ He was recapitulating in his own work the recent stages in the history of painting and, if he did not always manage to correct his romanticism by his determination to be objective and realistic in his portraits, he at least succeeded more often in his still lifes. In these he was now attaining a real mastery, a precision of observation allied to a vigour of execution. Still lifes were more suited to his purpose than imaginative compositions, since they were free of the disturbing personal element, and enabled him to devote himself entirely to problems of technique.

Zola owned a black marble clock, which he had probably inherited

* Zola: *L'Oeuvre.*
† Zola: *La Fortune des Rougon*, MS. page 62.
‡ Zola: *L'Oeuvre.*

from his father. Cézanne used it, together with a few other objects – a shell, a vase, a cup, a lemon – for the subject of a canvas which in its power and simplicity was undoubtedly one of the major successes he had achieved since he had begun to paint.

He offered it to Zola. But Zola was no longer interested in Cézanne's pictures. All he now saw in Cézanne was a man in tragic conflict with his art, a man who struggled and swore in 'a long desperate effort',* and who was chief character for one of his future books. Zola's enthusiasm for painting had almost ceased since the Battle of the Salon, which had no doubt been largely the basis for it in the first place. He could think of nothing now but his *Rougon-Macquart*, of the 'enormous work of which he was dreaming.'† Since May he had been working on the first volume, *La Fortune des Rougon*, turning out chapters with the regularity of a machine.

In September, Paul Alexis, having at last decided to leave home, arrived in Paris, and Valabrègue took him to see Zola in the Rue de la Condamine. Zola, who was tired of being surrounded only by painters, made him welcome, and they soon became friends. Cézanne painted a conversation piece of Alexis reading to Zola.‡ In its own way the picture was a companion piece to Manet's portrait of Zola. But the pupil surpassed the master. Cézanne was emerging as a great painter at the very moment Zola had decided that he was irremediably condemned to impotence in his profession, that he was a man 'crushed by art.'§

* * *

By the beginning of 1870, Cézanne had been away from Provence for a year. He was rarely to be absent from Aix for so long again. The fact was that, in spite of his boorishness and mistrust of women, he had fallen for the charms of one of his models, a tall, fair girl, with good features, an attractive figure and dark, thoughtful eyes. Her name was Marie-Hortense Fiquet. He was thirty-one and she nineteen. Born at Saligney in the Jura, on 22 April, 1850, Hortense had come to Paris

* Zola: *L'Oeuvre*.

† Ibid.

‡ This picture, *Paul Alexis lisant à Zola*, was found by chance in 1927 in the attics of the writer's house.

§ Zola: *L'Oeuvre*.

with her parents when she was very young. Her mother had been dead some years and her father had a modest job in a bank. She made her living as a pattern-weaver but earned a little extra money on the side as a model. In Cézanne's eyes she had one great virtue as a model: patience. Posing, however, bored her; she was by nature gay, vivacious and talkative. Whichever quality it was that appealed to Cézanne, it was certainly not her liking for painting nor her knowledge of it, for painting held no interest for her at all.

Without knowing it, Hortense played an essential part at this important moment in Cézanne's creative life. She brought a certain stability to his existence. Thanks to her, his frustrated sensuality was allayed and the liaison enabled him to overcome his romantic fantasies. He was on the point of achieving what he had longed for so ardently: the disciplining of his internal stresses so as to attain control of the art of which he dreamed, his only passion in life.

Cézanne knew he was reaching his goal. Mocking his own romanticism, he painted a canvas entitled *Une Moderne Olympia*, a caricature of Manet's picture, in which he depicted himself gazing at a star in an operetta. The picture was only partially successful; but he did not care. He only needed to persevere. When Manet, at the Guerbois, asked him what he was going to send to the Salon, he replied: '*Un pot de merde*.'

Repeating his joke of three years before, he selected the portrait of Emperaire and a nude to submit to the Hanging Committee, and took them to the Palais de l'Industrie on the last possible day, 20 March. He was given an hilarious ovation. A journalist-caricaturist named Stock, who happened to be there, interviewed him, and he replied with a mock profession of faith: 'Yes, my dear Monsieur Stock, I paint as I see, as I feel – and I have very strong feelings. Those others feel and see as I do, but they daren't do it. They go in for Salon painting. But I dare, Monsieur Stock, I dare. I have the courage of my convictions – and,' he added, at once mocking and prophetic, 'he laughs longest who laughs last.'

His pictures were rejected. 'But I am none the worse for it,' Cézanne wrote to a friend in Aix, whom he informed, as if it were a matter of no importance, that Honoré, Gibert's son, had been accepted, as had

Solari, Bazille, Sisley, Renoir, Pissarro and Manet. At this Salon of 1870, Fantin-Latour exhibited a huge canvas – *Un Atelier aux Batignolles* – in which he depicted some of the habitués of the Guerbois – Zola, Renoir, Monet and Bazille among them – grouped round Manet at his easel. Cézanne was naturally not among the élite.

On 31 May, Zola, alarmed by rumours of war, married Gabrielle Meley at the Mairie of the XVIIth Arrondissement. Cézanne, with three other friends from Aix, Solari, Roux and Alexis, was a witness.

A few days before, Zola had received a letter from Théodore Duret:

'I hear talk of a painter called, I think, Cézanne or something of the sort, who comes from Aix and whose pictures have been rejected by the Hanging Committee. I seem to remember your telling me in the past of a very eccentric painter from Aix. Is he the same man who was rejected this year?

'If he is, would you be kind enough to give me his address and a letter of introduction, so that I may go and make the painter's acquaintance and see his work.'

The day before his wedding, on 30 May, Zola replied to Duret:

'I do not feel I can give you the address of the painter of whom you write. He shuts himself up a good deal; and is going through an experimental period. In my opinion, he is quite right to let no one into his studio. Wait till he has found himself.'

CHAPTER FIVE

The Peace of the Sea

> Sieyès was asked: 'What did you do during the Revolution?' He replied: 'I lived.'

ON 19 July, 1870, the Imperial Government declared war on Prussia. Napoleon III's Empire was tottering. In January, at the funeral of the journalist Victor Noir, who had been assassinated by Pierre Bonaparte, people on the boulevards were shouting: 'Vive la République!' Encouraged by the Empress, Napoleon III fell into the trap Bismarck had set for him with the famous Ems telegram of 13 July.

'When the war has lasted a year, there will not be a single gaiter-button lacking!' declared Marshal Lebœuf. It would be difficult to imagine a more appalling state of unreadiness in a country. Nothing had been organised: military stores contained no food, munitions or uniforms; there were no ambulances; the military staffs had been issued with maps of Germany, but none of the frontier. Mobilisation was entirely haphazard. The chaos was incredible. Soldiers were unable to find their regiments; general officers could get no information as to the whereabouts of their commands, which often existed only on paper. The Garde Mobile was called up; but there were neither arms nor uniforms to issue to them, and they were put to drill with broom-handles. No more than 250,000 men could be put into the line. Though accepted 'with a light heart' by Émile Ollivier, Président du Conseil, the war began disastrously.

The crisis that was stirring all France failed to move Cézanne. He left the flat in which he was living with Hortense at 53, Rue Notre-Dame-des-Champs and quietly disappeared. He went to Provence and installed Hortense in the house on the Place de l'Église at l'Estaque. He had no doubt told his indulgent mother of his liaison; but Louis

Auguste knew nothing of it. Had he known, he would no doubt have been very angry, concluding that Hortense was an adventuress and after his fortune. Louis Auguste, who was now seventy-two, had retired from business and, in agreement with his partner Cabassol, had closed the bank.

Though he was living with Hortense at l'Estaque, Cézanne often went to spend a day or two in Aix. He does not appear to have been on the call-up lists. In any case, mobilisation in Provence was proceeding with remarkable slowness. To the chaos and widespread difficulties of the general mobilisation, Provence was contributing a profound indifference. The war was a long way off and the population remained completely unaffected by the catastrophic news from the east, where the French armies, during that month of August, were suffering defeat after defeat.

Cézanne also remained unconcerned. He was painting! Never had l'Estaque with its great bright bay and circle of hills seemed so beautiful. In the distance, under a golden haze, lay Marseilles, its port filled with ships, and the low hill of Notre-Dame-de-la-Garde stood out against the rugged background of the Marseilleveyre. Nearer at hand, at the foot of the rocky spurs, the tile kilns of Saint-Henri smoked amid the red earth. From the seashore, the streets of l'Estaque rose steeply towards a tumble of white rocks, against which the pines stood out in a quivering emerald green. Inland, the country was all peaks and gorges, with here and there a lonely house. Below lay the sea, on which the rocky islands seemed to float. There was peace here; and Cézanne spent his days painting among the rocks between sea and sky. He was struggling to become objective and put on canvas precisely what he saw.

On 2 September, at Sedan, Napoleon III surrendered to the enemy with 83,000 men. Two days later the Republic was proclaimed in Paris. At ten o'clock at night, in Aix, the Republicans invaded the Hôtel de Ville, removed the insignia of the defunct régime, announced the supersession of the city councillors, and elected new ones by acclamation; among them were Louis Auguste, Baille and Valabrègue who had returned from Paris, and also an olive oil merchant, an old friend of Cézanne's, Victor Leydet.

To Cézanne's surprise, Zola arrived in l'Estaque, with his mother and Gabrielle. He was seeking a refuge in Provence for the two women. The Prussian armies were advancing on Paris, and Gabrielle had been 'so afraid'* that Zola had hurriedly left the capital. *La Fortune des Rougon* had begun as a serial in *Le Siècle* in June; but the invasion had put a stop to its publication.

It had also prevented Zola continuing work on the second volume of the *Rougon-Macquart*, *La Curée*. Zola was profoundly disturbed by the crisis and no longer had the heart to work. 'This appalling war,' he said, 'has made the pen drop from my hand.' During the previous month, on 5 August, in an article in *La Tribune*, entitled *Vive la France*!, he had expressed with considerable violence, and a fine contempt for danger, his disgust with the Empire; the Imperial Parquet was proceeding against him; but happily the Empire was at its last gasp. It now occurred to him that the fall of the Empire would provide a logical conclusion to the cycle of the *Rougon-Macquart*. Zola felt sure, as he told Cézanne, that their 'period' was about to begin.

In the meantime, he stayed with Cézanne, who remained as impervious as ever to political events, and painted away as if nothing had happened. Zola was short of money and exasperated by his forced inactivity. Now that his mother and Gabrielle were in safety, he wanted to return to Paris. But events moved too quickly for him, for on 17 September Paris was besieged. Leaving Cézanne to the peace of l'Estaque, Zola went to live at 15, Rue Haxo in Marseilles. By arrangement with Arnaud, the editor of the *Messager de Provence*, who had serialised his *Mystères*, he made plans with Marius Roux, who had also taken refuge in the Midi, to start a daily newspaper, *La Marseillaise*, to which Valabrègue was to contribute.

The Government had decided to fight to a finish. Paris had armed 500,000 men and was resisting. On 7 October, Gambetta left the capital by balloon to organise the defence of the provinces and raise new armies to fight the Prussians. Despite the surrender of Bazaine at Metz, on the 27th, when 163,000 men were taken prisoner, fighting was going on everywhere: on the Loire, around Paris, in the north and in the

* Zola: letter to Edmond de Goncourt, 7 September, 1870.

east. Even the Municipal Council of Aix issued a proclamation: 'Let us arise, Citizens, and march as one man!'

Marius Roux, however, admitted to Zola that these patriotic proclamations contained more humbug than heroism. Baille and Valabrègue were members of the recruiting committee for the Garde Nationale. According to Roux, it was absurd to take them or their functions seriously. 'Let us march, indeed! They're nice ones!' Nor did Louis Auguste seem to be taking his duties very seriously either. He appeared in the minutes of the Council on nearly every occasion as 'absent for reasons unknown.' His wife was, nevertheless, a patroness of the International Society for Aid to the Wounded.

On 18 November, Cézanne was informed that the municipality of Aix had elected him to the Committee of the Drawing School by fifteen votes out of twenty (the largest majority obtained). However, he took no more interest in it than he did in the war, and attended the meetings with no greater frequency than his father attended those of the Council.

Whether he was in l'Estaque or in Aix, Cézanne imperturbably carried on with his work and paid little attention to anything else. In bad weather he painted portraits, or scenes with groups of figures, often drawing his inspiration from illustrations in the fashion magazines read by Hortense and his sisters. These second-rate illustrations were enough to set his imagination working, although it needed no very great spur. 'I don't need anything to excite me,' he said. 'I can do that for myself.' He was now beginning to bring the same objectivity to his portraits as to his still lifes; to his eye, that was what his models were: a face was similar to an apple, insomuch as it afforded precisely the same opportunity to plumb the secrets of nature.

La Marseillaise was selling badly; and Zola, realising that it must shortly close down, had taken it into his head to become Sub-Prefect of Aix. He took a few soundings, but discovered that the prefectorial administration was unfortunately in as great a state of chaos as was the military. No one seemed to know who had nominated the present Sub-Prefect of Aix. Zola, being short of money, grew impatient and, on 12 December, leaving his mother and Gabrielle in Marseilles, set off for Bordeaux, to which the Government of National Defence had retreated, in an endeavour to hurry through his nomination. But his canvassing proved abortive. In the end, on 19 December, he succeeded, as an alternative, in becoming secretary to one of the ministers, Glais-Bizoin, whom he had met in the past on *La Tribune*. Happier about his immediate future, Zola was able to look forward optimistically to the end of the war. 'If we're clever about it,' he wrote on 22 December to Marius Roux, 'we shall make a triumphant return.'

But the war went on. General Chanzy's troops were fighting desperately on the Loire. On 27 December, the Prussians began to bombard a starving Paris.

In Paris and in Aix the weather was appalling, alternating between snow and rain. At l'Estaque, the sea was grey and rough, and the sky lowering; pine and rock were covered with a layer of dirty, yellow snow. The general mobilisation was continuing, and Cézanne had received his call-up papers.

He had not, however, responded to them; and during the preceding weeks he had been regularly seen in Aix, where people were beginning to say that the banker's son ought to be in uniform. The police went out to the Jas de Bouffan to fetch him. 'He left two or three days ago,' his mother told them. 'When I hear where he is, I'll let you know.' But Cézanne had made no secret of his retreat at l'Estaque, and the authorities very soon discovered where he was. In the meantime, informers had also denounced Zola, not realising that he had left l'Estaque. On 2 January, Marius Roux's father overheard in a café that four Gardes Mobiles and a corporal had received orders to seek out defaulters in the suburbs of Marseilles; among the names mentioned were those of Cézanne and Zola.

What happened is not known. It may well be that Baille and Valabrègue brought pressure to bear on the Committee or, again, which is more than probable, the Garde Mobile brought little enthusiasm to its duties. In any case, Cézanne made no attempt to conceal his whereabouts. War and mobilisation had no reality for him; while the hard winter, of which everyone was complaining, afforded an opportunity for further researches. He painted and studied nature, seeking solutions for one problem after another. Still torn by the conflict and contradiction between the two poles of his nature, Cézanne was devoting all his efforts to reconciling the irreconcilable. During these days of January and February, when the thaw was setting in, he painted *La Neige fondante à l'Estaque*. In the meantime, the army had been defeated at Mans, Saint-Quentin and on the Doubs. Paris surrendered on 28 January, and France had lost the war. The Garde Mobile was unlikely to disturb Cézanne now.

The snow had melted and l'Estaque had come into its own again: red-tiled roofs, rocks, pines and a calm sea. Cézanne continued to paint.

* * *

It was now May, and Zola had been back in Paris since 14 March, living in his house in the Batignolles, which had been occupied for a time by refugees. On 18 March, *Le Siècle* had begun publishing the serial of *La Fortune des Rougon* again, though for a time Zola feared that the single copy of the manuscript had been lost. On the very same day, the Commune insurrection began.

For over two months, Zola lived a difficult life in Paris to the sound of gunfire; he was twice arrested, once by the insurgents, and a second time by government supporters. Threatened a third time with arrest and detention as a hostage, he managed to escape to Bonnières, where he waited for the troubles to come to an end. On 28 May the government troops destroyed the Commune with much bloodshed. Zola returned to Paris, impatient to get to work again. 'We are the writers of tomorrow,' he said. But where was Cézanne? Zola had heard nothing of him for months. Since Alexis was going to the south, Zola asked him to look up their friend.

Alexis went to l'Estaque, but Cézanne was not there. He was told that he had gone to Lyons 'to wait till Paris stopped smoking.' But Zola guessed this was not true. He pressed Alexis to make enquiries at the Jas de Bouffan. At last, at the beginning of July, contact was re-established. On 4 July, Zola wrote to Cézanne: 'I'm living quietly in the Batignolles again, as if I had emerged from a bad dream . . . I have never been more hopeful nor had a greater desire to work. Paris is being reborn. As I have often told you, our reign is at hand. My novel, *La Fortune des Rougon*, is in the press. You can't imagine the delight I take in correcting the proofs . . . I feel rather sorry that all the fools aren't dead, but it consoles me to think that we are all still alive. We can take up the struggle again.'

Their reign might be at hand, but Cézanne merely shrugged his shoulders. He wanted to work a little longer in this fine summer weather of 1871; and then he would pack his bags.

The Painter Abused

PART THREE

[1872 - 1882]

CHAPTER ONE

The Banks of the Oise

The secret of the strong is ceaseless self-restraint.—BARRES

ON their return to Paris, Cézanne and Hortense went to live at 5, Rue de Chevreuse, in the same house as Solari.

The capital was binding up its wounds from the two sieges. Solari, who, with Courbet, had taken part in pulling down the Vendôme column during the Commune, was now working on repairs to the Louvre. The painters of the Batignolles group had undergone very diverse experiences during the war. Contrary to what Zola had said in his letter to Cézanne, one of them, and not the least gifted, was dead. Bazille, who had enlisted in the third regiment of Zouaves, had been killed on 28 November during the attack on Beaune-la-Rolande. Guillemet had served in the Garde Mobile. Renoir had been a trooper in the Cuirassiers, and been set to groom horses first in Bordeaux, and then in Tarbes. Manet, who had joined the artillery after 4 September, had become a staff officer; to his horror, he had found himself under the command of Colonel Meissonier who, unable to forget aesthetic hatreds, had, it was said, sent his subordinate on all the most dangerous missions. But not all the painters of the Batignolles group had shown such patriotism. Like Cézanne at l'Estaque, Monet had taken refuge in London, where he had found Daubigny and Pissarro and had made the acquaintance of the art dealer Durand-Ruel, who was greatly interested in the new painting.

The meetings at the Guerbois had begun again, but many of the painters of the group had now left Paris. Absorbed in his Rougon-Macquart, Zola's appearances were less frequent. Cézanne scarcely went there at all. He seemed to want to stand aloof. Sullen and surly, he saw almost no one, not even Zola. Perhaps the turn his private life had taken was to some extent responsible. Hortense had been pregnant for some months, and this, whether he had wanted it or not, was a new tie.

Like Zola, Cézanne was one of those people who have not the courage to break off a relationship; for better or for worse, the first woman he loved was to be the only woman in his life. But unlike Zola, who transformed it into an ideal and a principle of life, Cézanne accepted the situation reluctantly, and it made him sour with himself and with others. One day in December, Solari heard furniture being moved down the stairs. It was Cézanne moving out, in search of an illusory peace elsewhere.

Cézanne went to live at 45, Rue de Jussieu. He had taken a little flat on the second floor, whose windows overlooked the wine market. It was not the quietest place he could have chosen. From dawn onwards, there was a continuous noise of rolling barrels. From his window he painted a view of the market, and the almost uniformly grey and brown tones, together with the brutally expressive drawing, are indications of the disquiet and sombre humour from which he was suffering at this time.

On 4 January, 1872, Hortense gave birth to a boy, whom his father acknowledged, and registered at the Mairie of the V Arrondissement under the Christian name of Paul. Soon afterwards, in February, Achille Emperaire created some slight diversion in Cézanne's life. Wishing to try his luck in Paris once again, the dwarf asked Cézanne to put him up. Cézanne obligingly agreed that Emperaire might share his 'hovel.'

Arriving from Aix, Emperaire came to stay in the Rue de Jussieu; but Cézanne soon regretted his offer of hospitality; a small flat, a squalling infant and a lodger were too much. Nor was Emperaire particularly grateful. He considered Cézanne 'very ill lodged'; moreover, the noise from the wine market – 'a clatter to raise the dead' – was intolerable. Emperaire, whose confidence in his own genius could not be shaken, was prepared to go to any lengths to get his work recognised. He would triumph over 'the great ones of the earth,' and conquer that 'monster,' bourgeois art. For him the Salon was the Promised Land; and to obtain entry to it he made call upon call, waited in the ante-rooms of ministers, harassed everyone he knew who might have influence, and indeed many he did not know. He conceived the most extraordinary plans. He intended to go to see Hugo, 'the

Great Victor,' 'the great poet of the Revolution,' to show him his sketches and 'ask his advice about two possible subjects for sending in to the Salon.' He was afraid of nothing and no one. 'Seeing the Giant does not frighten me,' he said of Hugo.

This grandiloquent and ingenuous assurance might have amused Cézanne at any other time. But now it made him impatient and the inevitable soon happened. Living under the same roof with him was clearly impossible. Emperaire had arrived in Paris on 18 February; a month later he left the Rue de Jussieu. 'I'm leaving Cézanne's flat,' he wrote to his friends. 'I must. As things are, I cannot escape the fate of the rest. I have found him forsaken by everyone. He no longer has one single intelligent or affectionate friend. Zola, Solari, and all the others never see him now.' Cézanne was 'the most extraordinary creature you can imagine,' a 'real monster if ever there was one (in the scientific meaning of the word).'

Nevertheless, Emperaire could not break completely with Cézanne, for the verdict on his entry for the Salon would be sent to the Rue de Jussieu. This year, Cézanne seemed completely unconcerned about the Salon. In conflict with himself, tormented by his art which was in process of evolution, he was far too preoccupied to bother to submit an entry to the Hanging Committee. Nor was he alone in this. Monet, Pissarro and Sisley, whose pictures Durand-Ruel was buying, and who were therefore less concerned with the Salon battle, had also abstained. But painters in general had high hopes of this first Salon under the Third Republic. They imagined the change of régime would also bring about a change in the outlook of the Hanging Committee.

Had they consulted Zola, he could have told them otherwise. The previous autumn, the Procureur de la République had sent for him to warn him to stop the serial publication in *La Cloche* of the second volume of his series, *La Curée*, which was being accused of immorality. Failing this, the paper would be prosecuted. Régimes might pass, but prejudices remained; and the painters were soon to be made aware of it. The Hanging Committee under the Third Republic showed no greater understanding than that of the Second Empire. Worse still, it considered anything new subversive; all painting that was not strictly academic was, in its view – and in the public's – to be classed with that of Courbet, suspect, dangerous, Communard and a threat to the social order.* The discontented demanded a Salon des Refusés, but with no greater success than in the time of M. de Nieuwerkerke.

* * *

Before the war, Pissarro had lived in Louveciennes, not far from the Marly aqueduct. The Prussians had pillaged his house and turned it into a slaughterhouse, using his canvases as butcher's aprons. On returning from London, Pissarro had decided to live elsewhere. For some years past he had been attracted by the lush meadows and watery skies of the Oise valley. For an open air painter the district was rich in subject matter. Pissarro chose the town of Pontoise, where he went to live at 26, Rue de l'Hermitage.

A determined open air painter, who had resolutely eliminated 'black, sienna and the ochres' from his palette, Pissarro was always trying to convince his friends of the advantages they would derive from a close contact with nature. Still as persuaded as ever of Cézanne's talent, he pressed him to come to Pontoise.

Cézanne had a great admiration for Pissarro. Above all he valued his balance and commonsense – virtues he himself so strangely lacked. Moreover, Pissarro was kindly, tactful and discreet. Certainly Cézanne could not at this moment return to Aix with an infant son and Pissarro might well be the man to help him with advice at this difficult juncture in the development of his art. Pissarro submitted to the influence of nature and this attracted Cézanne. He knew he must go farther in the conquest of himself and acquire still greater objectivity. But for this he lacked both knowledge and technique. Pissarro would teach him. In the summer, Cézanne took Hortense and his son to Pontoise. He went to stay at Saint-Ouen-l'Aumone, a suburb of the town, in the Hôtel du Grand-Cerf, at 59, Rue Basse.

Cézanne found the atmosphere at Pontoise most agreeable. Pissarro, who was over forty, was like an elder brother to him (Cézanne was

* During the Commune, Courbet, as President of the Fédération des Artistes, had suppressed the École des Beaux-Arts and the Académie des Beaux-Arts.

now thirty-three). Pissarro understood his character and knew how to make their relationship an easy one. His natural modesty and good humour disarmed Cézanne's touchiness and suspicion; and Cézanne felt at home in the house in the Rue de l'Hermitage, where he found Madame Pissarro equally kind.

There were two or three other painters in the neighbourhood with whom Pissarro and Cézanne formed a friendly group: a certain Béliard, the young Victor Vignon and, from time to time, Guillaumin, who, tired of being too poor even to buy sufficient food, had become a civil servant again in the Ponts et Chaussées of the city of Paris. The Pontoise countryside, the calm, fresh landscapes of the Vexin, delighted Cézanne. He set up his easel next to Pissarro's, worked and listened to his friend's advice.

In Pissarro's view, Cézanne's palette was too dark. 'We never paint light enough,' Daubigny had been saying for a long time past. 'Never paint except with the three primary colours and their immediate derivatives,' Pissarro told Cézanne. Pissarro painted with little touches so as to give his colours their full values and communicate to the subject the very palpitation of air and light. For things partake of the luminous atmosphere surrounding them; their true colour, their 'local tone,' is modified by the light. Thousands of reflections play over things, as indeed they colour the shadows, which are never truly black. Moreover, forms become diluted in light. Nature, as it presents itself to the eye, is no more than an appearance, but it is this appearance that must be caught. Such was the theory.

Pissarro encouraged Cézanne to look at a landscape and record precisely what he saw, to translate the sensations of his retina without seeking to interpret them in any way at all; he adjured him to get away from the 'self' and become merely the attentive and exact observer of external reality. Cézanne listened and applied himself to these precepts, persuaded of the excellence of the method. He copied one of Pissarro's landscapes, a view of Louveciennes, to acquire a better understanding of his friend's technique. Nor, at this moment, could any technique have been better suited to him or more conducive to the achievement of his immediate ambition. Though only 'temperament,' by which he meant initial force, could carry a man to his goal,

Cézanne realised that uncontrolled force was a vain waste of energy: true force was disciplined force.

Cézanne found considerable difficulty in pursuing the processes of analysis Pissarro recommended. In spite of himself, his temperament carried him away. While Pissarro, who was more conscientious and hard working than he was temperamental, had no difficulty in being objective, could go on quietly filling his canvas with his light brush strokes, Cézanne continually found himself laying his colours on with vigorous impatience. He struggled relentlessly to lay the Old Adam. Pissarro was certain, as he wrote to Guillemet, that Cézanne 'would astonish many painters who had been far too quick to condemn him.'

Nor was Pissarro alone in this belief. Not far from Pontoise, at Auvers-sur-Oise, a curious man by the name of Dr Paul-Ferdinand Gachet had come to live. He had been born in Lille on 30 July, 1828, and was about the same age as Pissarro. He had a practice in Paris in the Rue du Faubourg Saint-Denis, where he had lived till recently. He had married in 1868, and his young wife, who already had a daughter aged three, was not only pregnant again but suffered from consumption. In the previous April, Dr Gachet had therefore bought a big two-storyed house in the Rue des Vessenots, in Auvers; it had at one time been a girls' school and had a large terraced garden. He divided his time between Paris and the banks of the Oise.

The doctor had certain eccentricities. He was often to be seen in Auvers wearing a blue army surgeon's overcoat of 1870; in the summer he wore a white cap, in winter a fur one. He dyed his hair yellow, and on sunny days carried a white sunshade. Dr Gachet was interested in everything under the sun, and his views were inevitably heterodox. He was a free-thinker and a socialist; in medicine he practised homeopathy; and he was deeply interested in phrenology and palmistry.

From early youth he had been attracted to painting. He both painted and etched himself, and frequented artistic circles, while he also claimed to be descended from the Flemish painter John Mabuse. He had made friends with Daubigny, who also lived at Auvers, as well as with Daumier, who had now retired half-blind to the neighbouring

Valmondois. The doctor's tastes in painting, as in everything else, tended towards the new and the revolutionary. He admired Courbet; he frequented the cafés where the art of the future was being brought to birth; he knew and admired Manet, Monet, Renoir, Degas and, of course, Pissarro. He was vital, enthusiastic, and warm-hearted. He believed in a better future for humanity, and treated the poor of the district with secret charity. He also collected stray animals and filled his house with innumerable cats and dogs. He had met Cézanne at Pissarro's house and, having seen his work, had no doubt at all that he was a great painter. Delighted, as always, to make friends with an artist of talent, he persuaded Cézanne to come and live at Auvers, where he could lease a small house and be more comfortable than in an hotel room at Pontoise.

Cézanne moved to Auvers in the autumn. He went to live close to the Gachets, with whom he got on extremely well. The doctor was impulsive by nature, but Pissarro had warned him that, if he wished to remain on good terms with Cézanne, he must be tactful, avoid argument, never impose on him, and above all give him no reason to suppose that an attempt was being made to put 'the grapnel on him.' Moreover, his particular phobia of being touched or even brushed against must be respected. The doctor, however, paid little heed to these counsels.

Nevertheless, the admiration Gachet showed for his work soon gave Cézanne confidence. His temper improved. For the first time he found himself in a circle of friends who were passionately interested in his painting. Pissarro and Gachet were constant in their encouragement. The critic Duret, to whom Zola had refused to give Cézanne's address, wrote to Pissarro in December asking if it were possible 'to see something of Cézanne's,' for in painting, as he said, he was more than ever on the lookout for 'sheep with five legs;' and Pissarro immediately replied: 'If you are looking for sheep with five legs, Cézanne may well satisfy you, for some of his studies are quite extraordinary, seen with a vision that is unique.' And Daubigny, having seen Cézanne painting on the bank of the Oise one day, exclaimed: 'I've just seen a most extraordinary sketch by a young, unknown painter, a certain Cézanne!' And, indeed, everyone was feeling more optimistic. At the beginning of 1873, some of Pissarro's canvases were sold for quite reasonable prices in Paris, one of them even reaching 950 francs.* 'We're beginning to cut our way way through,' Pissarro said to Duret.

Cézanne seemed more contented. He liked the Auvers countryside. It had one major quality as far as he was concerned: perfect quiet. He was no longer so impatient with his work; he was discovering anew the fabulous richness nature yielded to the attentive and loving observer. No longer was he in search of the violent and rather naïve effects by which he had exploited his emotions. Absorbed now in the contemplation of his subject, he was devoting his whole power of concentration to the least nuance. The most banal object, the simplest landscape, were investigated with determined humility. It was now that the miracle occurred: at the very moment he no longer desired to be anything but an interpreter, a servant of nature, he began to express himself with a plenitude he had never before achieved. The more he subjected himself to nature, the more nature seemed to reveal the essential Cézanne on his canvas. In the process of discovering the richness of nature, he discovered his own, and they became fused into a wonderful unity – of which colour was the language.

Cézanne patiently learned its alphabet. As he gradually refined his visual acuity, so he became aware of the complex edifice of colour the world afforded. Those days at Auvers-sur-Oise in 1873 were wonderfully serene. He set up his easel by thatched houses, in fields and in roads, and painted. He painted Dr Gachet's house, Père Lacroix's, and the house known as The Hanged Man's. Whereas, in the old days, he had attacked his canvas with impetuosity, he now worked with a slow and ordered concentration, building his canvas up, touch by touch, with exquisite deliberation.

It did not come easily to him. He was never satisfied. He continually corrected and altered, superimposing layer upon layer of paint, achieving a granulated impasto that gave his canvas the warm opulence of a fine enamel. The closer he approached to reality, the richer it proved itself to be, and he would pursue his researches yet further. Day after day, week after week, even month after month, he would go back to the same canvas, trying always to achieve a little more. 'Leave that picture, Cézanne, it's perfect, don't touch it again,' Dr Gachet

* The equivalent of approximately £150 today.

would say, convinced that Cézanne would spoil it. Besides, the world kept changing; trees, sky and earth altered with the seasons; and some of his pictures, on which he worked too long, reflect the transformation.

Cézanne's relations with Gachet remained unclouded. He often went to the Rue des Vessenots to paint a still life. Gachet would supply him with fruit, jugs, vases, pieces of Italian pottery, honeycomb glass, and so on. Madame Gachet picked flowers for him, which he arranged in Delftware.

One day, Gachet and Cézanne were discussing Manet and his *Olympia*. The doctor greatly admired the picture. Somewhat irritated by Gachet's praise of it, Cézanne picked up his palette and at great speed painted another version of his *Moderne Olympia* of three years ago on the spot. The original picture had not been altogether successful, but now, with the new mastery he had acquired by patient attention to technique, he produced a work that was not only brilliant in colouring, light of touch, and delicate in its sensuality, but also most subtle in its irony. This extraordinary exercise in virtuosity delighted the doctor.

Gachet, who signed his work Van Ryssel (Flemish for 'from Lille'), was devoted to etching, which he preferred to painting. When he bought his house in Auvers, he had been able to fulfil a long cherished ambition by setting up a studio, with all the necessary paraphernalia for etching, in a barn. But he was not content to indulge in etching on his own; he was an enthusiastic propagandist for the medium. Guillaumin and Pissarro etched with him on occasion; and he tried to persuade Cézanne to attempt it too. Eventually he got his way; and Cézanne's first attempt, a reproduction of Guillaumin's *Vue de la Seine*, which belonged to Gachet, was followed by a portrait of Guillaumin himself (*Guillaumin au Pendu*). But after three more essays, Cézanne abandoned the medium, which clearly did not suit him.

Gachet not only gave Cézanne his friendship and encouragement, but from time to time helped him more materially by buying him a canvas. No doubt this did not cost him much; but it was a considerable help to Cézanne, who was very badly off. He had only the small allowance his father had given him as a bachelor with which to support himself, Hortense and the child.

No one, seeing Cézanne in his thick boots, waggoner's cloak, old cap or yellow straw hat, would have taken him for a rich banker's son. He was completely indifferent to appearances. But, despite his worn and neglected clothes, he had a certain presence. He was tall and well set up, held his head high and walked with a light step. His beard was ragged, but his eyes were quick and extraordinarily bright. Though he was perpetually dissatisfied with his work, he nevertheless knew that he was approaching truth in his art, and was therefore able to bear more easily the material difficulties of his life, even the fact that he often had to economise over the tools of his trade; he could frequently not afford canvas and had to paint on cardboard.

Pissarro and Gachet helped in more ways than one. When he was unable to pay his bill at Rondès, the grocer in the Rue de la Roche at Pontoise, Cézanne had suggested paying off the debt with canvases. Rondès enquired of Gachet whether he should accept this unusual offer. 'Take the paintings,' the doctor said, 'they'll be worth a lot one day.' And, on Pissarro's recommendation, one of the schoolmasters at the Pontoise school (which Pissarro's son attended), a man named Rouleau, bought some of Cézanne's pictures. 'He is like a beneficent god,' Cézanne said gratefully of Pissarro.

Socialist by political inclination, Pissarro had been friends before the war with a small colour-merchant, Julien Tanguy, whose opinions were similar to his own. Tanguy, familiarly known as Père Tanguy, was a Breton of some fifty years of age.* He came of a family of poor weavers from the neighbourhood of Saint-Brieuc, and had started life as a plasterer, married a pork-butcher's daughter and, for a time, had sold sausages at Saint-Brieuc.

He came to Paris ten years before the war and, having first found employment with the Compagnie de l'Ouest, had then become a colour-grinder in the well-known house of Édouard in the Rue Clauzel in 1865. Shortly afterwards he had set up on his own, prepared his own colours, and sold them from a barrow in the localities which the open-air painters, such as Monet and Pissarro, were then beginning to haunt.

Unfortunately, the Commune had been a disastrous period for Tanguy. No one knew exactly what had happened, except that he

* He was born at Plédran, in the Côtes-du-Nord, on 28 June, 1825.

had been taken prisoner, with arms in his hands, in the ranks of the Fédérés, had been sent to Satory, court-martialled and found guilty. Exiled to Brest (he escaped the execution squad by the skin of his teeth), he had mouldered there for many months. Eventually, through the good offices of an academic painter, Jobbé-Duval, who was a member of the Municipal Council of Paris, he was freed and returned to the capital, where he took up his old trade again. Since the Maison Édouard had left the Rue Clauzel, he opened a shop at No. 14 in that street. Pissarro had recommended customers and put Cézanne in touch with him.

Cézanne and Tanguy had made friends at once. The colour-merchant was attracted by Cézanne's work; he liked its originality, its novelty, and its technique, which was so different to 'official' art; and his sympathy was aroused by its revolutionary character. Père Tanguy was one of the kindliest of men. Though heavy in body and rather forbidding in appearance, his generous nature was reflected in his candid blue eyes. He was always ready to oblige a friend and to give a penniless painter credit – which was often prolonged indefinitely.

In his own way, Père Tanguy was a stoic. 'A man who lives on more than fifty centimes a day is a blackguard,' he would say. This was typical both of his generosity and his spirit. Having fought with the Fédérés and suffered imprisonment, he had become an out-and-out revolutionary. As a colour-merchant he supported the painters who were not accepted by officialdom. And these painters became, in a particular sense, *his* painters. They painted in clear colours; and he defended painting in clear colours. He associated it, in his kindly and ingenuous way, with the revolution. To give it a helping hand was to assist the coming of the splendid tomorrows he envisaged. Moreover, it gave him pleasure; and he hated the 'tobacco juice' colouring cherished by the bourgeois.

He was delighted to supply 'Monsieur Cézanne,' as he respectfully called him, with canvases and paints. And since his customer was always rather short of money, Tanguy was prepared to accept in exchange a few works which he would put up for sale in his shop in the Rue Clauzel. Cézanne was very grateful for the arrangement.

In 1874 there was once again considerable agitation among the younger painters. There had been many rejections for the Salon in the previous spring, though they had not much affected the painters of the Batignolles group, of whom Manet had been almost the only one to submit work. The others, realising that the Hanging Committee would never change its attitude, had not bothered to do so. Moreover, Manet's success in the Salon had tended to confirm their conviction: in *Le Bon Bock* he did not seem to have made any advance on his previous work.

Influenced as it was by Franz Hals, *Le Bon Bock* appeared to them 'old fashioned.' Manet's success was in their view an unenviable one: he had achieved official approval by making concessions – by putting 'water in his *bock*.' They felt they must make their own mark with the public outside the Salon. The young painters were in fact beginning to attract the attention of a few amateurs; and some of their canvases had achieved relatively high prices at auctions. They now decided to organise their own exhibitions.

They would be in more direct contact with the public, which would be able to gain a better understanding of their aims than when their canvases – or such of them as the Salon happened on occasion to accept – were scattered among a plethora of pictures in different styles. The idea had occurred to them before the war, but they had been unable to implement it owing to lack of funds. But things were different now; time had gone by; at whatever cost, young painters must emerge from the isolation to which the dictatorship of the Hanging Committee threatened to banish them for ever. They were all the more prepared to take the risk since Durand-Ruel, early in 1874, had ceased buying their canvases. He had found great difficulty in selling them. A number of collectors, who had been among his best customers, had lost confidence in him since he had become interested in Pissarro, Monet and Sisley; they believed he had lost all critical acumen, if he had not gone completely out of his mind. The economic crisis from which France had been suffering, since the brief period of prosperity following on the war, had also increased the painters' own anxieties as to their immediate financial future.*

* See *The History of Impressionism* by John Rewald. This important work deals in detail with the development of French art between the years 1855 to 1886. It is an inexhaustible mine of information and accurate references.

Pissarro, Monet and Degas were largely instrumental in making the exhibition possible. Pissarro was determined that Cézanne should take part in it. The public, which had never yet had an opportunity of seeing Cézanne's work, would at last be able to assess his talent.

* * *

In the meantime, Zola, whom Cézanne had probably not seen at all during these last months, was working stubbornly on his *Rougon-Macquart*. For the moment, however, his labours did not appear to be achieving their reward. The two first volumes of the series, *La Fortune des Rougon* and *La Curée*, had failed even to attain a *succès d'estime;* they had had very few reviews and a derisory sale. To add to his difficulties, his publisher had gone bankrupt. Charpentier, his new publisher, had published the third volume, *Le Ventre de Paris*, a few months previously, but it had had no greater success than the others. But Zola was undeterred. He was determined to complete the immense panorama on which he was engaged, and into it he put everything that he had ever known, seen or learned. In *La Fortune des Rougon*, he had depicted Solari; in *Le Ventre de Paris*, he had sketched, under the name of Claude Lantier, a portrait of Cézanne. It was, however, merely the sketch for a portrait he proposed to elaborate one day; and he looked on his old friend with 'a bitter, wounded pity,' as 'a failure of genius,' as the victim of 'an appalling, tormented impotence.'

CHAPTER TWO

The Public

> Success is everything, Monseigneur, and yet what does it prove? Nothing . . . It depends on time, place and circumstances.—ÉLÉMIR BOURGES: *Les Oiseaux s'envolent et les Fleurs tombent*

WHILE his friends were trying to organise the exhibition, Cézanne returned to Paris and went to live in a little two-storey house at 120, Rue de Vaugirard.

His parents, however, were pressing him to come to Aix. It was now the spring of 1874, and three years since he had left Provence. His prolonged absence was bound sooner or later to arouse the banker's suspicions. 'I have told you,' Cézanne wrote to his parents, 'that to be with you is a greater pleasure to me than you can imagine, but once in Aix I am no longer free, and when I want to return to Paris it is always a struggle; and though your opposition to my return is not absolute, I am always much concerned by your resistance to my leaving. I very much hope my liberty of action will not be hindered, and I shall hasten my return with all the greater pleasure.'

True though this might be, he naturally said nothing of the main reason that prevented his going to Aix. He was not happy about leaving Hortense and little Paul alone in Paris; and it was too risky to take them to Provence. He therefore kept putting off going to Aix himself, fearing he might be detained there overlong.

In the meantime, he was having considerable difficulty in paying his way, and he wanted his father to increase his allowance to 200 francs a month.* 'It would permit me,' he wrote with a not altogether convincing cunning, 'to stay for some time in Aix, and it will give me great pleasure to work in the Midi, which affords my painting so many opportunities. Believe me, if Papa will agree to this, I shall, I think, be able to pursue the studies I wish to make in the Midi.'

* Approximately £35 a month today.

Many of Cézanne's friends were much poorer than he was. Without the funds advanced by Degas, who had private means, and by Henri Rouart, an engineer who was prepared to spend money on painting, the exhibition could probably not have taken place. It would clearly have been impossible to ask the participants to pay much towards it. The exhibition was, however, giving rise to a great deal of discussion.

In the first place, the leader of the group, Manet, the only one of them all who cared about official recognition from the Salon, absolutely refused to take part in it. 'I shall never commit myself to appearing with M. Cézanne!' he declared. In his view Cézanne was nothing more than 'a mason who paints with his trowel.'

Nor was Manet any more appreciative of Renoir, whom he considered 'a good man gone astray in painting.'* And Pissarro, it must be admitted, had found it far from easy to get Cézanne accepted as a participant; his colleagues considered him either too daring or too bad. Indeed, some members of the group, Degas in particular, feared that the public would react violently to the pictures shown.

This group, which did not altogether approve of some of the participants, hoped to make the exhibition less provocative by drawing on a wider range of artists, particularly on those who were more conformist and exhibited in the Salon. As this would also reduce the individual share of the expenses, they succeeded in the end in getting their way.

Even then, however, some painters found the prospect far from reassuring and refused to take part. Among these was Guillemet, who was beginning to abandon his former enthusiasms, tending to look on them as the sins of youth, and was becoming increasingly attracted by money and success. He had achieved an honourable mention in the Salon of 1872 as the reward for submission. It was clear that the group lacked homogeneity; and, indeed, so afraid were they of appearing to found a new school that Renoir rejected the perfectly harmless title of 'La Capucine,'† which Degas had proposed giving to the group. The

* Vollard.

† The name of 'La Capucine' had occurred to Degas because Nadar, the photographer, had consented to lend the large premises he occupied at 35, Boulevard des Capucines, on the corner of the Rue Daunou.

exhibitors were to present themselves to the public simply under the appellation of the 'Société anonyme coopérative d'artistes peintres, sculpteurs, graveurs, etc.'

However, the exhibition was gradually organised. It was opened two weeks before the Salon, on 15 April; and it was to last a month. The public was to be admitted not only from 10 to 6, but also from 8 to 10; the price of entry was fixed at one franc.

On the suggestion of Pissarro, egalitarian as always, the rule was made that 'once the works have been arranged according to size, chance must decide where they are hung.' There were one hundred and sixty-nine paintings by twenty-nine artists. With Cézanne – who sent in *La Maison du Pendu*, an Auvers landscape and his *Moderne Olympia* – Monet, Renoir, Pissarro, Sisley, Guillaumin, Degas and Berthe Morisot were mingled painters, mostly invited by Degas, who were less likely to upset the public.

Degas was right to be anxious about the impact such an exhibition would make. The mere holding of it was a proclamation of independence, an assertion of a will to break with tradition and a defiance of the Hanging Committee of the Salon, the only recognised authority on art. It was clearly subversive. Such people were capable of anything, for were they not the spiritual brothers of the murderers of hostages and of the *Pétroleuses* of the Commune?

And, in fact, hardly had the exhibition opened when a flood of violent hostility, mockery and sarcasm was let loose. A crowd of visitors, occasionally threatening and sometimes hilarious, jostled its way into Nadar's premises. Contrary to Degas' expectations, the public completely ignored the more conformist works and devoted its entire attention to the pictures of the *Intransigeants*.

Their work was 'appalling,' 'stupid,' 'hideous!' 'This painting lacks all sense.'* All these so-called artists 'squint with their minds.'† They had something wrong with their eyes, like the hysterics in the Salpêtrière; one saw everything violent, another discerned 'hairdresser's blue in all nature.'‡ These painters were humbugs; they

* O'Squarr in the *Courrier de France*, 6 April, 1877.

† The opinion of a certain Guichard in a letter to the mother of Berthe Morisot.

‡ Huysmans in *L'Art Moderne*.

simply loaded a pistol with colours and fired it point-blank at the canvas!

Most of the serious critics, of course, paid no attention to this display of 'daubs.' The few who did condescend to notice the exhibition did so in virulent terms. Nevertheless, there were one or two who made a laudable effort to understand what they saw, even discovering certain merits in the work of Renoir, Monet, Pissarro and Degas. But that was as far as they could go. Clearly, they could not go so far as to acknowledge Cézanne, from whom no Hanging Committee, as Jean Prouvaire, the critic of the *Rappel*, remarked, 'has ever dreamed of the possibility' of accepting a canvas. Marc de Montifaud wrote in *L'Artiste* that Cézanne was 'a sort of madman, who seemed to paint in *delirium tremens*.' Cézanne was impossible.

Such a *succès de scandale* was bound to attract the attention of *Charivari*. One of its contributors, Louis Leroy, made the exhibition the subject of a humorous article, which he entitled *L'Exposition des Impressionnistes*. In it, he described a visit to the exhibition in company with an imaginary medal-winning landscape painter, who had been a pupil of Bertin, called 'Joseph Vincent.'

'He had come imprudently, thinking no harm; he imagined he was going to see the sort of painting one sees everywhere, good and bad, generally more bad than good, but not subversive of the great traditions of art, of the cult of form and respect for the masters. "Form? Masters? We want no more of them, my dear chap! We've changed all that."

'As he went into the first room, Joseph Vincent received a preliminary shock when he saw M. Renoir's *Danseuse*.

' "What a pity," he said to me, "that the painter, who has a certain sense of colour, does not draw better: his dancer's legs are as fluffy as the gauze of her skirts."

' "I think you're being hard on him," I replied, "the drawing seems to me very concise."

'Bertin's pupil, thinking I was being ironical, merely shrugged his shoulders without bothering to answer me.

'Assuming the most ingenuous air, I led him gently to M. Pissarro's *Champ Labouré*.

'At sight of this formidable landscape, the poor man thought his spectacles had misted over. He wiped them carefully and replaced them on his nose.

' "Good heavens!" he cried. "What on earth is that?"

' "Don't you see? It's white frost on deeply ploughed furrows."

' "Do you mean to say those are furrows, and that frost? They're merely scratches with the palette knife on a dirty canvas. It has neither head nor tail, neither top nor bottom, neither foreground nor background."

' "Perhaps. But the impression's there."

' "Well, it's a very odd impression! Oh, what's that?"

' "It's M. Sisley's *Verger*. I commend the little tree on the right to your attention; it's gay; but the impression . . ."

' "Don't talk to me about impressions! It's no good and never could be." '

The tour of the gallery continues in the same way. At Monet's *Boulevard des Capucines*, Joseph Vincent begins to snigger:

' "Ha! Ha! There's a good one for you! . . . There's an impression I don't know about . . . But, just tell me, what are all those little black marks at the bottom of the picture supposed to be?"

' "Why," I said, "they're passers-by."

' "Do you mean to say I look like that when I walk down the Boulevard des Capucines? . . . Great heavens above! Are you by any chance pulling my leg?"

' "I assure you, Monsieur Vincent . . ."

' "But those marks have been put on by the sort of process used for whitewashing stone fountains. Pif! Paf! Vli! Vlan! And there you are! It's disgraceful! Appalling! Enough to give one a stroke!" '

Under the influence of the paintings, Joseph Vincent soon becomes delirious and 'impressionist' himself. Catching sight of Monet's seascape, *Impression, Soleil levant*, he exclaims: 'Ah, there he is, there he is! I recognise him, Papa Vincent's favourite! *Impression*, I knew it! And, since I'm impressed, I know it must be an impression . . . And what freedom and ease of technique! Paper tinted in manufacture is more *réussi* than that seascape!" '

Cézanne's *Moderne Olympia* finally drives him mad.

'Père Vincent's classic mind, attacked from every side at once, became completely deranged. He came to a halt in front of the custodian whose duty it was to watch over these treasures and, taking him for a portrait, began criticising him somewhat emphatically.

' "Do you think he's bad enough?" he said, shrugging his shoulders. "Full face, he's got two eyes, a nose and a mouth! Surely no impressionist would have made such sacrifices to accuracy. With the useless details the painter has put into that face, Monet could easily have made twenty custodians!"

' "Move on, you!" said the "portrait."

' "Did you hear that? Why, he can even speak! The fool that daubed him must have spent quite a bit of time on him!"

'And to give his aesthetic views proper emphasis, Père Vincent began dancing a scalp dance in front of the bewildered custodian, shouting in a hoarse voice:

' "Ha! I'm impression on the warpath, I'm the avenging palette knife, I'm Monet's *Boulevard des Capucines*, I'm M. Cézanne's *La Maison du Pendu* and *Moderne Olympia*! Ha! Ha! Ha!" '

This was the first time that the Paris public had had the opportunity of seeing Cézanne's works; the welcome it gave them was even less encouraging than that received by his colleagues. His three pictures were daily targets for the more outrageous remarks, though he did not seem to care overmuch. And he was one of the very few exhibitors who succeeded in selling a canvas.

One day, a handsome man of some fifty years of age visited the exhibition of these painters who, since Louis Leroy's article, had been derisively nicknamed 'Impressionists.'* He looked at *La Maison du Pendu* and appeared somewhat baffled, clearly not caring much for the

* The term 'impression,' as applied to the new painting, if not that of 'Impressionism,' had been in use for some time. 'It is a real pity,' Théophile Gautier had written of Daubigny, 'that this landscape painter . . . contents himself with an *impression* and so much neglects details.' Of the same painter, Odilon Redon had similarly said in 1868 that he was 'the painter of a moment, of an impression.' Someone had even given Daubigny the title of 'Leader of the Impressionist School.' Moreover, Castagnary had written of Jongkind, in 1863, that 'everything lies in the *impression*.' The word 'impression' was also constantly used by Manet about his own work. (Quotations recorded by John Rewald in *The History of Impressionism*.)

picture. He began trying to explain his reasons to his son, who was with him. And yet, oddly enough, as he elaborated his criticism, he began to realise that the canvas had powerful qualities of composition and colouring. 'It's clear we don't understand what it's about,' he said suddenly. 'It obviously has first class qualities. I must have something by this painter.' And Count Armand Doria, the great collector, who had defended Corot twenty years before, bought *La Maison du Pendu* on the spot.

There was one man, Zola, who could have replied to the attacks on the Impressionists. But Zola was no longer interested in painting nor in the painters for whom he had fought in the past. His sole reason for going to the Boulevard des Capucines was to take notes which would one day be useful to him for the novel of which Cézanne was to be the hero, and to watch the reactions of the mocking crowd. 'People were elbowing their way through the crowd roaring with laughter . . . Each canvas had a success all its own; people were shouting to each other to come and look; and witticisms were being bandied about . . . The heat was making faces red; and in each face there was a stupid, gaping mouth, that of an ignorant fool, condemning the paintings, making every sort of crass and irrelevant criticism, accompanied by that inane and malicious laughter, which only the sight of original work can draw from bourgeois imbecility.'* Zola was concentrating to the exclusion of all else, on his *Rougon-Macquart*, of which the first four volumes (the latest, *La Conquête de Plassans*, had just been published) were hardly selling at all.

Did Zola discuss Cézanne's canvases with him? It would seem improbable. From now on Zola was to maintain a prudent silence about his friend's work. Nevertheless, Cézanne and Zola remained loyal to their old friendship, and Zola had paid tribute to it this year in his *Nouveaux Contes à Ninon*, for which he had used some of his Aix memories. Yet, little by little, life was driving them apart, as it had already separated them from Baille. Nowadays, Cézanne never saw anyone but painters; and Zola saw only writers. Cézanne very seldom appeared at Zola's 'Thursdays,' particularly since Madame Zola appeared to have little liking for the poor failure of an artist, with his

* *L'Oeuvre.*

neglected clothes and unrefined language. Moreover, the ex-flower-seller of the Place Clichy had even less liking for Hortense. The Cézannes were clearly not her class!

Cézanne, who had made up his mind to go to Aix as soon as the exhibition was over, had promised to go first to Pontoise to say good-bye to Pissarro. But it would seem that he had not accepted the jeers of the critics and the jibes of the public with as much serenity as he would have liked people to think. Towards the end of May, he slipped away from Paris without saying good-bye to anyone.

CHAPTER THREE

The Shouting and the Silence

Nous voulons nous donner de vastes et d'étranges domaines
Où le mystère en fleurs s'offre a qui veut le cueillir
Il y a là des jeux nouveaux des couleurs jamais vues
Mille phantasmes impondérables
Auxquels il faut donner de la réalité.

GUILLAUME APOLLINAIRE

LOUIS AUGUSTE was not mellowing with age. He had always been authoritarian, and now, at seventy-six, had become something of a tyrant. No longer having a bank through which to exercise his almost maniacal avarice, he showed it in the most futile details. Cézanne was as helpless against him at thirty-five as he had been as a child.

Louis Auguste felt considerable resentment against his son, whom he accused not only of betraying his hopes, but of making himself an object of ridicule to the Paris papers. He treated him with a sort of churlish pity, bullied him, and delighted in denying him anything he wanted, in particular, of course, an increase in his allowance; he was also continually changing his mind as to whether he would allow him to return to Paris. He opened all his son's letters, with the result that Cézanne was unable to receive news of Hortense and little Paul.

Despite these vexations, Cézanne managed to settle down in Aix. He was delighted to see his mother, to whom he probably admitted that he had a son. And he was happy to see Provence again; its landscapes confirmed him in the belief that colour was really 'the realm in which our minds and the universe meet.' He forgot his Paris disappointments and serenely set to work. He was sure of himself and of the path he was pursuing. When he saw in the newspapers that Guillemet, who had now become entirely academic, had won a medal of the second class in the Salon, he said: 'It simply goes to prove that if you follow the path of virtue, you are always recompensed by men, but not by painting.'

One day, Honoré Gibert, who had succeeded his father as head of the Aix Museum and Drawing School in 1870, asked Cézanne whether he might visit his studio. Having read articles about the Impressionists, he 'wanted to see for himself just how dangerous this painting was.' Cézanne good-humouredly agreed, but told Gibert ironically that by examining his 'products' he would get no truly precise idea of the 'progress of the evil,' and that in order to do so he needed 'to see the work of the great criminals of Paris.' 'Upon which, he came,' Cézanne told Pissarro, 'but when I told him for instance, that you replaced modelling by a study of tones, and tried to make him understand from nature, he closed his eyes and turned away. But he said he understood, and we parted on good terms . . . He's a good chap and encouraged me to persevere, for patience is the mother of genius, etc.'

At the end of June, Valabrègue arrived from Paris and gave Cézanne a letter from Hortense: everything was all right in the Rue de Vaugirard, and the child was well. Reassured, Cézanne continued working. He was painting landscapes, and treating them as if they belonged to the neighbourhood of Pontoise or Auvers: damp skies, rich vegetation, forms melting into an impalpable halo of mist, an abundance of green and blue.

Pissarro's pupil had now become a true Impressionist. Yet, unlike his colleagues, Cézanne was not temperamentally content merely to record 'impressions'; he had an innate need to organise his canvas, to give it order, rhythm and unity, an intellectual coherence. Impressionism had certainly taught him the essentials and, above all, the importance of colour; but there was an element of superficiality about it which left him dissatisfied.

* * *

By September, Cézanne was back in Paris with Hortense. The months of solitude and meditation in Aix had been of the greatest value to him. The future seemed full of promise. What did the yapping of a few curs matter? Cézanne knew the day would come when the merits of his painting would be recognised.

He was so persuaded of it that, though usually he was uncommunicative about his art, he wrote to his mother: 'I am beginning to find that I am better than all those about me, and you know that a good opinion of myself has only come with knowledge. I still have to work, though not to achieve that perfect finish, which is admired by fools. For this, which is so appreciated by the crowd, is only the handicraft of a workman, and makes the resulting work inartistic and commonplace. I have to try for a perfection which is truer and more expert. And, believe me, the moment always comes when one imposes oneself, and earns more fervent and more convinced admirers than those who are merely deluded by empty appearances.' Nor was he any less sanguine about his future material success. 'It's a very bad moment for sales, the bourgeois are loth to part with their money, but it will pass.'

Never had he been so sure of himself. With his high, prematurely bald forehead, his long hair falling over his neck, his thick beard and dark, intelligent eyes, he gave an impression of maturity and power. He was reaching port. As he told his mother, from now on he had merely to study nature with a passionate and scrupulous attention in order to achieve his longing to become one day a painter without equal.

On his return to Paris, he had found the circumstances of his friends far from encouraging. The only evident result of their exhibition in the spring had been obloquy. They were rarely able to sell their work; and, when they could, it was to part with canvases for as little as forty francs* merely to get enough to eat. The more unfortunate were suffering cruel poverty. But their difficulties, a consequence of the ostracism to which all the Impressionists were subjected, bound them with even closer ties. They helped each other when they could; and enjoyed a warmth of mutual friendship. There was but one ray of light in these dark days: during the summer, they had made the acquaintance of Gustave Caillebotte, a young man of twenty-six, who was devoting himself to their cause.

A member of a family of the *grande bourgeoisie*, grown rich in commerce, Caillebotte, who had been born in Paris, had inherited a considerable fortune on the death of his father the previous year. Since he had no need to earn his living, he was able to devote himself entirely to his numerous and disparate hobbies: naval construction,

* Approximately £7 today.

horticulture, philately and painting. In the previous year, he had entered for the examination of the École des Beaux-Arts, and had been successful. He had then become a pupil in Bonnet's studio, but had soon been disillusioned by the official academic teaching.

During the summer, however, he had met Monet and Renoir, and through them the whole Impressionist group. Attracted by their talent, he was doing all he could to help them. Slender, with a pale face, delicate features, chestnut hair and rather melancholy grey eyes, Caillebotte had not only a remarkable distinction of manner but also fine moral qualities: he was tolerant, loyal, modest and level-headed. To his new friends he was a Maecenas, sheltering them and feeding them, lending or giving them money, and frequently buying their work.

His purchases, however, were more often dictated by his wish to help than by any other consideration. 'Does no one want it? Very well, I'll take it,' he would often say. But even Caillebotte's generosity could not relieve the general distress.

Cézanne found no happier atmosphere at Zola's. The novelist was still waiting fretfully for success. In the six months that had elapsed since *La Conquête de Plassans* had been published in May, it had sold no more than one thousand seven hundred copies. Worse still, not a single critic had noticed it. During the hot months of the summer – the temperature in Paris had reached 93° in July – Zola had been writing *La Faute de l'Abbé Mouret*, the fifth novel of his series, and had described, under the name of Paradou, the Domaine de Galice, near Aix, to which he, Cézanne and Baille had so often made excursions in the past. Determined at all costs to win a public, he had filled the book with luxuriant and lyrical descriptions as well as pages of feverish sensuality. Zola himself said that he was now 'obsessed by a passion for precise analysis.'* But this was far from being the case. If Cézanne was now cured of his romantic tendencies, Zola seemed on the other hand to have lapsed into a more lush romanticism than before.

Cézanne at once started to work. He was studying the great masters, and was inspired by them to paint a number of canvases, which he considered more than mere exercises; they were an intellectual

* *Nouveaux Contes à Ninon.*

investigation into the craft of painting. The Impressionists' pursuit of the fugitive play of light and the importance they attributed to the ephemeral sensations of the retina were satisfying him less and less.

He was obsessed by the need to express the permanent reality that existed beneath the quivering iridescence of light; he refused to accept the immediate sensation alone; he felt a need to analyse it, submit it to the test of his intellect and impose order on it. Impressionism was both a revolution and a conquest, but he felt that it would achieve its full significance only when it had become part of the continuity of painting, and had revivified the tradition of art.

For Cézanne, this quest on which he was engaged was infinitely more important than anything else. Like any other artist, he wanted approbation; but he was indifferent to success as such. For him, success could never be a goal, but only a consequence. And this was why he was unable to accept Zola's discontent with any seriousness; and why, in his heart of hearts, he was not interested in the projects of his painter friends.

In this year, 1875, the group were proposing to hold another exhibition. However, in the hope of raising money, they intended in the first place to hold a collective sale at the Hôtel Drouot. Cézanne took no part in it and, in the event, had no need to regret his abstention. The sale took place on 24 March and nearly provoked a riot. As each picture was put up for auction, the audience howled with indignation. There was such jostling and argument in the sale-room that the crowd might well have come to blows had not the auctioneer sent for the police. But the more serious outcome was that the sale was a fiasco, despite the support of Caillebotte, Théodore Duret and others, who defended the Impressionists and did what they could to push the prices up. The seventy-three canvases sent in by Renoir, Monet, Sisley, Berthe Morisot and others, all went for absurdly low prices. Albert Wolff, the critic of the *Figaro*, took advantage of the occasion to say: 'The impression made by the Impressionists is that of a cat walking over the keyboard of a piano, or of a monkey that has laid hands on a paint-box.'

As a result of the uproar, which was more hostile than they had ever imagined, Cézanne's colleagues lost courage and gave up the idea of holding an exhibition. By way of compensation the sale at the Hôtel Drouot made them a new friend, Victor Chocquet, who was a collector, though on a comparatively small scale, a great admirer of Delacroix and, by profession, an official in the Direction Générale of the Customs.

Among the few people in the sale-room who had supported them against the outraged crowd, the painters had noticed Chocquet, a tall, middle-aged man, with silver hair and a rather ascetic face, who wore a small beard. He had spoken in their favour with great vigour, though without ever losing his temper. They had wondered who he could be.

The day after the sale, Renoir received a letter complimenting him on his pictures and asking him to paint a portrait of Madame Chocquet. The previous spring, Chocquet had intended visiting the exhibition in the Boulevard des Capucines, but he had been discouraged by his friends. By chance, he had attended the sale at the Hôtel Drouot, and he had not regretted it. Renoir's canvases had reminded him a little of the work of his favourite Delacroix, of which he owned an important collection. Renoir and Chocquet quickly became friends, for Chocquet was a true lover of art, caring neither for fashion nor for the market value of his pictures.

He was far from rich and, to buy the pictures he liked, saved money on food and clothes. He may not have possessed a proper winter overcoat, but he had superb taste. Art was a necessity to him.

Chocquet might easily have risen to a higher grade in his department, but he refused to be exiled from Paris. To promotion, he preferred the opportunities the capital afforded of visiting antique shops, print-merchants and booksellers. His taste and discernment, his unwearying patience, and the folly of the times that held even Delacroix in contempt, had enabled him to fill his flat in the Rue de Rivoli with splendid treasures. Renoir was astounded by the veritable museum he found there. Chocquet had twenty canvases by Delacroix, as well as a great number of his water-colours and drawings; Courbets, Manets, a delightful Corot; XVI century, Louis XIII, Régence, Louis XV and Louis XVI furniture; a collection of antique clocks; Nevers and Lorraine pottery; and Sèvres, Compagnie des Indes, Tournai, Chantilly and Saint-Cloud porcelain.

As soon as he met Chocquet, Renoir thought at once of Cézanne. If there was anyone who could appreciate Cézanne's art, Chocquet was that man. He took Chocquet to Père Tanguy's shop to see Cézanne's work. Renoir had made no mistake; Chocquet's reaction was immediate. He bought one of Cézanne's *Baigneuses* on the spot. 'How splendid it will look,' he said, 'between a Delacroix and a Courbet!' They returned to the Rue de Rivoli with it. On the threshold of his flat, Chocquet suddenly became anxious: would his wife approve his purchase? 'Listen, Renoir, do me a good turn. Tell my wife the Cézanne belongs to you, and then forget to take it with you when you leave. Like that, Marie will have time to get used to it before I admit to her that it's mine.'

The admission cannot have been long delayed, for Chocquet was anxious to make Cézanne's acquaintance. Could Renoir persuade him to come to the Rue de Rivoli? Cézanne came and it was a meeting of two enthusiasts. 'Renoir tells me you like Delacroix,' Cézanne said as soon as he arrived. 'I am devoted to Delacroix,' replied Chocquet. 'Would you like to see my collection?' The collector and the painter made a tour of the pictures, and then emptied the drawers of their water-colours and drawings. Soon Delacroix' work was spread all over the furniture, over the rose-coloured silk of the Louis XVI chairs, and over the carpet. Down on their knees, Chocquet and Cézanne looked, admired and gave free rein to their enthusiasm. Overwhelmed by emotion, they both burst into tears. A great friendship had begun.

In Chocquet, Cézanne found 'moral support.' Chocquet showed a wonderful understanding of Cézanne's artistic intentions. He looked on Cézanne as the great contemporary master. Whenever he discussed painting, he invariably brought the conversation round to Cézanne, who became 'his painter.' Cézanne frequently dined with Chocquet, they saw each other constantly, and the basis of their friendship was an almost religious enthusiasm for Delacroix. In Chocquet's company Cézanne forgot his fear of the 'grapnel.' He painted Chocquet's portrait and, no doubt under his friend's influence, an *Apothéose de Delacroix*, in which he portrayed him beside Pissarro, Monet and himself.

Since January, having left the Rue de Vaugirard, Cézanne had been living on the Île Saint-Louis, where Guillaumin was occupying Daubigny's old studio at 13, Quai d'Anjou. Cézanne sometimes worked with Guillaumin on the quays of the Seine, but he more often pursued his researches alone.

Since he could only rarely afford models, and though his wife sat for him occasionally, he was constrained to paint himself, which he did again and again over the years. There was nothing egocentric in his approach to these self-portraits, no self-confession, no attempt to reveal his own mystery. He was indifferent to the truth about himself and simply painted himself as he might have done a plate of cakes, seeking solutions to certain technical problems. And so it was with his studies of *Baigneurs* or *Baigneuses* – a theme suggested to him, no doubt, by the memory of the old days on the banks of the Arc – in which he experimented with the problems of composition.

These canvases, as far as Cézanne was concerned, were preparatory exercises for the work he dreamed of being able to do one day. To him they were of no importance; and little Paul, who was now three and a half, was allowed to play with them and batter them to his heart's content. Cézanne was amused by the child's destructiveness. 'My son tears open the windows and the chimneys; the little beast is perfectly aware that it's a house!' he exclaimed. But the child destroyed far fewer canvases in play than his father did in exasperation.

Obsessed with the complicated problems of his work, Cézanne lived the life of a recluse. When he did go out, it was to the Rue Clauzel to see Père Tanguy, buy colours and leave with him a canvas or two that seemed to him more or less satisfactory. On occasion, if he met a friend in the shop, he would allow himself to be taken to the Nouvelle-Athènes, the café in the Place Pigalle, where the ex-habitués of the Guerbois now met. But he rarely stayed long.

He disliked cafés and the sort of discussions that took place in them. With a few exceptions, Cézanne preferred the society of the uneducated to that of artists, since they never talked of painting and had no occasion to make silly remarks about it. He loathed the pretentious. There were a few artists and critics at the Nouvelle-Athènes who understood what he was aiming at, but there were others, such as the splenetic Duranty, who made no effort to conceal their contempt for this rather sullen painter whose clothes were always stained with paint. 'If Cézanne puts so much green on his canvases,' Duranty said sarcastically, 'it must be because he imagines a kilogramme of green to be greener than a gramme.'*

Shut away in his own world, Cézanne was gradually losing contact with the realities of life. When he laid aside his palette, he was bewildered by things that bore no relation to his preoccupations. To some he must have seemed almost half-witted; and he was becoming increasingly shy. The less awkward he tried to be, the clumsier he became.

The least social difficulty paralysed him. One day he was asked to dine with Nina de Villard. She was young, pretty, an excellent pianist, and a real 'princess of Bohemia.'† She liked the society of painters. There was no formality in her house; her guests simply sat down to dinner when they happened to arrive. If they were very late, the dishes were warmed up for them. Many of the habitués of the Nouvelle-Athènes were her constant guests and it was probably one of them who gave her Cézanne's address.

The invitation caused him much perplexity. In the end, after a great deal of anxious pondering, he decided to go to Nina de Villard's house in the Rue des Moines on the appointed day. He rang the door-bell. There was no answer. He rang again. There was still no answer. Very disconcerted, he was wondering what to do, when the door was suddenly opened. A lady's maid in a negligée, her corsage unbuttoned, and splendid golden hair reaching to her knees, asked him what he wanted. Cézanne had arrived much too early. In dismay, he muttered vague excuses and beat a hasty retreat.

Nevertheless, he was to return to the Rue des Moines. Like many other artists, he found its warm and welcoming atmosphere to his liking, and there he could meet such friends as Paul Alexis and Dr Gachet. There, too, he met a young musician, named Cabaner, who immediately became passionately interested in his painting.

Like Chocquet, Gachet and Tanguy, Cabaner became one of his

* Gauguin was later to write: 'A kilo of green is greener than half a kilo. Young painter, you must meditate this truism.'

† Léo Larguier.

most enthusiastic supporters. Not, alas, that this was likely to carry much weight with the more serious minded, for Cabaner was less known for his music than his wit. He was a strange man; and there was all the greater merit in his whole-hearted admiration for Cézanne, since he was well aware that he himself was a failure.

Though gifted with imagination and an original talent, unlike Cézanne he was unable to exploit his natural gifts, for he was utterly incapable of application, of making that daily effort which, in the long run, produces great creative work. He was a Catalan from Perpignan; short, thin and rather sickly in appearance; and he directed a constant flow of mocking wit not only at others, but at himself. When his talent as a composer was praised, he would say: 'Oh, I shall be better remembered as a philosopher.' He also said: 'My father was much the same kind of man as Napoleon, but less stupid.' But he had a talent for friendship and Cézanne could count on him for 'moral support.'

It was now fifteen months since Cézanne had left Aix and it was time he returned for a while to allay his father's suspicions, if nothing else. The thought that his father might cut off his allowance terrified him. He was well aware that he was quite incapable of earning his living. He knew no trade and had no aptitude for anything except the painting of pictures which, still so imperfect in his eyes, were nothing but objects of mockery. If his father, in a moment of irritation, stopped supporting him, he and his family would starve.

This year, 1876, Cézanne's friends organised another exhibition. But Cézanne took no part in it. On the other hand, he sent a canvas to the Salon which the Hanging Committee rejected as usual. When the exhibition opened in April, he was already in Aix.

* * *

The weather in Provence this spring was bad. Rain alternated with frost. At the Jas de Bouffan the fruit blossom and the vines were frozen and Louis Auguste was not in very good humour.

Thanks to Chocquet, who sent him catalogues and newspapers, Cézanne was able to get news of his friends' exhibition, which was being held in Durand-Ruel's premises in the Rue Le Peletier. It had an appalling press. Wolff, for instance, wrote in *Le Figaro:* 'The Rue Le

Peletier has bad luck. After the burning down of the Opéra,* a new disaster has fallen upon the district . . . Five or six lunatics, of whom one is a woman, a group of unfortunate people obsessed with ambitious folly, are showing their works there. There are people who would roar with laughter at them. For my part, I feel sad . . . It is an appalling spectacle of demented human vanity.' He went on in this tone for a whole column, accusing 'the members of this circle of vain and noisy mediocrity' of having 'raised the negation of everything that is art to the status of a principle. They have attached an old painting rag to a broom-handle and made a standard of it . . . I know some of these regrettable Impressionists; they are charming young people, utterly convinced that they have found the right path. It is a distressing spectacle.'

In spite of the persistent bad weather, Cézanne went for his usual walks about the countryside. Once again, he was bringing what he had learned to these landscapes that he felt he understood more intimately year by year. And how very different they were from those painted by his friends amid the little villages of the Île-de-France, the river banks, the undulating hills and soft reflections. Here, the land was hard and triumphantly mineral. Its outline was vigorous, precise, and permanent. Impressionism could not render the concrete realities of this landscape. He must achieve what was enduring in it by moving towards disciplines of greater austerity.

At the beginning of June he went to l'Estaque, where the inhabitants were inclined to look at him askance. 'If looks could kill, I should have been dead long ago,' he said. He did not care, for amid these solitudes of hill and sea, he could meditate in peace on the problems of painting.

'It's like a postcard,' he wrote to Pissarro, 'red roofs against a blue sea . . . The sun is so terrifying that, so it seems to me, objects are silhouetted not only in black and white, but in blue, red, brown and violet. I may be wrong, but it seems to me to be the antithesis of modelling.' Chocquet, whose portrait he had painted in Paris, had commissioned him to do two little landscapes. He was working hard on them, and he almost regretted having to return to Paris at the end of

* The Opéra had been in the Rue Le Peletier since 1821. It was burned to the ground during the night of 28 October, 1873.

July. Owing to the fact that the trees kept their leaves – the pine, the olive, the cypress, the ilex and the laurel – the Provençal countryside did not change overmuch with the seasons. It permitted the patient analysis of which Cézanne felt increasingly in need. 'There are some subjects that require three or four months' work,' he said. But he intended to return to l'Estaque for a long stay as soon as he could. He had never understood Provence so well; and for his art, which was so very personal, and already so different from the painting of his friends, such a long stay was an absolute necessity.

Cézanne must have realised that he was moving farther and farther away from his friends, the Impressionists. But he was too grateful to them to contemplate denying them or separating himself from them. Without them, and Pissarro in particular, he would never have become the painter he now was. He would go on struggling with them. And yet the Salon oddly enough had become for him a sort of Promised Land. He refused to renounce all hope of reaching it. The day must surely come when his canvases would be admired and admitted there. But the years were passing; the days of defiance and aggressiveness were over: and, as he himself said, it was now his most 'neutral' works he intended submitting to the Hanging Committee.

* * *

Paris, to which Cézanne returned in August, was alive with talk of Zola and his new novel, *L'Assommoir*. In March, he had published the sixth volume of his series, *Son Excellence Eugène Rougon*, which like the previous ones had achieved very little success. But, on 13 April, the newspaper *Le Bien Public* had begun serialising *L'Assommoir*, and it had immediately become the object of frenzied discussion. It was bitterly attacked for its immorality; and so many readers had cancelled their subscriptions to the paper that, on 6 June, *Le Bien Public* was forced to stop the serial. On 9 July, however, Catulle Mendès, who was editor of *La République des Lettres*, took over the serialisation. The caricaturists were having a field day.

The Impressionists, however, had had no similar success during Cézanne's absence. Apart from a few eccentrics, no one believed in their future. Zola, on the other hand, though he might be accused of immorality and pornography, was granted talent, though he was blamed for misusing it. Albert Wolff, on the very day that he called the Impressionists 'madmen,' had declared that *Son Excellence Eugène Rougon* was 'the work of a great writer.' He 'lacks tact, I know,' he said, 'but his work is of the greatest interest and of incontestable validity.' But he would not allow that the Impressionists had talent. Even the critics from whom they had a right to expect understanding, such as Duranty, who was an habitué of the Nouvelle-Athènes, were lukewarm in their approbation.

Had Cézanne's friends not met Caillebotte, who spared neither money nor trouble in their cause, it is unlikely that they would have had so early an opportunity of showing their work to the public again. Caillebotte was determined, cost what it might, that an exhibition should be organised no later than 1878. He was himself an extremely odd character and, though only twenty-eight, was persuaded he might die at any moment. 'All my family die young,' he would say. He therefore drew up a will that autumn in which he stipulated, since he did not want his demise to prevent help for his friends, that the necessary sum, thirty or forty thousand francs, or more if necessary,* should be paid out of his estate to ensure that the exhibition should be held 'in the best possible conditions.' He had no doubt whatever that the proper place for the Impressionists was in the Louvre. Since getting to know them, he had bought many of their works and in his will he left them to the nation. 'Since I wish the gift to be accepted, and so that the pictures shall not be relegated to an attic or to some provincial museum, but hung in the Luxembourg and later in the Louvre, it is necessary that a certain period of time shall elapse before this clause can be executed, until the public, I do not say understands, but accepts this painting. This period may well be twenty years or more. In the meantime, my brother, Martial, and failing him another of my heirs, shall keep them.'

His conviction of an early death did not prevent Caillebotte devoting himself actively to the proposed exhibition. Throughout the autumn and winter, he worked continuously to that end. 'The exhibition will take place; it must take place,' he wrote in January to Pissarro. There

* Today some £5,000 to £7,000.

was considerable difficulty in finding premises, for Durand-Ruel had leased his gallery for a year. In the end, Caillebotte overcame every obstacle, and arranged for the exhibition to take place, not in a year's time, but the following spring.

It was hoped that, on this occasion, the number and the quality of the canvases displayed would compel the public and the critics to realise the importance of the new painting and disarm the many who were prejudiced against the work of the group. Besides, in this exhibition the group would present itself with greater homogeneity. No one outside the group would be represented. Indeed, on Renoir's suggestion, they decided to name it 'The Impressionist Exhibition.' As Renoir remarked, it would say unequivocally to the passer-by: 'You will find here a kind of painting you do not like. If you come in, that is your own fault; you will not be reimbursed the ten sous entrance fee!'

Full of confidence, the group made plans to exhibit their best work. Cézanne, for his part, intended sending in fifteen canvases: still lifes, studies of flowers, landscapes, the portrait of Chocquet, a study of a woman's face, another of bathers, and some water-colours. The public should have a comprehensive view of his work.

Cézanne was now thirty-eight, and it was high time he should cease to be considered merely a crazy painter and that people should begin to recognise him as the great artist he was in process of becoming. Zola had at least realised his ambitions and had become the 'most read' novelist in France.

On 4 April, in a huge apartment on the second floor of 6, Rue Le Peletier, the third exhibition of the Impressionists opened.

In that succession of high rooms there hung a marvellous collection of pictures, bright, beautiful and sunlit. It was the springtime of modern painting. In the first room were the Monets and Renoirs: Monet's views of the Gare Saint-Lazare, and his *Dindons blancs;* Renoir's *La Balançoire* and, in the big room, his *Bal au Moulin de la Galette*. And in this room too, in the place of honour, were the Cézannes and the Berthe Morisots. Farther on were the Guillaumins, landscapes by Sisley, his *Pont d'Argenteuil* and *Les Inondations de Marly*, landscapes of Pontoise and Auvers by Pissarro, Caillebottes, and more Monets. Degas held sway in another room. Some two hundred and forty carefully selected canvases summed up everything Impressionism had to say that was at once new and authentic.

The first visitors, of whom many were distinguished, showed far greater discretion than had the public at previous exhibitions. 'Even those,' wrote a journalist in the *Siècle*, 'who had come to criticise, halted before more than one picture in admiration.' Some journalists went so far as to say that the Impressionists, by appealing directly to the public, showed 'a certain courage,' and that this attitude 'proved their great good faith.' In short, everything seemed to be going well and, as the *Courrier de France* said: 'One might think that the hostility the Impressionists aroused in their early days was, perhaps, due to the clumsy, and perhaps rather brutal, expression of a profound astonishment.'

However, the Impressionists would have been gravely mistaken to rejoice too soon. In spite of a few cautious articles, the press in general castigated them as firmly as it had done in the past. To give the exhibition publicity, a young man, Georges Rivière, on Renoir's advice, was publishing a little paper, *L'Impressionniste*, for the duration of the exhibition.

In the first number, of 6 April, Rivière regretfully had to announce in an open letter to *Le Figaro*, that, with rare exceptions, the press was 'unanimous in its recriminations.' As a result, the public changed sides. Encouraged and supported by a flow of virulent articles, mocking, rowdy crowds jostled their way through the exhibition. 'It is impossible,' wrote Barbouillotte in *Le Sportsman*, 'to stand for more than ten minutes before some of the more sensational canvases in the gallery without feeling seasick . . . That is perhaps why some people were saying: "You must admit some things are well rendered." '

Amid the crowds that thronged the exhibition, Chocquet, who was very hurt by the contempt expressed for the Impressionists, did his fighting best. Every day, from opening to closing time, he was there, indefatigably eloquent, politely insistent, amiably vehement, endeavouring to convince the public how wrong they were to scoff at these masterly works. They took him for a harmless lunatic.

In the Rue Le Peletier and on the Boulevard des Italiens, hawkers were crying *L'Impressionniste;* but few copies were sold. People saw in it merely an attempt to gain notoriety and solicit support at all costs.

In the evening, after the crowd had gone, for the exhibition closed at five o'clock, Cézanne would sometimes go to the Rue Le Peletier to see his friends: Chocquet, Renoir, Caillebotte, Pissarro and Rivière would often be there. He would sit in silence, listening to their talk. Chocquet, still excited by the arguments of the day, would announce that the public's incomprehension must soon cease, that its eyes must ineluctably be opened, but Cézanne was not reassured.

Though his friends had given him the place of honour, it was at his paintings above all others that the crowd jeered. His canvases, and in particular his portrait of Chocquet, were the highlights of the exhibition; but they seemed to arouse an automatic response of laughter and sarcasm. Cézanne was a madman, a 'monster,' a Communard, subversion itself! Even such visitors as were prepared to listen to Chocquet's arguments remained completely hostile to Cézanne's work, and the few critics who on occasion showed some indulgence towards Monet, Renoir or Pissarro, were pitiless in their condemnation of Cézanne.

He was, wrote *Le Petit Parisien*, 'a real intransigent, hot-headed and fantastical. When we look at his bathers, his head of a man, his female figure, we must admit that the impression nature makes on us is not *that* which the painter feels.' 'If you visit the exhibition with a woman in an interesting condition, pass rapidly by M. Cézanne's *Portrait d'Homme*,' said the celebrated Leroy in *Charivari*. 'That very strange head, the colour of boot-tops, might impress her too vividly and infect her child with yellow fever before ever he made his entry into the world.' 'When children play with paints and paper, they do better,' said Roger Ballu in *La Chronique des Arts et de la Curiosité*.

Cézanne said nothing. He had worked with extraordinary determination to achieve a technique, had paid a heavy price in self-discipline, and had expended such patience and tenacity in the slow development of his art, that to be rewarded merely with insults could not be other than bitterly disappointing.

Georges Rivière tried to reply to the criticisms levelled at Cézanne in *L'Impressionniste:*

'The artist who has been most subjected to attack and maltreatment during the last fifteen years by both press and public is M. Cézanne.

There is no outrageous epithet that has not been hurled at him, and his works have been, and still are, continually mocked. One newspaper called the portrait of a man he exhibited this year "Billoir in Chocolate!"* The jeers and insults result from an insincerity that no one even attempts to dissimulate. People go to look at M. Cézanne's pictures with the intention of venting their spleen . . . For my part I know no painting less deserving of mockery than his. M. Cézanne is not only a painter, but a great painter. People who have never held brush or pencil have said he cannot draw, and have accused him of imperfections that are in fact merely the refinements of immense knowledge . . . His still lifes, so beautiful and precise in the relationships of their tones, have the grave quality of truth. Every picture by this artist moves one, because he is himself greatly moved when confronted by nature and has the technique to transmit his emotion to his canvas.'

Rivière went on to quote the view of one of his friends:

'The painter of the *Baigneurs* belongs to the race of giants. Since he cannot be compared with anyone else, people find it easier to deny him his due. Yet he has his admired counterparts in the history of painting; and if the present does not render him justice, the future will class him with his peers, among the demigods of art.'

* * *

Cézanne was far from combative; he belonged to the type who surrenders the field when attacked and has no other concern than to disappear. The uproar aroused by his paintings saddened him and gave him a great desire for silence and solitude. He longed to be left in peace.

The criticism to which his work had been subjected had not, however, seriously impaired his self-confidence; his researches into the technique of painting seemed to him as important as ever. But his present level of achievement was in his own eyes still so very far from the ideal he envisaged, that he was inclined to wonder whether there was not after all some truth in the criticisms he had suffered and whether the results he had so far obtained were not wholly insufficient,

* This was the portrait of Chocquet. Billoir was a murderer who had cut up a woman into small pieces in Montmartre; he was guillotined on 26 April.

22. Paul Cézanne aged about 36 [*c.* 1875]

23. Portrait of Cézanne [*c.* 1880]. Lithograph by Renoir

24. Renoir at the Château des Brouillards, Montmartre, in the early 1890s

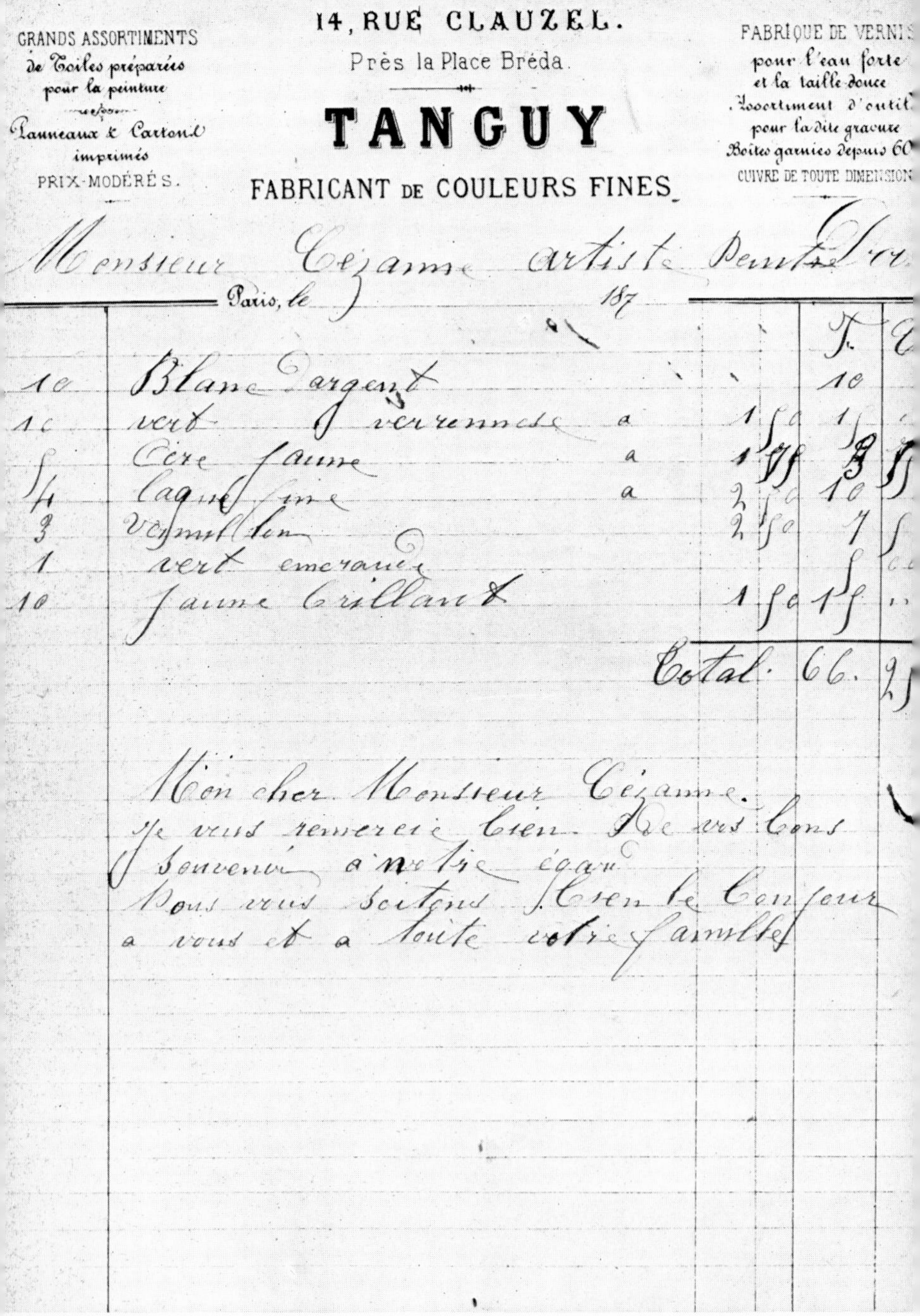

GRANDS ASSORTIMENTS
de Toiles préparées
pour la peinture
Panneaux & Cartons
imprimés
PRIX-MODÉRÉS.

14, RUE CLAUZEL.
Près la Place Bréda.

TANGUY

FABRICANT DE COULEURS FINES

FABRIQUE DE VERNIS
pour l'eau forte
et la taille douce
Assortiment d'outils
pour la dite gravure
Boîtes garnies depuis 60
CUIVRE DE TOUTE DIMENSION

Monsieur Cézanne artiste Peintre Doit

Paris, le 187

				F.	C.
10	Blanc d'argent			10	
10	vert veronnese	a	1 50	15	
5	Ocre jaune	a	1 75	8	75
4	laque fine	a	2 50	10	
3	vermillon		2 50	7	50
1	vert emeraude			5	
10	jaune brillant		1 50	15	
			Total	66.	25

Mon cher Monsieur Cézanne.
Je vous remercie bien de vos bons
souvenir à notre égard
Nous vous soitons bien le bonjour
a vous et a toute votre famille

25. Père Tanguy: Bill for paints supplied to Cézanne [undated]

26. Émile Zola [*c.* 1877]

N° 5

GRANDS ASSORTIMENTS
de Toiles préparées
pour la peinture
Panneaux & Cartons
imprimés
PRIX MODÉRÉS

14, RUE CLAUZEL.
Près la Place Bréda

TANGUY

FABRICANT DE COULEURS FINES

FABRIQUE DE VERNIS
pour l'eau forte
et la taille douce
Assortiment d'outils
pour la dite gravure
Boites garnies depuis 60 fr
CUIVRE DE TOUTE DIMENSION

Avoir à
Monsieur Cézanne — Doit

Paris, le 187

1873 Août	5	Reçu à compte espèces	10	
1874 avril	1	d° d°	10	
Mai	15	d° d°	20	
Juin	1	d° d°	20	
8bre	25	Vendu un tableau	50	
9bre	1	d° d°	50	
d°	30	d° d°	50	
1876 Mars	20	Reçu	52	50
	30	Vendu un tableau	50	
Xbre	30	d° d°	50	
1877 8bre	26	Reçu	50	
1879		Reçu dans le courant de l'année	480	
1880 Janv	15	Reçu	200	
1884		Vendu un tableau	200	
1885		d°	150	
			1442	50

27. Père Tanguy: Account for sale of paintings by Cézanne between 1873–1885

28. Paul Cézanne in his Paris studio [1894]

whatever his friends might think of them. For him, art was so grave a matter that it could be approached only with the utmost humility. Had he perhaps been guilty of presumption? Sickened by the uproar, he determined to disappear and work in silence till the day came when he could say with confidence: 'I am Cézanne.'

Indefatigably he went to work on his accustomed themes: still lifes, portraits and self-portraits. He painted Hortense in many poses, sitting in a big red chair, sewing, or with still hands against the background of the olive-coloured wall-paper of their Plaisance flat.

They were now residing at 67, Rue de l'Ouest, behind the Gare Montparnasse. Cézanne lived a curiously restricted life. His friends had risked another sale at the Hôtel Drouot, but he refused to take part in it. He had made himself ridiculous enough in the Rue Le Peletier; and the presence of his work among that of his friends was likely only to embarrass them. Meanwhile Hortense took in sewing from time to time to increase their income; but they were often very short of money.

At one such moment Cézanne took a canvas, *Baigneurs au Repos*, with which he was reasonably satisfied, and set off to see if he could find a buyer for it. He happened to meet Cabaner in the street. The musician asked if he might see the picture. Cézanne unwrapped it and put it up against a wall. 'It's come off fairly well, hasn't it?' Cabaner greatly admired it; as Renoir was to say of it, it was 'a diamond!' Moved to tears by this unaccustomed appreciation, Cézanne, forgetting that he was short of money and had intended selling it, presented Cabaner with the picture. He was 'very happy,' he said, that his picture should go 'to someone who likes it.'

Cézanne often went out to Pontoise to paint with Pissarro; or, again, he would go and join Guillaumin in the Parc d'Issy-les-Moulineux. But his work was now beginning to diverge profoundly from that of his Impressionist friends.

As the years went by, the Impressionists were becoming increasingly absorbed in rendering the play of light to the exclusion of almost everything else. In their canvases, objects dissolved into a coloured mirage and they had almost entirely abandoned the expression of space and volume which had been the essential preoccupation of all painting

29 (opposite). Paul Cézanne at Barbizon, Fontainebleau Forest [1894]

since the Renaissance. Cézanne could not admit any of this. He could not allow that all the diverse elements of nature should be neglected for one alone.

His peasant atavism made him instinctively distrustful of the brilliant and the superficial. Like all peasants, he had a fundamental regard for solid reality. As a painter, it was reality he desired to render in its totality. He was aiming at something more than the Impressionist analysis of light, which had taught him so much.

It seemed to Cézanne that the intellect should have its say. The Impressionists, with a sort of poetic abandon, limited themselves to the spontaneous registering of the sensations nature inspired in them. But Cézanne was no longer prepared to admit that the registering of a mere sensation was enough. 'The artist,' he declared, 'does not simply note his emotions as a bird sings: he composes.' Painting should be no mere reflection of the superficial and transitory aspects of the world, but should elucidate its innate structure, assert the latent order behind the apparent chaos.

Though Cézanne often painted the same landscapes as Pissarro, the path of the Ravine or the Côte des Boeufs at Pontoise, his canvases had nothing in common with those of his friends, except their liveliness of colour. To his friends, colour was an end in itself, but to Cézanne it was a point of departure, the element he must use to achieve painting's plenary verities.

These verities, Cézanne was well aware, he could discover only in Provence; and he intended returning there in the winter for a long stay. This time, whatever the risks, he would take Hortense and his son with him.

Zola, whose financial difficulties had been eased by his success – his publisher had just paid him 18,500 francs* in royalties for the first thirty-five printings of *L'Assommoir* – was spending the summer at l'Estaque, where he was writing his next novel, *Une Page d'Amour*, and eating quantities of bouillabaisses, shellfish, and spiced dishes, 'a mass of delicious filth.'

Cézanne asked him to inform his mother of his plans, but without telling his father. 'If by December,' he wrote, 'she could find me a little

* Approximately £3,500 today

lodging of two rooms in Marseilles, not expensive, but not in a district where there are too many murders, I should be grateful. She might send a bed and bed clothes there . . .' But, a little later, Cézanne changed his mind: the 'plan' seemed to involve 'certain difficulties,' and he gave it up.

Though still in Paris, he might well not have been, for all his friends saw of him. Sometimes he remained invisible for weeks on end. He had practically ceased going to the Nouvelle-Athènes, where some of the habitués had never even set eyes on him. He was already becoming something of a legend, and there were many anecdotes current about him, mostly of a disagreeable sort. But one night, when out for a solitary walk, he came to the Place Pigalle and went into the café. His blue painter's smock, paint-stained coat, and shapeless, greasy hat, created something of a sensation. 'He had a great success!' Duranty wrote sarcastically in a letter to Zola.

Though Cézanne might produce this effect on the habitués of the Nouvelle-Athènes, this was not the case with a young stockbroker to whom Pissarro introduced him. This young man, Paul Gauguin, was working in the Banque Bertin in the Rue Laffitte. He was twenty-nine, comfortably off, and obsessed with painting. He had taken lessons at the Académie Colarossi, had sent a canvas in to the Salon the previous year, and it had been accepted. But academic art had not satisfied him for long; the new painting attracted him. He had met Pissarro, who had told him of the Impressionists' theories, and now Pissarro introduced him to Cézanne.

Gauguin did not take to Cézanne as a man; his slovenliness, his obscene language, and that self-dissatisfaction which concealed so much pride, irritated him. But what an artist he was! From time to time Gauguin bought canvases by Pissarro, Cézanne and their friends. No doubt this was his principal merit in their eyes at this time.

* * *

At the beginning of March, accompanied by Hortense and little Paul, Cézanne set out for the Midi.

CHAPTER FOUR

Storms

> My kind family, an excellent one moreover for an unfortunate painter who has never known how to do anything . . .—CÉZANNE: Letter to Zola, 1 June, 1878

CÉZANNE was very much mistaken if he imagined he was to find perfect peace in which to paint. The presence of Hortense and little Paul severely complicated his life in the Midi.

In principle Cézanne was living in Aix, but it was at l'Estaque he wanted to work. Moreover, for fear of gossip reaching Louis Auguste, Cézanne thought it better to stay at l'Estaque alone. He had therefore installed Hortense and Paul in Marseilles, at 183, Rue de Rome. He wasted a great deal of time going from place to place, though the railway had been built some three years previously, for Marseilles was ten kilometres from l'Estaque and thirty kilometres from Aix.

The fact was that Cézanne had to be exceedingly careful because of Louis Auguste's attitude. It seemed probable that the old fox had heard something, for he clearly had some suspicion of his son's liaison. He watched him narrowly, and was always trying to surprise evidence that his suspicions were correct. He opened all Cézanne's letters addressed to the Jas de Bouffan.

Cézanne was ill at ease and played a careful game; he went to Aix as often as possible and there appeared at every meal, as his father insisted. Louis Auguste was now eighty and Cézanne thirty-nine (his baldness and a certain stoutness made him look even older), but his father still treated him as if he were a schoolboy.

Nor was this all Cézanne had to put up with. His old colleague Villevieille had now left Paris and established himself permanently in Aix, where, with a few pupils, he was painting religious pictures for colonial missions. Whenever his pupils saw Cézanne, they shouted insults after him, mocking his long hair and, no doubt, his notoriety as an Impressionist. Villevieille had obviously pointed out Cézanne as the typical subversive artist.

Then, in the middle of March, little Paul developed bronchitis; and when Cézanne's anxiety was at its height, Louis Auguste opened a letter to him from Chocquet and found the proof he had been searching for. Chocquet had unfortunately mentioned 'Madame Cézanne and little Paul.' Louis Auguste was at once furious and triumphant; he stormed and raved, and asserted that he was going to put an end to his son's bohemian way of life.

With his back to the wall, Cézanne lied with obstinate desperation, denying the facts against all the evidence. Louis Auguste threatened to reduce his allowance. He would give him a hundred francs a month.* Since he had no responsibilities and only himself to support, he should be able to manage very well on it. He would give him a hundred francs, no more, perhaps even less, possibly nothing at all!

Cézanne was dismayed; his financial circumstances were difficult enough already. His debt to Tanguy had been constantly increasing. Before leaving Paris he had given the colour-merchant an I.O.U. for 2,174 francs 80 centimes.† What was to happen if his father put his threats into effect? His son in Marseilles needed medical attention. How on earth could he earn his living?

It never occurred to him for an instant that the situation was somewhat paradoxical, since he was legally already in possession of his share of the inheritance. When Louis Auguste retired from business, he had made over his fortune to his children so as to avoid death duties. As far as he was concerned, it was of course a legal fiction; he could not conceive that anyone would dare to contest the fact that he was still master of his own fortune.

But to take his stand on his legal rights and defy his father was more than Cézanne could contemplate. But what was he to do? In his difficulty he turned to the only man who was in a position to help him: Zola. 'Please do the best you can,' he wrote humbly, 'among your friends and through your influence to help me find a job, if you think it at all possible.' By return of post, Zola, who was no doubt as sceptical

* About £17 today.
† Some £350 today.

about Cézanne's abilities in this direction as was Cézanne himself, advised his friend to do all he could to keep his allowance and offered in the meantime – no one ever appealed to Zola's generosity in vain – to help him financially if it became necessary.

Though relieved from anxiety for the immediate future by this letter, Cézanne was still extremely worried. His relations with his father remained tense. Louis Auguste, exasperated by his son's denials, set traps for him and cross-questioned his acquaintances. There was no doubt that he was certain of the existence of a grandson, for Cézanne wrote to Zola: 'He says he wants to disembarrass me of him.' Cézanne redoubled his precautions. However, anxious about his son's health, he went one day to Marseilles, where he was delighted to find the child recovering. Unfortunately, he missed the train back. Since he must at all costs put in an appearance at dinner, there was no alternative to walking the thirty kilometres from Marseilles to Aix. It was a forced march and, in the event, he was an hour late.

At the end of March Louis Auguste was still taking a sadistic pleasure in keeping his son in suspense. Cézanne had received an invitation from his Impressionist friends to participate in another exhibition. But at the moment he had other worries. In any case, a repetition of the furore aroused by the exhibition the year before could only discredit him further and it was now his ambition to be officially recognised and accepted by the Salon (to which end he had again submitted a painting). He was still very dissatisfied with his work and he felt there was little in common now between his painting and that of his friends. Yet he did not wish to give an impression of letting them down, and so he asked Zola to lend him the canvas he had painted before the war, in which he had depicted Zola's black marble clock. Soon after he heard that the exhibition had been abandoned.

At the beginning of April, Louis Auguste cut Cézanne's allowance down to a hundred francs. Cézanne argued in vain, though he had in fact feared he would get nothing at all. His father was adamant; and Cézanne was obliged to ask Zola to send Hortense sixty francs.*

From time to time he risked a hasty visit to Marseilles. On one

* Approximately £9 10s. today.

occasion, he made the journey with Gibert. On the way, as he gazed out of the window at the countryside, at Mont Sainte-Victoire and the rocks above Beaurecueil, he said: 'What a splendid subject!' To which, Gibert replied: 'The lines are too symmetrical.' 'Those chaps,' Cézanne grumbled, 'have the eyes of professors.' But he had no heart for a fight. The jeering of the newspapers and the public, the insults of Villevieille's pupils, and the contempt with which he was treated by the inhabitants of Aix, combined with his father's attitude towards him, were all calculated to depress and induce a state of chagrined humility in him. 'I am working; but without much result and outside the general trend,' he wrote briefly to Zola.

Everything was going wrong for Cézanne at this time. His mother, who was his only real support in his struggle against his father, now fell gravely ill. This event made Louis Auguste all the more difficult to deal with. On 1 May, as in the previous month, he gave his son no more than the hundred francs allowance, and this compelled Cézanne to ask Zola's help to the extent of another sixty francs. A few days later, Cézanne heard from Zola that the Salon Hanging Committee had rejected his canvas. 'I very well understand,' he wrote sadly to Zola, 'that it could not possibly be accepted because of my point of departure, which was too far removed from the goal I wished to attain, that is to say the representation of nature.'

Soon after the situation brightened a little. Cézanne's mother was out of danger and very shortly up and about again, and Louis Auguste did not seem to be getting much further towards the indisputable proofs he required. Cézanne hoped he would grow weary of the whole business. In the meantime, the old man categorically refused to increase the allowance beyond the one hundred francs a month and Cézanne had to continue asking Zola for help. During June, no doubt for reasons of economy, he moved Hortense and little Paul into another flat, at 12, Vieux-Chemin de Rome.* He himself escaped from Aix during the first fortnight of July to keep his convalescent mother company at l'Estaque, thereby reaping the double advantage of avoiding his father's bullying and having an opportunity of enlisting his mother's help.

* Today, Rue d'Italie.

Cézanne's mother did not much care for Hortense; in her eyes, Hortense was an intruder who had stolen her son. But she was tolerant and made the best of things as they were. She was becoming devoted to little Paul, whom she had seen several times, and Cézanne became less harassed and began to make plans again. He hoped to spend the winter in Marseilles and return to Paris in the spring. Then, if Zola agreed, he would go and work in the neighbourhood of Médan, where the novelist had just bought a little house.

In the meantime, at the Jas de Bouffan, Louis Auguste had opened a letter to Cézanne from his landlord in the Rue de l'Ouest. On leaving Paris, Cézanne had left the key of his flat with Antoine Guillaume, a cobbler in the Rue de Vaugirard, who was a friend of his. But there was at this time a Universal Exhibition taking place in the capital; and when some of his relations came to Paris for it, the cobbler put them up in Cézanne's flat. The landlord, unaware of the circumstances, wrote to Cézanne complaining that he had sub-let his flat without permission. Louis Auguste leapt to the conclusion that his son 'was hiding women in Paris.' 'The whole situation is becoming a sort of musical comedy,' Cézanne wrote.

But Cézanne could be as stubborn as his father. He tried to persuade Louis Auguste to allow him enough money to live in Marseilles during the winter. 'I would thus be able to stay on as long as possible.' But it was no use, Louis Auguste would not give in. Then, early in September, a third compromising letter arrived at the Jas de Bouffan. It was to Hortense from her father and had been forwarded to Aix. 'You can imagine the result,' Cézanne wrote to Zola. 'I violently deny the whole thing and, since Hortense's name fortunately does not appear in the letter, I merely say that it is written to some woman or other.'

Quite suddenly the sky cleared. 'Papa,' wrote Cézanne, 'has fallen for a charming little maid we have in Aix.' Love had an emollient effect on the old man; he stopped bullying his son and gave him three hundred francs.* 'Unprecedented,' said Cézanne happily. He could now go on painting with a relatively quiet mind.

* * *

* Approximately £50 today.

In the middle of September, Cézanne's mother left l'Estaque to return to Aix for the vintage. Cézanne himself went to spend his nights in Marseilles, where he had taken yet another flat, not far from the Central Market, at 32, Rue Ferrari,* returning to work at l'Estaque each morning. He did not much care for Marseilles; it was, so he said in a letter to Zola, 'the French oil capital, as Paris is the butter capital: you have no idea of the overwhelming arrogance of this savage population; it has but one instinct, that of making money . . .'

One day, in Marseilles, Cézanne chanced to meet Huot, who had been with him at the Drawing School. Huot had done well for himself. He had become an architect, and two years running (1865 and 1866) had been awarded the Gold Medal at the Salon. In Marseilles he had the important job of principal architectural inspector to the Compagnie Immobilière. He showed a certain condescension towards the painter and, during their conversation, he happened to ask Cézanne if he still saw Zola. 'Sometimes,' Cézanne replied, rather amused. Did he still get letters from him? 'Only recently,' said Cézanne. Huot was astonished. How very strange that the famous novelist should still be in contact with this ill-dressed dauber. However, on the strength of it, he gave Cézanne his card and invited him to call. 'You see how useful it is to have friends,' Cézanne wrote when giving Zola an ironic account of the meeting.

Another day, he saw Marion in the distance, by the door of the Faculté des Sciences, where his young admirer of the old days – Marion was still no more than thirty-two – was now Professor of Zoology. But Cézanne did not speak to him. He had been wounded too often and was on his guard against rebuffs. He was afraid of men who had succeeded. He sometimes saw Emperaire, who lived in the most appalling poverty in Aix. He even wrote to Zola asking him to recommend Emperaire 'for some job, however small it may be.'

At the beginning of November, Hortense had to return to Paris in

* This information is based on a letter from Cézanne to Zola dated 19 December, 1878. The edition of Cézanne's *Correspondance* has it (page 154) 'Rue Ferrière.' But this is a misreading. The original letter is in the manuscript department of the Bibliothèque Nationale.

a hurry.* For over a month, till the middle of December, Cézanne, who had had to borrow a further hundred francs from Zola, remained alone with his son at l'Estaque. He lived in constant fear of his father arriving unexpectedly. For Louis Auguste had been only briefly distracted by the servant girl and had begun his investigations again. The weather was appalling and Cézanne could not work. He stayed at home and read Stendhal's *Histoire de la Peinture en Italie*, with that scrupulous attention he devoted to everything he did. As for little Paul, he was, as his father affectionately remarked, 'terrible on all counts.'

At last Hortense returned from Paris. The weather improved and Cézanne was able to begin painting again.

'As you say, there are some wonderful subjects here,' he wrote to Zola. 'It's a question of rendering them, and I'm not sure of my success; I began to see nature rather late; it is full of interest however.'

He was humble and melancholy. In a few days' time, on 19 January, he would be forty years old.

* The reason for her hurried journey is unknown. Hortense, Cézanne told Zola, 'has had a little adventure in Paris. I shan't put it on paper, but I'll tell you about it when I return, though it is not very important.'

CHAPTER FIVE

Resignation

> And I said, O that I had wings like a dove: for then would I flee away, and be at rest. Lo, then would I get me away far off: and remain in the wilderness.—PSALM LV. Verses 6 and 7

WHEN Cézanne returned to Paris in March, he found his Impressionist friends much divided. Renoir and Sisley had decided to try their luck at the Salon. They were therefore excluded from the forthcoming Impressionist exhibition – the fourth – which was to open in the Avenue de l'Opéra. Some members of the group were unrelenting on this point: to submit works to the Hanging Committee of the Salon amounted to treason.

This did not worry Cézanne in the least. He intended to try and obtain admission to the Salon and had no intention of exhibiting with the Impressionists, for he felt it was likely to diminish his chances with the Hanging Committee. When Pissarro pressed him, he declined the invitation, pleading the 'difficulties created by his sending work to the Salon.'

At the same time, he paid 'a little insinuating visit' to Guillemet, who by dint of making concessions had achieved a position of sufficient importance in the official world of art to have been appointed a member of the Hanging Committee. Putting his pride in his pocket, Cézanne asked him for his support with his colleagues, those 'hard-hearted judges.'

It was a curious and indeed humiliating overture, since Cézanne had no respect whatever for Guillemet's facile work and was certainly quite incapable of concealing the fact. He no doubt hoped that, if he were hung in the Palais de l'Industrie, the general view taken of his work might thereby be changed. To achieve this, he was prepared to go to any lengths, other than those of conformism and compromise which were the best passports to the Hanging Committee. Guillemet, who was a good friend, promised to plead his cause.

Having made these arrangements, Cézanne quitted Paris in April for Melun. He left the keys of his flat with Tanguy so that he might show his canvases to prospective purchasers, should there be any.

* * *

At Melun, Cézanne lived as if cut off from the world, devoting himself to the complex and difficult task of endeavouring to resolve the fusion of light, which decomposed objects, with the construction that gave them spatial reality. He was endeavouring 'to make of Impressionism something solid and durable like the art of the museums.'

Utterly absorbed in this task he lost all track of the days. From time to time, he received a letter (in spite of Guillemet's support, he had once again been subjected to what he called the 'harsh guillotine': the Hanging Committee had rejected his work), or he made a brief trip to Paris. In June, Zola suggested that he should spend a fortnight with him at Médan.

The year before, when telling Flaubert of his purchase, Zola had said that it was 'a rabbit hutch' of a house. It cost 'nine thousand francs,* and I'm telling you the price so that you shall not be too impressed. Literature,' he added, 'has paid for this modest country retreat, which has the double advantage of being far from a station, and of having no single bourgeois in the neighbourhood.' But the 'rabbit hutch,' which had originally been built by a waiter from the Café-Américan, was very soon enlarged. Zola now spent eight months of the year in the country and was constantly building on to his house.

The little village of Médan, consisting of some two hundred inhabitants, lay among trees on the banks of the Seine. It had now become Zola's headquarters, and he had many visitors: friends, admirers, writers, actors, painters, publishers and editors. Cézanne, by nature a recluse, must have been somewhat bewildered by all the talk and the continual coming and going at Médan; but Zola delighted in it.

Success and money had at last enabled Zola to indulge in those things

* Approximately £1,500 today.

he had always wanted. He could now be himself. To Cézanne, for whom a rickety table, an old bed and a ragged chair had always sufficed, the master's huge study with its great desk, its Louis XIII armchair, and its monumental chimney-piece bearing in huge gold letters the inscription '*Nulla dies sine linea*,' was a matter for considerable astonishment.

Throughout the house every piece of furniture was laden with china, pewter, brass, ivories and wood-carvings, an astounding display of knicknacks, while the walls were lined with armour and tapestries in naïve luxuriance. With singularly tasteless romanticism Zola had mingled periods, styles and countries, the Turkish with the Gothic, the Japanese with the Venetian, the authentic with the false, decorating an alcove with a rood screen, a ceiling with an ivory angel, juxtaposing an exquisite eighteenth-century statuette and a valueless piece of pottery, all in fantastic profusion. Médan may not have had a single bourgeois before Zola went to live there, but this was certainly no longer the case. Cézanne said he felt as if he were visiting a minister.

Nevertheless Zola was as friendly and affectionate as ever. Indeed, he may even have been a trifle too obviously so; it was so very clear that fortune had failed to smile on his old friend. Poor Cézanne! In the old days, at Aix, he and Baille had also had their dreams. But such was life: some it destroyed, and others it exalted. And now, in his triumph, Zola was surrounded not by his old friends but by strangers. Except for the faithful Alexis, none of his disciples, none of those whom the jealous called the 'Messieurs Zola' came from Aix, neither Céard nor Hennique, neither Huysmans, nor that tough-looking man who loved yachting, drink, food and women, Guy de Maupassant. Zola's kindness was all compassion.

In spite of the disconcerting atmosphere of Zola's house, and the continual coming and going of people whom he did his best to avoid, Cézanne quite enjoyed his stay at Médan. The countryside with its water meadows and orchards, its rows of willows and poplars along the Seine, was delightful. He painted by the river, where the silence was broken only by the occasional whistle of a train.

* * *

About 20 June Cézanne returned to the austerities of Melun. There he rose early, spent the day painting, and went to bed a little after eight. He was sometimes engaged on the same subject for weeks at a time. Nothing came easily to him. As the years went by, he became ever more exacting.

In October he wrote to Zola asking for seats for the play based on *L'Assommoir*, which had been playing at the Ambigu since January. Writing to thank him, he said: 'They could not have been better seats, and I didn't sleep at all.'

The winter of 1879 was an exceptionally hard one, and all the more disagreeable because of a fuel shortage. There were forty degrees of frost in December and the snow was deep and frozen hard. In the ordinary way, Cézanne avoided painting snowscapes. The snow melted too quickly and gave him no time to perfect his picture. But now the frost looked like lasting, and he set up his easel in the nearby forest of Fontainebleau.*

The extent to which Cézanne's life was restricted to the dimensions of his canvas was remarkable. Zola always sent him his books as soon as they appeared. In February, Cézanne received his friend's new novel, *Nana*. 'It's a magnificent work,' he wrote, 'but I fear the newspapers have entered into a conspiracy not to mention it. Indeed, I have seen no announcement or review of it in the three little papers I take. And this vexes me, because it is indicative of a profound lack of interest in art . . .' Zola must have been amused by the letter. What desert could Cézanne be living in not to have heard even a remote echo of the extraordinary uproar *Nana* was creating? For the last four months no one had been talking of anything else. Since its serialisation had begun in *Le Voltaire* in October, the whole country had been discussing its courtesan heroine with either enthusiasm or indignation. There had been enormous publicity – posters, prospectuses, advertisements in the newspapers and sandwichmen on the Boulevards – and the scandal spread throughout France. Zola's 'naturalism' had its partisans and its detractors everywhere. His enemies were denouncing him as obscene; the newspapers were full of caricatures; and there were popular songs

* According to Jean de Beucken, Cézanne was inspired to paint this picture by a photograph.

being sung in the streets: *Belle Nuna, fais pas ta tata; Nana, la Vestale de la Place Pigalle; La Femme à papa, c'est Nana*, etc. Everyone was talking of Nana; you could not escape her. As Céard said: 'It's becoming an obsession, a nightmare.' On 15 February, when *Nana* was published in volume form, 55,000 copies were sold in the first twenty-four hours.

But Cézanne had heard nothing of all this.

* * *

Cézanne returned to Paris in March. He went back to the Rue de l'Ouest, but this time to a fifth-floor flat at No. 32.

His life in Paris was very nearly as quiet as it had been at Melun. He saw an occasional friend, Tanguy, Zola, Guillaumin, or the unhappy Cabaner, who was suffering from consumption, and reduced to playing the piano in a café-concert in the Avenue de La Motte-Picquet. Cézanne naturally went often to the Louvre, where he studied the Poussins. This, he felt, was what he must achieve; he must remake 'Poussin entirely from nature.'

He was painting still lifes and self-portraits in his studio, but he was also attempting to compose subject pictures of bathers. He worked without models, using old studies for the human form. Models still made him shy. One day he engaged a professional. She undressed and posed in the nude. 'Monsieur, you seem embarrassed,' she said. He sent her away.

Zola had done his best to bring his friend out of his shell, to get him to meet people and take him into society. But he had no success. Paralysed with shyness, Cézanne was terrified of parties and unknown faces. Zola had taken him to the salon of Charpentier, the publisher, in the Rue de Grenelle, to which many celebrities came: Rochefort, Sarah Bernhardt, Mounet-Sully, Gambetta, Massenet, Jules Ferry, Edmond de Goncourt, Octave Mirbeau and Alphonse Daudet among others. But nothing would induce Cézanne to go there a second time, though the Charpentiers were always very hospitable to painters, and had helped his friend Renoir with commissions for portraits.

The brilliant and the witty made him conscious of his own insufficiency. He knew neither how to behave, nor what to say; and he was peculiarly adept at making solecisms.

Zola did not persevere for long. For the last three years he had been living in the bourgeois Rue de Boulogne,* in a huge apartment, furnished in exactly the same way as the house at Médan. He asked Cézanne to one of his evening parties. It had not occurred to Cézanne to change; moreover, he made it clear that he thought Zola's guests, in their evening clothes, both snobbish and pretentious. Almost the only words he uttered during the whole evening were to say to Zola: 'Don't you think it's a bit hot, Émile? Do you mind if I take my coat off?'

Yet these profound differences, both of temperament and position, did not apparently affect their relationship. Cézanne never took advantage of his friend. He had never, for instance, tried to impose Hortense on the Zolas, who clearly preferred to ignore her. Nor did he force himself on them. He was somewhat embarrassed by Zola's celebrity and, when writing to Zola, he sometimes ended his letters with such remarks as this of 1 April: 'I am your grateful old schoolfellow of 1854.' In spite of Guillemet's support, Cézanne had again been rejected for the Salon, while canvases by both Renoir and Monet (who had now also made up his mind to desert the Impressionist exhibitions) had been accepted. But, owing to the manifest ill-will of the authorities, they were so badly hung that the two painters determined to send a letter of protest to the Minister of Fine Arts.

They asked Cézanne to request Zola to get the letter published in *Le Voltaire* with a few words of introduction. 'The few words,' Cézanne wrote to Zola, 'should tend to show how important the Impressionists are and the profound curiosity they have aroused.' But he did not, he added, wish to influence Zola in any way. 'I have more than once,' he said, 'been placed in the position of having to ask you to do things which may embarrass you. I am merely a go-between, no more.'

Zola, however, went further than this. On 18, 19, 21 and 22 June, he published a series of articles in *Le Voltaire* protesting against the treatment of Renoir and Monet, and giving his views, with all the authority he had now acquired, on Impressionist painting. 'They are treated as practical jokers,' he said, 'as charlatans mocking the public

* Today, the Rue Ballu.

and going to any lengths to advertise their works, while on the contrary they are in fact convinced and austere observers. People seem to be unaware that most of these strugglers are poor men dying in misery of hunger and fatigue. These martyrs to their beliefs are singular practical jokers.'

Zola also pointed out that, though people were denigrating the Impressionists, they were busy copying their technique – 'They are flying with our wings,' said Degas – and were adulterating it by painting canvases of a 'corrected Impressionism, toned down, brought within the comprehension of the crowd.' 'It is,' he wrote, 'a mounting and irresistible flood of modernity, which is gradually sweeping over the École des Beaux-Arts, the Institute, and all the accepted techniques and conventions . . .'

It was nevertheless surprising that the Impressionists had not succeeded in making their mark. Great creators are inevitably recognised in the end. Had not Zola himself, in spite of every obstacle, every attack, finally triumphed! But the same public that had been compelled to recognise his talent would not admit that of the Impressionists. What was one to conclude? Surely the public that had accorded *L'Assommoir* and *Nana* such success was not blind, nor could it be so excellent a judge in one direction and yet a bad one in another. Alas, one was led to a most painful conclusion. If the Impressionists failed to achieve recognition, it could be only because their work did not come up to their intentions: 'It is because not a single artist of the group has forcefully and definitively realised the new formula they have invented . . . They are all precursors. The man of genius has not yet been born. One can see what they are trying to do and one can agree with it, but one looks in vain for the masterpiece which would make the formula triumph, and before which all heads would be bowed.'

These remarks were naturally not very popular among the Impressionists, although Cézanne, for his part, could accept them with a good grace. His opinion of Impressionism as such was not, after all, fundamentally so very different from Zola's. Nor could he really disagree with what Zola had written about himself: 'M. Paul Cézanne has the temperament of a great painter; he is still struggling with his researches into technique and remains closer to Courbet and Delacroix.' It was obvious to Cézanne that Zola, out of friendship, had tempered his critical judgment in so far as it concerned himself.

In July Cézanne again went to stay with Zola at Médan. He did not much care for the atmosphere there, the hangings and the servants, Zola working at his monumental desk, the copious and over-elaborate meals, the writers throwing their sales figures in each other's teeth. Why did he go? Was it really out of friendship for Zola? Or due to the curious restlessness, the instability, that were continually impelling him to move from place to place? Or, again, was it so that he could escape from Hortense? Their love was now dead; they had become strangers. It was another of life's deceptions.

Sometimes Cézanne disappeared, unable to bear the continuous performance played at Médan, or because he disliked some of Zola's friends: Busnach, for instance, who had adapted *L'Assommoir* and *Nana* for the stage, a gross, cynical and vulgar man, who churned out quantities of operettas and melodramas. 'A great man arrived while I was there,' complained Cézanne. 'M. Busnach! One is no longer anyone when such a great man as he is about!'

Cézanne was easily crossed. One day Madame Zola posed for him in the garden serving tea. Unfortunately the picture would not come out as Cézanne wished. Madame Zola heard him swearing to himself under his breath. Suddenly Guillemet joined them and made a joke. Cézanne lost his temper, broke his paint brushes, rent the canvas and went off shaking his fists.

* * *

Cézanne returned to Paris at the end of August. Except for a handful of loyal friends, few people knew anything of him. No one had seen his pictures and he was known only as the eccentric whom Duranty had described under the name of 'Maillobert.'

Duranty had died in April the previous year. He had left a posthumous volume, *Le Pays des Arts*, which Charpentier had just published. In this book, an imaginary young painter goes to visit various artists in their studios, among them Cézanne, who is referred to as 'that mad Maillobert, whom a few young men talked about in the studios:'

'As I was about to knock at the door, I heard a parrot screaming inside. I knocked. "Come in!" someone shouted with an almost exaggerated Midi accent.

'Hardly had I got inside, when I thought: "I'm in the presence of a madman!"

'I was bewildered both by the place and the man. Dust and dirt were everywhere, broken pots, rags, bits of plaster, dried mounds of clay, all lay about in heaps as if it were a rag-picker's premises. There was a nauseatingly musty smell. The bald painter, who had an enormous beard and two peculiarly long teeth that seemed to hold his lips half open, looked at once youthful and old, indescribably sordid and, as it were, the symbolic divinity of his studio. He waved to me and gave me a smile which might have been either mocking or insane.

'As my eyes fell on the quantity of huge canvases hanging all round the room, I was rooted to the spot by their appalling colour.

' "Ah," said Maillobert with a nasal, sing-song, very Marseillais accent, "so Monsieur is a lover of painting? Here are my little scraps from the palette," he added, pointing to the most gigantic canvases . . .

'At that moment, the parrot cried: "Maillobert is a great painter . . ."

"He's my art critic," said the painter with a terrifying smile . . .

'Then, as he saw me looking curiously at a number of large chemist's jars standing on the ground and bearing abbreviated Latin inscriptions: *Jusqui. – Aqu. Still. – Ferrug. – Rhub. – Sulf. Cup.*:

' "They're my paint-box," said Maillobert. "I show the others that I achieve the true painting with drugs, while they only manufacture drugs with all their fine colours! You see, painting depends on genius . . ."

'He dipped a spoon into one of the chemist's jars and brought out a trowelful of green which he applied to a canvas on which a few lines indicated a landscape; he twisted the spoon round and one could just see that the daub was intended to be a field . . .

' "In two hours," he said, "I cover four yards of canvas, and they talk about painting with a palette knife! I only use my palette knife these days for cutting cheese, and I've given my brushes to the laundress's children for drumsticks." '

Cézanne was much mortified and longed to avenge himself by being hung in the Salon. 'Paul is still counting on you for you know what,' Zola had written recently to Guillemet. But every spring brought another disappointment, and the Salon of 1881 still hung no canvases by Cézanne.

After this latest failure, Cézanne left Paris at the beginning of May and went to stay at Pontoise, at 31, Quai du Pothuis.

Before leaving, he asked Zola to write a preface to the catalogue of a sale some painters were organising for the benefit of Cabaner. Cabaner was dying. Life had shown him no mercy right to the end.

* * *

For Cézanne Pontoise was another Melun, with the difference that his solitude was not so complete: Pissarro was there, faithful as ever to the banks of the Oise.

In spite of the fact that Cézanne no longer exhibited with the Impressionists, their friendship had remained as warm as ever. They had both suffered disappointments and this created a mutual bond of sympathy. Pissarro had great difficulty in selling sufficient canvases to keep his family going. More often than not, he lived in dire poverty.

Now passed fifty, he had had no semblance of success. Like Cézanne, he was prematurely aged; with his white beard and hair, he looked like some melancholy patriarch. Yet he showed no bitterness. His difficulties had diminished neither his charm nor his kindness. Cézanne often went painting with him. He painted views of the mill at La Couleuve, of the Galet hill and of Cergy village. He was working more slowly than ever, with thin, short brush strokes, simplifying in order to give his canvases a rigorous and rhythmical construction.

Sometimes the two painters went to Auvers to see Gachet. But the doctor's house was no longer the happy place it had been in the past. Madame Gachet had died of consumption six years before and the doctor still mourned her.

There had been a change, too, in his professional life. Two years before, in 1879, he had been involved in a railway accident at La Chapelle when on his way to Paris. Disregarding his own injuries, he had tended the other passengers. The Compagnie des Chemins de Fer du Nord had rewarded him by making him their doctor for the Herblay-Auvers sector. He was now living three days a week at

Auvers, where a governess looked after his children and house. Despite his domestic troubles, he, too, painted in his leisure time and could understand a little of Cézanne's bitterness, for he had never succeeded in getting a picture into the Salon himself.

Pontoise was only some fifteen kilometres from Médan. Cézanne planned to go there across country and on foot. 'I think,' he wrote to Zola, 'that I can make it.' But his younger sister, Rose, who was twenty-seven, had just married a young bourgeois of Aix, Maxime Conil; and they informed him of their intention of visiting Paris. 'You can just see me taking them round the Louvre and the other picture galleries,' Cézanne wrote sarcastically. However, Rose fell ill, which put a stop to their sight-seeing and Cézanne 're-embarked them' for Aix.

He had several works on the stocks, some painted by grey weather and some by sunshine. 'I'm working a little, but very inadequately,' he said, as usual minimising his efforts.

But there was one man, at least, who was watching these efforts with extreme attention. Gauguin, the stockbroker, had come to spend his holidays at Auvers, to be near Pissarro and Cézanne. He was still painting as an amateur; but he was becoming increasingly bored with his profession, which took up too much of his time and strength, and was longing to devote himself entirely to art. He was earning a considerable amount of money – one year he made 40,000 francs* – and had put aside 15,000 francs with which to buy pictures. His collection, consisting mostly of works by the Impressionists, included twelve Cézannes.

Cézanne was naturally flattered by the interest this young man of thirty-three took in his work. And yet, was it not perhaps a little too insistent? Was this Gauguin, who was always much too well dressed, by any chance trying to put 'the grapnel on him?' Was he trying to pilfer his methods and technique? Cézanne's suspicions were aggravated when, after Gauguin's departure, Pissarro received a letter from him written in a somewhat flippant style: 'Has M. Cézanne found the precise formula for a work which everyone will accept? If he should find the recipe for compressing the extravagant expression of all his

* Approximately £7,000 today.

sensations into one single and unique process, I pray you try to make him talk in his sleep by administering one of those mysterious homeopathic drugs, and come immediately to Paris to tell us of it.'

The summer was coming to an end and Cézanne, tired of Pontoise, left for the south in October. On the way, he stayed for a week at Médan, where Zola told him that Baille was on the road to success. Thanks to a match with a rich wife, he was about to become an important manufacturer of spectacles and binoculars in the Rue Oberkampf; the firm supplied the Ministry of War. 'It's always a pleasure to see one's own generation succeed,' said Zola. But what would Zola and Baille have thought if they re-read the letters they had written in their youth? If they met now, Zola would talk of his sales and Baille of his order-book.

* * *

Cézanne left Aix almost at once for his refuge at l'Estaque. His father, who had still not completely uncovered his secret, now tended to let him alone. He was still very curious, but more kindly disposed. 'It seems I've got grandchildren in Paris,' Louis Auguste had recently told a friend. 'One day, I shall have to go and see them!'

Nevertheless he continued to open his son's letters whenever he got the chance. He was thus the first to read the little book Paul Alexis had just published on Zola (*Émile Zola, Notes d'un Ami*), in which he described the boyhood of the 'inseparables.'

'The copy you were kind enough to send me,' Cézanne wrote to Paul Alexis, excusing himself for his delay in thanking him, 'fell into the impure hands of my family in Aix. They took care to tell me nothing about it. They opened the envelope, cut the pages and read it all through while I was waiting beneath the peaceful pine. But I got to hear about it in the end. I demanded it, and now I'm in possession of it and am reading it.' Cézanne confessed how moved he was to see the 'things of the past' recalled, and to find quotations from the youthful verses of Zola, 'he who is still content to remain our friend.'

Yet Cézanne's attention must have been arrested by the passage in which Alexis discussed the novel about painting which Zola had been contemplating for a long time past:

'His principal character is ready to hand,' Alexis wrote. 'It is the painter, dedicated to modernity, who appears in *Le Ventre de Paris:* Claude Lantier . . . I know that in Claude Lantier he intends to make a study of the terrifying psychology of artistic impotence. Around this central man of genius, the sublime dreamer whose production is paralysed by a flaw in his nature, will move other artists, painters, sculptors, musicians, writers, a whole company of ambitious young men who set out to conquer Paris: some fail, some more or less succeed; but they are all case histories of the sickness of art; variations on the present neurosis. Naturally Zola will be compelled in this book to lay his friends under contribution, and to record their most typical characteristics. As far as I am concerned, if I find myself in it, and even if I'm not flattered by it, I promise not to sue him.'

Cézanne knew very well that the Claude Lantier of *Le Ventre de Paris* was himself. But now, at the beginning of 1882, he was not going to worry about what Zola might think of his painting, or of what he might write about his destiny as an artist. For this year, at last, Guillemet was to get him into the Salon.

Every member of the Hanging Committee had the right to nominate a rejected work. It was what was known as hanging a work 'for charity.' The teachers sitting on the Committee generally used this right on behalf of one of their pupils. Guillemet and Cézanne had come to an agreement that this far from distinguished means of entry should be used on Cézanne's behalf. Apart from anything else, it was somewhat ridiculous for Cézanne to be presented as 'Guillemet's pupil.' Nevertheless he would be hung in the Salon at last.

In the meantime Cézanne was working at l'Estaque with Renoir, who was on his way back from Italy. Unfortunately, Renoir developed pneumonia. Cézanne nursed him devotedly. 'I can't tell you how kind Cézanne has been to me,' Renoir wrote to Chocquet. 'He mobilised his whole family to help me. We're having a big farewell dinner at his house with his mother, for he is returning to Paris, and I am compelled to stay somewhere in the Midi on my doctor's strict instructions.' The whole household had done their best for him. Cézanne's mother had prepared delicious dishes. 'At luncheon she gave me a *brandade de* *morue,*' said Renoir. 'I think it must be the ambrosia of the gods recovered. One should eat it and die.'*

Meanwhile, the Impressionists in Paris were intending to hold another exhibition and asked Cézanne to participate. But he replied that he had nothing to show. Now that the doors of the Salon were opening to him it was hardly the moment to risk the mockery that an Impressionist exhibition was bound to arouse.

In March, as Renoir had told Chocquet, Cézanne was in Paris, anxiously awaiting the opening of the Salon.

Guillemet had kept his promise, but alas, Cézanne's canvas – a portrait† – went completely unnoticed. The only mention was a passing one by a journalist of the *Dictionnaire Vèron* who said that 'the shadow in the eye-socket and on the right cheek gives promise of a future colourist.'

The irony of the situation lay in the fact that this time failure seemed irremediable.

* 'It was from this stay at l'Estaque,' Renoir recorded, 'that I brought back a magnificent water colour by Cézanne, *Les Baigneuses* . . . I was with my friend Lauth one day, when he was suddenly taken short. He said: "You don't happen to see any trees about, other than pines?" "Splendid, here's some paper!" I cried. It was a most exquisite water-colour, which Cézanne had discarded among the rocks after spending twenty sessions on it.'

† What portrait this was is unknown. The catalogue merely says 'Portrait de M.L.A.' It has been suggested that it was of Cézanne's uncle and godfather, Louis Aubert.

Mont Sainte-Victoire

PART FOUR

[1882 - 1895]

CHAPTER ONE

Isolation

This world is not made for me, nor I for it.—DIDEROT

IN October, Cézanne returned to Aix feeling he never wanted to come back to Paris. Before leaving the north, however, he went to stay with Zola, but even this friendship seemed empty to him now. Success had had a deplorable effect of Zola, Cézanne thought, and he had become 'a beastly bourgeois.' Coming in late one day, tired, untidy, laden with his painting equipment, Cézanne surprised an ironical glance between Zola and a servant. He determined never to come to Médan again. The fact was that his sensitive nature was smarting under his repeated failures. It was not so much that his friendship for Zola had lapsed; indeed, he had merely to think of the past for the warm affection of those early days to be renewed; but he felt at an intolerable disadvantage. Particularly since Madame Zola was apt to make it evident that his coarse manners, stained clothes, silences, moods and solecisms made him no more desirable a visitor than those deplorable cousins of hers who regularly descended on Médan with extended palms, drawn as if by a magnet to the novelist's golden fame. Cézanne decided he would not go and see his friend again. It was better to disappear and live in isolation.

He went to ground in the Jas de Bouffan and saw no one. When he did go into the streets of Aix and happened to meet people he knew, he showed no sign of friendliness. He was becoming increasingly misanthropic. When he met Baille's brother, Isidore, who had become a lawyer, he merely muttered that he looked 'a nasty little legal blackguard.' Nor was he any easier in temper with his family. When his sister Rose arrived with her husband to 'lie in' at the Jas, Cézanne filled the house with his 'outcries,' in which he was more or less supported by his sister Marie, who had become an exceedingly autocratic old maid, and did not see eye to eye with the young couple.

Cézanne was now forty-three. His head was bald, his skin grey, his eyelids drooped and his face bore lines of defeat. The outlook was sombre and he began to believe that he was finished. He thought of Marguery, the gay friend of his youth, who had killed himself the previous summer by jumping out of a window of the Palais de Justice. Cézanne was profoundly concerned about his own fate. His present isolation aggravated this feeling and, in November, he wrote to Zola that he had decided to make his will.

Should he die in the near future his sisters would automatically inherit from him, but in no circumstances did he wish this to happen. He wanted his mother and little Paul to be his heirs. But how was this to be achieved and made legally watertight? He turned to Zola once again, asked him to draft his will and keep it for him because 'the document might be stolen here.'

But these sombre concerns did not prevent his working. 'I am still working a little, though I am doing nothing else,' he wrote to Zola.

It was becoming increasingly clear that only in Provence could Cézanne be completely himself. Only here could he pursue his researches into painting as he conceived it. If he were ever to fulfil himself, it would be face to face with Mont Sainte-Victoire and the Étoile hills, whose masses were so boldly defined in the clear air of Provence. He knew this countryside so well that for him it was no longer subject to the changes of the days and seasons. Behind the chance play of light he could see the unvarying and immutable truths of the rocky landscape. Here, the very earth seemed in tune with his basic need to construct, to reduce forms to their essentials, and impose an almost geometric severity on the chaotic appearance of things. Remote now from the artistic circles of Paris, in his lonely contemplation of his native province he was beginning to understand what were the basic necessities of his art. He was no painter of the north or of the Île-de-France; he was the painter of this hard geological land. Classicism was after all a Latin quality; and it was only in the Midi that one could remake Poussin from nature.

Life was not 'very gay' at the Jas de Bouffan, Cézanne wrote to Zola. His brother-in-law and his sister Rose were still there, and their baby squalled. He was harassed by his father, while his sister Marie, who had become increasingly religious, nagged him to regularise his relations with Hortense. 'Marry her, why don't you marry her!' she kept saying. Cézanne would leave the house in a fury; sometimes staying away for days. But he could not be happy anywhere now.

No painting has greater balance, discipline and serenity than that of Cézanne; yet no one could be more unstable than the man who created it.

He often went to Marseilles. There, behind the Church of the Réformés, he would walk up the slope of the Cours Devilliers,* climb the stairs of an old house and visit Adolphe Monticelli, whom he would find sitting at his easel in an untidy attic that was half living-room half studio. Cézanne had made great friends with this brother in failure. Monticelli was some fifteen years older than Cézanne but was still a handsome figure of a man; tall in spite of rather short legs, he had a high forehead and a splendid red beard. Till 1870, Monticelli had lived in Paris, but had then returned permanently to Marseilles. At one time he had been something of a dandy. With white collars and cuffs, a velvet cape, pearl-grey gloves and a gold-knobbed cane, he had been like 'a portrait by Titian that had come out of its frame.'† But now he tended to neglect his appearance. He still loved opulence, luxury and splendour; but since he had no money, his imagination had to suffice. His life was one long dream of magnificence, and his painting was of Venetian scenes and Watteau-like *fêtes galantes*. He adored beautiful women and, in his canvases, he depicted them laden with jewels, gold, feathers and brocades in shadowy and mysterious gardens. He was devoted to opera and tzigane bands, and would hurry home to his attic after a performance, 'light all the candles he could find' and paint 'as long as he had the strength.'‡

'I give myself the luxury,' he declared, 'of placing fine notes of colour on my canvases; a rich yellow and a velvet black give me supreme pleasure.' He sold his works in order to live, but he would never demean himself to argue about the price. He was profoundly disinterested in success. Unlike Cézanne, incomprehension and

* The Cours Franklin Roosevelt today.

† Louis Brès.

‡ Paul Guigou.

mockery did not affect him in the least. The two painters often went off on expeditions together. Once they wandered, haversack on back, for a whole month among the hills between Marseilles and Aix. Cézanne was in lyrical mood and declaimed Virgil.* He was persuaded that Monticelli possessed 'private secrets of trituration.'† He never tired of watching him at work.

Monticelli, according to Cézanne, had 'temperament.' He was the heir to Delacroix, a baroque romantic who abandoned himself to his luxuriant imagination. Cézanne could see himself in him, for at bottom their natures were not dissimilar. But Cézanne, in his determination to seek a form of classical expression, had bridled his. The struggle between his intelligence and his instinct was a poignant one and the search for reality a tragic accompaniment to his creative life. 'I see the planes moving, and the straight lines sometimes seem to sag.' Cézanne envied Monticelli's facility and his happy capacity to be content with what he was instead of striving for the impossible.

* * *

In March Rose and her husband left the Jas de Bouffan. 'I think,' wrote Cézanne to Zola, 'that my outcries will have results and that they will not come back to the country this summer.'

A little later, he went to stay at l'Estaque with Hortense and took 'a little house with a garden . . . just above the station,' in what was known as the Quartier du Château, the Château Bovis. Cézanne lived 'at the foot of the hill.' Behind his house, the rocks rose up among the pines. In front lay the huge bay, strewn with islands, and in the distance the hills of the Marseilleveyre.

In May Cézanne heard of Manet's death; he was fifty-one. 'Manet's catastrophe' no doubt re-awakened his own apprehensions, for he went with his mother to Marseilles to see a solicitor and drew up a will, which he sent to Zola, his mother keeping a copy.

'I am painting as always,' he wrote to Zola. 'There are fine views here, but they don't necessarily make good subjects. Nevertheless, when the sun is setting, and one goes up to the heights, there is a

* Reported by J. Gasquet.

† Tabarant.

splendid panorama over Marseilles and the islands, which makes a very decorative effect in the evening.' Since Cézanne avoided invention as far as he could, he took endless trouble to find viewpoints from which a landscape made a composition in itself. He was obsessed by l'Estaque and its neighbourhood; and his single preoccupation was to render its beauty on canvas. But he felt his way hesitantly and discarded canvas after canvas in dissatisfaction. He longed to combine in one unique and marvellous picture all the diverse components of the landscape: the intense blue of the Meditteranean, the rugged mass of the Marseilleveyre, the houses nearer at hand with their tiled roofs, and the green semi-circle of the pines. He had moved far from Impressionism now. With a strict and deliberate simplification he arrested the ever-shifting movement of time and imposed eternity on his subjects. The world stood still. Water and foliage seemed to exist in a sort of mineral dream. Nor was there any human presence; merely an ineffable silence. 'The sky always, and the limitless in nature attract me . . .' he said.

The year 1883 went by like a dream. That summer he spent a few weeks at the Jas de Bouffan. But, in November, he was back in l'Estaque, where his mother soon came to live with him. There were no interruptions to his concentration. From time to time he saw Monticelli in Marseilles; but Monticelli had lost much of his enthusiasm and his joy in life; his mother had died and left him greatly mourning; his health, too, had deteriorated.

At the end of December, however, Monet and Renoir, who was on his way back from Italy, paid Cézanne a visit.

A little later, in February, Valabrègue came to see him. 'We walked round the town together,' Cézanne wrote. 'We remembered some of the people we had known in the past, but how remote we were from all sentiment!' The friendships of the past had fallen away. Villevieille, for instance, who hated Cézanne's painting, looked on him with contempt. There were others who were still polite, but they were inclined to pity him, which he found exasperating. He had little in common with them now.

Indeed, Cézanne was very isolated. Zola's books were almost the only messages that reached him from the outside world. 'Thank you very much for sending it to me,' he wrote on one occasion, 'and for not forgetting me in the remoteness in which I live.' His solitariness oppressed him. He seemed to be painting in a desert. He had no one to talk to, no confidant in his moments of depression. His father, mother, sisters and Hortense were all incapable of understanding his painting, and the almost maniacal obstinacy that drove him on to produce work that was despised. Sometimes, when he thought of Goya and the Duchess of Alba, he would sigh. It seemed to him that he had missed everything in life, even the sweet and consoling love of a woman who would have helped him triumph over fate, bear his failure, and strengthen him to face the future.

Hortense, who was continually complaining of being condemned to live in Provence, sat for him merely to avoid scenes. To have to sit still for hours on end was no pleasure to her, particularly since Cézanne categorically forbade her to move. She had to sit 'like an apple.' 'Does an apple move?' he roared.

Once again Cézanne tried to break out of the oppressive circle of his isolation. He applied to Guillemet, asking his help for a portrait he had sent in to the Salon. Unfortunately the privilege of 'charity,' which Guillemet had invoked on his behalf two years before, had been abolished. There was nothing he could do, and the Hanging Committee rejected the canvas.

Disheartened though he must have been, Cézanne worked laboriously on: l'Estaque landscapes, bathers, portraits – of Hortense, his son and himself – and still lifes. With infinite patience, he organised the subjects of his still lifes, which he looked on as exercises and experiments. He arranged fruit, pots, knives, napkins, glasses of wine, bowls and bottles, blending or contrasting their colours, graduating their light and shade, slipping coins under the peaches and apples till the arrangement on the table assumed a design that satisfied his eye. 'The composition of colour!' he said. 'That's the whole secret. It was thus that Veronese composed.'

And yet, what if he were wrong? What if these arrangements were sublime only in his eyes. Perhaps he was as deluded as Frenhofer in *Le Chef-d'Oeuvre Inconnu*?

Cézanne had read this short novel by Balzac over and over again. For ten years, Frenhofer, a painter of genius, had been working on a canvas, *La Belle Noiseuse*, his masterpiece, which he concealed from prying eyes. But one day, intoxicated with success, he consented to show his picture. There was nothing to be seen but a confused mass of colours, a chaos of unrelated lines, from which emerged, by some miracle, one exquisite naked foot, which had 'escaped from the incredible, the slow and progressive destruction.'

When Cézanne looked at his own canvases he wondered whether they really made sense, or whether, like Frenhofer's *La Belle Noiseuse*, they were illusory, 'merely a sort of formless mess.' It was a strange coincidence that Balzac should have placed in Frenhofer's mouth phrases that Cézanne could have uttered today almost without the alteration of a word.*

'Frenhofer,' says one of his friends, 'is a man passionately devoted to art, who sees higher and further than other painters. He has thought profoundly about colour, about the absolute truth of line; but, as a

* 'Nature,' says Frenhofer, 'comprises a series of curves which interlace. Strictly speaking, drawing does not exist! . . . Line is the means by which man renders the effect of light on objects; but there is no line in nature, where everything is full: it is in modelling that one draws, that is to say one detaches things from their environment; the distribution of light alone gives bodies their appearance! . . . Perhaps it would be better not to draw a single line, but to attack an object by the centre, dealing first with the features that are most highly lit, and then go on later to the darker parts. Is this not what the sun, the divine painter of the universe, does?'

This may be compared with the following statements made by Cézanne:

'Light and shade are a relationship of colours; the two principal accents differ not by their general intensity but by their peculiar sonority.

'Pure drawing is an abstraction. Drawing and colour are not distinct since everything in nature is coloured.

'The form and contour of objects are revealed to us by their oppositions and contrasts which are the result of their particular colouring.

'One draws in the process of painting. Precision of tone gives at once the light and the shape of an object. The more the colour harmonises, the more precise becomes the drawing.

'Line and modelling do not exist. Drawing is a relationship between contrasts or simply the relationship between two tones, white and black.' (Recorded by Léo Larguier.)

'In an orange, an apple, a ball or a head, there is a culminating point; and that point is always – in spite of the terrible effect: light and shade, the sensation of colour – the nearest to our eye; the edges of objects recede towards a centre placed on our horizon.' (From a letter to Émile Bernard.)

result of his researches, he has begun to doubt even the object of his researches.'

'I am Frenhofer,' said Cézanne.

Like Frenhofer's, Cézanne's face was 'marked by the weariness of age, and still more by the thoughts that undermine both body and mind.' He was forty-six, but looked ten years older. He suffered agonies from neuralgia which, he said, deprived him at times of his lucidity.

Like Frenhofer, Cézanne suffered and doubted, moved blindly forward along his solitary path, wondering with anguish whether he was producing works of eternal value or merely mirages, whether he had dedicated his life to painting in vain.

CHAPTER TWO

The Bell-Tower of Gardanne

Car j'ai, pour fasciner ces dociles amants,
De purs miroirs qui font toutes choses plus belles:
Mes yeux, mes larges yeux aux clartés éternelles!

BAUDELAIRE: *La Beauté*

IN the spring of 1885, Cézanne fell in love with a servant girl at the Jas de Bouffan, called Fanny. She was healthy, vigorous, robust and not afraid of hard work. 'You'll see how good-looking the maid at the Jas is,' Cézanne said; 'she's just like a man!'*

Cézanne completely lost his head. One day, in his studio, he began drafting a letter to Fanny on the back of a drawing:

'I saw you, and you let me kiss you; from that moment I have been deeply disturbed. You will forgive a friend, who is tortured by anxiety, taking the liberty of writing to you. I do not know what view you will take of the liberty, which you may think a great one, but how can I bear the despondency that oppresses me? Is it not better to show one's feelings than to hide them? Why, I asked myself, conceal one's torment? Is it not a solace to suffering to give it expression? And if physical pain can find some amelioration in the cries of the sufferer, is it not natural, Madame, that mental sorrows should seek appeasement in a confession made to an adored being?

'I know well that this letter, whose premature and hazardous despatch may seem indiscreet, has nothing to recommend me to you but the kindness of . . .'†

* * *

Cézanne was far too unskilful to be able to conceal the adventure from his relations for long and they immediately turned on him.

* Reported by Jean de Beucken in *Un Portrait de Cézanne.*

† The rest of the draft has disappeared.

Hortense, who was well aware that the only remaining links between herself and Cézanne were the child and the paltry habits of sixteen years of life in common, bitterly defended her threatened security. Without being aware of it, she had an ally in Marie, who nevertheless despised her. Cézanne had already run far enough off the rails with his painting, his mistress and his illegitimate child. In no circumstances must he be permitted to add to them the absurd scandal of another immoral affair. He must marry Hortense; and the quicker the better.

Marie undertook to get Louis Auguste's consent. In June, Louis Auguste would be eighty-seven and his mind was failing. He was often detected hurrying off with what he hoped was a casual air to bury a handful of gold coins in the garden. Marie had acquired increasing authority at the Jas, though she left her father the illusion of power.

Cézanne attempted to put up a fight to preserve his new-found happiness, which he felt was giving him back his youth and his confidence in life. It appears, however, that Marie had sacked Fanny without delay.* Cézanne, for whom the slightest obstacle became a mountain, began making complicated plans. On 14 May, he asked Zola's help: 'I am writing to you,' he said, 'in the hope that you will be kind enough to do something for me. I want you to do me a service, which will mean nothing to you, but will be of great importance to me. It is to receive a few letters for me, and to forward them to the address I will give you later. I don't know whether I am mad or sane. *Trahit sua quemque voluptas!* I turn to you and implore your absolution; how happy the good are! Don't refuse me this service, I don't know where to turn.' But he must have felt rather embarrassed at always importuning Zola when he was in difficulties, and he added this curious postscript: 'I am insignificant and can do you no service; but since I shall die before you, I'll ask the Almighty to keep you a good place.'

But if Cézanne thought he was going to escape his sister, he was mistaken. In his battles with his father, he had always won in the end; he had agreed, promised and lied; but his yielding had been only simulated; Louis Auguste had been met with an exhausting non-

* There is much that remains obscure about this adventure.

resistance, which led him to retire from the field so that his victories were ultimately converted into defeats.

But these tactics were of no avail against Marie. She understood her brother far better than did Louis Auguste; and she was not to be taken in by such manoeuvres. She rated and nagged him incessantly. His life became intolerable. Desperately clinging to his love for Fanny, he struggled on, but the moment came when he realised he was cornered between Marie and Hortense. Panic-stricken, he seemed to have no other resort but flight. In the middle of June he fled to the north, and took refuge with the Renoirs at La Roche-Guyon.

He could not, however, prevent Hortense from following him with young Paul. In the past Hortense had let him go where he wished. She had never been concerned at his long absences. But things were very different now. She had no intention of allowing the father of her child to leave her. And the child, whom Cézanne adored, was her best card. The Renoirs, who must have been rather surprised by this sudden eruption, welcomed the discordant couple as best they could.

Hortense told them of her troubles. Cézanne pretended to indifference and tried to paint a view of La Roche-Guyon. But he was in such a state of agitation that he found it difficult to concentrate on his work. He was awaiting letters from Fanny, which Zola, whom he had kept informed, was to forward to the Poste Restante. But no letters came. Was Fanny faithless? Cézanne was very unhappy. He could stay at La Roche-Guyon no longer. Zola, who was at the moment in Paris, was soon due at Médan and Cézanne intended to stay with him. On 27 June, he asked Zola to let him know when he reached home.

But the days went by. Zola had not answered by 3 July. Cézanne wrote again. There was no letter from Zola on either the 4th or 5th. Cézanne was furious. And then, on the 6th, he suddenly realised he had forgotten to go to the Poste Restante to get his mail. There he found a line from Zola, who could not understand why Cézanne was in such a state of agitation. 'What is going on?' Zola was now at Médan, but his wife was ill. 'Can't you wait a few days?' he asked. But this was precisely what Cézanne could not do. Fanny had still not written. To stay at La Roche-Guyon any longer was out of the question. On 11 July, Cézanne suddenly left for Villennes, which was next door to Médan. At the first sign from Zola, he would go there at once. Moreover, while at Villennes, he intended borrowing Zola's boat from which to paint. But it was the eve of 14 July and Villennes was *en fête*. Cézanne was unable to find a room; the Sophora, the Berceau and the Hôtel du Nord were all full. He had to go down the Seine to Vernon, where he eventually managed to get into the Hôtel de Paris. He informed Zola on the 13th. But within forty-eight hours he had changed his mind and had decided impulsively that he would return to Aix. He had capitulated; and Marie and Hortense had won.

Nevertheless, before going back to the Midi, he decided he must stay at Médan. But the delay till Zola could have him seemed terribly long. Now that he had made his decision, he was in a hurry to leave Vernon. At last he got a line from Zola inviting him for the 22nd.

* * *

It was three years since they had met.

Les Rougon-Macquart had now reached thirteen volumes. *Au Bonheur des Dames* had appeared in 1883, *La Joie de Vivre* in 1884, and *Germinal* in March of this year. The presses were turning out Zola's books in ever increasing numbers. Even his old works, which had made no mark at the time of publication, were now finding a large public. For his *Thérèse Raquin*, which he had published in 1868, Zola had received royalties amounting to 13,000* francs. He was a rich man, would soon be as rich as old Louis Auguste. He was also a big eater and growing fat. He weighed fifteen stone and measured forty-four inches round the waist – figures that were a measure of his success, as were the yearly additions and embellishments to Médan. With every successful novel, a new wing, outbuildings or more land were added. The garden extended into a park, an avenue of limes had been planted, hothouses, pigeon lofts and a model farm built.

It seemed to Zola that Cézanne's failure and incapacity had been finally proved during these last three years. Now, on top of everything else, here was this ridiculous affair with a woman! Cézanne was clearly as incompetent to manage his life as he was his genius. 'I am chaste,' Zola sometimes said. 'Another woman than my wife? That's the way

* Approximately £2,000 today.

to waste time!' But it was clear that Hortense was partly responsible. Zola had never approved the liaison.

He hoped to show in his forthcoming book, of which Cézanne-Lantier would be the hero, not only 'the struggle of the artist against nature,' but also 'the struggle of woman against art.' However that might be, *chasque toupin trovo sa cabucello*,* as they said in Provence; God made people and paired them off. Poor Paul! Who would have thought in those distant schooldays that it would all come to this? It was a tragic failure. 'Incessant struggle, ten hours' work a day, the devotion of his whole being. Then, what? After twenty years of passionate endeavour, to end up like this . . .' In spite of his long friendship with Cézanne, Zola had yielded to his wife's prejudices. In the circumstances, it was hardly fitting that this failure's canvases should continue to hang where visitors could see them. They were relegated to the attic.† Zola was upset and rather embarrassed. On his huge desk, there reposed a manuscript to which he added a few pages every day. It was the manuscript of his next novel, the fourteenth volume of the *Rougon-Macquart* series, *L'Oeuvre*, the novel of which Claude Lantier – or Cézanne – was the hero. He had begun writing it two and a half months ago and now Zola's central character was here under his eye.

But Cézanne did not linger at Médan. In his nervous state, he found its ostentation intolerable. He suddenly called to mind the letter Zola had written to him at the end of the war of 1870: 'I feel rather sorry that all the fools aren't dead, but it consoles me to think that we are all still alive. We can take up the struggle again.' When Zola made a parade of his acquaintances and told him that he had recently dined 'with a great man,' Cézanne could not resist reminding him of his letter: 'All the same,' he said, 'if all the fools had died, you'd have to eat your stew at home, alone with that bourgeoise of a wife of yours!'

Zola was offended, and the two friends parted.

A few days later, much concerned as always about his health and

* Provençal for: 'Every pot finds its cover.'

† Zola possessed about ten of Cézanne's works, among which were: *Le Poêle dans l'Atelier*, *l'Enlèvement*, *La Pendule de Marbre noir*, *Une Lecture chez Zola*, *L'Estaque* and two portraits.

terrified by the thought that he might be suffering from diabetes, Zola left with his wife for Mont-Dore to take the cure.

* * *

Cézanne returned to the Jas de Bouffan, over which Marie now reigned; and there, grumbling and discontented, he surrendered. 'If I only had a family who didn't interfere, everything would be all right.' Though shaken by his emotional crisis, he began working again.

Disliking the atmosphere at the Jas, he went every day to Gardanne, a small town of some four thousand inhabitants ten kilometres from Aix, where Hortense was now living. It was, of course, all over between them. He had accepted his fate. His life was dust and ashes. 'A brothel in the town, or what have you, but nothing else. I pay – it's a disgusting word – but I need peace, and at a price I can get it,' he wrote to Zola.

Cézanne had found a subject for painting in Gardanne. The old houses rose steeply along the narrow streets to a mound on which stood a square bell-tower, and with his brushes Cézanne explored its forms and organised its volumes. Painting may have been like a hair shirt to him; he was nervous, unhappy and disgusted; but never before had he approached a landscape with such profound understanding.

CHAPTER THREE

Claude Lantier

> The latest to appear is always a monster, the black sheep of the flock. The artistic history of recent times is there to prove the truth of this fact, and simple logic is sufficient to make one conjecture that it will inevitably happen again, so long as the public will not place itself at the sole viewpoint from which a work of art can be judged sanely.
> —ÉMILE ZOLA: *Édouard Manet* (1867)

CÉZANNE, finally tiring of journeying from Aix to Gardanne every day, decided to live in Gardanne with Hortense, who was very soon to become his legal wife. They planned to be married in the spring.

They lived in a flat in the Boulevard de Forbin, a pretty street lined with four rows of plane trees, at the foot of the old town. Cézanne's worries had affected his health; he felt tired and physically weak. 'I should like to have had the intellectual balance that characterises you,' he wrote to Chocquet . . . 'But chance has denied me so firm a base, it's the one regret I have in the world.' Sometimes, in the evenings, he went to the café to meet the local doctor and Jules Peyron, a civil servant, who occasionally sat for him. He bought a donkey to carry his painting things, but it gave him a great deal of trouble. Sometimes it would trot on far ahead of him, and at others stick its toes in and refuse to move at all. Neither kindness nor beating could make it see reason. In the end Cézanne simply had to give in to its whims.

His expeditions sometimes lasted several days; he ate with the peasants and, if they had no bed available, he slept in their barns. He painted Gardanne and its bell-tower, its old mills, and also Mont Sainte-Victoire rising in the distance, its base partly obscured by the Mont du Cengle. His thoughts were increasingly preoccupied by the silent majesty of these bare hills. 'There are treasures to be captured in this countryside, which have not yet found an interpreter worthy of the riches they reveal,' he wrote to Chocquet.

Occasionally, on a Sunday, Marion, with whom he had renewed contact, came to visit him. For the last six years Marion, who was now nearly forty, had been director of the Natural History Museum of Marseilles, but his artistic enthusiasms were still very much alive and he continued to paint as an amateur. He and Cézanne once more set up their easels side by side and, while they painted, Marion talked of the geology of this countryside, and of the cataclysmic pressures that had determined its structure. As Cézanne listened to him, the plain, the hills, the strata of the rocks, and the pyramid of Mont Sainte-Victoire gradually assumed a profound existence of their own, that must somehow be interpreted with little paint and much simplicity.

* * *

On the morning of 23 February, Zola was writing the last pages of *L'Oeuvre*, in which Claude Lantier, in despair at his artistic impotence, had hanged himself. He was being buried in the Saint-Ouen cemetery. At the graveside, Claude's friend, the novelist Sandoz (Zola), was standing beside an old painter named Bongrand.

'It seemed to him,' Zola wrote, 'that his youth was being buried; it was the best part of himself, his illusions and enthusiasms, that the sextons were putting into a hole in the ground . . . They lowered the coffin into it, the aspersorium was passed round. It was all over . . .'

Zola went on:

'Everyone was moving away, the surpliced priest and the choirboy disappeared behind the green trees, and the neighbours dispersed, loitering among the graves and reading the inscriptions.

'And Sandoz, as he was about to leave the half-filled grave, said: "We alone knew him . . . And there's nothing left, not even a name!"

' "He's happy now," said Bongrand, "he has no picture on the stocks in the earth he's sleeping in . . . It's better to go than to work unremittingly to produce crippled children as we do; children that are always imperfect, lacking legs or heads, and fail to come alive."

' "Yes, one has to put one's pride in one's pocket, resign oneself to the *more or less* and cheat with life . . . I carry my books through to the end, but I despise myself because I feel they are incomplete and untrue, in spite of all the effort I expend on them."

'Their faces pale, they walked slowly away, side by side, past the white graves of children, the novelist then at the height of his powers and fame, the painter growing old, and immensely celebrated.

' "At least there was one man who had both courage and logic," Sandoz said. "He admitted his impotence and killed himself . . ." '

On the last page, Zola wrote:

' "Christ, eleven o'clock!" said Bongrand, looking at his watch. "I must go home."

'Sandoz exclaimed in surprise.

' "What! Eleven o'clock already!"

'He looked round in despair at the low gravestones, across the huge cemetery that seemed strewn with cold rows of pearls, and still blinded with tears, he said: "We must go back to work." '

Zola must have heaved a sigh of relief as he came to the end, for he was being pressed by the editor of *Le Gil Blas* which was publishing his new novel as a serial. 'I'm thankful to have finished it, and I'm very pleased with the end, what's more,' he wrote to Henri Céard.

The serial aroused a great deal of comment in the art world. It was known to be a *roman à clef*. There was much dissatisfaction among the Impressionists, to whom it seemed that Zola was betraying his old friends. 'They get no further than sketches,' he had written, 'they are recorders of hasty impressions, there is not one among them who seems to have the power to become the awaited master.'

Zola certainly gave proof in his novel – if proof were needed – that he understood nothing about painting. The artists of whom he wrote were Impressionists, but he described their works in terms that would have been more suited to the worst kind of academic art. But was the public likely ro realise this? More probably it would take it as an encouragement to jeer at the Impressionists once again.

L'Oeuvre marked a break. To the Impressionists, Zola appeared to have gone over to their adversaries. At the very moment they were beginning to find a small public Zola was castigating them as impotent failures. Monet wrote to Zola: 'I have been struggling for a long time now, and I fear that at the very moment we are getting somewhere, our enemies will use your book to confound us.'

But who was Claude Lantier? Was it Manet, as many people

thought? It occurred to no one in Paris to suggest the name of Cézanne. That name meant little to anyone. To a schoolboy, who asked him for the key to the characters in his novel, Zola replied evasively: 'What is the use of giving you names? They are all failures of whom you have doubtless never heard.'*

Cézanne received a copy of *L'Oeuvre* at Gardanne. If the originals of Zola's characters were an intriguing mystery to the public and even to some of the author's friends, this was not the case with him. With considerable emotion he read the descriptions of their youth together, of the Collège Bourbon, of their rambles in the Aix countryside, of swimming in the Arc, and of their dreams of fame.

All their old friends were there, drawn more or less true to life: Baille, who in the novel was an architect called Dubuche; Solari, who remained the sculptor he in fact was under the name of Mahoudeau; and Alexis (Jory), Guillemet (Fagerolles), Chaillan (Chaîne) . . . The Thursday dinners at Zola's, the meetings in the Café Guerbois (the Café Baudequin), the story of Solari's crumbling statue and the holidays at Bennecourt in 1866 were all there. Cézanne found his attitudes, his gestures, his own words recorded. When Lantier said that the day would come 'when a single original carrot would be pregnant with revolution,' it was undoubtedly himself speaking. And so was the painter who 'struggled unceasingly,' 'worked madly,' was ravaged by doubts, and mocked by the public; who lamented that he could not realise his intentions, destroyed his canvases, and 'kicked the furniture' when his work did not come out as he hoped. There could be no possible doubt about all this.

As he went on reading, he found the portrait Zola had drawn of him increasingly intolerable. Zola had made it perfectly plain that he considered him a hopeless failure, a pathetic character, an abortive genius who would never succeed. Cézanne wept as he read the five hundred pages containing the condemnation of his whole life. So this was what his friend thought of him!

It was not that he expected Zola to understand. But that his friend's opinion of him should be so brutally expressed, that he should see no redeeming feature, and that he should identify him with this crazy,

* The schoolboy was Gustave Coquiot, the future art critic.

pusillanimous, hysterical character, confounded him. He knew very well, of course, how Zola had concocted *L'Oeuvre*. In his usual way he had accumulated quantities of notes, assembled his memories, asked all his friends for information concerning every aspect of the world of art, the picture dealers, the collectors (even Chocquet appeared in the novel under the name of M. Hue), the tools of the trade, the models and the intrigues of the Salon. And then he had simply sat down and written his book, ingenuously and without malice. He had not intended to wound. It had never occurred to him that he might do so. He had simply wanted to write a book.

Cézanne was also aware that Claude Lantier was a composite character; and, as a character, suffered from the Rougon-Macquart heredity. But this, in a sense, made the book the more atrocious. For, though he was writing a work of fiction, Zola had made it clear what he thought of Cézanne's work. It was evident to Cézanne that he inspired Zola with nothing but pity, and pity was more wounding than insult. Where was their friendship now? The misunderstandings which had partially eroded it through the years, were here made tragically manifest. Their friendship had survived only through compromise, a tacit silence about the work that was Cézanne's whole life. Cézanne had accepted that silence, had been able to delude himself that, in spite of everything, it was implicit with a certain modesty. But now it was revealed as nothing but a lie. Finally, Zola had made Claude Lantier kill himself!

But, in fact, when a painting failed to come out right, you did not kill yourself; you put it on the fire and began another. It seemed probable that Zola had put as much of himself into Claude Lantier as he had of Cézanne. Perhaps, like Lantier, Zola would have killed himself had he suffered constant indifference and contempt.

In a sense, the whole book could be reduced to terms of social ambition; popular success, money, the need to be revered as a master; all this was true of Zola, who in his heart was gnawed by doubts from which he could escape only by continual and fantastic labour.

To Cézanne there now seemed to be little use in continuing to pretend to friendship. It would be unworthy of what they had been to each other for so many years. He could not bear the thought of a parody of their relationship; and his disappointment was irremediable. Everything was finished between them. He would reply to Zola; but in no circumstances would he admit that he had been mortally wounded. He would behave as if nothing had happened, as if *L'Oeuvre* had caused him no pain at all. Assuming a studied calm, he wrote Zola a brief letter of acknowledgment:

Gardanne, 4 April, 1886.

My dear Émile,

I have just received *L'Oeuvre*, which you were good enough to send to me. I thank the author of *Les Rougon-Macquart* for this kind token of remembrance and ask him to permit me to clasp his hand at the thought of bygone years.

Ever yours under the impulse of past times.

Paul Cézanne.

It was an embarrassed and impersonal note and the last he would ever write to Zola, his old friend.*

* * *

Three weeks later, on 28 April, Cézanne married Hortense at the Aix Mairie. The ceremony was only a formality. Cézanne gave a luncheon to the witnesses, among whom were his brother-in-law Conil and his friend from Gardanne, Jules Peyron, while Hortense went back to the Jas de Bouffan with young Paul (who was now fourteen) and her parents-in-law. The next day, when the religious ceremony took place in the church of Saint-Jean-Baptiste in the Cours Sextius, no one was present except Maxime Conil and Marie.

Life went on exactly as before.

During her stay at the Jas, Hortense had realised that for her parents-in-law, and above all for Marie Cézanne, she would never be anything but an intruder. She was only tolerated. There was no question of her having a real place in the Cézanne family.

Louis Auguste was merely clinging to life now, and Marie reigned

* A few years later, Vollard saw Cézanne furiously tear a canvas to pieces merely at the mention of *L'Oeuvre*.

at the Jas. She ran everyone and everything and interfered in her sister's and brother's married lives. Difficult, meddlesome and outspoken, she terrified Hortense, who returned thankfully to live at Gardanne – which was what Marie desired. Cézanne's mother desired it too, for Paul remained her favourite child, and she wanted to see as much of him as possible, and on his own.

She was jealous of Hortense; and her son's affection for her encouraged her in this. Cézanne undoubtedly preferred to come to the Jas by himself. He still looked on it as his real home; and he often stayed there, leaving Hortense behind at Gardanne. Now that his friendship with Zola was dead, his mother's love was the one consolation in his loneliness, and in his disappointments in art, marriage and friendship. It was a shelter from a hostile world. At the Jas, he could once more become the child who in the past had taken refuge from Louis Auguste's anger in the safety of his mother's skirts. Marie, too, regained all her old prestige in his eyes. She was, he said, 'really the eldest.' He was continually astonished by the fact that she always knew exactly what she wanted, and that she was so clever at sorting out family difficulties, which seemed to him insoluble, quite apart from the fact that the last thing he wanted was to have to deal with them himself.

* * *

In November 1885 Monticelli had had a stroke, and he died on 29 June, 1886.

At about the same time Cézanne paid a short visit to Paris. He went to Père Tanguy's shop, the only place in the capital where his work could now be seen.

Tanguy had failed to grow rich as a picture dealer. The canvases which painters had pledged with him for tubes of paint rarely found buyers. His narrow, crowded shop was cluttered with pictures by Cézanne, Gauguin, Guillaumin, Pissarro, and also by a Dutch painter who had recently come to Paris and for whom Tanguy had developed a great affection: Vincent Van Gogh.

Nor could Tanguy get very good prices for those works he did sell. As far as Cézanne, his favourite painter, was concerned, he had divided his canvases into two categories: the small and the large. He sold the small ones for 40 francs and the large ones for 100.* It was true, of course, that Tanguy was not a very good salesman. He was apt to become attached to a picture and ask some absurd price for it, such as four, five or even six hundred francs, to discourage a customer from buying it. Nor was he prepared to gossip about Cézanne or any other of *his* painters with people he did not know. Since 1870, he had been in considerable fear of the government. How was he to know these strangers were not police spies? Suppose the government, on the pretext that they were revolutionaries, threw the painters of the 'School,' as Tanguy called it, into prison? Silent and taciturn, he would go into the back shop and bring out canvases done up in a parcel, which he would slowly unwrap; then, one by one, his eyes clouded with emotion, he would place them on chairs and wait for the customer's decision without uttering a word. Only to the habitués would he talk a little, and they were for the most part young artists. Waving a finger, he would say: 'Look at that sky! That tree! It's come off, hasn't it? Look at that, and that!' But young artists could not afford to buy. Tanguy gradually succeeded in communicating his enthusiasm for Cézanne to them, but he remained as poor as ever. Not that this prevented his sharing the little he had: it would have been an insult to refuse an invitation to his frugal table. He was in continual financial difficulties. Only the year before, when on the point of being sold up by his landlord, and had had to send a pressing appeal to Cézanne who, through the years, had accumulated a debt with him that now amounted to rather more than 4,000 francs.†

In his isolation in Provence Cézanne was unaware that the canvases he had left with Tanguy were attracting increasing attention among the shop's habitués; and that some went there, as if to a museum, to study his work and discuss it. Pissarro, too, was ever more admiring and even, on occasion, bought some of his friend's canvases. He told his

* Approximately £7 and £17 today. 'There were also,' reported Vollard, 'canvases on which Cézanne had painted studies of various subjects. He left it to Tanguy to separate them. These little studies were intended for art lovers who had not a 100 francs, nor even 40. And so Tanguy, scissors in hand, could be seen cutting out little subjects, while some poor purchaser, handing him a *louis*, waited to take away three apples by Cézanne.'

† Approximately £700 today.

sons: 'If you want to learn to paint, look at Cézanne.' Three years before, in 1883, he had reproached Huysmans, who had just published his *L'Art Moderne*, for having made no more than a very slight allusion to Cézanne. 'Will you permit me to say, my dear Huysmans, that you have allowed yourself to be carried away by literary theories which are applicable only to the school of Gérome . . . modernised?'*

Gauguin, who had given up the stock-exchange and the bank three years previously to adopt the uncertain profession of painter, was becoming increasingly sure that Cézanne's work would sooner or later be of outstanding importance, and poor though he now was, refused to allow his wife to sell his Cézannes. In the previous November, he had written to her about two of them: 'I am attached to my two Cézannes, which are rare of their kind, for he has completed few of them, and one day they will be very valuable indeed,' he prophesied.† Pissarro and Gauguin had taken to Tanguy's shop a young painter, called Paul Signac, who was a fervent adherent of 'divisionnisme.' He was sufficiently impressed by Cézanne's work to buy a landscape painted in the valley of the Oise. And there were many other young artists who came to see Tanguy's Cézannes, notably Émile Bernard, then aged eighteen, who at once became an enthusiastic supporter.

* 'Cézanne's personality,' Huysmans replied, 'is profoundly sympathetic to me, for I know through Zola his efforts, vexations and defeats, when he is struggling to succeed in a work! Yes, he has temperament and is an artist, but taken all in all, if I except a few still lifes which come off, the rest, in my opinion, is not viable. It's interesting, curious and thought provoking, but there is certainly something wrong with his eyes, which, so I am told, he realises himself . . . In my humble opinion, Cézanne's work is typical of unsuccessful Impressionism. After all, you must realise that after so many years of struggle, it can no longer be merely a question of more or less manifest intentions, made more or less apparent, but of complete works, serious offspring, which are not jokes, or curious cases that might find a place in some Dubuytren Museum of painting . . .' This is obviously an echo of Médan opinion. Huysmans was one of Zola's intimate circle.

† In a letter to Émile Schuffenecker, of 14 January, 1885, Gauguin said: 'Look at Cézanne, that misunderstood man, whose nature is essentially mystical and oriental (his face is like an old Levantine's), his form has all the mystery and oppressive tranquillity of a man lying down to dream, his colour has the gravity of the oriental character; he is a man of the Midi, and spends whole days on the tops of mountains reading Virgil and gazing at the sky; his horizons are lofty, his blues very intense and his reds have an astonishing vibrancy.'

They at least gave hope for the future. Perhaps in the end, people's eyes would be opened and the 'School' would triumph. Meanwhile, it was a pity that Zola had written *L'Oeuvre*. 'It's not right! It's not right!' lamented Tanguy. 'I would never have thought it of M. Zola, who is such a nice man and the friend of these gentlemen! He hasn't understood them! It's a great misfortune!'

Cézanne was doubtless pleased to hear from Tanguy that his work was not held in quite such contempt as he supposed. But, though in itself encouraging, it could not matter much to him that a few artists, as unknown and despised as himself, should admire his painting; it did not affect the basic problem. Nor was he in sympathy with the work and intentions of many of these young painters. As is so often the case with the great creators, men who live in their own universe and are concerned only with their own dreams and their own researches, Cézanne was never able to appreciate work that showed too great a divergence from his own.

One day during this summer, Tanguy invited him to luncheon to meet Van Gogh. Though they shared many enthusiasms, particularly an admiration for Delacroix, Cézanne was not favourably impressed by the Dutchman's passion and frenzy, which were as manifest in his conversation as in his painting. Cézanne was both surprised and rather shocked. He could not understand Van Gogh at all, and his work aroused his disapproval. 'In all sincerity,' Cézanne said, 'you paint like a madman!'

* * *

Before returning to the Midi, Cézanne went to stay for a while with Chocquet at Hattenville, in Normandy.

Victor Chocquet was now very comfortably off, having received an unexpected legacy. But it had brought him little happiness, for the death of his only daughter had clouded his old age. He was a sad and melancholy man.

While at Hattenville, Cézanne painted another portrait of him. But the painter did not stay long in Normandy. He returned almost at once to Aix, to Hortense, Marie, his mother, and the Jas de Bouffan, to the hills and the grandeur of the Provençal countryside. He had few illusions left; it would have needed a greater self-confidence than his to be able to convince himself, at the age of forty-seven, that there could be any change in his fortunes now. If he continued to paint, it was purely from compulsion.

On 23 October, Louis Auguste died in Aix at the age of eighty-eight.

CHAPTER FOUR

The Big Pine

> There is a passing moment in the world. Paint it in its reality! Forget everything else for that.—CÉZANNE

LOUIS AUGUSTE left each of his three children 400,000 francs.* It provided Cézanne with an income of some 25,000 francs,† but made no difference to his way of life. Once he had paid his keep and bought his painting materials, money held no interest for him. He disliked luxury in any form, and the idea of spending money on amusements simply did not occur to him.

Hortense, on the other hand, took a different view. Until now, she had been forced to live a parsimonious life, which had been aggravated by constantly moving house. She had not particularly minded these changes of scene as such, for she liked travelling and staying in hotels; but to go on living as if they still had no more than 150 francs a month seemed to her quite absurd. When you had money, you might as well take advantage of it. Under the disapproving eye of Marie, who considered Hortense extravagant, Cézanne gave his wife whatever money she asked for. Hortense enjoyed the little pleasures of life and she was bored in Provence; she wanted to return to Paris and soon announced that the climate of the Midi did not suit her.

But, at the moment, Paris had nothing to offer Cézanne. He was obsessed by Mont Sainte-Victoire, and painted it from many different viewpoints. Since his brother-in-law, Conil, had bought the property of Montbriant, not far from the Jas de Bouffan, two years before, he frequently went and set up his easel there.

He had found an ideal subject. Stretching away towards the mountain lay the valley of the Arc, cut on the right by the horizontal line of the viaduct. It made a perfect picture. He also often

* Approximately £65,000 today.

† Approximately £4,000 today.

went into the hills overlooking the Tholonet road,* and he took a room in the Château Noir, near the Bibémus quarry where, thirty years ago he, Zola and Baille had walked in the pine-woods, reciting verses.

Now he probed and analysed, and in doing so Cézanne came to the remarkable conclusion that symmetry imposed on objects in representation was a lie. When you examined a form attentively and minutely, you saw that the part on which the light fell increased in size, expanding in a wealth of tones, while that part which lay in shadow was reduced, attenuated and unified. Similarly with the verticality and stability of objects. It was not thus they presented themselves to the eye; it was the mind that lent them these characteristics. Symmetry and verticality were merely intellectual habits. Obsessed with the desire to paint exactly what he saw, Cézanne pondered whether to take his fidelity of vision to its ultimate extreme and refused to adhere to what was universally accepted as truth.

The effect on his painting was considerable; the sides of a vase (as in *Le Vase Bleu*) were no longer in proportion, the walls of a house tilted, and the world seemed to reel.† Cézanne had ceased to belong to his period as a painter. Now he was moving towards the future. Solitary, uncertain and self-doubting, he pondered painfully on what he was about. Could he be wrong? Physically he was becoming weaker, and he felt unhappy and persecuted. Life was gradually crushing him. He was becoming afraid of everything, of ordinary daily life, of people and their 'grapnels,' of the silent forces of the earth. He was afraid of death and of the beyond.

In his alarm, he abandoned himself increasingly to the influences of

* Today, the Route Paul-Cézanne.

† René Huyghe and Bernard Dorival have analysed this temporary characteristic of Cézanne's art. 'In us,' writes René Huyghe, 'life has made indissoluble the sensation and the idea we have of it, to such an extent that perfect sensory exactitude becomes a human inexactitude. In his obsession to achieve a sensory absolute, Cézanne strayed from the familiar and the recognised to the extent that the public accused his eye of error when his only fault was to yield to an over rigorous precision . . . The Latin,' René Huyghe continues, 'knows only one extreme: that of logic . . . There is a madness of truth as there is a "madness of the cross." Cézanne knew it and lived it and it is that which gives his work its ardent and dramatic quality.'

his mother and sister. Yielding to Marie's persuasion, he had even begun going to church. A church was a refuge. 'I still feel I have a little time left on earth: but afterwards? I believe I shall survive, and I don't want to run the risk of roasting *in aeternum*.' Though he mistrusted priests, and mingled both suspicion and irony with his respect for religion, he went to confession and communion, and found a certain peace and consolation in the services.

Scorned as an artist, he was uncertain whether his audacities were inspired by greatness or delirium. To be able to go on, to advance a little further, he had to struggle unremittingly against self-doubt. Every aspect of his life seemed to be one of unrelieved failure. And now his acceptance of at least one form of conformity was the reverse of a medal whose obverse was heroism.

* * *

'On the farther bank of the Seine, the Quai des Ormes* was bordered by little grey houses, chequered on the ground floor by the wooden fronts of shops while, above, the wavering line of their roofs stood out against the sky; the horizon . . . was bounded by the blue slates of the roof of the Hôtel de Ville on the left, and the lead dome of Saint-Paul on the right . . . Strange shapes crowded the water, a dormant flotilla of rowing boats and gigs, a wash-boat and a dredger, moored to the quay; then, over by the other bank, lighters full of coal and barges full of stone, dominated by the gigantic arm of an iron crane.'

It was thus Zola described in *L'Oeuvre* the north bank of the Île Saint-Louis, where his hero, Claude Lantier, had his studio. It was here, at 15, Quai d'Anjou, that Cézanne came to live on his return to Paris in 1888. Guillaumin, who was his neighbour at No. 13, very probably told him of the vacant flat.

No. 15, Quai d'Anjou is a seventeenth-century house, probably built by Louis Le Vau in about 1645 for Nicolas Lambert de Thorigny, President of the Chambre des Comptes. No. 17, nearby, is the famous Hôtel Lauzun, where Baudelaire lived for some time in his youth.

* Today the Quai de l'Hôtel-de-Ville.

Cézanne's flat, on the second floor, overlooked the Seine and the quays. It was a peaceful district and had always attracted painters.*

But Cézanne could find no peace. His health was becoming increasingly precarious and he felt incapable of remaining long in the same place. Sometimes he worked at the Quai d'Anjou, sometimes in a studio he had leased in the Rue du Val-de-Grace; or, again, he left Paris and fled to the banks of the Marne. Chocquet had asked him to decorate his house in the Rue Monsigny, and he made two sketches before abandoning the project.

On the other hand, he was working hard in his studio in the Rue du Val-de-Grace on a *Mardi Gras* subject, for which his son, dressed as Harlequin, and the son of Guillaume the cobbler, dressed as Pierrot, were his models. For hours on end the boys were made to hold their poses, for Cézanne would tolerate neither fatigue nor weakness. One day Guillaume's son fainted.

Nearly every afternoon Cézanne went to work in the Louvre, to consider and reconsider his art in front of the Poussins, the Rubens and the Veroneses. 'The Louvre is the book from which we learn to read,' he said.

He went to Chantilly, where he stayed in the Hôtel Delacourt. He remained there for five months, painting pictures that might well have been inspired by the Midi, for he treated the misty landscapes of the Île-de-France very much in the same manner as the harsher countryside of Provence. Wherever he was, whether in the north or in the south, he was now painting only 'Cézannes.' His art was continually evolving. Not only had he succeeded in fusing the contradictory elements of sensation and intellect, but he was softening the rigour and abstraction of his classicism. Maturely considered and strictly constructed, every canvas was alight with comprehension. He pursued his researches into the art of painting with the ardent and passionate determination of one whose work was not only loved but understood and eagerly awaited.

For all Cèzanne knew, this was certainly not the case. Cloistered in

* Daumier lived for seventeen years at 9, Quai d'Anjou. On the same bank of the Île Saint-Louis, Philippe de Champaigne lived on the Quai Bourbon, as did Meissonier, who built a medieval watch-tower there.

his isolation, he was still hardly aware that artists, art lovers and critics were visiting Tanguy's shop in increasing numbers to see his canvases. For some the shop was 'a chamber of horrors'; but, for others, it was a 'museum of the future.'*

Tanguy's devotion and the way he had of 'lowering his eyes to a picture with the tenderness of a mother imploring admiration of a beloved child,' impressed those who entered the shop in the Rue Clauzel. Were these pictures horrors? Or would they live? It was clearly time to assess this phenomenon Cézanne. On 4 August, *La Cravache* published an article by Huysmans, in which the writer tried to analyse Cézanne's art together with that of the second-rate Tisson and of a Sunday painter, the clown Wagner†: 'To sum up, he is a revealing colourist, who has contributed more than the late Manet to the Impressionist movement, but an artist with sick eyes who, in the wild misconceptions of his vision, has discovered the premonitory symptoms of a new art, and thus it would seem may be summarised the too neglected painter, M. Cézanne.'

As a constant visitor to Médan, Huysmans was certainly aware that Zola had used Cézanne for one of the characters in his book. Confusing the painter with the hero of *L'Oeuvre*, he attributed to Cézanne that sickness of the eyes which Claude Lantier had inherited. Cézanne's work disconcerted the critic so much that he had to explain his unease pathologically.

It is not known whether Cézanne ever saw Huysmans' article, though it was the first any critic had devoted to him since the Impressionist exhibitions. Nor do we know what happened to Cézanne during the next few months, beyond the fact that he was moving, haphazardly and unhappily, from place to place. But he was back at the Jas de Bouffan when Renoir passed through Provence in the winter.

Renoir was amazed by Cézanne's canvases. Never had he imagined that Cézanne could have attained to such power of expression. 'How does he do it? He can't put two touches of paint on a canvas without its succeeding.' To watch Cézanne at his easel, gazing at the landscape with 'ardent, concentrated, attentive and respectful' eyes was 'an

* Émile Bernard.

† The article was reprinted the following year in *Certains*.

unforgettable sight.'* As for Cézanne, the world around him ceased to exist when he concentrated on his subject. Every day he went back to the same place, working patiently and indefatigably on his canvas.

Renoir was convinced that here, living in obscurity, was one of the great artists of the world. But how disconcerting the man could be. Suddenly despairing of obtaining the effect he wanted, he would rip his canvas to pieces. Or he would go home to the Jas de Bouffan utterly depressed and discouraged, having discarded his canvas among the rocks of the hillside. It needed very little to exasperate him. When an old woman, carrying her knitting, came near while he was painting, Cézanne shouted in fury: 'Look at that old cow coming!' And, in spite of Renoir's protests, he gathered his painting things together and hurried off as if pursued by the devil.

Nor was it long before Renoir became the victim of Cézanne's ill-humour. He had been well entertained at the Jas de Bouffan, had enjoyed 'good fennel soups,'† prepared by Cézanne's mother who, like all good cooks, delighted in detailing her recipes. But, one day, Renoir, thinking no harm, unfortunately made a joke about bankers, and Cézanne – supported by his mother ('Really, Paul, in your father's house!') – turned on him.

Renoir left the Jas de Bouffan much upset.‡

* * *

Cézanne returned to the Quai d'Anjou.

In this year, 1889 – it was the year the Eiffel Tower was built – a Universal Exhibition was to be held in Paris and was to include an important Fine Arts section. Chocquet had been asked to lend one of his valuable pieces of furniture. He had agreed, but out of devotion to Cézanne had demanded, as a *quid pro quo*, that one of his friend's canvases should be exhibited; the organisers assented. *La Maison du Pendu* (which Chocquet had exchanged with Comte Doria for *Neige fondante en Forêt de Fontainebleau*) was selected.

* Reminiscences of Renoir reported by Gustave Geffroy in *La Vie Artistique*, Vol. III.

† Reminiscences of Renoir recorded by Ambroise Vollard in *En écoutant Cézanne, Degas, Renoir*.

‡ He went to live at Montbriant, which he had leased from Maxime Conil.

However, Cézanne had little reason to congratulate himself. Though the organisers had agreed to hang the picture, they had given no guarantee as to how they would hang it. They placed it high under the roof where no one could see it.

In the autumn, however, he received a letter from Octave Maus, secretary of the Brussels Art Society, which was called the 'XX,' inviting him to take part, together with Van Gogh and Sisley, in a forthcoming exhibition.

Cézanne hastened to respond to the 'flattering' invitation. He sent two landscapes and a *Baigneuses* to Brussels. The exhibition opened on 18 January in the Royal Museum of Modern Art. It was a further disappointment. He received 'not even the honour of a controversy!'* Only one journalist appeared to notice that his canvases were there; and he made the contemptuous comment: 'Sincere daubing.'†

Most of the Impressionist painters had now won at least a modest reputation and people were collecting their paintings. Some were paying as much as 2,000 francs for a Pissarro. The previous year, Théo Van Gogh, Vincent's brother, had even sold a Monet to an American for 9,000 francs.‡ Cézanne alone remained unknown and unappreciated. He was now fifty-one and already looked an old man. His beard and the hair that fell over his collar had turned white. His health was growing worse.

The cause had now been diagnosed. He was suffering from diabetes, and had to submit to a regime, though he did not always follow it. He sometimes had to interrupt his work from sheer physical debility. His disease increased his irritability and his temper became ever more difficult. He was often impatient, intolerant and rude. He would grow furious at the mere mention of a member of the Institute or a teacher at the École des Beaux-Arts. The slightest noise had become torture to him. A waggon's squeaking wheel or a street-seller's cry was apt to produce a convulsive fit of anger; and was liable to become a pre-

* Émile Bernard.

† *La Fédération Artistique Belge*, 26 January, 1890 (quoted by A. Vollard, in *En écoutant Cézanne, Degas, Renoir*).

‡ Approximately £1,500 today.

text for moving house. Even the quiet of the Île Saint-Louis was not enough; and he went to live in the Avenue d'Orléans.

Everything seemed to be going wrong. Chocquet had just died; and Cézanne was very distressed. In Chocquet he had lost not only a friend but also one of his greatest admirers. As for Hortense, she had no wish to return to Aix. Her father had recently died, and as she had to go to her native Jura to attend to family business, she wished to take advantage of the opportunity to go on to Switzerland. Cézanne wearily agreed. Marie was not on hand to put a stop to Hortense's plans, nor indeed to give her brother advice about the organisation of his family budget.

Cézanne had found an admirably simple solution for dealing with the family finances. He divided his income into twelve monthly parts, and then re-divided these into three equal parts: one for his wife, one for his son (who had turned eighteen in January), and one for himself. Unfortunately, Hortense frequently upset this arrangement by spending more than her share and then trying to appropriate as much as she could of her husband's. She found him a great deal more amenable than young Paul who, though utterly insensitive to his father's work, was no fool and had, indeed, much commonsense, a fact which Cézanne recognised with astonishment and admiration.

During the summer, therefore, at Hortense's insistence, they all three went to stay for a while in the neighbourhood of Besançon. Cézanne painted a few landscapes on the banks of the Ognon, a tributary of the Saône. Then they crossed the frontier and stayed at the Hôtel du Soleil, at Neuchâtel.

Hortense liked the town and the easy hotel life. She was in no hurry to move away. Cézanne, on the other hand, did not care for Switzerland at all. He felt out of his element. At the *table d'hôte*, in the hotel, he found himself among strangers to whom he had nothing to say. He was sullen and talked to no one, except a Prussian who showed him 'some sympathy.'* He tried to paint and set up his easel beside the lake or in the valley of the Areuse. But the Swiss landscape, so different from that of Provence, was alien to him, and his inability to seize on its character discouraged him. When, after some weeks, Hortense

* Letter from Alexis to Zola, 13 February, 1891.

finally decided to move, Cézanne left two canvases, with which he had made little progress, in the hotel.*

An unwilling tourist, Cézanne was led protesting first to Berne and then to Fribourg. Wandering through the streets of Fribourg, they came upon an anti-religious demonstration. Infuriated by what he saw and heard – 'There is nothing but that!' he used to say sometimes, pointing to the sky – Cézanne disappeared among the crowd. His wife and son, used to his sudden disappearances, were not much alarmed. However, when Cézanne failed to return to the hotel that evening, they became anxious and instituted a search. No trace of him was found till they received a letter from Geneva four days later telling them to join him there.

This incident was no doubt rooted in Cézanne's profound irritation with the whole Swiss journey rather than due to his religious susceptibilities. Hortense, however, was unmoved. She dragged her reluctant husband on to Vevey and Lausanne but by then Cézanne had had enough. It was now five months since they had left Paris and he wanted to go home; but Hortense refused to go to Aix; she wished to return to Paris. Together with her son, she took train for the capital, while Cézanne left angrily for the Jas de Bouffan.

* * *

Since he was a boy, Cézanne had been going to the Aix Museum to look at *Les Joueurs de Cartes* attributed to Louis le Nain. It was not a particularly good picture, but there was a quality about it that appealed to him. 'That's how I should like to paint!' he had said.

On his return to the Jas, he determined to paint a similar subject. He knew the difficulties of the task. There was no question, of course, of copying the rather banal composition of the Aix picture. He determined to take peasants for his models. He understood peasants, their secrecy and reserve, their slowness and deliberation, the complexity behind their apparent simplicity, better perhaps than any other painter.

He started by painting separate portraits of his models, who came from the Jas estate, in particular a gardener called Paulet, who was

* According to Rivière another artist found them and, using them for his own purposes, painted over them.

generally known as Père Alexandre. He was as delighted by their stillness and patience as he was excited by this new undertaking.

This unusual euphoria would appear to have given him for once the power to make a decision. He compelled his wife to come to the Midi by the simple process of reducing her monthly allowance. Hortense and young Paul arrived in Aix in February and Cézanne took a flat for them in the Rue de la Monnaie,* though he himself remained at the Jas de Bouffan. His real home was now more than ever with his mother and sister, 'whom he undoubtedly prefers to his wife!' wrote Paul Alexis to Zola. Alexis was at this time living in Aix, and derived considerable amusement from Cézanne's matrimonial difficulties. Alexis called Hortense 'la Boule' (no doubt the nickname current for her at Médan); while that 'urchin of a son' was called 'le Boulet.' 'If, as Cézanne hopes,' went on Alexis, 'the Boule and the brat take root here, there will be nothing to prevent his going to live in Paris for six months from time to time. "Hurrah for sunshine and liberty!" he cries.'

These optimistic arrangements, to which Alexis probably owed the affability with which Cézanne welcomed him (he gave him four pictures), were in sharp contrast to the tense relationship existing between the various members of Cézanne's family. Marie was constantly quarrelling with her mother, and was on bad terms with her sister Rose, whom she reproached with being too soft with her husband, Maxime, who gambled and indulged in promiscuous affairs. As for Hortense, she no longer saw either her mother-in-law or Marie, 'who,' declared Alexis, 'detests her'; and she was not on speaking terms with Rose.

In the middle of it all Cézanne continued to work on his *Joueurs de Cartes* as if nothing were the matter. He was perhaps not altogether displeased at being able to take his revenge on Hortense for the Swiss journey. 'My wife,' he said, 'likes nothing but Switzerland and lemonade.' From now on Hortense would have to be satisfied with her allowance. Supported by his mother and Marie, he felt 'in a position to resist'† Hortense's demands for money.

For his *Joueurs de Cartes*, Cézanne selected a large canvas seventy-

* Today, Rue Frédéric-Mistral.
† Alexis.

eight inches long. He painted five figures, three playing and two looking on. But he was dissatisfied with the result. Several times he made a fresh approach to the composition using smaller canvases and reducing the number of figures, first to four, then to two.* He suppressed everything but the essentials. In line, colour and the structure of the composition, he was searching for a simplicity and a subtlety which, once achieved, would be indestructible.

* * *

At Tanguy's shop, which he had now moved from 14 to 9, Rue Clauzel, Cézanne's canvases were being discussed more enthusiastically than ever. Some of the ex-pupils of the Académie Julian who, two or three years before, in 1889, had formed themselves into a group with symbolist tendencies which they called the Nabis, were regular visitors to the little shop. Among them were Maurice Denis, Édouard Vuillard and Paul Sérusier, the founder and oldest member of the group (he was thirty). The Nabis were disciples of Gauguin, and through Gauguin felt affiliations with Cézanne. It was true that many of them did not feel as immediate an enthusiasm for Cézanne's work as had Gauguin, who used to say as he set off to paint: 'Let's go and make a Cézanne.'† Some among them did not at first understand Cézanne at all. One day in 1890, for instance, Sérusier suggested to Maurice Denis that he should write about Cézanne in one of his critical articles. At that time Maurice Denis had never seen a Cézanne; but it so chanced that he met Signac that same day, and Signac took him to see his own collection of Cézannes.

Maurice Denis was disappointed by them. One still life, in particular, filled him with such horror that he decided never to mention the painter's name. Later, however, he altered his views; little by little, he began to understand 'the nobility and greatness' of Cézanne, and eventually became one of his most zealous supporters.

* There are five versions of *Joueurs de Cartes* extant: two in France, one in Great Britain and two in the United States.

† Gauguin wrote to Émile Schuffenecker in June 1888: 'The Cézanne you want from me is an exceptional pearl and I have already refused 300 francs for it; I cling to it like the apple of my eye and, even in the case of utmost necessity, I would part with it only after my last shirt.'

But who precisely was Cézanne? Tanguy's silence on the subject, and the veil of mystery he cast over Cézanne's painting, which was unusual enough in itself, left the field open to conjecture. None of these young men had ever met him. He lived in Aix it appeared. But who could be certain even of that? Gauguin claimed to have known him; but Gauguin was now in the Antipodes. Émile Bernard, who persuaded as many people as he could to visit Tanguy's shop, had to admit that he had never met Cézanne.

Some imagined that Cézanne was long dead and that the paintings were the work of an unknown genius being brought to light posthumously. Others thought he must be a 'myth,'* and that the pseudonym of Cézanne concealed the identity of some famous painter who feared to acknowledge such audacious work. It was true that some well-informed persons had said that Cézanne was Zola's Claude Lantier. But none of this took one much further.

Nevertheless, two critical studies devoted to Cézanne appeared one after the other in 1892. Georges Lecomte, in his book, *L'Art Impressionniste*, mentioned the 'very sound and integrated art which that marvellously instinctive painter frequently achieved' – but why the past tense? And Émile Bernard devoted to Cézanne the 387th number of *Hommes d'Aujourd'hui*. Cézanne, he wrote, 'opens a surprising door to art: painting for its own sake.' Analysing one of Cézanne's canvases, *La Tentation de Saint Antoine*, he discovered 'that power of originality and technique for which we are always searching and so seldom find in the work of the generation known today. And this makes me think,' added Bernard, 'of what Paul Gauguin said to me one day when talking of Paul Cézanne: "Nothing looks so much like a daub as a masterpiece." An opinion which seems to me to be cruelly true in the present instance.'

This remark, supposing he read it, was certainly calculated to impress a young man of some thirty years of age, who frequented Tanguy's shop and gazed with a somewhat indolent and feline eye at Cézanne's work. Ambroise Vollard, who was of Creole origin, had already begun to deal in art in an amateur way. He had little money, but was optimistic about the future. At the moment, he was doing

* Maurice Denis.

little more than look around. He had managed a few small deals and, in anticipation of hard times, had bought a barrel of ship's biscuits. He was prepared for a long and doubtless uncertain voyage. Vollard examined Tanguy's Cézannes; but Tanguy, under the spell of Émile Bernard's eloquence, had decided to sell no more of *his* painter's canvases. They were bound to increase in value soon; from now on he considered them 'a treasure without price.' Vollard, in his apparently casual way, listened to Tanguy and the conversation of the customers who frequented his shop. He soon realised that of all the Impressionists Cézanne alone had no proper dealer.

* * *

The *Joueurs de Cartes* finished – in so far as he could ever finish anything, for perfection was not of this world – Cézanne began his wanderings again. Paris and Provence attracted and repelled him in turn. He moved from one to the other in a vain search for serenity.

Early in the year 1894, he was in Paris, staying in the Bastille quarter at 2, Rue des Lions-Saint-Paul, near the Rue Beautreillis where he had lived some thirty years before, when attending the Académie Suisse. But he knew few people in Paris now. Even Père Tanguy had recently died.

Tanguy had suffered appalling agonies during his last weeks. He had been removed to hospital with cancer of the stomach; but when he realised the end was near, he had insisted on being taken back to the Rue Clauzel. 'I want to die at home, near my wife, and amid my pictures,' he declared. One night, he said to his wife: 'When I am no longer here, life will not be easy for you. We own nothing but our canvases. You will have to sell them . . .' He died next morning, 6 February.

Continually on the move, it was some time before Cézanne heard of Caillebotte's death, which occurred a fortnight after Tanguy's, on 21 February. Despite the presentiment which had led Caillebotte to make his will so long ago, he lived for another eighteen years; but had long ago retired to Gennevilliers, where he had caught a fatal chill pruning his roses.

By his will of 1876, Caillebotte had left his collection of pictures to

30. Paul Cézanne [1889]. Photograph for his card of admission as exhibitor in the International Exhibition, 1900

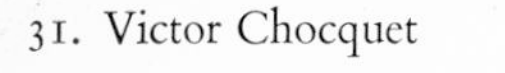

31. Victor Chocquet

32. Victor Chocquet. Drawing by Cézanne

33. Paul Cézanne, fils. Drawing by Cézanne

34. Paul Cézanne, fils

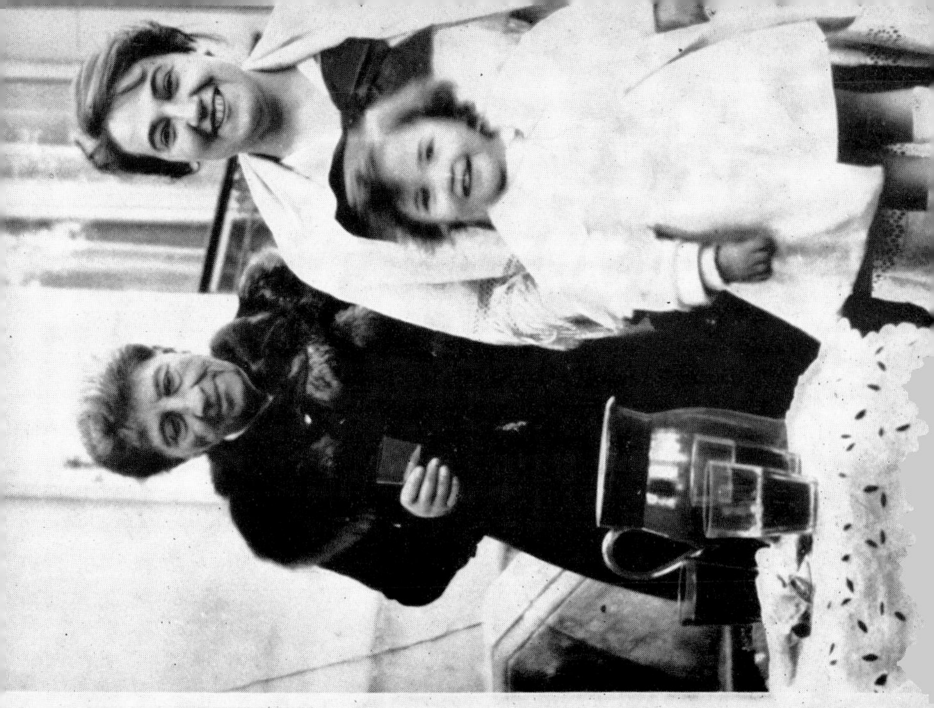

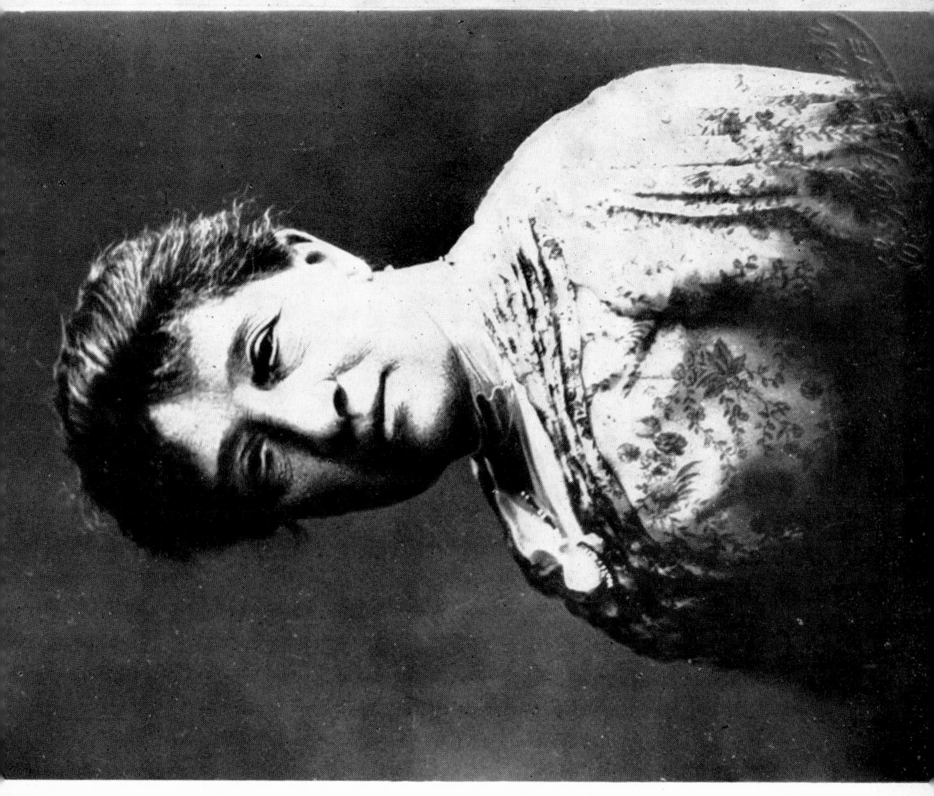

35. (left). Hortense Cézanne, the artist's wife [*c.* 1900]

36. (right). Hortense Cézanne towards the end of her life, with her niece, Mademoiselle Conil, and grand-daughter.

37. Cézanne in his studio at Aix, seated in front of the small version of his painting, 'Bathers'. Photograph by Émile Bernard [1904]

38. Cézanne's studio in the Chemin des Lauves, Aix [*c.* 1906]

39. Paul Cézanne in the garden of his studio at Aix, with Gaston and Madame Bernheim de Villers [*c.* 1904]

40.

42.

Cézanne at Les Lauves, Aix [*c.* 1904]

41.

43. Cézanne and Gaston Bernheim de Villers at Les Lauves, Aix [*c.* 1904]

44. *Hommage à Cézanne*. By Émile Bernard [1904]

the Nation. Apart from two Millets, it comprised three Manets, sixteen Monets, eight Renoirs, eighteen Pissarros, seven Degas, nine Sisleys and four Cézannes. What view would the authorities take of this bequest? Cézanne excepted, the position of the Impressionists had much improved in recent years. Their canvases were being bought; and often for comparatively reasonable prices. But the old quarrels were far from dead. At the very thought of such sacrilege to the Luxembourg, the traditionalist painters were bound to object. The Beaux-Arts authorities began considering their policy at the beginning of March, by which time the news of the bequest was widespread.

At this moment Théodore Duret decided to sell his collection. 'Your collection is admirable,' Duret once said to a great Parisian collector. 'It's splendid! I know only one better, and that's my own: it consists of nothing but Impressionists.' Duret's collection was auctioned at the Galerie Georges Petit, in the Rue de Sèze, on 19 March. The three Cézannes were bought for 650, 660 and 800 francs.*

But the prices could not compare with those attained by artists who had 'arrived'; a Monet, for instance, *Les Dindons blancs*, went for 12,000 francs.† Prices such as these staggered the experts, who had advised Duret to withdraw the Cézannes from the sale so as not to discredit the rest.

Indeed, so surprising were these prices, that the critic Gustave Geffroy seized the opportunity of writing an article about Cézanne. A week later, on 25 March, it appeared in the *Journal*:

'Cézanne,' he wrote, 'has become a sort of precursor acknowledged by the Symbolists, and it is quite clear, from the facts of the case, that there is a direct relationship, a precise continuity between the painting of Cézanne and that of Gauguin, Émile Bernard, etc. And this is also true of the painting of Vincent Van Gogh.

'For this alone, Paul Cézanne deserves to be given his due.

'It must also be said that there is a very evident intellectual link between Cézanne and his successors and that Cézanne has had the same

* Between, approximately, £100 and £130 today. The Duret collection consisted of three Cézannes, six Manets, six Monets, four Pissarros, three Renoirs, three Sisleys and eight Degas.

† Approximately £2,000 today.

theoretical and synthetical preoccupations as the Symbolist painters have now. Today, whether one wants to or not, it is easy to gain a clear conspectus of the development and general direction of Cézanne's art . . . Moreover, one has an increasingly strong and dominant impression that Cézanne does not approach nature with a theory of art or with the despotic intention of submitting it to some preconceived law, to some personal aesthetic formula. And yet, for all that, he is not without a plan, a convention and an ideal. However, they do not derive from art, but rather from his ardent curiosity and his desire to possess what he sees and admires.

'He is a man who looks closely about him, who is intoxicated by the spectacle before him, and wishes to record the emotions aroused in him by that intoxication within the limited space of the canvas. He sets to work and searches for the means of accomplishing this transposition with the greatest possible truth.'

Cézanne read this article at Alfort;* and no doubt he was much surprised by it. He wrote to the critic expressing his 'gratitude' for the 'sympathy' he had shown him. At the same time he must have realised that Geffroy was a friend of Monet, and that Monet, who never failed in kindness, may well have put the critic up to it.

In the meantime, Caillebotte's legacy was having considerable repercussions. The representatives of the Nation – Henri Roujon, Director of the Beaux-Arts, and Léonce Bénédite, Keeper of the Luxembourg – had accepted it in principle; but they were in fact trying to achieve some compromise with Caillebotte's brother, Martial, and with Renoir, who was an executor. They were well aware that they could not refuse the bequest outright. Nevertheless, to accept the whole of it, in accordance with the terms of the will, was more than they could bring themselves to agree to; and they prevaricated. Martial Caillebotte and Renoir realised from the first that they could not hope to succeed in getting Caillebotte's wishes observed in their entirety. The best they could expect was a partial realisation of his intentions. The discussions that ensued gave rise to passionate arguments in the press.

In April the *Journal des Artistes* began an enquiry into the current

* Today, Alfortville.

feeling about the legacy. Gérome responded with fury: 'We are living in a century of decadence and imbecility . . . The standards of society as a whole are visibly declining . . . This is a matter of paintings by M. Manet, M. Pissarro and others, is it not? I repeat, that for the Nation to accept such filth, there must be a great moral decline . . . They are madmen and anarchists! I tell you that people like that paint with their excrement at Dr. Blanche's* . . . People say it's a joke and that it doesn't matter . . . Well, I don't agree, it's the end of France as a nation.' The historic painter, Benjamin Constant, took a similar view. 'Protest, and protest vigorously,' he wrote. 'These people are not even humbugs. Their paintings don't exist, they're sheer anarchy.' 'To hang the pictures you mention in the Luxembourg,' opined Lecomte du Nouy, 'would create a deplorable example, for young people might be diverted from serious work . . . It's madness.' And the portrait painter, Gabriel Ferrier, declared: 'I don't want to say much about those people, because I don't know them and don't want to know them. Whenever I see any of their work, I hurry away as quickly as I can . . . My opinion is categorical: they should be treated to kicks in the backside.'

All the replies to the enquiry were not so intransigent. Tony Rodert-Fleury wrote more intelligently: 'One should be prudent and reserve one's judgment . . . That which surprises today may perhaps be the painting of tomorrow . . . We should respect all new experiments as interesting. Impressionism is still in the experimental stage; but the day a man of robust genius and sound education makes it acceptable, we shall perhaps have a new art.'

As for Gyp, the spritely author of *Mariage de Chiffon*, who had also been asked for her views, she wrote: 'These pictures are to be placed in the Luxembourg, and I think it a very good thing because I adore them. I rather belong to that school myself, I'm very Champ-de-Mars. I like painting which is alive and in which you can breathe good sunny air, and I don't like canvases painted in cellars.'

Gaston Leseaux came to the defence of the Impressionists in *Le Moniteur* on 24 March, 1894: 'The hanging of these canvases so full of art and thought will show up the emptiness that resides within certain frames, the sumptuous banality of Bouguereau, Detaille and company.

* A famous alienist of the period.

Lack of space, if not the taste of the authorities, will force these painters to move out to Carpentras or Landerneau . . .'

While this controversy was raging, the sale of the Tanguy collection took place at the Hôtel Drouot on 2 June. Madame Tanguy, following her late husband's advice, had decided to turn their stock into cash. But though the sale was organised by the writer Octave Mirbeau, the prices were not as high as had been hoped.

The only respectable price was paid for a Monet, which found a buyer at 3,000 francs (approximately £500 today). Six Cézannes went for a total of 902 francs (£150), their prices ranging from 95 to 215 (£16 to £35). But many works by other painters went for no more. Though the Pissarros all went for over 400 francs (£65), the six Gauguins failed to average 100 francs each (£17), the Guillaumins ranged between 80 and 160 francs (£13 to £26), a Seurat went for 50 francs (£8 10s. 0d.) and a Van Gogh for 30 francs (£5). The sale as a whole brought in 14,621 francs,* which nevertheless seemed quite a handsome sum to Madame Tanguy, who had been poor all her life.

Despite the low prices, the auctioneer congratulated one of the buyers on his courage. The buyer was none other than young Ambroise Vollard, who bought five out of the six Cézannes. He was, however, somewhat embarrassed by the compliment since he had not the money to pay for his purchases and had to ask for time.

* * *

* The equivalent of more than £2,000 today. It is interesting to compare these prices with those currently paid for the works of the academic painters. In 1876, a canvas by Cabanel was sold for 56,500 francs; in 1888 *Le Charmeur de Serpents* by Gérome for 95,500 francs; in 1886, 100,450 francs had been paid for a Bouguereau; and in 1887 Meissonier's *Friedland* had gone for 336,000 francs (some £60,000 today).

Subject to a possible error in identification, Cabanel's *Aglaé*, which had been sold for 26,000 gold francs in 1876, went at public auction in 1937 for 2,000 paper francs.

In our own day, however, one canvas by an academic painter has reached a reasonably high price: in 1954, at the Bessonneau sale, Benjamin Constant's *Bazar au Maroc* went for 350,000 francs (approximately £350). But, as *L'Oeil* remarked, one may well wonder 'whether the purchaser at the Bessonneau sale did not take the *Bazar au Maroc* to be an unexpected work by the author of *Adolphe*.'

Some eight years earlier, Claude Monet had gone to live near Vernon, in the village of Giverny. In the autumn, Cézanne went to join him. He was touched by Monet's kindness and friendliness and, moreover, he greatly admired Monet's work. 'The sky is blue, isn't it? And it was Monet who discovered it . . . Monet is nothing but an eye; but, my God, what an eye!'

Though he was living at the inn, Cézanne frequently went to see his friend. Monet gave him what he now required more than ever: 'moral support.' Cézanne's moods of enthusiasm and despair were alternating at this time with disturbing frequency. He was irritable and nervous. His quick, piercing eyes, his excited talk and wild appearance astonished and were inclined to alarm those who did not know him. The American painter, Mary Cassatt, who was a friend of Monet, thought he was 'a cut-throat'* the first time she saw him. But she quickly revised her opinion when she discovered that the brigand was shy, timid and gentle. 'I'm like a child,' Cézanne said of himself.

Towards the end of November, Monet invited Geffroy, Mirbeau, Rodin and Clemenceau to Giverny. 'I hope Cézanne will still be here and of the party,' he wrote to Geffroy, 'but he's so odd, so shy of seeing new faces, that I fear he may let us down, in spite of the fact that he very much wants to meet you. What a tragedy that the man should not have had more support during his life! He is a true artist, but has reached a point where he doubts himself too much. He needs his self-confidence bolstering; he was very grateful for your article!'

The party took place on 28 November. Despite Monet's fears, Cézanne was there. Indeed, he was exceptionally sociable that day. He was clearly delighted to meet these famous men: Geffroy, to whom he was manifestly grateful, Mirbeau, whom he considered 'the greatest writer of his time,' Rodin, 'the prodigious hewer of stone,' a 'man of the Middle Ages,'† and Clemenceau, the terrible politician.

Indeed, he seemed over-excited and Monet's friends were struck by it. He roared with laughter at Clemenceau's jokes. Taking Mirbeau and Geffroy aside, he remarked with tears in his eyes: 'M. Rodin is not

* Letter from Mary Cassatt to Mrs Stillman, quoted in *The Graphic Work of Mary Cassatt*, by Adelyn D. Breeskin (Bittner, New York, 1948).

† Joachim Gasquet.

at all proud, he shook my hand! A man who has been decorated!' Luncheon cheered him still further. He became confidential. He disowned the painters who claimed to derive from him and accused them of having robbed him. With much sighing and groaning, he said to Mirbeau: 'That M. Gauguin, just listen to this! . . . Oh, that M. Gauguin! . . . I had a little sensation, a tiny little sensation. It was nothing in particular . . . No bigger than that . . . But it was my own little sensation. Well, one day, that M. Gauguin took it from me. And he went off with it. He trailed the poor thing about in ships! . . . Across America . . . Brittany and Oceania, across fields of sugar-cane and grapefruit . . . to the land of Negroes and I don't know where else. How do I know what he's done with it? And what can I do now? My poor little sensation!' And after luncheon, when they were all walking in the garden, Cézanne fell on his knees on the path before Rodin 'to thank him once again for having shaken his hand.'*

A little while later, Monet decided to give another party, a luncheon in honour of Cézanne. He invited Renoir, Sisley and some other friends. Cézanne arrived late and the party had already gone in to luncheon. As soon as Cézanne had sat down, Monet made a little speech assuring him of their affection and the sincere and profound admiration they all felt for his art. Unfortunately Cézanne was in one of his black moods that day and, while Monet was speaking, he bowed his head and wept. Then, looking reproachfully at him, he said: 'Must you also mock me, Monet?' He got to his feet and, in spite of his friends' dismayed protests, hurried away.

Not long afterwards, having seen nothing of Cézanne for several days, Monet became anxious and went to enquire after him. Cézanne had left Giverny. Not only had he failed to say good-bye to Monet but he had discarded a number of canvases on which he had been working at the inn.

* * *

In the spring of 1895, it occurred to Cézanne that he might paint Gustave Geffroy's portrait. Geffroy was an important art critic, and Cézanne thought that if he could make a good job of it, the Hanging Committee of the 'Salon de Bouguereau' could hardly refuse to hang

* Gustave Geffroy: *Claude Monet, sa Vie, son Oeuvre.*

it. Why, they might even award him a medal! One morning in April, Cézanne wrote to the critic:

'Dear Monsieur Geffroy,

'The days are lengthening and the weather growing warmer. I am unoccupied all morning till the hour when a civilised man eats. I propose coming to Belleville to shake you by the hand and submit a proposal to you which I have been considering off and on for some time . . . Very cordially yours,

'Paul Cézanne, painter by inclination.'

Geffroy, who was no doubt curious to watch Cézanne at work, agreed to the proposal. Cézanne set to work with great enthusiasm. He knew it would take him a long time, and he suggested painting Geffroy sitting in an armchair at his desk, his back to a bookcase. On the table were a few papers, an open book, a little plaster cast by Rodin and a flower in a vase. Till the portrait was finished, none of these might be moved; and so that Geffroy might resume his precise pose, Cézanne marked the position of the chair on the floor with chalk. The flower was a paper one; he worked so slowly that natural flowers were of no use to him; the 'damned bastards' faded too quickly.

Cézanne went to Belleville practically every day. He seemed in excellent humour and painted with a sustained fervour that astonished the critic. As the canvas took shape, Geffroy considered it to be 'of the first order.'* Cézanne had so far only sketched in the face. 'That will come last,' he said. As he worked, he talked about painting and painters. Geffroy mentioned Monet. 'He is the greatest of us all,' said Cézanne. 'Monet, why, I add him to the Louvre!' The new schools and *divisionnisme* made him laugh: 'I like Baron Gros, how do you expect me to take such nonsense seriously!' There were, however, certain subjects that were taboo. Cézanne growled when Geffroy tried to explain Impressionism – Monet in particular – by relating it to 'Renan, the latest atomistic hypotheses, to biological development and the general trend.'† In Cézanne's view, all this was nonsense.

* Geffroy: *op. cit.*

† Joachim Gasquet.

Moreover, the critic's radical political views and his support of Clemenceau irritated Cézanne. He was prepared to admit that Clemenceau had 'temperament,' but to agree with his views was quite impossible! 'You see, I'm too weak!' Cézanne explained. 'And Clemenceau could not protect me! Only the Church can do that!'

Cézanne undoubtedly felt at his ease with Geffroy. He often had luncheon with the critic, his mother and his sister. He sometimes even went with Geffroy to a tavern by the Saint-Fargeau lake. He was able to forget his disappointments and become expansive. One day, he remarked: 'I want to astound Paris with an apple!'

It was at this time that Cézanne met Francisco Oller again – his old friend from the days of the Académie Suisse. Oller had just returned to France after many years abroad. He had come from Puerto Rico. But he had worked also in Spain, where he had been honoured with a royal commission: an equestrian portrait of Alphonso XII. Oller had changed since Cézanne last saw him; he was sixty-two and 'old and shrivelled.'* He was astonished by the work that was now being done in France; the clear tones of the Impressionists dazzled him.

In his present mood, Cézanne was delighted to see him; Oller had travelled far, though not along the road to success. Cézanne gave him the freedom of his studio in the Rue Bonaparte, paid some debts for him, and lent him a small sum of money, Oller naturally maintained as close a relationship with Cézanne as he could.

The painting of Geffroy continued; by June there had been some eighty sittings. But Cézanne was becoming depressed; he felt the portrait would never be finished, that he would never be able to 'realise' it as he wished. Perhaps Zola had been right after all: he was nothing but a failure, a miserable spoiler of canvases. He saw the Salon and the medal escaping him. How presumptuous he had been to put Geffroy to all this trouble! Completely losing his confidence he sent to Belleville for his easel and painting things together with a word of excuse to the critic. He had been wrong ever to attempt the work; would Geffroy please forgive him; the portrait was beyond his capacity; he must abandon it.

* Letter from Pissarro to his son Lucien, 23 March, 1895.

Geffroy was taken aback by this sudden abdication, particularly since the portrait was half finished. He persuaded Cézanne to come to Belleville and assured him that he had begun 'a very fine work'; he owed it to himself to complete it. The sittings continued; but Cézanne's heart was no longer in his work.

One morning at this time, Cézanne saw Monet in the Rue d'Amsterdam; but immediately turned away, 'lowered his head and disappeared into the crowd.'* Another day, on the quays of the Seine, he saw Guillaumin and Signac. They clearly wanted to talk to him, but Cézanne signed to them to continue on their way. He worked at the portrait for a week more. Then the inevitable happened: he left Paris without a word.

Oller, who was clinging to Cézanne as closely as he could, knew that he proposed leaving for Aix, and decided to go with him. Cézanne, in exasperation, told Oller to meet him at the Gare de Lyon at a certain time, 'in the third class compartments.' He had determined to rid himself of Oller's importunities by travelling first class himself. But Oller was not easily discouraged. Having searched the station in vain for Cézanne, he came to the conclusion that he had left by an earlier train; decided to follow him and took the next train to the south. At Lyons, however, in order to check on Cézanne's whereabouts, he sent a telegram to young Paul in Paris asking him where his father was. The reply confirmed his suspicions: Cézanne was at the Jas de Bouffan. In the meantime, Oller had five hundred francs stolen from him in the hotel. He hurried on to Aix and immediately informed Cézanne of his arrival. 'If that's the case, come round at once. 'I'm expecting you,' Cézanne replied briefly.

Cézanne was in a highly nervous condition. Oller found him violent, sardonic and proud. 'I'm the only one of them who has "temperament," ' he shouted. 'I'm the only one of them who knows how to use a red . . .' Pissarro was 'an old fool.' Monet was merely 'sly.' 'They've none of them got guts!'

What Oller had said to infuriate Cézanne, we do not know but, on 5 July, he received a peremptory letter:

'Monsieur,' (Cézanne crossed out the 'dear'),

* Geffroy.

'The autocratic tone you have used towards me for sometime past, and the rather too cavalier manner with which you allowed yourself to address me, at the time of your departure, are more than I can stomach.

'I have determined never to receive you again in my father's house.

'The lectures you have allowed yourself to read me have now therefore borne their ultimate fruit. So good-bye.'

On his return to Paris Oller told everyone that Cézanne was a 'cad' and a 'madman.' He retailed to anyone who would listen what Cézanne had said about his friends. Pissarro was hurt; he thought Cézanne's behaviour 'clearly crazy.' Dr Aguiard, who was a friend of theirs, thought Cézanne irresponsible. 'Is it not sad and pitiful,' Pissarro wrote to his son Lucien, 'that a man endowed with such genius should be so unbalanced?'

Cézanne was living alone at the Jas de Bouffan with his mother, who was now aged eighty-one and an invalid. Marie had taken a flat in the town, mother and daughter having at last found their temperaments hopelessly incompatible.

Remembering how kind Monet had been to him, Cézanne wrote him a letter expressing his regret for having left without saying good-bye. 'I have temporarily had to give up the study I was making of Geffroy, who so generously placed himself at my disposal, and I am rather embarrassed by the insignificant results I obtained, particularly after so many sittings, and all the alternating enthusiasms and discouragements. But here I am, back in the Midi, from which I should perhaps never have emerged to throw myself into the chimerical pursuit of art.'

Cézanne might well talk of the 'chimerical pursuit of art,' but he knew very well that he would continue to paint until he had drawn his last breath. He would go to his easel at five o'clock in the morning and work till night, without a thought for anything else – his illness, Hortense, or the fifty-six lost years. 'There is a passing moment in the world. Paint it in its reality! Forget everything else for that,' he exclaimed. 'I want to lose myself in nature, grow with her again, grow like her.' Nature was the great and permanent tragedy; everything had to die. Victory was pregnant with its own defeat. There was no permanence or stability about the world, only a perpetual interplay of tragic and shadowy forces in which death was triumphant though life was constantly renewed. In the canvases he was painting now, the houses crumbled; individual trees were lost in a swarming, all-pervasive verdure; the very rocks were alive. Week after week, Cézanne went to Montbriant to paint one big pine, and he endued it with almost human qualities.

The Lyricism of Evening

PART FIVE

[1895 - 1906]

CHAPTER ONE

Ambroise Vollard

> Monsieur,
>
> In your literary columns [*Excelsior*, 6 February, 1938], you say: 'If M. Maillol has been able to make a living for so many years, it is above all due to the generosity and intelligence of M. Ambroise Vollard.' I was naturally much flattered to see the word 'intelligence' applied to me. On the other hand, I am embarrassed by the attribute of 'generosity' in the relations between a dealer and an artist; it seems to me that it is rather like saying that, by purchasing a piece of land in which he thinks he will find gold, the purchaser is being generous to the vendor of that land.
>
> AMBROISE VOLLARD: Letter to Édmond Jaloux

IN 1893, Ambroise Vollard had opened a little shop at 39, Rue Laffitte. At that time the Rue Laffitte was the centre of art dealing in Paris. All the big dealers had galleries there; Durand-Ruel, Bernheim-Jeune, Tempelaere and many others. Vollard had already held an exhibition of drawings by Manet and another of Forain's; but now – two years later – he planned to do much more than this.

Vollard brought more guess-work than intuitive response to a work of art, and he was well aware of it himself. For him pictures were, in the first place, objects of speculation.

Whether he bought Roybets and Ziems, or staked everything on the notorious Cézanne, the essential thing was to make no mistake concerning the future. He was indefatigable in his questioning of people whose judgment about painting seemed to him sound. And he was a very good listener.

Extremely astute, he affected ingenuousness; alert and active, he pretended to indolence. But from beneath their half-closed lids, his eyes would sometimes shine like those of 'a jaguar lying in wait.'* Pissarro deplored the fact that there had never been a one-man show

* Louis Vauxcelles.

of Cézanne's work; and he encouraged Vollard to organise one. Renoir and Degas supported the suggestion and Seurat, before his death in 1891, had said the same thing.

The negotiations over the Caillebotte legacy had come to an end the previous May, after more than a year. The officials had reluctantly accepted thirty-eight of the sixty-five canvases. On what basis they finally made a selection among these 'deplorable' works is unknown. Renoir described several meetings at which, as executor, he had been present. His own painting, he said, was 'a subject of anxiety' to Roujon, the director of the Beaux-Arts. 'The only canvas of mine they admitted with confidence,' said Renoir, 'was *Le Moulin de la Galette*, because Gervex (an academic painter) figured in it. They looked on his presence among my other models as a sort of moral guarantee. He was also prepared to accept, though without much enthusiasm, Monet, Sisley and Pissarro . . . But when it came to Cézanne! Those landscapes composed with the balance of a Poussin, those pictures of bathers in which the colours seem to have been ravaged from the old makers of faience, in fact all that supremely sapient art! . . . I can still hear Roujon saying: "This one doesn't even know what painting is!" '

However, Cézanne entered the Luxembourg. The officials rejected his *Bouquet de Roses* and his *Baigneurs au repos*, but accepted two of his canvases: *L'Estaque* and *Une Cour de Ferme à Auvers-sur-Oise*.*

In consequence, Gérome and some of the teachers at the École des Beaux-Arts threatened to resign in protest against the 'Luxembourg scandal,' declaring that 'they could no longer teach an art whose every law was violated by the pictures admitted to the museum.'† And Vollard began to consider even more seriously the advice of those who

* Degas was the only artist whose works were all accepted by the officials. They consisted of seven pastels, on which the administration placed an average estimated price of 4,070 francs. Monet had eight canvases accepted (average estimated price: 5,750 francs) out of sixteen; Pissarro seven (average estimated price: 1,857 francs) out of eighteen; Sisley six (average estimated price: 1,333 francs) out of nine; Renoir six (average estimated price: 5,000 francs) out of eight. Manet's *Le Balcon* and *Angelina* (valued together at 13,000 francs) were accepted, but his *La Partie de Croquet* was refused. Cézanne's works were valued at 750 francs each, the lowest price of all. His *Baigneurs au repos* was the canvas Cézanne had given to Cabaner; it is now in America, in the Barnes Foundation.

† Tabarant.

were trying to persuade him to hold a Cézanne exhibition. The moment had perhaps come for a decisive gamble.

Vollard did not know where Cézanne was. Nor did Pissarro, who had offered to lend some canvases for the exhibition. Having discovered that Cézanne had been painting in the forest of Fontainebleau, Vollard went there and found traces of him at Avon, then in Fontainebleau itself. He was told Cézanne had returned to Paris, but no note had been made of his address. It was merely remembered that the name of the street in which he lived was composed 'of the name of a saint and that of an animal.' Could it be the Rue des Lions-Saint-Paul? Vollard determined to visit each house in turn, and discovered that Cézanne had been living at No. 2. But the elusive artist had left for Aix in June. However, Hortense and young Paul were still in the flat and Paul promised to write to his father at once and tell him of the dealer's proposals. A few days later he told Vollard that Cézanne had agreed. This was followed by the arrival of nearly one hundred and fifty canvases without stretchers, rolled up in a bundle.*

* * *

Vollard's project appeared to arouse no particular enthusiasm in Cézanne. At Aix he continued to lead his solitary life, broken only by an occasional meeting with such old friends as Emperaire and Solari.

Solari had been no more successful in achieving his ambitions than had Emperaire. An impenitent bohemian, he had worked in many places; Lyons, Blois, Reims and Tarascon. He spent his life dreaming of grandiose works, very few of which ever came to fruition. He was now living in Aix, in an old outbuilding in the Rue du Louvre,† which he had more or less turned into a studio.

Both Emperaire and Solari were very poor and, from time to time, Cézanne would give them a good meal. One day in November, the three of them, together with Solari's son, Émile, made an excursion into the hills to the Zola dam. Young Solari, who was twenty, and wanted to become a writer like his godfather Zola, was much amused

* It is not known on what terms these canvases were sent to Vollard.

† Today, Rue Maréchal-Joffre.

by the strange pair Cézanne and Emperaire made. 'You might think it was a dwarf Mephistopheles leading an old Faust,' he said.

Cézanne and his friends went up past the Château Noir to the Bibémus quarry, then down to Saint-Marc, where they lunched under a fig tree on food bought from a labourers' canteen. In the afternoon, they went on to Le Tholonet, where they dined. Emperaire, who was not very used to wine, got rather drunk; on the way back, he fell and hurt himself rather badly.

A few days later, Cézanne and the two Solaris decided to climb to the top of Mont Sainte-Victoire, some 3,000 feet. It was too hard a climb for Emperaire. In spite of his diabetes, Cézanne was still a great walker. The night before they slept at Vauvenargues so as to start the climb at dawn. Cézanne was in particularly good humour and reminisced with Solari about their youth.

When young Solari pointed to some plants beside the path and remarked that, though they were green, they looked blue, Cézanne said in astonishment: 'The brigand! He has discovered at a glance, at the age of twenty, what it has taken me thirty years to see!' Having lunched near the summit, they turned back towards the valley. Cézanne, excited by the memories of his youth, tried to climb a pine. But he was tired and not as agile as he had once been. 'Do you remember, Philippe,' he said, 'how easily we used to do it!'

* * *

In the meantime, the one-man exhibition in Vollard's gallery had opened.

Vollard had placed in his window the *Baigneurs au repos*, which formed part of the Caillebotte bequest and had been refused by the authorities. This was a deliberate provocation. Vollard's housekeeper was alarmed. 'I fear Monsieur will be much criticised by his customers for putting a picture of naked gentlemen in the window!'

From the opening day, Cézanne's friends were continually in the gallery. The works exhibited* belonged to every period of his creative

* According to Vollard's reminiscences, the following works among others were displayed: *La Léda au Cygne*, 1868; *Le Festin*, 1868; *Portrait de l'Artiste par lui-même*, 1880; *La Maison abandonnée*, 1887; *Étude de Baigneuses*, 1887; *La Forêt de*

life and gave a complete and significant conspectus of his development. Even in people who knew Cézanne well and who had been able to keep in touch with his work through the years the exhibition aroused extreme astonishment. 'My enthusiasm is nothing compared to Renoir's,' Pissarro wrote to his son, Lucien. 'Even Degas has succumbed to the charm of this refined savage, Monet, all of us . . . Are we wrong? I don't believe so. The only people who don't yield to Cézanne's charm are precisely those painters and collectors who have shown us by their errors that their sensibilities are defective.'

Monet, in his desire to pay homage to his old and unfortunate friend, immediately bought three canvases. Degas also bought one or two. Pissarro proposed an exchange. He wrote: 'Was I not right in 1861, when Oller and I went to see that odd Provençal Cézanne, in the Atelier Suisse, making studies which were derided by all the untalented in the school, among them the celebrated Jacquet, who declined ages ago into the pretty-pretty and whose works fetched their weight in gold?'

The exhibition caused a considerable stir in the Paris art world. Vollard's gamble was turning out singularly well. The exhibition had come at the precise moment when it was likely to make the greatest effect. The cultivated public had become used to the Impressionists; and it had now been prepared to contemplate (if not comprehend) with a certain serenity work that went beyond Impressionism. Cézanne might surprise, indeed he might still shock, but he could no longer be ignored.

Tanguy's fervent admiration and the enthusiasm of the young painters, who had taken Cézanne as a master and sought instruction from his canvases, had quietly and gradually laid a basis for the revelation that was this exhibition of 1895. It was as if a crystallisation had taken place. On 16 November, Geffroy wrote in *Le Journal:* 'He is

---

Chantilly, 1888; *Le Grand Pin*, 1887; *Portrait de Mme Cézanne, dans la serre*, 1891; *Les Bords de la Marne*, 1888; *Portrait de l'Artiste par lui-même*, 1890; *Jeune Fille à la Poupée*, 1894; *Sous-bois, Forêt de Fontainebleau*, 1894; *Mme Cézanne au Chapeau vert*, 1888; *Baigneuses devant la Tente*, 1878; *Portrait de M. Louis Guillaume*, 1880; *Le Déjeuner sur l'Herbe*, 1878; *La Corbeille de Pommes*, 1885; *L'Estaque*, 1883; *Le Jas de Bouffan*, 1885; *Auvers*, 1880; *Gardanne*, 1886; *La Lutte*, 1885; *Portrait de Mme Cézanne*, 1877. (The dates given by Vollard should be accepted with caution.)

great and authentic, ardent and ingenuous, violent and subtle. He will go to the Louvre, and there is more than one canvas here destined for the museums of the future.'

The importance and obvious influence of the exhibition was so evident that it was bound to be greeted with fury in certain quarters. Cézanne, who till yesterday had been utterly and safely ignored, suddenly became the object of considerable animosity. He was exciting both envy and hatred. One day the painter Quost walked into Vollard's gallery and, pointing furiously to a picture, enquired what 'the damned thing was supposed to be?' Vollard replied in his lethargic, cynical way that 'being no painter, art critic or collector,' he could give 'no authoritative opinion;' all he could do was to show him that 'the catalogue gave the title as *Fleurs*.'

'Flowers!' exclaimed Quost. 'Has that painter of yours ever looked at a flower? I, Monsieur, have lived for years with flowers on the most intimate terms! Do you know what my peers have nicknamed me? The Corot of the Flower, Monsieur! Corollas, stamens, calyxes, stems, pistils, stigmas, pollen, how often have I not drawn and painted them! Three thousand studies of detail, Monsieur, before even daring to attack the least of wild flowers! And yet I don't sell!'

The measure of this jealousy was made manifest by an article in the *Journal des Artistes* on 1 December, by Georges Denoinville, entitled: 'The Limit.' Denoinville began by remarking that Cézanne's canvases were not signed:

'Not signed! Incredible, isn't it? Particularly in a period of publicity such as this . . . can it be due to some feeling of restraint or modesty in the artist, or is it merely an overwhelming pride?

'Let us unmask him! Césanne (*sic*) have the courage of your convictions! It's a musical name, isn't it? It attracts you, ladies, does it not? But alas, and alas again, the painting does not! . . .

'Indeed, I have no doubt that your pretty eyes will refuse to admire such insane productions and I can see you expressing your holy horror, your red lips curled in disdain, while you fly in disgust from the nightmare of these atrocities in oil, which go beyond all permissible practical-joking. One may get away with pulling the world's leg, but not to this extent! . . .

'The most astounding thing about it is that one meets well-known art critics, whose names we shall not mention from proper respect, who praise these inanities to the skies! That comradeship should sometimes lead to minor dishonesties is excusable till the moment comes when it is a matter of imposing names on the public and making it take sows' ears for silk purses! . . .

'Some of our colleagues are doing a bad job, for credulity has limits and confidence bounds!'

Such articles, which reiterated the tone of the press at the time of the first Impressionist exhibitions and had a certain anachronistic quality about them now, were in fact rare. Most of the criticism, sometimes favourable, sometimes not, was at least serious in tone. Thadée Natanson, in *La Revue blanche*, 1 December, 1895, remarked how profound Cézanne's influence now appeared to be. 'Apart from the purity of his art which has no meritricious attractions,' wrote Natanson, 'he has another quality of all precursors which attests his mastery: he dares to be rough, almost savage, and carries things through to their conclusion, in contempt of all else, with the single-mindedness of all initiators who wish to create something of original significance.'

Similarly, Arsène Alexandre, in an article in the *Figaro*,* entitled 'Claude Lantier,' reminded his readers of Zola's *L'Oeuvre* and the mythical personality with which Cézanne had been endued:

'The opportunity has arisen to state that he really does exist, and that his life has indeed not been altogether useless to others . . . It has been suddenly discovered that Zola's friend, the mysterious Provençal, the inventive but imperfect painter, so wild and yet so clever, is a great man.

'A great man? Perhaps not altogether, if one discounts the enthusiasms of a season, but he has the strangest of temperaments and, consciously or not, the younger school has borrowed much from him.'

Arsène Alexandre also incidentally attacked Zola. He accused him of having, in *L'Oeuvre*, 'exaggerated his characters, altered the facts to suit himself and introduced a lyrical romanticism into things that were quite simple.' There was little delay before a reply came from Médan. A friend of Zola, Thiébault-Sisson, the critic of the *Temps*, wrote of

* 9 December, 1895.

Cézanne in almost precisely the same terms Zola had used ten years before of Claude Lantier:

'Such he was when he came to Paris from Aix-en-Provence, in 1857 (*sic*), to find an artistic formula, as Émile Zola, his intimate friend, came in search of a formula for literature; and such he remains today, retiring, shy of the world, not only avoiding appearances in public, but also of allowing his works to appear, because he remains today as he has always been, incapable of self-judgment, and unable to derive from a new conception all the profit that cleverer people have derived from it, in a word, too incomplete to be able to realise what he himself had first seen, and produce his full measure in definitive works . . .'*

The public, of course, did not always grasp Cézanne's intentions. As Pissarro remarked, many people were 'bewildered' by his canvases. Nevertheless, a number of buyers appeared on the scene, such as Auguste Pellerin, the margarine king, and a great collector, also the ex-King of Serbia, Milan Obrenovitch IV, who nevertheless uttered a cry from the heart: 'Why don't you advise your Cézanne to paint pretty young women?' On the whole, Vollard was much encouraged.†

* *Le Temps*, 22 December, 1895. Other articles appeared in *L'Art Français* (23 November), *L'Art International* (25 November), *Mercure de France* (January 1896), etc.

† According to Vollard's reminiscences, he sold pictures at this exhibition at prices varying between 10 and 700 francs (approximately 30/– to £100 today). Twenty-five years later Auguste Pellerin, speaking to Vollard of the picture he had bought on this occasion, said: 'One of your colleagues has been trying to do me down. If you will believe me, he had the impudence to offer me 300,000 francs for that Cézanne!' (300,000 francs in 1920 would be the equivalent of approximately £6,000 today.)

CHAPTER TWO

The Springtime of the World

> I breathe the virginity of the world. I am assailed by a sharp sense of its hues. I feel as if I were aglow with all the hues of the infinite . . . I become one with my picture. We are an iridescent chaos. I come to my subject and lose myself in it. I think vaguely. The sun gradually pervades me, like a distant friend, warming and fecundating my laziness. We germinate.—CÉZANNE

FOR some little while past there had existed a society of amateur painters, the Friends of the Arts, at 2, Avenue Victor Hugo in Aix. They had made Villevieille their president.

As a result of the sensation Cézanne's work had created in Paris, the society began to wonder whether it ought to exclude that 'bad and much decried painter, who was nevertheless a native of Aix,'* from its next exhibition. It finally decided to invite Cézanne to contribute some paintings and two delegates were sent to see the painter. Cézanne was so surprised and delighted by this invitation from his fellow citizens that he offered each of his visitors a canvas. The first, too embarrassed to refuse, accepted the present, but the second felt that courtesy had limits. 'My wife,' he said, 'has a horror of modern painting.'

The Friends of the Arts were considerably embarrassed by the two pictures Cézanne submitted, a *Champ de blé* and a *Sainte-Victoire.*† Where could they hang these monstrosities so that they should not attract too much attention? It was finally decided to put them over the entrance door; but even in this position they were spared neither laughter nor derision. Was this really what people in Paris liked? It was incredible. A local critic, who wrote his review in verse, produced a mocking quatrain about the *Sainte-Victoire:*

* Marcel Provence: *Le Cours Mirabeau.*

† This was *La Sainte-Victoire au grand Pin* now in the Courtauld Collection.

A travers les rameaux des pins géants, on voit
Se profiler en bleu le mont Sainte-Victoire.
Si la nature était ce que ce peintre croit,
Ce sommaire tableau suffirait pour sa gloire.

In spite of these affronts, Cézanne attended the closing banquet, where he felt very much out of his element. When one of the speakers solemnly declared: 'Gentlemen, our period will be known as that of Cabanel and Bouguereau,' Cézanne could bear it no longer. 'Your Bouguereau,' he shouted amid an appalled silence, 'is the greatest idiot of the lot!'

Cézanne was much more downcast by the contempt of the local critics than he was rejoiced by the echoes of success that reached him from the exhibition in Paris. Numa Coste, who saw him fairly frequently at this time, was struck by his morose air; he was very depressed and filled with 'dark thoughts.'* Yet he was now being talked about in all the Paris studios and, what was more, his work was beginning to sell. His success, despite certain hostile criticism, was becoming incontrovertible. But Cézanne could not believe in it. He had reached a point where he was incapable of giving appreciation its due, whilst every attack on him reopened old wounds.

One Sunday in the spring he went to the Café Oriental, on the Cours Mirabeau,† with Numa Coste, Solari and an old schoolfellow, the baker Henri Gasquet, who had now retired from business. Dusk was falling over the town and Cézanne, sitting at a table on the terrace, was watching the Sunday crowd strolling in the Cours. He had just come from visiting his sister Marie after Vespers, and for once was tidily dressed, wearing a black tie and a clean coat. Suddenly a young man came up and told him shyly how much he had admired his two canvases in the Friends of the Arts' exhibition. The tribute was too sudden and too unexpected for Cézanne. He turned red in the face, got to his feet, gave the young man a 'terrible glance' and, banging the table with his fist, upsetting the bottles and glasses, shouted: 'Don't you make game of me, young man!' Then he fell back in his chair, tears in his eyes, having recognised the baker's son, Joachim. 'Henri, my

* Numa Coste: Letter to Zola, April 1896.
† The Cours had been renamed in 1876.

dear Henri, please don't joke about this – is it really true your son likes my paintings?' 'He would be terribly upset not to meet you,' replied the baker. Then Cézanne, turning to Joachim, said: 'Sit down there.' His voice was trembling. 'You're young. You don't understand. I don't want to paint any more. I let myself go . . . But listen, I'm an unfortunate man and you mustn't hold it against me. How could I believe that you like my paintings, when you've seen only two of my canvases, and all those bastards who write in the papers about me have never understood the first thing? Oh, they've hurt me, those people have! . . . It's the *Sainte-Victoire* that hit you in the eye. There now, you liked that canvas . . . I'll send it round to you tomorrow. And I'll sign it! . . .' Henri Gasquet, the baker, had, like Louis Auguste, fathered an artist – a poet. Joachim, his only son, had been extremely precocious from the first. Hardly had he left school before he was founding reviews, jellygraphed with the help of one of his father's workmen. Like Zola, Cézanne and Baille in the past, Gasquet and his friends – Joseph and Charles Maurras, Xavier de Magallon, Emmanuel Signoret, Paul Souchon, Jean Royère and José d'Arbaud among them – asserted their faith in poetry and beauty. The 'student with the blue eyes,' as Gasquet was called, looked like a young god. He was just twenty-three; and in the January of this year, had married the 'most beautiful girl in Provence,' Marie Girard, queen of their literary circle.

For a week past Joachim Gasquet had talked of nothing but Cézanne's canvases, they had 'intoxicated' him; and his young wife shared his admiration. He had also told his father of them. And now he addressed Cézanne as 'Maître.' 'Be quiet, young man, be quiet. I'm just an old fool who feels like weeping to listen to you.'

For the next week, Cézanne and Joachim Gasquet saw each other every day. They went for long walks in the Aix countryside and Cézanne took heart in the company of the young poet, and from the warmth and sincerity of his admiration. And if we are to believe Gasquet,* he talked as he had never talked before, explained what he was trying to accomplish in painting, and enthusiastically pointed out the splendours of that landscape of which he hoped to leave an image

* Cf., John Rewald: *Cézanne, Geffroy et Gasquet*, (Quatre Chemins Éditart), Paris, 1959 [Editor].

behind him. 'The great classic countries,' he said, 'our own Provence, and Greece and Italy, as I imagine them to be, have a spiritual quality about their light, while their landscapes seem to shimmer with a smiling, acute intelligence . . . Look at Sainte-Victoire, how it soars with such an imperious thirst towards the sun, and how melancholy it is at evening, when all that ponderous mass relapses! . . . Its contours rose out of the fire. And there is still fire in them. By day, the shadow seems to retreat quivering from them as if afraid. Up there is Plato's cave: see how, when the great clouds pass, their shadows tremble on the rocks, as if burning, and are absorbed at once by a fiery mouth. For a long time I did not know how to paint Sainte-Victoire, because I imagined the shadow to be concave, like other people who don't look, whereas – look there! – it's convex, it's taking flight from its centre. Instead of pressing down, it's evaporating, becoming fluid. It's turning blue and mingling with the movement of the air. But if you look over there to the right, at the Pilon du Roi, you'll see that the light is still, humid, glittering. It's the sea . . . That's what has to be rendered.'

Cézanne seemed to be blossoming with the almond trees. He was in a highly emotional state. He would stop to look at a cloud, or to pick up a handful of earth and knead it lovingly. 'It's the first time I have seen the spring,' he said.

He painted portraits of Gasquet, his wife and his father. He was happy, excited, and for once prepared to talk about himself. One evening, on returning with the poet from a long walk, he said what he had never said before, and perhaps had not dared to think: 'There is only one living painter, and it is I!'

Having made the claim, however, he was consternated, fell silent, and seemed almost to shrivel up, as if some disaster had overtaken him.* He hurried away and, by next morning, had gone to earth in the Jas de Bouffan, and refused to see the young poet. Two days later, on 15 April – Gasquet had gone to the Jas in vain each day – he received a note from Cézanne:

'Dear Monsieur, I am leaving for Paris tomorrow. Please accept this expression of my best wishes and most sincere greetings.'

However, a fortnight later, Gasquet was much surprised to see

* All the quotations in these passages are from Joachim Gasquet.

Cézanne in the Cours Mirabeau coming home from painting. Gasquet was about to hurry over to him, but was deterred by Cézanne's astonishing appearance: the painter seemed 'depressed, crushed, disheartened.' Much concerned, Gasquet merely saluted him; but Cézanne appeared not to see him. Next day, however, Gasquet received the following letter:*

Aix, 30 April, 1896.

'Dear Monsieur Gasquet,

'I met you this evening at the lower end of the Cours. You were accompanied by Madame Gasquet. Unless I am mistaken, you seemed very angry with me.

'If you could see inside me, the man within, you would not be so. Don't you understand the sad state to which I am reduced? I am not master of myself, I am a man who doesn't exist, and it is you, who claims to be a philosopher, who wants to finish me off. But I execrate the Geffroy[s] and those fools who, by writing an article for fifty francs, have attracted the attention of the public to me. All my life, I have worked to earn my living, but I believed one could do good painting without attracting attention to one's private life. Of course, an artist wants to succeed intellectually as much as possible, but the man himself should remain obscure. His pleasure must be in his work. Had it been granted to me to succeed, I should have stayed in my own little corner with my few studio colleagues, with whom I used to go out and have a drink. I still have a good friend from those days – but, there it is, he has never succeeded, though he is a damned sight better painter than all those bemedalled and decorated daubers who make you sick. And do you still expect me to believe in anything at my age? Besides, I am like one dead. You're young, and I can understand your wanting to succeed. But what remains to me in my solitude but to eat humble pie? If it were not for the fact that I am passionately fond of the configuration of my native country, I should not be here.

'But I've bored you enough with all this, and now that I have explained my position to you, I hope you will no longer look at me as if I had committed a physical attack on you.

* Reproduced on pp. 270–272, courtesy of Bibliothèque Méjanes, Aix-en-Provence.

'I hope, dear Monsieur, in consideration of my advanced age, that you will accept my most heartfelt good wishes.'

Much upset by this letter, Gasquet hurried to the Jas. Cézanne received him with open arms. 'Don't let's say another word about it,' he said, 'I'm an old fool. Sit there. I'm going to paint your portrait.'

* * *

During these long years of work, Cézanne had largely exhausted the resources of the Jas de Bouffan and its immediate neighbourhood. He was increasingly attracted by the hills of Le Tholonet. No longer content with only a room in the Château Noir, he took a little cottage near the Bibémus quarry. He could leave his painting things in it, and lunch there on bread and cheese, while reading Lucretius or Vigil.

Out at the cottage one day, he heard that Zola was in Aix, staying with Numa Coste. For the moment, he remembered only that they had so often gazed at these Tholonet landscapes together; he forgot all else, *L'Oeuvre*, the incomprehension and contempt, the pity, 'and many other things too, including that damned bitch of a maid who used to watch me out of the corner of her eye as I wiped my feet on the door-mat before going into the salon.' He felt sure that Zola would not dare to come and see him, so he would go to see Zola and shake him by the hand. He hurried off to Aix. On the road he met an acquaintance. Where was Cézanne going in such a hurry? Oh, to see Zola, of course! Had Cézanne not heard what Zola had said about him only yesterday? When asked if he would go to visit Cézanne, Zola had replied, or was supposed to have replied: 'What's the point of going to see that failure?'

Pierced to the heart, Cézanne turned about and went back to Le Tholonet.*

* * *

* At about this period, Zola published another and last article on painting. (*Le Figaro*, 2 May, 1896.) Having visited the exhibitions of that year, he realised to his surprise that the light tones of the Impressionists were now dominant. With some melancholy, he remembered the campaign he had conducted for this painting thirty years before in *L'Evénement*. 'I come to and tremble. Was it really for this I fought? For this bright painting, for these spots of paint, these reflections, this disintegration of light? Lord, was I mad? It's hideous and horrifies me! Oh,

Ambroise Vollard was very pleased with the results of his exhibition. With any luck he would be able to establish Cézanne. But first he needed more merchandise. He had kept in close touch with Cézanne's son, whom he quickly realised to be a good businessman, and now he determined to go to Aix.

From what he had heard, Cézanne seemed inclined to give his canvases away to anyone who fancied them, or simply to leave them about – had not Renoir found a water-colour of the *Baigneuses* in the hills at l'Estaque? It seemed to Vollard that all he had to do was to go to Aix and gather up Cézannes with which to replenish his stock. Hortense and young Paul arrived in Provence a few days before him.

Vollard much enjoyed his brief stay in Aix; and he was considerably diverted by Cézanne. In the studio at the Jas de Bouffan, he saw for himself that the painter's habit of slitting up his canvases with a palette knife was no legend; while outside, hanging in a cherry tree, was a still life Cézanne had thrown out of the window in a moment of discouragement. Cézanne himself was at his most cordial, delighted to welcome a dealer who took such an interest in his work. Vollard found him just as odd as he had been led to expect. He was amused by the painter's favourite expressions: 'Life's so terrifying!' 'They won't put the grapnel on me'; and by his disconcerting humility: 'You must understand, M. Vollard,' Cézanne explained, 'that I have a little sensation, but I can't manage to express it; I'm like a man who possesses a gold piece but cannot use it.'

Vollard had been warned of Cézanne's extraordinary irritability, and

---

the vanity of argument, the uselessness of formulas and schools! And I left the exhibitions of this year wondering in anguish whether I had done wrong in the old days. No, I did my job, I fought the good fight. I was twenty-six, and I was on the side of the young and the brave. What I defended then, I would still defend, because it was the audacity of the moment, the standard that had to be raised in enemy territory. We were right only because we were enthusiastic and had faith. What little we did that had truth is accepted today. And if the path we opened has become banal, the fact remains that we widened it so that contemporary art might make its way along it.' A curious and somewhat ambiguous article, in which Zola both rejoiced and grieved. In passing, he mentioned Cézanne, that 'great but abortive painter . . . whose qualities of genius are all that people look for today.' As Gustave Geffroy aptly remarked, the article was 'a sort of victory fanfare played as a funeral march.'

Aix, 30 avril 1896.

Cher Monsieur Gasquet,

Je vous ai rencontré au bas du cours ce soir, vous étiez accompagné de Madame Gasquet. Si je ne me trompe vous m'avez paru fortement fâché contre moi.

Si vous pouviez me voir en dedans, l'homme du dedans, vous ne le seriez pas. Vous ne voyez donc pas à quel triste état je suis réduit, pas maître de moi, l'homme qui n'existe pas et c'est vous qui voulez être philosophe, qui voulez finir par m'achever. Mais je maudis les Geffroy et les quelques drôles qui pour faire un article de 50 francs, ont attiré l'attention du public par moi. Toute ma vie, j'ai travaillé pour arriver à gagner ma vie, mais je croyais qu'on pouvait faire de la peinture bien faite sans attirer l'attention sur son existence privée. Certes, un artiste désire s'élever intellectuellement le plus possible, mais l'homme doit rester obscur. Le plaisir doit résider dans l'étude. S'il m'avait été donné de réaliser, c'est moi qui serais resté dans mon coin, avec les quelques camarades d'atelier, avec qui nous allions boire chopine. J'ai encore un brave ami de ce temps-là, eh bien, il n'est pas arrivé, n'empêche pas qu'il est bougrement plus peintre que tous les galvaudeux à médailles et décorations, que c'est à faire suer, et vous voulez qu'à mon âge, je croie encore à quelque chose, d'ailleurs je suis comme mort. — Vous êtes jeune, et je comprends que vous vouliez réussir. Mais moi, ce que je puis faire dans ma situation, c'est de filer doux, et n'était que j'aime énormément la configuration de mon pays, je ne serais pas ici.

Mais je vous ai assez ennuyé comme ça, et après que je vous ai expliqué ma situation, j'espère que vous ne me regarderez plus comme si j'avais commis quelque attentat contre votre sûreté. —

Veuillez, cher monsieur, et en considération de mon grand âge, agréer mes meilleurs sentiments et souhaits que je puisse faire pour vous. —

Paul Cézanne

he was particularly careful of what he said. However, when Gustave Moreau's name came up in conversation during a meal, Vollard casually remarked that he was said to be 'an excellent teacher.' This was too much for Cézanne. 'All the teachers,' he shouted in sudden fury, putting his glass down with a bang that broke it, 'are idiots, bastards and eunuchs; they've got no guts!' But in the face of Vollard's obvious consternation, he calmed down and said with a nervous laugh: 'The important thing, you must understand, M. Vollard, is to get rid of the schools, all the schools.' Nevertheless, Cézanne expanded under the influence of Vollard's visit. When they were walking together with young Paul in the garden of the Jas, Cézanne noticed the canvas hanging in the cherry tree. 'Son,' he said, 'we must get *Les Pommes* down. I'll try to carry that study further.'

Vollard, however, found it less easy to acquire Cézannes in Aix than he had expected. People were suspicious of the dealer. Since, with the exception of Gasquet and his friends, no one in the town took Cézanne's efforts seriously, what were they to make of Vollard? Was he pulling their legs or merely a fool? Many who possessed Cézannes refused to part with them or even show them to him. A certain countess, who had relegated hers to the attics, flatly refused to sell them to him:

'But I tell you, they're not art!'

'They're worth money, though,' Vollard said. 'And suppose the rats . . .'

'Very well, let my rats gnaw my Cézannes!'

The dealer's presence in the town soon became known, and caused much excitement among the local artists. If Vollard was buying paintings, they could show him some good ones, not daubs such as that madman Cézanne painted. Vollard did his best to discourage them. 'It's much too well painted to find a buyer in Paris; they don't care for good painting there.' One of these painters had been given two or three canvases by Cézanne, and Vollard asked if he might see them. 'Cézanne is a friend,' the painter replied. 'And, you see, I don't like my friends being laughed at. So that no one should be able to sneer at them in my presence, and since it was a pity to waste good canvas, I've painted over them.'

Nevertheless, Vollard was not altogether unsuccessful. One day, a man came to see him, produced a Cézanne out of a parcel and said: 'I won't take less than 150 francs.'* Vollard bought it on the spot. The man was delighted and said: 'Come with me!' He took Vollard to a house where he saw a number of Cézannes lying amid a heap of junk, a cracked chamber pot, old shoes, a bird cage and rusty tools.

The people of the house seemed rather suspicious of Vollard but eventually made up their minds to sell him the paintings for 1,000 francs. Vollard handed them a note. They examined it carefully, and said they must get the bank to authenticate it. This done, they said Vollard might take the Cézannes away. As he was leaving the house, they shouted after him from an upper window: he had left one behind; and they threw a Cézanne landscape down to him.

* * *

In spite of the good news Vollard had brought from Paris, Cézanne soon relapsed into depression. He had been too battered throughout his life to be able to take heart at a few indications of interest. Besides, he had been a stranger for so many years to the artistic circles of the capital that he could no longer grasp the importance of their approval. In his heart of hearts, he was much more concerned with the opinion of his neighbours.

His health seriously undermined by diabetes, he went to Vichy in June to take the cure. On leaving Vichy, he returned to Aix, but not for long. He left again almost immediately for Talloires, in the neighbourhood of Annecy. From there he wrote to Solari: 'When I was in Aix, I thought I should be better off elsewhere: but now that I'm here, I regret Aix. My life is beginning to be sepulchrally monotonous.'

At the end of August, after working for two months at Talloires, where he painted a view of the lake which, in its serenity and sober eloquence, is one of his most successful pictures, Cézanne went to Paris. He was annoyed at being unable to find a studio that suited him. Nor did he care for the Rue des Dames, in the Batignolles, where he was living. Towards the end of December, he moved to another flat, 73, Rue Saint-Lazare, where he was kept to his bed for three or four weeks with a bad attack of influenza.

* Approximately £25 today.

In the spring of 1897, the room reserved to the Caillebotte bequest was opened in the Luxembourg. Cézanne's satisfaction at being represented in a national collection was not unmingled with bitterness; once again the paintings were subjected to attack: 'The exhibition of this heap of excrement in a national museum publicly dishonours French art.'* Eighteen members of the Institute, headed by Gérome, sent a letter of protest to the Minister of Public Instruction, and there was even a question asked in the Senate.†

Cézanne soon grew tired of life in Paris. In May, he took refuge in the forest of Fontainebleau, staying at Marlotte and then at Mennecy; but by the end of the month he was back in Aix. 'I am very done up,' he had recently written to Gasquet. 'I ought to be more sensible and realise that at my age I should not longer have illusions, and that they'll always let me down . . . I won't say I envy you your youth, that's impossible, but your vigour and your inexhaustible vitality.'

Cézanne was delighted to see the Gasquets again. He liked going to their house. It was in the Rue des Arts-et-Métiers and seemed a haven of peace to him, for everywhere else in the town he was looked on as

* The opinion of an anonymous official painter quoted by Thiébault-Sisson in an article in *Le Temps* (9 March, 1897).

† The line taken by Gérome and his friends did not meet with unqualified approval. Thiébault-Sisson, in the article quoted above, wrote: 'Whether it [the Académie] desires it or not, Impressionist art has justified itself and produced masterpieces, whatever one may say. If reservations can be made about such and such a work by such and such an artist, the timeliness of the Impressionist experiment cannot be doubted. One may even say that it has been of greater benefit to those who have not adopted its formulas than to its adepts themselves. How many painters have cleaner palettes, brighter colour and a more subtle and perceptive vision because of it! It may perhaps be a transitory art; but it is certainly not a negligible one; and by the mere fact of its existence the State owed it to itself to show it in precisely the same way as it does the official art protected by the Académie. The protest [made by the eighteen members of the Institute] will therefore be vain. The indifferent will be amused, the sceptical will smile, and the spiteful will not fail to remark that this protest might well have emanated, not from artists whose ideal has been offended, but from tradesmen exasperated by the progress of a rival business. I know that the spiteful will be wrong, but the mockers will be with them, as the protesters will find to their cost.' Martial Caillebotte, for his part, would not accept the arrangement of 1895 as final. He hoped that in time the State would alter its decision and accept the canvases it had rejected. For twelve years, till 1908, he tried to break down the official hostility. He failed completely.

a maniac. Ever since his exhibition at Vollard's, he had been the object both of envy and slander. His success in Paris could not be forgiven him when so many 'sound' Aixois painters, who had been hung in the Salon, were languishing for lack of recognition. Nor was he forgiven for being his father's son.

The old rancours Louis Auguste had aroused were transferred to Cézanne. He felt hunted and would dodge down side-streets, hugging the walls. One day, he heard someone say as he went by: 'Painters like that ought to be put up against a wall and shot!'

With the Gasquets he felt safe at least. He was warmed by their admiration; and the Gasquets' friends listened to him with respect. 'I'm a plain man. You mustn't pay me compliments and lie to me from politeness.' He had been derided for so long that he found it difficult to believe that praise did not conceal some 'interested stratagem.'* But the praise of these young writers and poets – Jean Royère, Xavier de Magallon, Édmond Jaloux and José d'Arbaud – was sincere. And Cézanne was moved by it; often to the point of tears. But a moment later he would be roaring with laughter. He would talk about his art in a voice that was 'slow, meticulous, and with an intonation that was at once fond and caressing.'† 'Look how tenderly the light loves apricots, it takes them whole, enters into their very flesh, illuminates their every side! But it is miserly with peaches, of which it makes only one half luminous.' He was entirely absorbed in painting. Yet, knowing how fond Marie Gasquet was of music, he would ask her, out of gratitude, to go to the piano and play him some piece of Weber from *Oberon* or *Freischütz*. But he generally fell asleep; and Marie Gasquet would play *fortissimo* so that he would wake and not be embarrassed. And Cézanne would begin to talk of painting again: 'An artist, you see, must create his work as an almond tree its blossom, or a snail its slime . . .' Then he would suddenly fall into a reverie, perhaps watching the 'play of light and shade'‡ on his closed fist. Or he would speak shyly of the future: 'I may perhaps have come too early. I have been the painter of your generation rather than of my own.' But he was

* Édmond Jaloux: *Les Saisons littéraires*.
† Édmond Jaloux: *Fumées dans la Campagne*.
‡ Gasquet.

utterly without pretension. He was like a peasant who, disappointed in the previous harvest, hopes for a clement season in the coming year. His own youth was dead, as were most of his youthful friendships. But these young people were another springtime.

For several years past Cézanne had been trying to bring to fruition a big canvas of *Baigneuses,* which he wanted to make his masterpiece. 'It will be my picture,' he said. 'As in *Le Triomphe de Flore,** I want to marry the curves of women to the shoulders of the hills. But the focal point? I can't find the focal point . . . Tell me, what shall I group them round? Ah, Poussin's arabesque! He knew all about it, that chap . . .!' He was continually returning to this project, making sketch after sketch. But the work presented enormous difficulties, since he was painting without models. For the postures of his bathers, he was using sketches he had made at the Académie Suisse in his youth. He was even more afraid of getting a woman to pose for him now than he had been in the past. To justify his shyness, he said that he had now passed the age for 'denuding a woman to paint her.' Besides, women were calculating and would certainly try to 'put the grapnel on him.' And what a scandal there would be in Aix if he shut himself up in his studio with a model! As a result, he was frequently in difficulties with his picture. 'Look, you see women,' he said one day to José d'Arbaud, 'bring me some photographs . . .' D'Arbaud was somewhat taken aback by the request, since Cézanne had failed to explain the purpose for which he required them.

But there was much else about Cézanne that surprised his young friends: for instance, the incredible labour that went into the canvases they so much admired. Cézanne would sometimes stand, brush in hand, staring at his subject for a quarter of an hour or more without adding a touch of paint to his canvas. 'My eyes are sometimes so fixed on what I'm looking at,' he admitted to Gasquet, 'that they feel as if they were going to bleed . . . Tell me, do you think I'm a little mad? . . . I sometimes wonder, you know.' One afternoon, Gasquet and Xavier de Magallon went out to meet the painter in the Tholonet hills. When they reached the Bibémus quarry, they saw him, fists clenched, tears in his eyes, stamping up and down in front of a canvas he had just slit

* By Poussin.

in half. The *mistral* was blowing and carried the canvas away. Gasquet and Magallon ran to pick it up. 'Leave it! Leave it!' cried Cézanne. 'This time I was really going to express myself . . . It was there, the whole thing was there . . . But it just wouldn't come. No, no! . . . Leave it!' In a fury he trampled the canvas to pieces and then sat down and sobbed. Suddenly shaking his fist at the young men, he cried: 'Go away! Go away, can't you!'

* * *

On 25 October Cézanne's mother died. She was eighty-three and had been in a decline for a long time, almost completely crippled physically and failing mentally. Cézanne had done everything in his power to make her last days happy. He had hired a carriage, taken her out for drives, and been wonderfully attentive and affectionate. Her death upset him greatly; so much of his life disappeared with her, for she had been more of a 'moral support' to him than anyone else in the world. When she lay dead, he felt he must have some memorial of her at the last. He wanted a drawing and went to get his pencils. But then it occurred to him that he was not worthy: a 'sound' painter, a respected artist, was required rather than a failure such as himself. He hurried off to Villevieille and asked him to make a drawing of the dead woman for him.

CHAPTER THREE

The Bonfire at the Jas

A picture? . . . Forty sous of canvas and colours, or a hundred thousand francs of genius.—BALZAC

THE Dreyfus Affair was stirring France to her depths. Violent passions were splitting the country into two enemy camps, breaking up old friendships, and even dividing families. Dreyfusards and anti-Dreyfusards attacked each other with unparalleled fury. Amid the lies and the invective there were, however, gestures both noble and courageous. Zola had emerged as a defender of Dreyfus. At the beginning of the year, on 13 January, 1898, he had published an open letter to the President of the Republic in *L'Aurore*, to which Clemenceau gave the title 'J'accuse.'

Cézanne was no more disturbed by the Dreyfus Affair than he had been by the war of 1870. Under the influence of the virulently anti-Dreyfusard circle in which he lived, he contented himself, when people mentioned Zola, by saying: 'He has had his leg pulled.' He would cut Forain's anti-Dreyfusard cartoons from the newspapers and remark: 'How beautifully drawn it is!' These were his only known reactions to the Affair.

Though he still indulged in a good deal of swearing at his easel, when things were going comparatively well he was liable to burst into song:

La peinture à l'huile
C'est bien difficile,
Mais c'est bien plus beau
Que la peinture à l'eau . . .

'It's so good and so terrible to attack a blank canvas,' he said to Gasquet.

At the beginning of the year, Cézanne had another death to mourn: on 8 January Emperaire died. He was nearly seventy, and in his whole life there had not been one glimmer of success. He had lived unknown, and often hungry, in his attic, dreaming of beauty and fame, and to the very last he had done exercises on the trapeze in the vain hope of growing taller. There were two or three of Emperaire's pictures hanging in a cheap eating-house in the Passage Agard. Cézanne went there from time to time merely to look at them.

Painting, the Gasquets, Solari and his sister Marie now made up his whole life in Aix. Since the funeral of his mother, Cézanne had not dared go back to the Jas de Bouffan, which now gave him a sense of irremedial absence and loss. Yet he did not want the Jas to be sold, as Marie and the Conils did so that their inheritance might be equally shared; and he did his best to prevent it. But he had never succeeded in having his way in such matters.

Fortunately, he could always withdraw into his painting. One day, showing Gasquet a still life on which he was working, he said: 'People think a sugar-basin has no physiognomy, no soul. But it changes every day. You have to know how to approach those fellows, how to coax them . . . Those plates and glasses talk among themselves: interminable secrets . . .'

* * *

In May and June, Vollard held another exhibition of Cézanne's works in Paris; but Cézanne himself did not return there till the autumn. He went to live near Hortense and his son, in the Villa des Arts, at 15, Rue Hégésippe-Moreau, which curved round the side of the Butte Montmartre. The locality had the charm and peace of the countryside.

Cézanne's son was now the centre of his affections. And in him, though he was so very different and so much a stranger to his own concerns, he was aware of those qualities he himself lacked: an ability to get on with people, sound commonsense, and a capacity to cope with life. 'The boy' – who was now twenty-six – 'is more competent than I am,' he said; 'I have no practical sense.' He realised that his son was indifferent to art; but 'with him as intermediary, the difficulty I have in understanding the practical things in life will be smoothed out.' Aware that the demand for his father's work was increasing, young Paul, together with Vollard, set about looking for buyers. Cézanne was delighted and offered him a ten per cent commission on sales.

Thanks to his son and Vollard he hoped one day to earn 6,000 francs* a year with his brush; though, as young Paul pointed out, he should paint more female nudes, since these were 'much more easily sold.'

Vollard was as enthusiastic as ever about Cézanne's work. He did not pay the painter very much, but on the other hand he was prepared to take everything Cézanne produced, the least sketch, even the ripped canvases. This devotion to his work moved Cézanne; and it was no doubt an anodyne to his wounded pride. But there were still moments when he turned suspicious and muttered sombrely against the dealer. 'He's up to something, something criminal,' he would say. And then he would clear his studio, burn his sketches and the canvases he despaired of finishing or which did not seem to him sufficiently 'realised.' There would be that much less to speculate on.

At such moments of depression, even the most overt proofs of interest in his work could not console him. When the Berlin National Gallery bought two of his pictures, all he said was: 'Well, that won't make them accept me for the Salon!' Success was coming too late and was too removed from the kind of success he had always imagined. Had he been accepted by the Salon, had the Hanging Committee awarded him a medal, or the government the Légion d'Honneur, it would have given him far greater reassurance as to the value of his work. Nor would he any longer be affected by the ill-natured derision of his native town. 'Do you like Cézanne?' someone had said in public. 'I hate him. And I am speaking for posterity.' And Henri-Modeste Pontier, the new director of the Museum and Drawing School, who had succeeded Honoré Gibert in 1892, had sworn that, as long as he lived, no canvas of Cézanne should mar the Aix Museum by hanging beside that work of sculpture which had not only made his own reputation in the Salon of 1877, but was now such an honour to the gallery: *Ixion, roi des Lapithes, torturé pour avoir aimé Junon.*†

Could it be possible, Cézanne wondered, that between himself and the official hierarchy of successful painters, with their plethora of important commissions, posterity would choose him, a poor mocked old man? Was this not a fantastic dream from which he would awaken

* Approximately £1,000 today.
† Henri-Modeste Pontier kept his word. He died in 1926.

to find that his leg had been pulled by certain people in the most monstrous fashion?

But as soon as he picked up his brushes he forgot these painful questionings. He would work unremittingly to the end. 'I have sworn to die painting, rather than fall into the degrading second childhood that overtakes so many old men . . .' he said.

* * *

Vollard wanted Cézanne to paint his portrait. And Cézanne, who rarely found a model who would submit to his demands, agreed with alacrity.

When Vollard arrived at the Rue Hégésippe-Moreau for the first sitting, he was surprised to find that Cézanne had erected a sort of dais for him in the middle of the studio. There was a chair placed on a packing-case, which was in turn balanced on 'four meagre supports.' Vollard inspected it with some concern, but Cézanne reassured him: 'There's no danger of your falling, Monsieur Vollard, provided you keep your balance. Besides, when one sits one mustn't move.' The sitting began. Vollard had not realised that Cézanne looked on people 'as apples' when they sat to him. Eventually Vollard fell asleep and the whole dais collapsed. 'Idiot!' cried Cézanne. 'You've destroyed the pose!' Vollard determined to fortify himself with black coffee in future.

The sittings took place every morning from eight o'clock till half-past eleven. In the afternoon Cézanne went to the Louvre or to the Trocadero to draw from the masters. He retired early to bed, but always got up during the night to look at the sky. His constant concern was whether there would be a clear grey light for the next day's sitting.

But there were many other necessary conditions; and Vollard drew up a list of them: it was essential that Cézanne should be satisfied with the studies he had done in the museum the previous day; there must be no noise in the neighbourhood of the studio, particularly no barking dog,* or, indeed, anything else to distract Cézanne's thoughts. 'When I'm working, I need to be left in peace.'

* 'One day, accompanied by his son, I went to see Cézanne,' recorded Jean Royère . . . 'He seemed in a furious temper. "There's a dog been barking over there for the last hour!" he cried as we came in. "I've had to stop work." '

Nevertheless, during these days of 1899, Cézanne was in comparatively good humour. Such canvases of his as appeared in the sales were finding buyers at increasingly high prices; and these successes appeared to be gradually making him less bitter. In April, on Monet's suggestion, a sale was organised for the benefit of the children of Sisley, who had died in poverty on 29 January. A Cézanne went for 2,300 francs (approximately £400 today). And, in May, at the sale of Count Armand Doria's collection, Cézanne's *Neige fondante en Forêt de Fontainebleau* went for 6,750 francs (approximately £1,000 today). The public was flabbergasted, shouted that it was an imposture and demanded the name of the purchaser. A stout man with a beard got to his feet and said: 'I am the purchaser, and my name is Claude Monet.'

Cézanne was working on his *Baigneuses* at the same time as on the portrait of Vollard, and one day he told the dealer that he had at last made up his mind to have recourse to a professional model. Vollard was astounded: 'What, Monsieur Cézanne, a naked woman!' 'Oh, Monsieur Vollard,' replied Cézanne, 'I shall engage only a very old hag.' The painter did not, however, make use of her services for long. No one knew how to pose today and 'yet I pay dearly enough for a sitting: it costs four francs, twenty sous more than before 1870.'

The experiment having been a disappointment, Cézanne returned with all the greater enthusiasm to Vollard's portrait. The dealer showed an almost angelic patience. 'You're beginning to know how to sit,' said Cézanne, thinking he was paying him the most splendid of compliments. 'And you're useful to me as a study.' Quite insensible to fatigue himself when painting, Cézanne was incapable of realising that his model might be tired. It was his son who tried to give him a sense of reality: 'If you make Vollard come so often, you'll end by exhausting him, and if you exhaust him, he'll pose badly.' 'Son, you're right,' said Cézanne. 'One should humour one's model. You've got practical sense.'*

Vollard was as careful as ever not to give Cézanne a pretext for one

* The frequency with which the models for his portraits are shown leaning on their elbows can be explained by Cézanne's demands on them; as can also the fact that many of them look rather cramped and stupid with fatigue.

of his tempers. He was afraid for the fate of his portrait. Having lavished so much patience and suffered so much discomfort, he wanted it to be finished. He had seen too many of Cézanne's canvases destroyed in a fury. He talked as little as possible, and avoided the subjects of painting and literature.

Chocquet's widow died early in July and his collection was put up for sale. It included thirty-two of Cézanne's works. There was also a Delacroix that Cézanne much coveted, a large water-colour called *Fleurs*. Vollard, who was delighted to have an opportunity of obliging Cézanne, proposed buying it and giving it to Cézanne in exchange for one of his own pictures. In the meantime, Vollard had looked up Delacroix' catalogue and told Cézanne that the picture was described as a water-colour in which the flowers were placed at random against a grey background. 'Wretch!' cried Cézanne furiously. 'Do you dare to tell me that Delacroix painted at random!' Vollard tried to calm the painter down. 'What do you expect?' said Cézanne. 'I love Delacroix.'

As far as Cézanne was concerned, no work, however far advanced it might be, was ever really finished. After a hundred and fifteen sittings he abandoned Vollard's portrait, with the hope of returning to it one day 'when I have made some progress.' 'You must understand, Monsieur Vollard, that the outline escapes me. But I'm not displeased with the shirt-front,' he said.

* * *

During the summer Cézanne went to Montgeroult in the neighbourhood of Pontoise.

At Marines, a few kilometres to the north, there lived a young painter called Louis Le Bail and, at Pissarro's suggestion, he visited Cézanne.

Cézanne was flattered by the admiration of his young colleague; he was becoming less diffident and less unsociable now that there were increasing signs that people were truly interested in his work. At the Chocquet sale, which had been held on 1, 3 and 4 July at the Galerie Georges Petit, his canvases had fetched unusually good prices. Several had been sold for over 2,000 francs. His *Mardi Gras* had gone for

4,400 francs and *La Maison du Pendu* for 6,200. Altogether, the thirty-two Cézannes had made over 50,000 francs.* Dealers and big collectors had bid against each other for some of his works. Durand-Ruel, encouraged by Monet, had bought fifteen canvases and Isaac de Camondo, the rich banker, had to fight for *La Maison du Pendu*.†

Cézanne often went out to paint in company with Le Bail. On some such excursions he was in a particularly good mood and unusually communicative. 'It does me good,' he said, 'I'm glad to be able to let myself go.' He courteously answered Le Bail's questions about his views on the art of painting. But theoretical speculations seemed to him fruitless. 'We'll go and put our absurd theories into practice,' he would say ironically as they set off to paint. Feeling that Le Bail was sympathetic, Cézanne revealed his most secret thoughts. When Le Bail asked him whose pictures he liked best, he confessed, with mingled pride and humility, that he would prefer his own above all others, if he could realise what he sought.

Nevertheless, his touchiness and self-doubt were always latent; the least incident could arouse them. One day, when the two painters were working together, a young girl stopped and looked at their canvases. Indicating Le Bail's, she said it was the better. Cézanne was very much upset; he was utterly unable to take the girl's ignorance into account. The next day he clearly tried to avoid Le Bail. But the days were over when such an incident could affect him for long. He tried to explain away his ill-humour: 'You should be sorry for me,' he said. And then

* The equivalent of over £8,000 today. His works had increased ten times in value since the Tanguy sale five years before. It is interesting to compare the prices of the Cézannes at the Chocquet sale with those fetched by the canvases of other artists sold at the same time: 9,500 francs were given for a Delacroix; 290 francs for a Corot; 2,750 francs for one of the Courbets; 13,500 for Manet's *Paveurs de la rue de Berne;* 11,500 for Monet's *Vue d'Argenteuil;* and 20,000 francs for Renoir's *À la Grenouillère.*

† Vollard, who had a tendency to exaggerate the picturesque side of things, records that Camondo said to him about *La Maison du Pendu:* 'Well, yes, I've bought a picture which is not yet accepted by everyone! But I'm covered. I have an autographed letter from Claude Monet, who gives me his word of honour that this canvas will become famous. If you come to see me one day, I'll show you the letter. I keep it in a pocket nailed to the back of the picture to confute the ill-disposed, who think I'm crazy to have bought my *Maison du Pendu.*'

he added, still rather anxious: 'Out of the mouths of babes and sucklings . . .'

Another day, two horsemen came up while Cézanne was painting and tried to engage him in conversation. Cézanne growled at them and they rode off. When they had gone, Le Bail told him they were Baron Denys Cochin, a great collector who owned several of Cézanne's pictures, and his son.* Cézanne bitterly reproached himself for this solecism and it worried him for several days. He wrote to Le Bail: 'I am very upset by the false position in which I have placed myself. Though I have not had the honour of knowing you for very long, I am venturing to ask your help to repair my blunder. What ought I to do? Tell me and I'll be most grateful to you.'

The letter is pathetic in its embarrassment and forms a curious contrast to another Le Bail received from him a little later. Cézanne had moved from Montgeroult to Marines and he had asked Le Bail to come at three o'clock every day, knock at his door and awaken him from his siesta. One afternoon, since Cézanne gave no sign, Le Bail went into his room. Unaware of the painter's hatred of being touched, he must have shaken him awake. Cézanne was furious and wrote Le Bail a savage letter:

'Monsieur,

'The rather discourteous way in which you take the liberty of entering my room is not calculated to please me. In future, please have yourself announced.

'Please give the person who calls for them the glass and the canvas which were left in your studio.'

* * *

At Aix, where Cézanne now returned, the Jas de Bouffan had been sold. This saddened him, and one evening he appeared at the Gasquets almost in tears. Not only had the Jas been sold, but a bonfire had been made of furniture and other objects which he had been keeping 'like

* It is recorded that the son said: 'Look, Father, there's Cézanne.' 'How do you know he's Cézanne?' 'But, look, Father, he's painting a Cézanne.' Several writers have recorded this anecdote. *Se non è vero . . .*

relics.' No one had informed him that the destruction was to take place. 'They didn't dare to sell them. They were poor things, dust-traps! So they burned them . . . The armchair in which Papa used to take a nap . . . The table at which he had done his accounts since he was a young man . . . They have burned all that remained to me of him . . .'

Exiled from the house that held so many memories, Cézanne thought of buying the Château Noir, but his offer was refused. So he decided to live in the town, at 23, Rue Boulegon, a handsome house in the street in which Louis Auguste's bank was once situated. Cézanne lived on the second floor and arranged a studio in the attic. His sister Marie found a housekeeper for him: Madame Brémond. Forty, sensible, kind and an excellent cook, she looked after him most efficiently, made him keep to his diet, and in fact took the place of the absent Hortense.

Cézanne would be sixty-one next January. For some men this is still comparative youth, but for him it was decrepitude. He was in need of rest. At times he doubted whether he would ever go back to Paris again. He would have liked 'to be a monk like Fra Angelico, so that his life might be ordered once and for all and, freed from all cares and anxieties, he might paint from dawn to dusk, meditating in his cell, never to be interrupted in his meditations, nor distracted from his effort.'* He always rose at dawn and went to early Mass – 'Mass and a douche are what keep me going,' he said – then he would go to his studio and draw from plaster casts for an hour before returning to his current canvases. Later he would break off to read his favourite authors: Apuleius, Virgil, Stendhal or Baudelaire.

After luncheon, he would go out to paint in the neighbourhood of the Château Noir. Since he now had to husband his strength, he had come to an arrangement with a local cabman to drive him. The four-wheeler would come to the door at two o'clock every day, and as they drove out towards Le Tholonet, Cézanne sometimes talked to the cabman. 'The world doesn't understand me,' he said on one occasion. 'And I don't understand the world. That's why I've retired from it.' Sometimes he would sit up suddenly and cry excitedly: 'Look at those blues, the blues under the pines . . .' Cézanne gave the cabman a canvas to mark his appreciation of his services. 'Well, the man seemed quite

* Gasquet.

pleased. He said "thank you." But he left the canvas behind. He forgot to take it away,' he told Gasquet sadly.

The retired life Cézanne led gave rise to all sorts of gossip in Aix, and boys chased him and threw stones at him in the streets. His oversensitiveness and his complex imagination no doubt led him to exaggerate the hostility shown him.

CHAPTER FOUR

The Old Man of the Rue Boulegon

It is night. The gushing fountains are talking more loudly.
And my soul is a gushing fountain too.—NIETZSCHE

AT the end of 1899, Cézanne, after some hesitation, sent two still lifes and a landscape to the fifteenth exhibition of the Société des Artistes Indépendants, which had been founded in 1884, and had raised the Salon des Refusés to the level of an institution. There was no hanging committee; any picture sent in was hung automatically.

In 1900, Cézanne was surprised – for this almost amounted to official recognition – to have three of his works hung at the Centennale de l'Art Français, at the Petit Palais, in Paris, during the International Exhibition. This was due to the intelligent and obstinate determination of Roger Marx, an Inspector of the Beaux-Arts, who had long ago been won over to his work and that of the Impressionists.

Roger Marx had had considerable difficulties with the Institute, but in the end Cézanne had been voted admission, much to the fury of Gérome. On 1 May, at the opening of the Centennale, when Gérome was showing round Loubet, the President of the Republic, he hurried him through the room in which the Impressionists were hanging and said: 'Don't stop, Monsieur le Président. This is a disgrace to French art!'

In spite of Gérome and his colleagues, the triumph of the Impressionists was now a fact; and Cézanne's own success was foreseeable. The importance of the Aixois painter was becoming increasingly recognised. In the spring of 1901, he exhibited again with the Indépendants and also with the Libre Esthétique in Brussels, the group which had succeeded the 'XX.' His pictures were currently selling at between 5,000 and 6,000 francs.* At a recent sale, a canvas had fetched 7,000 francs.†

* Between approximately £850 and £1,000 today. This information is to be found in a letter from Pissarro to his son Lucien.

† Approximately £1,200 today.

Perhaps an even more significant fact was that one of the old habitués of Tanguy's shop, Maurice Denis, had just painted an *Hommage à Cézanne*. Grouped round a Cézanne still life were Odilon Redon, Sérusier, Bonnard, Vuillard, K. X. Roussel, Ambroise Vollard and some others. Denis included himself in the picture, and it was clear that these young painters at the dawn of the new century wished to express their admiration for Cézanne, whom they looked on as a master. When exhibited at the Salon de la Société Nationale des Beaux-Arts, and later at the Libre Esthétique, the picture aroused a great deal of interest. It was bought by a young writer called André Gide.

While his name was becoming known in the world, and his work continually finding new admirers, Cézanne was pursuing his regular routine in Aix. But he was undoubtedly happier. Perhaps, after all, he had not been wrong, had not worked in vain. Though there were still outbursts of irritability, there was nevertheless a greater serenity. But the struggle to achieve work that satisfied him went on unceasingly.

The further Cézanne carried his researches, the more wonderful the world appeared and the more difficult it became to express its inexhaustible riches. His canvases were increasingly fervid and lyrical. Like all great artists, he seemed to have found the secret of another youth in his old age. He had acquired a new, an almost impetuous freedom of expression. His pictures of Sainte-Victoire and Château Noir blaze like gems. Never had he been in such close communion with the trees, the rocks and the sky.

He was clearly gaining in both confidence and hope, for in November he decided to build a studio. He bought a site on the slope of a hill to the north of the town on the Chemin des Lauves.* It consisted of about an acre planted with olives, cherries and almonds, and included an old tumbledown cottage. He knew exactly what he wanted and commissioned an architect to carry out his plan. The cottage was to be pulled down and replaced by a building with a ground and first floor. Downstairs there were to be two small rooms and upstairs the studio. This was to be twenty-five feet long, twenty feet wide and fifteen feet high, and was to be lit by a huge expanse of glass on one side and two

* Lauve is a Provençal word meaning 'flat stone.' The Chemin des Lauves is today the Avenue Paul-Cézanne.

big windows on the other. It was all to be simple and efficient with no superfluous ornament. From the studio, Cézanne would have a splendid view over Aix, where the bell-tower of the cathedral of Saint-Sauveur rose above the roofs of the houses, to the hills beyond, with the chain of the Étoile and the Pilon du Roi closing the horizon.

These arrangements made, Cézanne went back to work. He was now compelled to admit that the younger generation was interested in him, and that Maurice Denis' *Hommage* was sincere. People came to see him and to listen to him talk. Gasquet introduced to him a young man called Léo Larguier from the Cévennes, whose ambition was to become a poet, and who was doing his military service in Aix. A few days later, Cézanne received a visit from another soldier, who was also in garrison in the town, the Marseilles painter Charles Camoin, and was much touched by his enthusiasm. 'A new era in art is on the way,' Camoin assured him.

Cézanne made these young soldiers welcome. They were in their early twenties, and he enjoyed their company. He considered they were 'very well balanced'; and they were a 'moral support' to him. He often invited them to a meal and gave them chicken or duck stuffed with olives. With them, he was at his best and liveliest; indeed, he surprised them by his kindliness. They were surprised, too, by the austerity in which he lived. A round polished walnut table, six chairs and a sideboard with a bowl of fruit were all the furnishings of his dining-room; there was not even a picture on the walls. He astonished them also by the way he talked of his 'feebleness' and the difficulty he had in 'realising' a painting as he wished: 'I feel I can get so far, but there is a point beyond which I cannot go.' They were impressed by the youth of his mind compared to the physical decrepitude which was becoming increasingly obvious. As he poured wine for them (it was 'no better than the wine in the canteen'*), he would quote – for his memory was as good as ever – the Latin and French poets.

But his conversation naturally consisted almost entirely of the 'damned business of painting.' He talked of Monticelli and Tanguy; and was not always kind about his old friends. On occasion he would call Monet a 'blackguard,' Renoir 'a pimp' and say that Degas 'lacked

* Larguier.

guts!' And yet, at other times, he would speak most warmly of them: 'Monet? The finest painter's eye that has ever existed.'

'A thousand painters ought to be killed every year,' he declared one day when in a particularly happy mood. 'But who should be given the job of selecting them?' Camoin asked. 'We, of course, damn it!' said Cézanne. And from time to time, emphasising his remark by banging the table, he would exclaim: 'Say what you like, I'm every inch a painter!' Then, turning serious, he would touch the objects on the table with a delicate finger, a bottle, a glass, a dish, and point out how they mutually reflected each other. 'Look at that!' he would say. And, if he became absorbed, he would quit the room and disappear. Larguier and Camoin knew it was useless to try and lure him back to finish his meal. Forgetting all about his guests, he would have gone to work in his studio on some problem that had been worrying him.

On Sundays Cézanne sometimes went to the barrack gate and waited for his friends. Dressed in their képis with pompons, red trousers and white gaiters, the soldiers would go with him to Mass at Saint-Sauveur. Coming out of church, Cézanne was often surrounded by a crowd of beggars. He had change ready and distributed it quickly, looking rather frightened. There was one beggar who seemed to terrify him and he always put a five franc piece in his bowl. 'That's Germain Nouveau, the poet,' he whispered to Larguier one Sunday.

Germain Nouveau had been a friend of Rimbaud and Verlaine, and had led one of the more curious lives of the period. At one time he had gone mad and become an inmate of Bicêtre. But, for many years past, he had been a religious vagabond, making pilgrimages to Rennes and to Santiago de Compostela. In 1898, ragged and verminous, he had returned to Aix, where he had spent his youth and where, so he believed, the demons could not find 'a field of action as in Marseilles or Paris.'* Everyone was rather afraid of him; and even the clergy could find no means of getting rid of this ecstatic who went each morning to communicate in every church in the town.

O mon Seigneur Jésus, semeur de paraboles
Qui contiennent l'or clair et vivant des symboles,
Prenez mes vers de cuivre ainsi que des oboles . . .

* Léon Vérane: *Humilis, Poète errant.*

Cézanne explained to his friends that religion was for him 'a moral hygiene.' 'Since I'm a weak character, I lean on my sister Marie, who leans on her confessor, who leans on Rome.' But he did not linger on these matters. Having taken what he called his 'slice of the Middle Ages,' he returned to his more permanent preoccupations.

One afternoon, when the company, in which Larguier was a corporal, was engaged in manoeuvres on the Tholonet road, he asked permission of his officer to go up to the Château Noir, where he knew Cézanne was working. He saw the four-wheeler standing beside the road and found Cézanne cleaning his palette. Cézanne drew his attention to the prodigality with which he used colours and exclaimed: 'I paint as if I were Rothschild!'

That evening, when Larguier had returned to barracks and was in charge of a squad doing arms drill, he saw Cézanne's four-wheeler coming down the road. He gave his squad the order: 'Present arms!' Cézanne took his hat off and stopped the cab. Larguier told him he had given the order to pay homage to a great painter. 'But you've done the most terrifying thing!' Cézanne said with a despairing gesture. 'Most terrifying, Monsieur Larguier!'

* * *

The friends of the past had either disappeared or were dead. Marion had died in 1900; so had Valabrègue; and Paul Alexis had been struck down with an embolism the following year. Of his old friends he now saw only Solari, with whom he sometimes spent an evening discussing painting. And yet for Cézanne life somehow always seemed to be beginning anew.

During the course of the summer, the Pavillon des Lauves was finished. Hoping to please, the architect had adorned it with terracotta mouldings and wooden balconies. Cézanne angrily ordered them to be removed. He moved his easels and a few pieces of furniture into the new studio and engaged a gardener called Vallier, who on occasion served him as a model. He intended, if he lived long enough, to finish his *Grandes Baigneuses* there. So as to be able to look at his picture in the open air, he had a slit made in the wall of the studio through which the huge canvas could be lowered into the garden.

Cézanne was now a sick man and prematurely ageing. At the beginning of this year, 1902, Vollard, who was being more attentive than ever, had come to visit him, and had shortly afterwards sent him a case of wine. The art dealers Bernheim had bought some canvases from his son, a move which had caused Vollard considerable anxiety. In the spring Maurice Denis had begged Cézanne to exhibit once again with the Indépendants, and from time to time young painters and writers would come to the Rue Boulegon to call on him. His fame was spreading and Mirbeau had even tried to get him the Légion d'Honneur, though without success. Roujon, the Director of the Beaux-Arts, to whom he spoke about it, said: 'Oh, no, Monet if you like! Monet doesn't want it? Let's give it to Sisley then. What? Dead is he? Would you like Pissarro? Choose any one you like, but don't talk to me of Cézanne.'

Fame seemed to be leavened not only with praise but with insult, envy and scorn. How sadly Zola must have thought of the dreams of their youth when he had been prosecuted and convicted after his manifesto 'J'accuse,' and had fled to England to escape imprisonment, insulted, defamed, his life threatened! Fame was also the blindness that was slowly falling on Degas, the rheumatism that was paralysing Renoir, and Cézanne's own illness that was inexorably taking its toll.

It was now that Cézanne heard of Zola's accidental death. During the night of the 28 September, in Paris, the novelist had been asphyxiated in mysterious circumstances by the fumes of a charcoal stove.* In spite of all that had happened to destroy their friendship, Cézanne burst into tears at the news and shut himself up in his studio. His youth was truly dead now.

* * *

In the autumn, for the first time in his life, Cézanne took a few days holiday. Larguier had just been demobilised, and his parents, desiring to thank the painter for his kindness to their son, invited him to stay in the Cévennes.

Cézanne took Hortense and Paul, who were visiting him in the Midi. Throughout their brief stay Cézanne was in high good humour,

* Mystery still surrounds Zola's death. It is not impossible that the 'accident' was in fact murder.

patiently tolerant of much that at any other time would have infuriated him. The Larguiers gave a luncheon in his honour to the notables of the district. Out of politeness to the painter, they talked of the rare pictures they had chanced at one time or another to see. More fortunate than the rest, the clerk to the magistrates' court was able to boast a framed portrait of himself in chalk, drawn with three lines – and with what extraordinary dexterity! – by an itinerant artist at the Alais fair; 'and if Monsieur and Madame Cézanne would take a glass of muscat with him tomorrow, he would be delighted to show it to them . . .'

On his return to Aix, Cézanne felt rather lonely. Now that Larguier and Camoin had left, he saw almost no one. He had broken off relations with the Gasquets. 'I have no business in their salon, I am always saying: "*Nom de Dieu!*" ' And young Gasquet, in spite of being a poet, had a very material outlook on life. Though his admiration for Cézanne was clearly sincere, it would seem that he gave an impression of wishing to put 'the grapnel' on his canvases. Whatever the cause of the break, Cézanne was furious. 'Don't talk to me of the Gasquets, male or female!' They and their like were 'unspeakable; they belong to the clan of intellectuals, and what a crowd they are, good God!'*

Solari was now his only real friend in Aix. He would often give him dinner, either in the Rue Boulegon or at Mère Berne's restaurant at

* The reasons for Cézanne's quarrel with the Gasquets are not altogether clear. 'It seems certain, however,' writes John Rewald, 'that after one or even several quarrels, the two men avoided each other, and that on Cézanne's part a fairly pronounced disdain took the place of a sincere friendship. It may have been that Gasquet was lacking in tact and showed a too evident desire to obtain some of Cézanne's canvases. Though the painter was often happy to present his works to the few friends who admired them, he did not appreciate a too obvious wish to receive them as presents.' Jean de Beucken says that 'Joachim Gasquet not only believed in Cézanne's genius, but also in the talent of Solari, whose canvases he collected . . . foreseeing a rise in value. The poet,' continues Jean de Beucken, 'was trying to make a corner in the painter who had given him several canvases . . .' This author even goes so far as to use the word 'double dealing' about Gasquet. Finally, Édmond Jaloux in his *Saisons Littéraires* records that 'Gasquet himself never wished to explain his break with Cézanne.' Among the Cézannes owned by Gasquet are mentioned: *La Sainte-Victoire au Grand Pin*, *Les Marronniers du Jas de Bouffan*, *Le Grand Pin*, *La Vieille au Chapelet*. Gasquet did not apparently wait long before turning these works into cash. And this, in the view of some authorities (Édmond Jaloux) was what brought about the quarrel, since it both aroused Cézanne's suspicions and hurt his pride.

Le Tholonet, and in his company Cézanne could 'let himself go.' Late one night the neighbours heard a terrible clamour coming from his flat; they hurried off anxiously to Madame Brémond. She reassured them: it was only Cézanne and Solari arguing about painting. It may have been on this occasion that the two friends inadvertently drank a whole bottle of brandy.

The sympathy and admiration his work was now arousing enabled Cézanne at last to acknowledge his own worth. One day, in a moment of anger, he declared: 'In France there are over a thousand politicians in every administration, but there is only one Cézanne every two centuries.'

He was working with ever increasing fervour. Sometimes, on coming home from painting, he was so tired he could hardly stand or speak. After a quick dinner, he would fall exhausted into bed. But he was up again at dawn next morning, obstinately, and apparently indefatigably, setting off to work. 'I am working stubbornly,' he wrote to Vollard at the beginning of 1903, 'I have caught a glimpse of the Promised Land. Am I to be like the great leader of the Jews or am I to be allowed to enter it? . . . I have made some progress. But why so late and so painfully? Is Art really a priesthood that demands the total adherence of the pure in heart? I regret the distance that separates us, for on more than one occasion I would have had recourse to you for some moral support.'

Where in Aix was he to find the 'moral support' he needed? Not from his sister Marie. Rigid and austere, Marie was now the incarnation of family dignity. Utterly insensitive to her brother's painting, and embarrassed by the scandals it had aroused, she could do no more than see to it that he lived in decent circumstances, committed no deplorable eccentricity, and did not waste his money. Vexed by his generosity to the beggars at Saint-Sauveur, she had ordered Madame Brémond not to let him leave the house with more than fifty centimes in his pocket. Nor could he find 'moral support' in Madame Brémond. One day, when he was out, she burned his sketches for the *Baigneuses* – those horrible 'naked women.'*

* A woman, who sold wine and liqueurs on the Place des Trois-Ormeaux, asked Madame Brémond: 'How is Monsieur?' 'Not very well!' 'Is Monsieur painting?'

In March, Zola's widow decided to sell a great part of the novelist's collections, among which were ten Cézannes. These paintings, all of which dated from the painter's youth, fetched prices, as the *Gazette de l'Hôtel Drouot* oddly put it, 'well above the demand,' varying between 600 and 4,200 francs.* Zola's fame, the notorious part he had played in the Dreyfus Affair, and the mysterious circumstances surrounding his death created considerable if morbid interest in the sale. The anger the novelist had aroused had not entirely abated; seizing his opportunity, the polemical writer Henri Rochefort, a virulent anti-Dreyfusard, wrote a vitriolic article about Zola and his friends.

Since there were Cézanne canvases in the sale, Henri Rochefort, who was unaware that they had been gathering dust in the Médan attics for years, and knew nothing of the background to *L'Oeuvre*, identified Zola's views on painting with those of Cézanne, and as a corollary Cézanne's political opinions with those of Zola. He published his article, 'The Love of the Ugly,' in *L'Intransigeant*, on 9 March.

'Yesterday,' he wrote, 'when I went to a pre-view of the Zola sale, I expected to find the whole group of intellectuals with smarmed hair, and all the pretentious supporters of Dreyfus. I imagined they would be there in serried ranks, ready to persuade the visitors to enthusiasm and to extol the exquisite taste and knowledge of art of the author of *Pot-Bouille*.

'But these people are peculiarly cunning. They knew the taunts to which they would be exposed, Jews or Jew-lovers as they are, free-thinkers to the marrow, by putting in an appearance among the triptychs of Christ's Passion and the painted wooden statuettes of saints,

* Approximately £100 to £700 today. It is interesting to compare the fact that a Monet fetched 2,805 francs and a Pissarro 900 francs. Madame Zola still had one other canvas by Cézanne: it was forgotten in the attic at Médan and found only in 1927. As an indication of Zola's lack of artistic sensibility, it may be mentioned that he had a great admiration for a very academic work by Debat-Ponsan, *La Vérité sortant du Puits*. At the sale it fetched 350 francs. Debat-Ponsan is supposed to have said: 'I'm a gold medallist, I am! When your Monet can say as much, we'll discuss matters.'

'Oh, such horrors! I've just come down from burning a whole heap of naked women. I can't leave them for the family's sake. What would people say?' 'But some of them may be good.' 'They're horrors!' (From the partly unpublished recollections of Mademoiselle E. Décanis, the Wine-Merchant's daughter.)

martyrs and Virgins, which make this collection one of the most astonishing accumulations of religio-catholic bric-à-brac that ever encumbered a house.

'One might have been visiting one of those shops of religious knick-knacks in the neighbourhood of the Place Saint-Sulpice . . .

'The modern canvases Zola had mingled with these dregs from the shops created unmitigated hilarity among the crowd. There were ten paintings, landscapes and portraits, signed by an ultra-Impressionist called Cézanne, which would have aroused Brisson himself to gaiety.

'People were laughing in particular at the head of a dark, bearded man whose cheeks, which seemed to have been painted with a trowel, gave him a look of having eczema. The other paintings by the same artist seemed to be a direct defiance, not only to Corot and Théodore Rousseau, but also to Hobbema and Ruysdael.

'Pissarro, Claude Monet and the other eccentric open-air painters who practised *pointillisme* – those who were called the "confetti painters" – were academical, almost members of the Institute, compared to this strange Cézanne whose work Zola collected.

'The experts organising the sale have themselves shown a certain embarrassment; in cataloguing these fantastic things, they have accompanied each entry with the reticent comment: "A work of early youth."

'If M. Cézanne was still at the breast when he made these daubs, we have nothing to say; but what are we to think of the leader of a school, which the lord of Médan had pretensions to be, who did his best to propagate such pictorial insanities? And he even wrote articles on the Salon in which he had the presumption to dictate to French art!

'Has this hapless man never looked closely at a Rembrandt, a Velasquez, a Rubens or a Goya? For, if Cézanne is right, all these great painters are wrong. Watteau, Boucher, Fragonard, Prud'hon no longer exist, and it only remains, as a supreme manifestation of the art dear to Zola, to set fire to the Louvre.

'We have often asserted that there were Dreyfusards long before the Dreyfus Affair. All the sick and twisted in mind, the half-witted and the perverse were ripe for the coming of the Messiah of Treason. If one sees nature as Zola and his vulgar painters interpreted it, patriotism and honour may well appear in the guise of an officer handing his country's defence plans over to the enemy.

'The love of physical and moral ugliness is a passion like any other.'

This grotesque article delighted Aix. Here was the truth at last! Three hundred copies of *L'Intransigeant* were distributed during the night, slipped 'under the doors of everyone who was suspected in one way or another of being in sympathy with Cézanne.'* Cézanne himself received many copies. Rochefort's article was flung in his face, accompanied by insults and threats. Anonymous letters urged him to 'free the town he disgraced of his presence.'* There was an incredible uproar. Cézanne's son, who was in Paris and had no idea of what was going on in Aix, innocently told his father of the article and said that he had kept a copy for him. 'There is no point in sending it,' Cézanne replied, 'I find copies of *L'Intransigeant* pushed under my door every day, quite apart from those that reach me through the post.'

Horrified by this persecution, Cézanne hardly dared to leave the house. It was ironic that their friendship, which had cost him so much suffering when Zola was alive, should now, when Zola was dead, be used for an attack on him on grounds which had never in fact existed. Life was the most hideous of frauds.

* Gasquet.

CHAPTER FIVE

The Last Season

> O Seigneur! j'ai vécu puissant et solitaire,
> Laissez-moi m'endormir du sommeil de la terre!
>
> ALFRED DE VIGNY: *Moïse*

ONE morning in February 1904, when Cézanne was coming downstairs to go to the Pavillon des Lauves, he met a young man with a beard and a great shock of hair, who said: 'M. Paul Cézanne, if you please?' Cézanne politely took off his hat. 'Here he is! What do you want?'

His early visitor was Émile Bernard. Since those distant days when he had first become enthusiastic about Cézanne's work in Tanguy's shop, Émile Bernard had travelled widely. He had just returned from Egypt, where he had spent eleven years. Having landed at Marseilles with his wife and his two children, he hoped to realise his long-cherished dream of meeting Cézanne, his 'old master.' Cézanne welcomed him so warmly that he decided to stay in Aix for a month.

Cézanne, who was always delighted to find someone with whom he could 'let himself go,' was soon on very friendly terms with Bernard. He even offered him the use of the ground floor of his studio. Bernard, for his part, hoped 'to learn something from a man who knew so much,' and they saw each other constantly.

In spite of the diabetes, which was slowly ravaging him – his eyes were 'swollen and red, his features puffy, his nose rather purple' – Cézanne painted incessantly. 'I make progress every day,' he told Bernard; 'that's the essential thing.' Though he was constantly at work on his *Grandes Baigneuses*, he still found time to paint landscapes at the Château Noir and still lifes in his studio. Bernard was astonished by the unremitting labour with which Cézanne tried to achieve perfection.

He watched a still life of three skulls change colour and form almost every day.

The *Grandes Baigneuses* was clearly 'in a state of utter confusion.' Bernard, working on the ground floor, could hear Cézanne pacing to and fro in the studio above; and he often saw him come down to sit in the garden, deep in thought, and then hurry upstairs again. Cézanne saw a still life Bernard was painting, found fault with it, and wanted to correct it. But when Bernard handed him his palette, he exploded: 'Where's your Naples yellow? And where's your peach black? Where are your raw Sienna, your cobalt and your burnt lake? . . . You cannot paint without those colours.'*

During those rare moments when Cézanne was not actually painting or worrying about his work, he was very good-humoured and even, on occasion, gay. When he went to dine with the Bernards – they had taken a little flat in the Rue du Théâtre – he played with the children and dandled them on his knee, remarking that he was a 'Père Goriot.' Nevertheless his thoughts were rarely absent from his work for long. Then he would fall silent and the children had to be sent to bed, out of his way.

He was continually reiterating his views on painting to Bernard, asserting that 'one had to return to classicism through nature, that is to say through sensation'; that 'all nature was modelled on the sphere, the cone and the cylinder'; and that 'drawing and colour were not two different things.' 'One draws in the process of painting,' he said; 'the more the colour harmonises, the more precise the drawing becomes. When the colour has reached its full richness, the form has reached completeness. The secret of drawing and modelling resides in the contrasts and relationships of tones.' Cézanne's convictions were becoming increasingly 'absolute,' said Bernard. He reviled the school of the Beaux-Arts, Bouguereau and the Salon. 'Work regardless of anyone, and achieve mastery. That should be the artist's goal,' he said;

* Émile Bernard made a note of the components of Cézanne's palette at this time. They consisted of the following: brilliant yellow, Naples yellow, chrome yellow, yellow ochre, raw Sienna, vermilion, red ochre, burnt Sienna, rose madder, crimson lake, burnt lake, Veronese green, viridian, terra verde, cobalt, ultramarine, Prussian blue and peach black.

'the rest is not worth Cambronne's word.'* Bernard felt as if he were talking, not to a painter, but to painting itself, 'living painting.' Cézanne existed only in terms of his brush, and everything he saw nourished his preoccupation with painting. When dining with the Bernards he would often gaze at length at the fruit, the dishes, the glasses, the plates, or study the faces of his hosts 'in the play of the lamp-light and the shadow.'

One day he invited his new friends to accompany him on a walk in the hills above Château Noir. He astonished them both by his agility and the fact that he continued to talk about painting, even though at times they had to climb on all fours. 'Rosa Bonheur was the hell of a woman; she knew how to devote herself utterly to painting,' he said, as he scrambled among the rocks. On the way home, he discussed his favourite poets, and declaimed Baudelaire's *La Charogne*.†

Cézanne's alternating enthusiasms and bursts of anger were increasingly marked. When Pissarro died at the age of sixty-three,‡ he remembered with gratitude the days at Auvers-sur-Oise where 'the humble and colossal Pissarro' had taught him the laws of Impressionism, 'he was a father to me . . .' A moment later, his hatred of progress would break out in angry sarcasms and he was furiously waving his stick at a road surveyor and his engineers, those maniacs who made everything so ugly with their straight lines.§ But his disease was wearing him down. His anger, though still harsh, was no longer sustained. 'Don't

* General Cambronne was in command of one of the last squares of the Old Guard at Waterloo. It was then that he is supposed to have uttered the now legendary remark: 'The Guard dies but does not surrender.' According to another version, however, he made use of an obscenity which has been known ever since as 'Cambronne's word.' *Translator's note.*

† On the back of an *Apothéose de Delacroix*, Bernard discovered these lines written by Cézanne; they are somewhat Baudelaireian in inspiration:

'Voici la jeune femme aux fesses rebondies.
Comme elle étale bien au milieu des prairies,
Son corps souple, splendide épanouissement;
La couleuvre n'a pas de souplesse plus grande,
Et le soleil qui luit darde complaisamment
Quelques rayons dorés sur cette belle viande.'

‡ In November 1903. A few months earlier, in May, Gauguin had died in the Marquesas.

let's talk about it any more, I'm too tired, too exhausted. I ought to be sensible, stay at home and do nothing but work.'

Bernard had not been warned of Cézanne's hatred of being touched. One afternoon, returning from painting, Cézanne tripped and Bernard put out a hand to steady him. The old painter turned on Bernard in fury, swore at him, and hurried away to his studio. Bernard followed in bewilderment. When he entered the ground-floor rooms Cézanne appeared, 'his eyes starting out of his head.' Bernard tried to make his excuses, but Cézanne refused to listen to him and cried: 'No one shall touch me! No one shall put the grapnel on me!' Then he hurried upstairs to his studio and banged the door so violently that the whole house shook.

Bernard was much upset and left the Pavillon des Lauves imagining that he would never see the painter again. Yet that very evening, to his utter surprise, Cézanne came to visit him as if nothing had happened, nor did he make any reference to the scene. The next day Bernard went to see Madame Brémond and told her what had occurred. She reassured him. To anyone who knew Cézanne his behaviour was not at all surprising. 'I have orders never to touch him,' she said, 'not even with my skirt as I pass.' A little later Cézanne asked Bernard to forget the incident. 'Don't pay any attention, these things happen in spite of me. I can't bear being touched. It is something that dates from very long ago.'

Bernard, who had a marked liking for theoretical discussion, was constantly questioning Cézanne: 'On what do you base your perspective? What do you mean by the word "nature"? Are our senses sufficiently perfect to be able to record what you call nature without error?' These ratiocinations irritated Cézanne. 'Believe me, none of that is worth Cambronne's word,' he said. 'These things are thought up by university professors . . . Be a painter, not a writer or a philosopher.' But Bernard kept returning to the charge.* 'Do you know,'

* Émile Bernard was to become the champion of neo-classicism.

---

§ Writing to Paule Conil, his niece, in September 1902, about l'Estaque, he said: 'What is called progress is simply an invasion of bipeds, who are not satisfied till they have transformed everything into odious quays with gas-lamps or – which is even worse – electric light. What times we live in!'

Cézanne cried angrily one day, 'that I consider all theories ridiculous.' And he walked off, muttering: 'The truth is in nature and I shall prove it.'

But these clashes were soon forgotten. When the Bernards' stay came to an end, Cézanne was sad at parting with them. They had brought animation and warmth into his life. Solitude closed about him again. His disease was worrying him and he suffered from constant headaches and always felt tired. Bernard tried to continue their discussions by letter; but Cézanne was far from eager. His strength was declining, and he had less liking than ever for intellectual exercises of this nature. 'The artist,' he replied briefly to Bernard, 'should beware of the literary mind, which so often leads a painter from the right path – the concrete study of nature – to lose himself for far too long in intangible speculations.' Bernard was writing a long study on Cézanne for *L'Occident*.* Cézanne thanked him. 'But,' he added, 'I always come back to this: the painter must devote himself entirely to the study of nature, and endeavour to produce pictures which are directly informative. Talk about art is almost valueless.'

Bernard thought Cézanne's letters very disappointing. While he had been able to discover the elements of an aesthetic theory in his correspondence with Van Gogh in the past, he could extract nothing from Cézanne but rare and vague indications. In Bernard's view, all questions of art ought to be capable of precise definition. He even began to wonder whether Cézanne had any clear idea of the problems he was trying to resolve; whether, in fact, Cézanne was intelligent.

Cézanne's correspondence, when compared with Van Gogh's, is certainly rather disappointing. It throws but the faintest rays of light on either the artist or the man. Cézanne was no theoretician, It was only with brush in hand that he wanted to think. He was not motivated by

* It appeared in July. Deeming Cézanne a 'painter with a mystical temperament,' Bernard wrote: 'Whatever the Master may think of his own work, and he is far too harsh on himself, it dominates all contemporary painting, imposes itself by the quality and originality of its vision, the beauty of its technique, the richness of its colouring, its serious and durable qualities, and its amplitude. It attracts us by its conviction and its sane doctrine, it persuades us of the manifest truth it records and, in the present decadence, affords a salutary oasis. Affiliated to Gothic art in its exquisite sensibility, it is nevertheless modern, new, French and instinct with genius.'

45. Cézanne in the countryside near Aix. A photograph by Émile Bernard [1904]

46.

CÉZANNE AT WORK

1906: Cézanne 'Sur le Motif' in the last year of his life. Photographs taken by the painter K. X. Roussel at Les Lauves

47.

48.

49. Cézanne and Maurice Denis. Les Lauves, Aix [1906]

50. *Cézanne working at Les Lauves*, 1906. Painting by Maurice Denis (seated right)

51. *Cézanne at Work*. Painting by Hermann Paul, the caricaturist, after a sketch from life [1906]

52.

53.

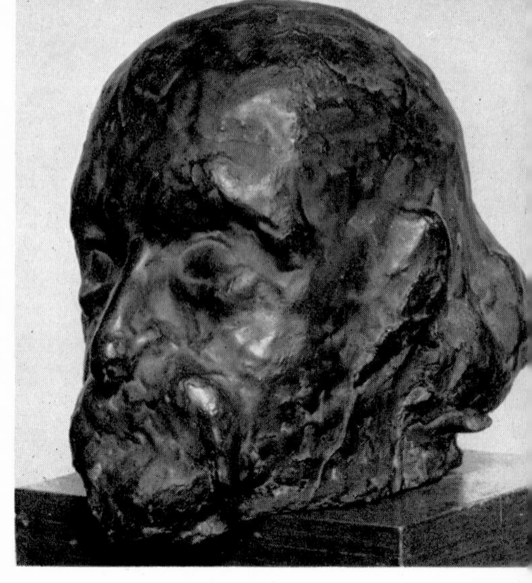

52. *Un Cézanne rêveur.* Terracotta bust by Philippe Solari [*c.* 1904]

53. Posthumous bronze of Cézanne by the Fauve painter Louis Valtat [1869-1952]

54. Le Château Noir, Aix

55. Monument to Cézanne at the Château Noir by Edith Vieil-Noë [1873-1935]

56. Bust of Cézanne by Henri Pontier [1842-1926], Director of the Musée Granet, Aix, who refused the admission of Cézanne's work

54.

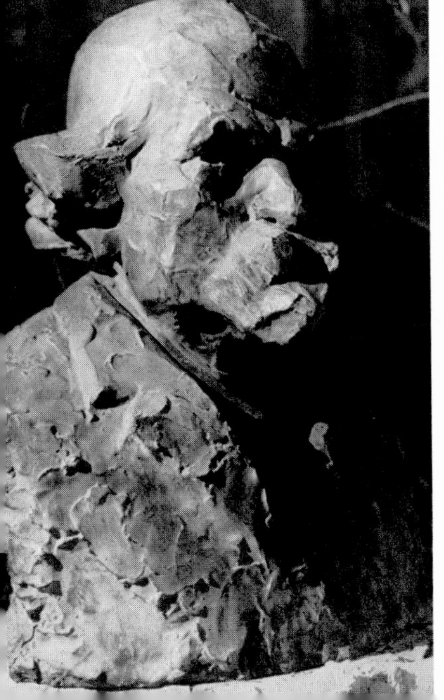

55.

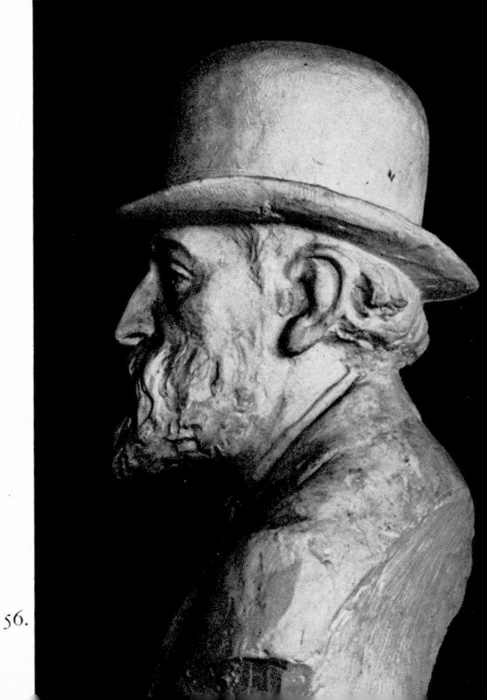

56.

57. Cézanne's studio in the Chemin des Lauves, Aix. A photograph taken after the death of Cézanne, at the time of Marcel Provence

intellectual considerations. He registered sensations and tried to give them an equivalent value on his canvas. His thinking was therefore, if one may say so, in terms of construction and above all colour, of which the latter alone could portray form. Since the problems with which he was concerned were purely plastic, Cézanne could have stated them only in lengthy and abstract arguments. And since explanations of this kind seemed to him of no importance whatever, and all that mattered to him was 'realisation,' he never tried to define in words what he was endeavouring to do. He avoided discussions and limited himself to repeating a certain number of formulas. Bernard had, indeed, some reason to suppose that Cézanne never clearly apprehended intellectually the problems he was trying to resolve. Of all the people who knew Cézanne, Bernard pushed his enquiries furthest, but without, it must be admitted, any appreciable result.

This, no doubt, explains to some extent why Cézanne's teaching has been so diversely (and so contradictorily) interpreted, why the Symbolists, the Fauves and the Cubists all claimed to derive from him. The painters who acknowledged him as a master generally did so on the basis of one or another of his remarks from which they elaborated an exclusive artistic theory. And Cézanne would certainly have hotly denied that these ideas originated with him. For him painting was a whole, and he would never have conceded, for instance, that painters might plead the authority of his remark - 'nature is modelled on the sphere, the cone and the cylinder' - to found the Cubist movement, which denied colour its pre-eminence.

* * *

Cézanne found the early summer heat rather trying and, as he oddly put it, he was 'under the stroke of cerebral troubles.' To conserve his energies he ceased going home to the Rue Boulegon for luncheon; and Madame Brémond brought him food to the studio. He was beginning to disintegrate physically.

The Salon d'Automne had been founded the year before and was entirely devoted to the new school of painting. This year its organisers, wishing to pay homage to Cézanne, had set aside a whole room for his works. Cézanne decided to go to Paris, where he hoped the cooler weather would do him good. He went to stay with his wife and son at 16, Rue Duperré, not far from the Place Pigalle. As soon as it was known that he was in Paris, many people came to call on him. He was touched by this token of admiration, but it quickly tired him and he escaped to Fontainebleau, though not for long. Without even waiting for the private view of the Salon d'Automne, he hurried back to his solitary life in Aix.

In the meantime the usual battle was taking place in Paris over the thirty works of Cézanne that had been hung (from 15 October to 15 November) in the Salon d'Automne, in the Grand Palais. The enthusiasm with which the young painters defended him was equalled only by the acrimony with which his enemies tried to discredit him.

'Painting that might have been done by a Madagascan' – 'One had to be a Goya to paint with mud' – 'Ah, Cézanne! Blessed are the poor in mind, for theirs is the kingdom of art' – 'It is impossible to imagine anything more incoherent: it is false, vulgar and mad' – these, among many others, were the kind of remarks made by critics for whom the very name of Cézanne still spelled horror.*

That young painters were profoundly interested in Cézanne, that his canvases were obtaining ever increasing prices in the sales, and that great collectors and foreign galleries were buying his work, had no effect whatever on the hostile critics; apparently nothing could persuade them even to make an attempt to understand. Their certitude had remained constant since the first Impressionist exhibitions. 'This artist is sincere,' wrote *Le Petit Parisien*, 'he has fervent admirers; no doubt he could paint differently . . . But he prefers to pour colours on to a canvas and then spread them with a comb or a toothbrush. And this produces landscapes, seascapes, still lifes and portraits . . . but by chance and at random, and the whole process recalls the patterns schoolboys make by folding a piece of paper over a blot of ink.' In short, Cézanne was a humbug and, as everyone knew, he owed his reputation entirely to Émile Zola.'†

* The quotations are from *Le Monde illustré*, *La République française*, *La Revue bleue* and *L'Univers*.

† 'Cézanne owes his reputation to Émile Zola,' wrote a certain Jean-Pascal in a pamphlet entitled *Le Salon d'Automne en* 1904.

It is doubtful whether Cézanne was even aware of these articles. He was busily at work, still hoping to make some progress before he died, and, as he wrote to Bernard in May, 'work that leads to progress in one's profession is sufficient compensation for not being understood by fools.'

* * *

An increasing number of people were journeying to Aix to see Cézanne and breaking in upon his seclusion. Visits from painters, writers, collectors and dealers* diversified the monotony of his life – 'the monotony which is engendered,' he wrote to Bernard, 'by the unremitting pursuit of the one and only goal, which at moments of physical fatigue creates a sort of intellectual exhaustion.'

Nevertheless, he worked stubbornly on. 'By work I shall prove I'm right,' he said. He had begun a portrait of Vallier, his gardener at the studio. 'If I bring the fellow off, it will prove my theory right.' He was also continually returning to *Les Grandes Baigneuses*. Would he ever bring it to a successful conclusion? He had been working on it in various forms for ten years. 'I hardly like to admit it,' he said. The peace of evening was descending on him; and it was with humility that he looked back at his long task, at the mass of work he would leave behind him.

Roger Marx wrote about his painting in the *Gazette des Beaux-Arts* and Cézanne sent him a note of thanks: 'My age and my health will never permit me to realise the dream of art I have pursued all my life. But I shall always be grateful to the intelligent art lovers who have seen – through all my hesitations – what I was trying to do to give my art a new impetus. I have never thought that one substitutes oneself for the past, one merely adds another link to it. Besides having the temperament of a painter and an ideal of art, that is to say a conception of nature, one should also have sufficient means of expression to be intelligible to the ordinary public and so achieve a reasonable place in the history of art.'

Cézanne received each of his visitors with the same rather melancholy simplicity. He showed them his works and told them his views on

* Among others may be mentioned: Hermann-Paul, Gaston Bernheim de Villers, Francis Jourdain, R. P. Rivière, J. F. Schnerb and Karl-Ernst Osthaus.

painting: 'Art that is not based on emotion is not art,' he would say; nevertheless: 'One must think, the eye is not enough, thought is needed.' When Francis Jourdain asked him what studies he would advise a young artist to undertake, he said: 'Copy his stove-pipe,' and he explained that, in his view, the most important thing of all was the play of light on a form and the means of rendering it on canvas.

In January, Camoin came to see Cézanne again. A little later, in March, Bernard returned to Aix. Cézanne had his wife and son with him and he invited Bernard to luncheon with them. Throughout the meal he kept glancing affectionately at his son and repeating over and over again: 'Son, you're a man of genius.'

When summer came, Cézanne, who found the heat increasingly trying, went once again to Fountainebleau. But he felt even less inclined than the previous year to face the noise and bustle of Paris. Meanwhile his work was arousing increasing interest there. The *Mercure de France*, on 1 and 15 August and 1 September, published the results of an enquiry into 'the present tendencies of the plastic arts.' Cézanne's importance was now so obvious that the *Mercure* devoted one question to him exclusively: 'Where do you place Cézanne?' The replies, as was to be expected, were very varied, admiration and enthusiasm being mingled with scorn and incomprehension. To some, he was 'a genius,' 'one of the great masters of French painting'; to others, 'a drunken scavenger,' 'a sour fruit.' Some thought his work would exercise a deep and lasting influence while others asserted that it would inevitably sink into oblivion.* And these disagreements became even more marked with the opening of the Salon d'Automne, which was showing ten Cézannes this year.

Cézanne, who had in the meantime returned to Provence, had the

* Among the odder replies the following may be quoted: 'Cézanne is a great artist who lacks education; his work is that of a rough and vulgar genius' (L. de la Quintinie). 'As for Cézanne, I take my stand. I respectfully avoid him' (Félix Vallotton). 'Cézanne's evident sincerity attracts me; his clumsiness astonishes me' (Henri Hamm). 'Cézanne is a forester with a tender heart like his skies and his fruits' (Paul Vernet). 'Cézanne? Why Cézanne?' (Fernand Piet). 'As for Cézanne, I will neither mention him nor think of him, since I am not concerned with selling his works' (Tony Minartz). 'Where do I place Cézanne? I regard him as pagans and heretics regard a dogma which is entirely incomprehensible to them' (Lucien-Hector Monod).

unexpected satisfaction of reading an article in praise of himself in *Le Mémorial d'Aix:* 'The painter Cézanne has recently been handed many bouquets by the most distinguished art-critics. M. Jean Puy says of him in the *Mercure de France*: "He has brought Impressionism back to the traditional and logical path. His teaching is immensely important..." Too little known in Aix, or too often misunderstood, we congratulate the painter Cézanne on his artistic success.'

But Cézanne was not deluded. He knew very well that he would die without one of his canvases being hung in the gallery of his native town; he knew that Pontier, its keeper, would never give way.

* * *

The carnival, which had been held in Aix for some fifteen years past,* gave Solari the opportunity to earn a little money. But while working on the decoration of the floats in January 1906, he contracted pneumonia. He was taken to hospital and died on the 17th. Cézanne had lost his last old friend.

A few weeks earlier, Solari had completed a bust of Zola for the town library. And Madame Zola had just given Aix, as a memorial to the novelist, the manuscripts of the *Trois Villes* series: *Lourdes, Rome* and *Paris*. On Sunday, 27 May, the municipality organised the unveiling of the bust. Cézanne was there, together with Madame Zola, Numa Coste and Victor Leydet, who was now vice-president of the Senate. In these faces, so marked by time, and in the bust sculpted by a dead hand, Cézanne saw his vanished youth. Even the Mayor of Aix reminded him of it, for his name was Cabassol, and he was the son of Louis Auguste's old partner. Cabassol, in his speech of thanks to Madame Zola, recalled the great part Aix, under the name of Plassans, had played in the novelist's work, and mentioned the friendship of the 'inseparables.'

Numa Coste rose to speak. He suffered from heart disease, which at times made his delivery breathless, while his voice quivered with emotion: 'We were then in the dawn of life, bursting with high hopes for the future. We were desirous of rising above the social morass in which impotent jealousies, spurious reputations and unhealthy ambi-

* The first 'Corso' was held in 1889.

tions lie stagnant. We dreamed of conquering Paris, capturing the intellectual centre of the world, and it was in the open air, in the depths of barren solitudes, by the banks of shady streams, and among the marmoreal hills, that we went off to forge arms for the gigantic struggle . . .'

How long ago were all those dreams of fame, those recitations of poetry among the rocky hills, those bathes in the Arc! 'When Zola had preceded the rest of us to Paris,' went on Numa Coste, 'he sent his first articles to his old friend Paul Cézanne, and kept us all informed of his hopes and prospects. We used to read his letters in the hills, under the shade of the green oaks, as if they were first bulletins from a battlefield . . .' Cézanne was visibly crying, overwhelmed by memories. So much of his life was here, epitomised in this bust of Zola; he was mourning for what they had been, for what he had been. His life was over.

Seigneur, vous m'aviez fait puissant et solitaire,
Laissez-moi m'endormir du sommeil de la terre.

(opposite) Cézanne: one of the last letters written to his son.

Aix, 25th July, 1906.

My dear Paul,

I received your welcome letter yesterday giving me your news; I am really sorry to hear of your mother's state of health, do all you can for her, see to it that she is comfortable, keeps cool, and has as much entertainment as circumstances permit.

Yesterday, Thursday, I should have gone to see the priest Roux. I could not go, and that is what will happen to the end, and it will be better so. He's a scrounger. I went to see your Aunt Marie about Marthe – that is another nuisance, at my age one should live an isolated life and paint.

Valier massages me, my back is a little better. Madame Brémond says my foot is better. I follow Boissy's treatment, it is atrocious. It is very hot. From eight o'clock onwards the weather is intolerable. The two pictures of which you sent me the photographs are not by me.

I embrace you with all my heart.

Your old father,

Paul Cézanne.

Remember me to Monsieur and Madame le Goupil, I am touched by their kind thoughts and they are so good to your poor mother.

P. Céz.

Aix, 25 Juillet 1906.

Mon cher Paul.

Hier, j'ai reçu ta
bonne lettre qui me
donne de vos nouvelles,
je ne puis que déplorer
l'état dans lequel se
trouve ta mère, donne
lui le plus de soins
possibles, cherche le
bien être, la fraicheur et
des divertissements appro-
priés à la circonst-
ance. — Hier, jeudi

je devais aller trouver le
ensoutané Rouxe. Je
n'y suis pas allé et tel en
sera ainsi, jusqu'à la
fin, ce sera ce qu'il y a encore
de mieux à faire. C'est un
paresseux! — A propos
de Marthe, je suis allé
voir ta tante Marie. —
c'est encore un têton, à mon
âge il convient de vivre
isolé et de peindre. —
Valtesse me fréquente, les ring-
vantum peu mieux, Madame
Brémond, dit que le pied va-
mieux. — Je suis le traite-
ment de Boissy, l'exté-

atroce. Il fait très chaud. —
Déjà huit heures, le temps est
insupportable. — Les
deux toiles dont tu m'as
envoyé la photographie ne
sont pas de moi. —
Je vous embrasse tous les deux
de tout mon cœur,

ton vieux père,

Paul Gauguin.

Donne le bonjour à monsieur
et à madame le Goupil. —
dont le bonheur me
touche et qui sont si gentils
pour ta pauvre mère.

[illegible]

Cézanne's disease was making increasing inroads on his vitality; and when depressed he often sadly quoted Vigny. He was only sixty-seven but he felt the end was near. With feverish desperation, he devoted the last ounce of his strength to his painting, trying always to advance a little further towards that goal which his increasingly exacting standards made ever more unattainable. Once again the Friends of the Arts of Aix asked him to exhibit with them, this time 'as of right.'* Cézanne insisted that his name in the catalogue be followed by the modest and grateful phrase: 'Pupil of Pissarro.' Perfection was unattainable; but perhaps the younger generation would take up his task where he had left it off. 'I am a landmark. Others will come . . .' he said to Maurice Denis who, together with K. X. Roussel, had made a pilgrimage to Aix.

* * *

It was now July and Cézanne had never felt the heat so severely. His kidneys were troubling him and his feet were giving him pain. In order to take advantage of the cool of early morning, he was at his easel by half-past four. But by eight o'clock he had to stop work; the temperature became 'unbearable,' his head swam, and he 'could no longer even think in paint.' The world seemed withered and blighted; the atmosphere was full of dust and 'of a lamentable hue.' The heat was 'odious,' 'stupefying.' Harassed by his physical pains, everything irritated him. He insulted a priest who called on him; and he had ceased going to Mass at Saint-Sauveur, since 'the old precentor, Poncet, has been succeeded by a fool of an abbé, who plays false notes on the organ . . . His playing positively hurts me.'

Yet, in spite of the heat, his weakness and giddiness, he forced himself to work, pursuing his 'researches,' and regretting his advanced age 'in view of my colour sensations.' At the end of July, a slight attack of bronchitis was not allowed to interrupt his painting for a single day. In August the weather grew hotter still; it was 'appalling.' In the afternoons, Cézanne made his cabman take him to the banks of the Arc, to the Trois-Sautets bridge, or to the fork of the Monbriant road. There, at least, under the tall trees that formed 'a vault above the water,' he

* 'Which did not prevent his works being very badly hung.' (John Rewald.)

could hope to spend a few relatively 'agreeable' hours painting. But 'the stench of the atmosphere is nauseating,' he wrote . . . 'The light is so foul that nature appears ugly.'

He realised with anguish that he would never succeed in rendering the prodigious complexity, the 'magnificent richness of colouring that is nature's.' He could, he said, work for months by the river 'without changing my place,' for the same subject, seen from different angles, provided such a variety of aspects when he leaned 'sometimes a little more to the right, sometimes a little more to the left.' If only the intolerable heat would cease! 'I seem to be living in a void,' he wrote to his son, whom he kept informed week by week of what he was doing and thinking, and also of the state of his health. 'Only you,' he wrote, 'can console me for my sad lot.' When he roused himself from his lassitude it was in exasperation. Pontier was 'a dirty cad'; the local intellectuals were 'a lot of bastards, cretins and scoundrels'; on all sides there was nothing but 'theft, complacency, conceit, rapacity, and the seizing of your work.'

During September, the heat moderated a little, and Cézanne enjoyed a visit from Camoin, with whom he could rail against Émile Bernard, who was still writing infuriating letters. This 'Emilio Bernardinos, a most distinguished æsthete,' he now agreed with Camoin to be 'an intellectual, congested by his memories of galleries.' And now, as summer drew to an end and the temperature declined, the weather was 'splendid,' the countryside 'superb.'

Cézanne was still devoting every moment to painting and, had it not been for 'his state of nerves,' all might still have been well. But then, at the beginning of October, his cabman had the insolence to raise his prices, asking for five francs to take him to Château Noir instead of the usual three. What presumption! The 'infatuated macrobian' – as Cézanne called himself – refused to give the cabman another penny. He would do without the cab and carry his traps himself. 'I see exploitation on every hand,' he said.

The rain, for which everyone had been longing, came at last, and there were heavy thunder-storms over Aix on 13 and 14 October. 'Nervous system much weakened,' Cézanne wrote. 'Only painting in oils keeps me going. I must continue.' And on the morning of the

15th, he wrote to his son that he had 'a little moral satisfaction . . . I continue to work with difficulty, but still I'm achieving something.' In a moment of pride, he added that, for the older painters, his contemporaries, he would be 'a disastrous rival.'

On the afternoon of the 15th, taking advantage of a fine interval in the weather, he hurried out to paint at a short distance from his studio. There was another storm, but in spite of the steady rain Cézanne went on working. Several hours went by and the rain continued. Soaked and shivering, he eventually decided to abandon his work and go home. Burdened with his easel, canvas and paint-box, he could do no more than crawl along. Suddenly he collapsed and fell in the road. A little later, the driver of a laundry cart found him, still lying in a coma, and took him back to the Rue Boulegon.

Madame Brémond sent for the doctor and informed Marie. In the meantime, Cézanne had come to in his bed. He was reluctant to obey the doctor's orders; while the doctor in his turn was surprised by the old man's vitality. The next morning, at his usual time, Cézanne went off to his studio intending to work on the portrait of Vallier. But the effort was too much for him. He felt very ill, and only with great difficulty managed to make his way home to the Rue Boulegon.

He felt faint and weak; the doctor came to see him and prescribed. Then pneumonia set in; but he refused to surrender. Madame Brémond, who could not lift him by herself, wished to engage a nurse. Cézanne stubbornly refused. Besides, he intended to start painting again. 'Monsieur,' he wrote to his colour merchant, on the 17th, 'it is now over a week since I asked you to send me 10 burnt lakes 7, and I have had no reply. What's going on? Please reply, and promptly.'

But his fits of impatience were becoming few and far between. He was rapidly declining. On the 20th, Marie wrote to young Paul that he should 'come as soon as possible,' that she considered his presence in Aix 'necessary.' Cézanne was delirious at times. In unconscious fury,

(opposite):

Funeral announcement of Paul Cézanne. The date of death is incorrect. Cézanne died on 22 October, 1906. The 'error' was intentional so that the interment might be postponed, without violation of the letter of the law, long enough to permit Cézanne's wife and son to reach Aix in time for the ceremony. (G. Mack).

Madame veuve Cézanne ;
Monsieur Paul Cézanne ;

Mademoiselle Marie Cézanne ;
Madame Conil, née Cézanne, et Monsieur Conil ;
Mesdemoiselles Marthe, Paule, Cécile, Amélie Conil, et Monsieur Louis Conil ;

Mademoiselle Marie Aubert ;
Madame Bourelly, née Aubert, Monsieur Bourelly et leur fils ;

Madame veuve Gilles ;
Madame et Monsieur Bonnefous, et leur fils ;

Et Mademoiselle Marie Conil ;

Ont l'honneur de vous faire part de la perte douloureuse qu'ils viennent d'éprouver en la personne de

MONSIEUR PAUL CÉZANNE

Artiste Peintre

leur époux, père, frère, beau-frère, oncle et allié, décédé à Aix le 23 octobre, à l'âge de 68 ans, muni des Sacrements de notre sainte Mère l'Eglise, et qu'on ensevelira demain

Mercredi 24 Octobre 1906, à 10 h. 1/2, paroisse Saint-Sauveur.

PRIEZ POUR LUI !

Maison mortuaire rue Boulegon, 23.

Aix, le 23 Octobre 1906.

Aix. J. Nicol — 6.400

he shouted the abhorred name of the Director of the Aix Museum: 'Pontier! Pontier!' In calmer mood, he asked for his son. On the 22nd, Madame Brémond sent a telegram to Paris: 'Both come at once. Father very ill.' Cézanne, in his delirium, muttered his complaints, or shouted his son's name. 'Paul! Paul!' he called, staring at the door.

But the door never opened on young Paul. Hortense had received Madame Brémond's telegram, but she had concealed it from her son. How could she go to Aix when she was busy with fittings at her dressmaker's?

Marie had gone out of the room for a moment, and Madame Brémond was left alone with Cézanne. She realised suddenly that she could no longer hear his breathing; he was lying very still. She went over to the bed. Cézanne was dead and his eyes were staring at the door.

INSTITUTION

CHRONOLOGY

There are in existence over 800 canvases by Cézanne, approximately 350 water-colours and a similar number of drawings. In his catalogue of Cézanne's work, Lionello Venturi attributes some 130 canvases to the early period (up till 1871); 160 to the so-called Impressionist period (1872–1877); 260 to the so-called Constructive period (1878–1887); and 250 to the so-called Synthetic period (1888–1906).

The hostility to Cézanne's work took a long time to disperse. On the other hand, the early influence his painting had exercised became profoundly important. It was both widespread and lasting. It is no exaggeration to say that it has nourished most of the great artistic movements of our time. Both the Fauves and the Cubists acknowledged Cézanne as their master. Braque, Matisse, Vlaminck, Picasso, Modigliani, Marquet, Derain, André Lhote and Delaunay were, among others, all subject to his influence and an extraordinary diversity of manner can be traced back to his art.

The importance attributed to Cézanne during the fifty years following his death may be gauged from this Chronology, in which I have listed the principal posthumous events affecting his work and reputation.

1906 The critic of the *Mémorial d'Aix* wrote on the morrow of Cézanne's death: 'I would wish the town of Aix to remember Cézanne, whose canvases are in the Luxembourg in Paris, in Berlin, and in the principal collections of Europe, though neither Aix nor Marseilles possesses even a sketch by him. Homage, though belated, is due to the memory of this painter whose fame is continually increasing . . . In the same way that we preserve . . . some of Zola's manuscripts, so we should be able to show visitors to our fine museum that we are not ungrateful, ignorant, narrow or behind the times, and that, when one of our fellow-citizens is an honour to our town, our town is anxious to commemorate him.'

October and November: Ten of Cézanne's canvases exhibited in the Salon d'Automne.

Émile Bernard organised a Mass for Cézanne in the Church of Notre-Dame de Lorette, in Paris.

1907 March: In the Viau sale, *Fruits* fetched 19,000 francs.

June: Exhibition of Cézanne's water-colours (79 works) in the Galerie Bernheim-Jeune, Paris.

October: Retrospective exhibition (56 works) in the Salon d'Automne.

On the advice of Léonce Bénédite, Keeper of the Musée du Luxembourg, the State refused the gift of Cézanne's paintings decorating the Jas de Bouffan, offered by M. Granel, its new owner.

Death of Numa Coste.

1908 *Death of Victor Leydet.*

1909 *Death of Doctor Gachet.*

1910 January: Cézanne exhibition (68 canvases and water-colours) at Bernheim-Jeune.

1911 Isaac de Camondo's bequest to the Louvre, which included several works by Cézanne: *La Maison du Pendu*, *Les Joueurs de Cartes*, *Le Vase bleu*, still lifes and water-colours.

1913 June: At the Marczell de Nèmes sale, *Le Buffet* sold for 40,000 francs and *Le Garçon au gilet rouge* for 56,000 francs.

1914 January: Cézanne exhibition (30 paintings) at Bernheim-Jeune.

The Cézannes of the Camondo bequest hung in the Louvre. Gustave Babin wrote in *L'Illustration* of 18 July: 'He [M. de Camondo] possessed the only landscape of Cézanne's which is acceptable to the clear-eyed, *La Maison du Pendu*, perhaps the only one in which the horizon is horizontal, in which the walls are vertical, in fact the only one which is not "all askew," in J. K. Huysmans' eyes Cézanne's prime merit. But he also rejoiced in the ownership of a sketch for *Joueurs de Cartes* – which serious newspapers have termed "famous" – as well as some other rather weak sketches by the same artist, and a not too mad Van Gogh. He had also acquired from such great artists as Manet canvases which will never count among their masterpieces, but which literature – or perhaps only art criticism – had extolled: I am thinking of *Lola.*'

1916 *Death of Villevieille.*

1917 *Deaths of Degas and Rodin.*

1918 *Death of Baptistin Baille.*

1919 February: At the Octave Mirbeau sale, *Au Fond du Ravin* sold for 41,000 francs.

Death of Renoir.

1920 March: At the S. Sévadjian sale, a bathing scene sold for 84,100 francs.

December: Cézanne exhibition (33 paintings, water-colours and drawings) at Bernheim-Jeune.

The Louvre bought *Les Peupliers.*

1921 February to March: Cézanne exhibition at the Kunsthalle in Basle.

November to December: Cézanne exhibition at P. Cassirer in Berlin.

Death of Joachim Gasquet.

1922 December: Cézanne exhibition at Bernheim-Jeune.

1923 At the suggestion of the painter Émile Lombard, an Aix municipal councillor, the Chemin des Lauves became the Avenue Paul-Cézanne.

1924 March: Cézanne exhibition at Bernheim-Jeune.

Death of Isidore Baille.

1925 June: At the Maurice Gangnat sale, *Le Pin de Montbriant* sold for 528,000 francs.

Charensol, in *L'Art Vivant* (1 December), reported a visit to the Aix Museum: 'I asked the concierge where the Cézannes were; she looked at me with profound contempt: "You, too!" she said, shrugging her shoulders. And she added: "No, Monsieur, we don't keep that sort of thing here."'

1926 June: Retrospective Cézanne exhibition (58 paintings, 99 water-colours) at Bernheim-Jeune.

A Paul Cézanne Society founded in Aix.

Deaths of Monet and Pontier.

1927 A painting by Cézanne (*Paul Alexis lisant à Zola*) discovered in the attics of Zola's house at Médan.

Death of Guillaumin.

1928 January: Cézanne exhibition in the Wildenstein Gallery, New York.

The paintings of the Caillebotte bequest went to the Louvre.

1929 Cézanne exhibition (43 canvases) in the Galerie Pigalle, Paris.

Auguste Pellerin bequeathed three Cézanne still lifes to the Louvre.

October: A monument to Cézanne by Maillol erected in the Tuileries Gardens in Paris.

1930 *Death of Madame Zola:* 80 letters from Cézanne found among the novelist's papers.

1931 May: Cézanne exhibition at Bernheim-Jeune.

1933 November to December: Exhibition of Cézanne water-colours at G. Seligmann, New York.

1934 November to December: Cézanne exhibition at the Museum of Art, Philadelphia.

1935 June: Exhibition of *Aquarelles et Baignades de Cézanne* at Renou et Colle, Paris.

July: Cézanne exhibition at Reid and Lefèvre, London.

1936 Spring: Cézanne exhibition (184 works) at the Orangerie, Paris.

August to October: Cézanne exhibition (173 works) at the Kunsthalle, Basle.

November to December: Cézanne exhibition (30 works) at Bignou, New York.

An American collector bought *Les Joueurs de Cartes* for $240,000.

Lionello Venturi published his Catalogue of Cézanne's Work.

1937 June: Cézanne exhibition (29 paintings and some water-colours) at the Reid and Lefèvre Gallery, London.

June to October: Exhibition *Le Maître Indépendant Paul Cézanne* (85 works) at the Salon des Indépendants.

September to October: Cézanne exhibition at the San Francisco Museum of Art. Cézanne exhibition (30 works) at Reid and Lefèvre, London. John Rewald published Cézanne's *Correspondance*.

1938 April: Exhibition *Quelques aquarelles de Paul Cézanne* at Bernheim-Jeune, Paris.

November to December: Exhibition *Dessins de Cézanne* at the Galerie Henriette, Paris.

1939 The centenary of Cézanne's birth marked by numerous publications and a variety of exhibitions.

February to April: Cézanne exhibition (35 works) at the Galerie Paul Rosenberg, Paris.

April: Cézanne exhibition at Rosenberg and Helft, London.

May: Exhibition *Reproductions et Livres de Cézanne* at the Galerie Magne, Paris.

May to June: Exhibition *Hommage à Cézanne*, at Bernheim-Jeune, Paris.

June to July: Exhibition *Cézanne's Centenary* (46 canvases, 30 water-colours, 20 drawings), at Wildenstein, London.

Exhibition *Le Centenaire du Peintre indépendant Paul Cézanne* (24 canvases, 38 water-colours and drawings), at the Société des Artistes Independants, Paris.

November to December: Exhibition *Cézanne's Centenary*, at Mary Harriman, London.

Exhibition *Centenaire de Paul Cézanne* (42 canvases, 17 water-colours, 20 drawings, autographs, souvenirs, photographs), at the Lyons Museum.

Cézanne exhibition at the Wildenstein Gallery, New York.

The French Post Office issued a stamp bearing Cézanne's head. In Aix, Marcel Provence, to mark the centenary, asked Cézanne's old cabman to drive his cab out along the Tholonet Road once more.

Death of Ambroise Vollard, who left a thousand million francs.

1940 February: Exhibition *Dessins de Cézanne*, at the Galerie Henriette, Paris.

April: Exhibition *Water-Colours by Cézanne*, at the Bignou Gallery, London.

1941 *Death of Émile Bernard.*

1942 December: At the Georges Viau sale, *La Vallée de l'Arc et la Montagne Sainte-Victoire* sold for five million francs.

1943 *Death of Maurice Denis.*

1944 *Death of K. X. Roussel.*

1947 January to February: Exhibition *L'Influence de Cézanne*, 1908–1911, at the Galerie de France, Paris.

February to March: Cézanne exhibition at the Cincinnati Museum of Art.

April: Cézanne exhibition (88 pictures) at the Wildenstein Gallery, New York.

Gift by an anonymous donor of a Cézanne self-portrait to the Louvre.

1951 Gift by Paul Gachet to the National Museums of France; it included three of Cézanne's canvases: *Une Moderne Olympia*, *Maison du Docteur Gachet à Auvers-sur-Oise*, *Petit Delft et fleurs*, and also numerous souvenirs of Cézanne.

1952 February to March: Cézanne exhibition (127 works), at the Institute of Art, Chicago.

April to May: The same exhibition in the Metropolitan Museum, New York.

May: At the Cognac sale, a Cézanne landscape sold for twenty million francs and a still life for thirty-three million francs.

1953 July to September: Cézanne exhibition (24 paintings, 26 water-colours and drawings), at Aix-en-Provence, Nice and Grenoble.

June to September: Exhibition *Monticelli et Le Baroque provençal* (23 Cézannes), at the Orangerie, Paris.

1954 July: The United States Embassy officially handed over to the Académie d'Aix the Pavillon des Lauves (Cézanne's Studio), which had been purchased by American subscriptions.

Summer: Exhibition *Hommage à Cézanne*, at the Orangerie, Paris.

August, at the Edinburgh Festival, and September to October at the Tate Gallery, London, Cézanne exhibition (65 canvases).

A Société Paul Cézanne founded in Paris.

Gift to the National Museums by Paul Gachet comprising four Cézanne canvases: *Bouquet de Dahlias jaunes*, *Carrefour de la rue Remy*, *Les Accessoires de Cézanne*, *Pommes Vertes*.

1955 July: A few of Cézanne's surviving friends met at the Pavillon des Lauves.

1956 Fiftieth anniversary of Cézanne's death.

1958 October: Cézanne's *Garçon au Gilet Rouge* was sold at Sotheby's, London, for £220,000. Until the sale on 24 June, 1959, of Ruben's *Adoration of the Magi*, the price realised by this picture was the highest ever recorded for a picture at an auction. In the same sale Cézanne's *Nature Morte: Les Grosses Pommes* sold for £90,000.

During this auction season, Cézanne's *Portrait de l'artiste par lui-même* sold for £32,000 and a *Portrait de Madame Cézanne* for £40,000.

1959 November: *Paysan en Blouse Bleue* by Cézanne, sold at Sotheby's, London, for £145,000.

BIBLIOGRAPHY

I

There are slightly more than two hundred of Cézanne's letters in existence, most of which have been collected in volume form by John Rewald (Paul Cézanne, *Correspondance*, Grasset, Paris, 1937. English Trans. Cassirer, Oxford, 1941; and *Cézanne, Geffroy et Gasquet*. Quatre Chemins-Editart, Paris, 1959). Further known letters consist of the following: one published by Jean Royère in an article on Louis Leydet, which appeared in *L'Amour de l'Art*, November, 1925; two to Octave Maus published by Lionello Venturi in *Les Archives de l'Impressionnisme* (Durand-Ruel, Paris–New York, 1939); and one to Achille Emperaire published by Victor Nicollas in *Achille Emperaire* (Aix-en-Provence, 1953).

There are also numerous relevant letters written either to Cézanne himself or to his friends and acquaintances. They form a valuable source of information, particularly the following: Zola's letters, collected in *Correspondance: Lettres de Jeunesse* (Charpentier, Paris, 1907) and *Correspondance: Les Lettres et les Arts* (Charpentier, Paris, 1908); letters to Zola from Monet, Pissarro, Solari, etc., in the manuscript department of the Bibliothèque Nationale in Paris (Catalogue Nos. 24150 to 24524 of recent French acquisitions); the correspondence of Camille Pissarro: *Lettres à son fils Lucien* (Albin Michel, Paris, 1950); the letters from Marion to Morstatt, published by John Rewald (*L'Amour de l'Art*, May 1938); letters from Renoir to Durand-Ruel published by Lionello Venturi in *Les Archives de l'Impressionnisme*, etc.

II

There is also a certain amount of contemporary evidence.

Émile Zola described his youth and that of his friends, Cézanne and

Baille, in *La Confession de Claude*, *Nouveaux Contes à Ninon*, *Documents littéraires* (the chapter entitled: 'Alfred de Musset'), *Nos Auteurs dramatiques* (the chapter entitled: 'Victor Hugo'); and his expeditions with Cézanne in the neighbourhood of Paris in *Aux Champs* (the chapter entitled: 'Le Bois'), which together with other pieces composes *Le Capitaine Burle*.

There are also useful sources of information – though they should be treated with a certain reserve – in Zola's works of fiction; and not only in *L'Oeuvre*. People, events and landscapes Cézanne knew appear, in varying degrees of disguise, in many other works. In *La Conquête de Plassans* Louis Auguste appears under the name of François Mouret; Solari, as Silvère, in *La Fortune des Rougon;* Claude Lantier, of *L'Oeuvre*, appears for the first time in *Le Ventre de Paris;* Gabrielle Meley inspired, though to an extent difficult to determine, *Madeleine Férat;* the holidays at Bennecourt form the background to the story *Une Farce ou Bohèmes en villégiature*, published in 1887–1888 in the *Anthologie contemporaine des Écrivains français et belges* (this story, which was not published in any collected edition during Zola's lifetime, appears in the *Oeuvres complètes); * Le Tholonet is described in *La Faute de l'abbé Mouret;* l'Estaque in *Nais Micoulin*, and so on.

From this point of view, Zola's working notes are of great value; they are to be found in the manuscript department of the Bibliothèque Nationale in Paris (Catalogue Nos. 10265 to 10355 of recent French acquisitions). Some have been published in the fifty volume edition of Zola's *Oeuvres complètes* (François Bernouard, Paris, 1927–1938), with notes and commentaries by Maurice Le Blond.

Other eye-witness accounts may be found in the following:

Alexis (Paul): *Émile Zola, Notes d'un Ami* (Charpentier, Paris, 1882).

Bernard (Émile): *Paul Cézanne* (in *L'Occident*, July 1904). *Julien Tanguy dit le 'Père Tanguy'* in *Mercure de France*, 16 December, 1908). *Souvenirs sur Paul Cézanne et Lettres* (Société des Trente, Paris, 1912). *Une Conversation avec Cézanne* (in *Mercure de France*, 1 June, 1921). *Souvenirs sur Paul Cézanne* (Michel, Paris, 1925). *Lettres inédites du peintre Émile Bernard à sa femme à propos de la mort de son ami Paul Cézanne* (in *Art-Documents*, June 1953). *Une Lettre inédite du peintre Émile Bernard à sa mère à propos de sa première visite à Paul Cézanne* (dans *Art-Documents*, November 1954). *L'Aventure de ma Vie* (unpublished MS.). *La Vérité sur Cézanne* (unpublished MS.). *Une Opinion de Cézanne* (unpublished MS.).

BERNARD (Mme Émile): *Souvenirs sur mon séjour à Aix-en-Provence auprès de Paul Cézanne en 1904 avec Émile Bernard* (unpublished MS.).

BERNHEIM DE VILLERS (Gaston): *Little Tales of Great Artists* (Quatre Chemins-Editart, Paris, E. Weyhe, New York, 1949).

BORÉLY (Jules): *Cézanne à Aix* (in *L'Art Vivant*, 1 July, 1926).

CAMOIN (Charles): *Souvenirs sur Paul Cézanne* (in *L'Amour de l'Art*, January 1921).

DENIS (Maurice): *Cézanne* (in *L'Occident*, September 1907), repeated in *Théories* (Bibliothèque de l'Occident, Paris, 1912). *L'Influence de Cézanne* (in *L'Amour de l'Art*, December 1920), repeated in *Nouvelles Théories* (Rouart et Waterlin, Paris, 1922). *Le Dessin de Cézanne* (in *L'Amour de l'Art*, February 1924). Preface to the catalogue of the exhibition *Centenaire du Peintre indépendant Paul Cézanne* (Société des artistes indépendants, Paris 17 March–10 April, 1939). *L'Aventure posthume de Cézanne* (in *Prométhée*, July 1939).

DUNOYER DE SEGONZAC (A.): *Du Musée de l'Acropole au Musée Dupuytren* (in *Le Figaro littéraire*, 2 April, 1955).

GASQUET (Joachim): *Cézanne* (Bernheim-Jeune, Paris, 1921). *Cézanne: What he said to me* (London, 1931).

GASQUET (Marie): *Biographie de Joachim Gasquet*, in JOACHIM GASQUET: *Des Chants, de l'Amour et des Hymnes* (Flammarion, Paris, 1928).

GEFFROY (Gustave): *Claude Monet, sa Vie, son Oeuvre* (Crès, Paris, 1924).

JALOUX (Édmond): *Fumées dans la Campagne* (La Renaissance du Livre, Paris, 1918). *Souvenirs sur Paul Cézanne* (in *L'Amour de l'Art*, December 1920). *Cézanne* (in *Marianne*, 22 February, 1939). *Les Saisons littéraires*, 1896–1903 (Librairie de l'Université, Fribourg, 1942).

Jourdain (Francis): *A propos d'un peintre difficile: Cézanne* (in *Arts de France*, 1946, No. 5). *Cézanne* (Braun et Cie, Paris, 1948). *Cézanne* (Braun et Cie, Paris, 1950). *Sans remords ni rancune* (Corrêa, Paris, 1953).

Larguier (Léo): *Le Dimanche avec Paul Cézanne* (L'Édition, Paris, 1925). *Én Compagnie des vieux peintres* (Albin Michel, Paris, 1927). *Cézanne ou le Drame de la Peinture* (Denoël et Steele, Paris, 1936). *Cézanne ou la Lutte avec l'Ange de la Peinture* (Julliard, Paris, 1947).

Osthaus (Karl-Ernst): *Dernière Visite à Cézanne* (in *Marianne*, 22 February, 1939).

Rivière (Georges): *Renoir et ses Amis* (Floury, Paris, 1921). *Le Maître Paul Cézanne* (Floury, Paris, 1923). *Cézanne, le Peintre solitaire* (Floury, Paris, 1933).

Rivière (R.-P.) et Schnerb (J.-F.): *L'Atelier de Cézanne* (in *La Grande Revue*, 25 December, 1907).

Royère (Jean): *Sur Paul Cézanne* (in *La Phalange*, 15 November, 1906). *Louis Leydet* (in *L'Amour de l'Art*, November, 1925). *Un Aixois, Joachim Gasquet* (*Souvenirs d'Enfance*) (in *Le Mémorial d'Aix*, 15 December, 1929). *Frontons* (Éditions Seheur, Paris, 1932).

Souchon (Paul): *Emmanuel Signoret* (La Couronne littéraire, Paris, 1950).

Vives-Apy (Ch.): *Le Peintre aixois Cézanne* (in *Le Mémorial d'Aix*, 16 February, 1911).

Vollard (Ambroise): *Cézanne* (Vollard, Paris, 1914). *Quelques Souvenirs* (Préface au catalogue de l'exposition Cézanne à la galerie Pigalle, Paris, 1929). *Souvenirs d'un Marchand de Tableaux* (Albin Michel, Paris, 1937). *En écoutant Cézanne, Degas, Renoir* (Grasset, Paris, 1938). *Paul Cézanne, his life and art* (London, 1924).

Further sources – mainly critical articles that appeared during Cézanne's lifetime – have also been drawn upon in the course of this book. The more important have been quoted in the text together with the appropriate references.

III

Cézanne's work has been catalogued by Lionello Venturi in his essential *Cézanne, son Art, son Oeuvre* (Rosenberg, Paris, 1936). It contains 1,619 items, of which over 800 are paintings (Vol. I: text; Vol. II: plates). This work is also provided with a comprehensive bibliography (containing 561 items), which is completed for the years 1936–1947 by Bernard Dorival's book, *Cézanne* (Tisné, Paris, 1948), comprising 220 further references.

In addition to the above, I am under obligations to many of the following works:

AGNEL (G. Arnaud d') and ISNARD (E.): *Monticelli, sa vie et son Oeuvre* (Éditions Occitania, Paris, 1926).

BADT (Kurt): *Die Kunst Cézannes* (Prestel Verlag, Munich, 1956).

BARR (Alfred): *Cézanne d'après les Lettres de Marion à Morstatt, 1865–1868* (in *Gazette des Beaux-Arts*, January, 1937).

BAZIN (Germain): *Cézanne et la Montagne Sainte-Victoire* (in *L'Amour de l'Art*, December 1938). *Monticelli et le Baroque provençal* (Édition de Musées nationaux, Paris, 1953).

BÉRHAUT (Marie): *La Vie et l'Oeuvre de Caillebotte*, catalogue of the Caillebotte exhibition (Galerie Wildenstein, Paris, 1951).

BERNEX (Jules): *Zola, Cézanne, Solari* (in *Les Cahiers d'Aix-en-Provence*, Autumn, 1923).

BERTRAM (Anthony): *Paul Cézanne*, 1839–1906 (Plates with an introduction by A. Bertram: Studio, London, 1929).

BEUCKEN (Jean de): *Un Portrait de Cézanne* (Gallimard, Paris, 1955).

BLÉMONT (Émile): Introduction to VALABRÈGUE'S: *L'Amour des Bois et des Champs* (Lemerre, Paris, 1902).

BOUCHOT-SAUPIQUE (Jacqueline): *Un Carnet de Croquis de Cézanne* (in *La Revue des Arts*, December 1951).

BOYÉ (Maurice-Pierre): *Cézanne et Antony Valabrègue* (in *Beaux-Arts*, 28 August, 1936).

BURGER (Fritz): *Cézanne und Hodler* (Munich, 1913).

CASSOU (Jean): *Cézanne, Les Baigneuses* (Éditions des Quatre-Chemins, Paris, 1947).

CATTAUI (Georges): *Le Centenaire de Cézanne. Pèlerinage à Aix-en-Provence* (in *Beaux-Arts*, 12 August, 1938).

Cézanne. Sketch Book, owned by the Art Institute of Chicago. Facsimile. (Curt Valentin, New York, 1951).

CHAPPUIS (Adrien): *Dessins de Paul Cézanne* (Éditions des Chroniques du Jour, Paris, 1938).

CHARENSOL: *Aix et Cézanne* (in *L'Art vivant*, 1 December, 1925).

COGNIAT (Raymond): *Cézanne* (Tisné, Paris, 1939).

COMBE (Jacques): *L'Influence de Cézanne* (in *La Renaissance*, May-June 1936).

COOPER (Douglas): *Au Jas de Bouffan* (in *L'Œil*, 15 February, 1955).

COQUIOT (Gustave): *Paul Cézanne* (Ollendorf, Paris, 1919). *Les Indépendants* (Ollendorf, Paris, 1921).

COURTHION (Pierre): *Rencontre de Charles Camoin* (in *Art-Documents*, July 1953).

DEFFOUX (Léon) et ZAVIE (Émile): *Le Groupe de Médan* (Payot, Paris, 1920).

DIMIER (Louis): *Sur l'Époque véritable du mot d'impressionnisme* (in *Bulletin de la Société de l'Histoire de l'Art français*, 1927).

DOITEAU (Docteur Victor): *La Curieuse Figure du docteur Gachet* (in *Æsculape*, August 1923-January 1924).

DORIVAL (Bernard): *Les Étapes de la Peinture française contemporaine*, Vol. I (Gallimard, Paris, 1943). *Cézanne* (Tisné, Paris, 1948 and House of Beric, London, 1949). *Cézanne* (Hazan, Paris, 1952).

DUBUISSON (A.): *Les Échos du Bois sacré* (Les Presses universitaires, Paris, 1924).

DURET (Théodore): *Monsieur Chocquet* (Preface to the catalogue of the Chocquet sale, Paris, 1899). *Histoire des Peintres impressionnistes* (Floury, Paris, 1906; English edit. 1910).

DURET (Théodore), WERTH (Léon), JOURDAIN (Frantz), MIRBEAU (Octave): *Cézanne* (Bernheim-Jeune, Paris, 1914).

ELDER (Marc): *À Giverny, chez Claude Monet* (Bernheim-Jeune, Paris, 1924).

FARON (Jean): *L'Âne de Cézanne* (in *Le Petit Var*, 2 March, 1938).

FAURE (Élie): *Les Constructeurs* (Crès, Paris, 1921). *Cézanne* (Braun, Paris, 1936).

FERNAND-DEMEURE: *Martyre et Béatification de saint Paul Cézanne* (in *La Grande Revue*, January 1939).

FLORISOONE (Michel): *Van Gogh et les Peintres d'Auvers chez le docteur Gachet* (special number of *L'Amour de l'Art*, Paris, 1952).

FRANCASTREL (Pierre): *L'Impressionnisme* (Les Belles-Lettres, Paris, 1937).

FRY (Roger): *Le Développement de Cézanne* (in *L'Amour de l'Art*, December 1926). *Cézanne: a study of his development* (Hogarth Press, London, 1927 and Macmillan, New York, 1952) (2nd Edition, 1952).

GACHET (Paul): *Cézanne à Auvers. Cézanne graveur* (Les Beaux-Arts, Paris, 1952).

GAUTHIER (Maximilien): *Le Comte Armand Doria* (in *L'Information artistique*, April 1955).

GEORGE (Waldemar): *Aquarelles de Cézanne* (Éditions des Quatre-Chemins, Paris, 1926).

GOWING (Lawrence): Preface to the Cézanne Exhibition in the Tate Gallery, London, 1954.

GUERRY (Liliane): *Cézanne et l'Expression de l'Espace* (Flammarion, Paris, 1950).

HUYGHE (René): *Cézanne* (Éditions d'Histoire et d'Art, Paris, 1936). *Paul Cézanne, un caractère et une vie* (in *Le Jardin des Arts*, November 1954).

BUYGHE (René) and REWALD (John): *Cézanne* (special number of *L'Amour de l'Art*, May 1936).

IMBOURG (Pierre): *Cézanne et ses Logis à Paris* (in *Beaux-Arts*, 20 January, 1939).

Isidore Baille (in *Le Mémorial d'Aix*, 5 October, 1924).

JAMOT (Paul): *Cézanne* (in *La Renaissance*, May-June 1936).

JEWELL (Edward Alden): *Cézanne* (The Hyperion Press, New York, 1944).

JOËTS (Jules): *Les Impressionnistes et Chocquet* (in *L'Amour de l'Art*, April 1935).

JOHNSON (Erle Loran): *Cézanne's Country* (in *The Arts*, New York, April 1930). *Cézanne's Composition* (University of California Press, Berkeley and Los Angeles, 1946).

JOURDAIN (Frantz): *Le Salon d'Automne* (Les Arts et le Livre, Paris, 1926). See DURET.

JOURDAIN, VAYSSIÈRE and GASTINE: *Notice sur la Vie et les Travaux de A.-F. Marion* (in *Annales de la Faculté des Sciences de Marseille*, Vol. XI, No. 1).

JUIN (Hubert): *Sur les pas de Paul Cézanne* (Librairie de l'Université, Aix-en-Provence, 1953).

KLINGSOR (Tristan-L.): *Cézanne* (Rieder, Paris, 1928). Engl. trans. by J. B. Manson (Bodley Head, London, 1925).

LANOUX (Armand): *Bonjour, monsieur Zola* (Amiot-Dumont, Paris, 1954).

LE BLOND-ZOLA (Denise): *Zola et Cézanne, d'après une Correspondance retrouvée* (in *Mercure de France*, January 1931). *Émile Zola raconté par sa fille* (Fasquelle, Paris, 1931). *Paul Alexis, Ami des Peintres, Bohème et Critique d'Art* (in *Mercure de France*, 1 March, 1939).

LE GOAZIOU (Alain): *Le 'Père Tanguy,' compagnon de lutte des grands peintres du début du siècle* (Floury, Paris, 1951).

LEYMARIE (Jean): *L'Impressionnisme* (2 vols., Skira, Geneva, 1955).

LOEB (Pierre): *Voyages à travers la Peinture* (Bordas, Paris, 1945).

LORAN (Erle): see JOHNSON (Erle Loran).

MACK (Gerstle): *Paul Cézanne* (Cape, London, 1935).

MAGLIONE (André): *Monticelli intime* (Barlatier, Marseille, 1903).

MAUPASSANT (Guy de): *Émile Zola* (A. Quantin, Paris, 1883).

MAUS (Madeleine-Octave): *Trente années de luttes pour l'Art* (1884–1914) L'Oiseau bleu, Bruxelles, 1926).

MEIER-GRAEFE (Julius): *Paul Cézanne* (Benn, London, 1927). *Cézanne und sein kreis* (Piper Verlag, Munich, 1918).

MIRBEAU (Octave): *Le Père Tanguy* (in *L'Écho de Paris*, 13 February, 1894). See DURET.

NÉGIS (André): *Adolphe Monticelli, châtelain des Nuées* (Grasset, Paris, 1929).

NICOLLAS (Victor): *Achille Emperaire* (Aix-en-Provence, 1953).

NICHOLSON (Benedict): *Cézanne: Paintings* (Drummond, London, 1946).

NOVOTNY (Fritz): *Cézanne* (Éditions du Phaidon, Paris, 1937 and Allen and Unwin, London, 1937).

PIA (Pascal): *Ambroise Vollard, marchand et éditeur* (in *L'Œil*, 15 March, 1955).

PROVENCE (Marcel): *Cézanne collégien* (in *Mercure de France*, 1 February and 1 August, 1925). *Cézanne et ses Amis. Numa Coste* (in *Mercure de France*, 1 April, 1926). *L'Année cézannienne* 1933 (Éditions du Feu, Aix-en-Provence, 1936). *Le Cours Mirabeau, trois siècles d'histoire*, 1651-1951 (Éditions du Bastidon, Aix-en-Provence, 1953).

RAIMBAULT (Maurice): *Une Lettre de Cézanne à Joseph Huot* (in *Provincia, Revue de la Société de Statistique, d'Histoire et d'Archéologie de Marseille et de la Provence*, 1937).

RAYNAL (Maurice): *Cézanne* (Éditions de Cluny, Paris, 1936). *Cézanne* (Skira, Geneva, 1939). *Cézanne* (Skira, Geneva, 1954, and Zwemmer, London, 1954).

REBATET (Lucien): *Le Coeur et l'Esprit de Cézanne* (in *La Revue universelle*, 15 June, 1936).

REWALD (John): *Cézanne au Louvre* (in *L'Amour de l'Art*, October, 1935). *Cézanne et Zola* (Sedrowski, Paris, 1936). *Une Copie par Cézanne d'après le Greco* (in *Gazette des Beaux-Arts*, February 1936). *Cézanne et son oeuvre* (in *L'Art sacré*, special number on Cézanne, 1936). *À propos du Catalogue raisonné de l'oeuvre de Paul Cézanne et de la chronologie de cette oeuvre* (in *La Renaissance*, March-April 1937). *Achille Emperaire, ami de Paul Cézanne* (in *L'Amour de l'Art*, May

1938). *Paul Cézanne: New Documents for the Years* 1870-1871 (in *The Burlington Magazine*, April 1939). *Cézanne, sa vie, son oeuvre, son amitié pour Zola* (Albin Michel, Paris, 1939 and London, 1950). *Cézanne: Letters.* Edited by J. Rewald, Transl. by M. Kay (Cassirer, London, 1941). *History of Impressionism* (New York, 1946). *Paul Cézanne: carnets de dessins, Preface et catalogue raisonné* (Quatre-Chemins-Editart, Paris, 1951). *Un Article inédit sur Paul Cézanne en* 1870 (in *Arts*, 21 July, 1954). *Cézanne, Geffroy et Gasquet* (Quatre-Chemins-Editart, Paris, 1959).

REWALD (John) and HUYGHE (René): see HUYGHE.

REWALD (John) and MARSCHUTZ (Léo): *Cézanne au Château Noir* (in *L'Amour de l'Art*, January 1935). *Cézanne et la Provence* (special number of *Le Point*, August 1936).

REY (Robert): *La Peinture française à la fin due XIXe siècle. La renaissance du sentiment classique* (Les Beaux-Arts, Éditions d'Études et de Documents, Paris, 1931).

RILKE (Rainer-Maria): *Lettres sur Cézanne* (Corrêa, Paris, 1944).

ROGER-MARX (Claude): *Le Paysage français de Corot à nos jours* (Éditions d'Histoire et d'Art, Paris, 1952).

ROGER-MILÈS (L.): *La Collection Chocquet* (Preface to the catalogue of the Chocquet sale, Paris, 1899).

SALMON (André): *Cézanne* (Stock, Paris, 1923).

SAN LAZZARO (G. di): *Paul Cézanne* (Éditions des Chroniques du Jour, Paris, 1936).

SCHMIDT (Georg): *Aquarelles de Paul Cézanne* (Éditions Holbein, Basle, 1952 and Macmillan, London and New York, 1954).

SHAPIRO (Meyer): *Paul Cézanne*, 1839-1906 (Thames & Hudson, London, 1954).

SILVESTRE (Armand): *Au Pays des Souvenirs* (A la Librairie illustrée, Paris, 1892).

STERLING (Charles): *Cézanne et les Maîtres d'autrefois* (in *La Renaissance*, May-June 1936).

TABARANT (A.): *Le Peintre Caillebotte et sa Collection* (in *Le Bulletin de la Vie Artistique*, 1 August, 1921). *Quelques Propos sur Cézanne* (in *Le Bulletin de la Vie Artistique*, 1 March, 1924). *Manet et ses Œuvres* (Gallimard, Paris, 1947).

TOLNAY (Charles de): *Cézanne et la Peinture en Europe* (in *La Renaissance*, May-June, 1936).

TOULOUSE (Docteur Édouard): *Émile Zola* (Société des Éditions scientifiques, Paris, 1896).

TOURETTE (Jean): *J'ai découvert des esquisses inconnues de Cézanne* (in *Les Lettres françaises*, 28 August, 1952).

VAUDOYER (Jean-Louis): *Beautés de la Provence* (Grasset, Paris, 1926). *Les Peintres provençaux de Nicolas Froment à Paul Cézanne* (La Jeune Parque, Paris, 1947).

VAUXCELLES (Louis): *Ambroise Vollard, curieux homme* (in *Beaux-Arts*, 28 July, 1939).

VENTURI (Lionello): *Sur les dernières années de Cézanne* (in *Minotaure*, 1936). *Les Archives de l'Impressionnisme* (Durand-Ruel, Paris-New York, 1939). *Paul Cézanne: Water-colours* (Cassirer, London, 1943). *De Manet à Lautrec* (Albin Michel, Paris, 1953).

VÉRANE (Léon): *Humilis, Poète errant* (Grasset, Paris, 1929).

VERGNET-RUIZ (J.): *Cézanne et l'Impressionnisme* (in *La Renaissance*, May-June, 1936).

WERTH (Léon): see DURET.

INDEX

Académie Colarossi, 179
  des Beaux-Arts, 50, 142
  Suisse, 68–72, 74, 81, 83, 87, 89, 94, 95, 240, 248, 277
  Julian, 238
Aguiard, Dr, 250
Aix-en-Provence, 19, 20, 22–24, 30–32, 35, 37–40, 42–45, 47–49, 51–53, 56, 59, 63, 64, 67, 69, 73, 76, 78, 81, 88, 91, 97, 99, 101, 103, 108, 110, 111, 119, 122, 123, 125, 128, 132, 133, 140, 142, 152, 160, 161, 163, 169, 180, 182, 184, 189, 197, 198, 203, 220, 226, 236, 237, 239, 249, 257, 262, 263, 265, 268, 275, 288, 290, 295, 296, 299
Alexandre, Arsène, 261
Alexis, Paul, 110, 119, 123, 126, 128, 134, 168, 189, 198, 199, 220, 235, 237, 293
Apollinaire, Guillaume, 160
Arc, river, 37, 40, 43, 124, 220, 228, 314
Aubert, Dominique, 97
  Elizabeth. *See* Cézanne, Madame
Austria, 35
Auvers-sur-Oise, 144, 145, 146, 147, 173, 196, 197, 302

Bail, Louis Le, 284–286
Baille, Baptistin, 36, 38–40, 42, 46, 47, 49–51, 54–56, 61, 62–65, 71, 73–76, 88, 90, 98, 108, 110, 112, 130, 132, 133, 158, 163, 220, 229, 265
  Isidore, 42, 55, 189, 198, 203
Ballu, Roger, 175
Balzac, 279
Barbouillotte, 174
Bargès Bank, 23
Barnes Foundation, 256
Barrès, 139
'Batignolles Group', 114
Baudelaire, 97, 211, 230
Bazille, Frederic, 86, 87, 89, 96, 104, 114, 117, 122, 128, 139
Beauté, La, 211
Béliard, 143
Belleville, 247–249
Bénédite, Léonce, 242
Bennecourt-sur-Seine, 108, 110, 220
Berlin National Gallery, 281
Bernard, Émile, 225, 232, 234, 239, 240, 241, 300–305, 307, 308, 315
Berne, 236
Bernhardt, Sarah, 191
Bernheim, Gaston, 307
  Jeune, 255, 294
Besançon, 235
Beucken, Jean de, 190, 211
Bibliothèque Nationale, 185
Bicêtre, 292
Bien Public, Le, 171
Bismarck, 129
Blanche, Dr. 243
Bonaparte, Pierre, 129
Bonnard, 290
Bonnet, 163
Bordeaux, 133, 139
Bouguereau, 244, 264
Bourges, Élémir, 152
Breeskin, Adelyn D., 245
Brémond, Madame, 287, 296, 972, 303, 316, 318
Bres, Louis, 205
Brest, 149
Briançon, 20, 21
Brussels, 289
  Art Society, 234
Busnach, 194

Cabanel, 244, 264
Cabaner, 168, 169, 177, 191, 256
Cabassol, 23, 37, 130
Caillebotte, Gustave, 162–164, 172–173, 175, 240, 242, 256, 258, 275
Martial, 242, 275
Camoin, Charles, 291, 292, 295, 315
Camondo, Isaac de, 285
Cassatt, Mary, 245
Castagnary, 123
Céard, 189, 191
Centennale de l'Art Français, 289
Certains, 232
Cézanne and Cabassol Bank, 23, 67
Cézanne, Geffroy et Gasquet, 265
Cézanne, Louis Auguste, 20–24, 28–31, 44, 52, 53, 55, 56, 58, 59, 61, 65, 67, 73, 74, 75, 91, 113, 125, 130, 132, 160, 169, 180–184, 186, 198, 212, 222, 227, 228, 276
Cézanne, Madame, 23, 56, 183, 184, 185, 237, 278. *See also* Aubert, Elizabeth
Marie, 23, 27–29, 41, 44, 66, 91, 92, 205, 212, 213, 216, 222, 223, 226, 228, 230, 235, 237, 250, 264, 280, 287, 293, 296, 316
Rose, 39, 59, 92, 112. *See also* Conil
village, 20
Cézanne, Paul, and acceptance by Luxembourg, 256; acknowledges his own worth, 296; always painting, 65; and apprenticeship to bank, 74; at Law School, 50; attracted by sculpture, 89; becomes more exacting, 190; becoming something of a legend, 179; begins going to Church, 230; and birth of son, 140; and boarding school, 31; and bohemian behaviour, 114–116; built own studio, 290; ceases to belong to his period as a painter, 316, 317; death of, 316, 317; and death of his mother, 278; and demands of a model, 283; and desire to render reality, 178; and difficulty in paying way, 152; discontented with his work, 73; and discovery of Paris, 67; and disease, 314; and early drawing, 28, 30; endeavours to resolve the fusion of light, 188; entirely absorbed in painting, 276; and examinations, 49; excited envy and hatred, 260; and exhibition at Aix, 263, 264; and experimenting with water colours, 120; fails examination, 83; falls in love, 90, 211; feels the heat, 305, 314; feels isolated, 207; has few illusions left, 227; and first exhibition, 157, 159; and first love, 47; gains in confidence, 290; goes to Paris, 65, 66; is happy and excited, 266; and hatred of being touched, 303; and his health, 231; and Impressionist Exhibition, 173, 174; is indifferent to money, 52; lives at Pontoise, 142; lives in indescribable disorder, 102; is looked on as an ill-bred boor, 115; and losing contact with world, 168; marries Hortense, 222; and moods, 71; and his Mother's love, 223; moves to new studio, 293; and music, 41; is never satisfied with his work, 146; is nervous, unhappy and disgusted, 216; is no longer ignored, 259; is now a sick man, 294; is object of mockery, 117; and one-man exhibition, 258, 259; and work, 132, 167, 250; paralysed with shyness, 191; plans to marry Hortense, 217; and poetry, 43, 44; and portrait painting, 111; and prestige, 110; receives call-up papers, 133; is rejected by Salon, 90, 103, 117, 122, 192, 200; remains alone and unappreciated, 234; requires moral support, 245; and school, 37-39; searching for serenity, 240; and sensitivity, 32; smarts under repeated failure, 203; and his son, 280; and success, 281; suffers from diabetes, 234; and support of revolt, 95; is sure of himself, 162; and temperament, 38; is utterly without pre-

tensions, 277; wept when he read *l'Oeuvre*, 220; and women, 51, 82, 126, 127; works with increased fervour, 296
Chaillan, Jean Baptiste Mathieu, 50, 51, 55, 61, 72, 81, 88, 108, 220
Champaigne, Philippe de, 231
Chantilly, 231
Chanzy, General, 133
Charpentier, 191, 194
Château Noir, 40, 290, 300, 302, 315
Chautard, 81, 82
Chocquet, Victor, 165, 166, 168, 170, 173–176, 181, 199, 200, 217, 221, 226, 231, 233, 235, 284
Chronique des Arts et de la Curiosité, 175
Cladel, Léon, 114
Claretie, Jules, 96
Claude Monet, sa Vie, son Oeuvre, 246
Clemenceau, Georges, 76, 245, 248, 279
Cloche, La, 141
Cochin, Baron Denys, 286
Colet, Louise, 19
Collège Bourbon, 31, 32, 38, 42, 48, 57, 69, 220
Confession de Claude, La, 94, 97, 98, 99, 101, 118
Conil, Maxime, 197, 222, 228, 233, 280
Rose, 197, 203, 206, 237. *See also* Cézanne, Rose
Paule, 303
Conquête de Plassans, La, 158, 163
Constant, Benjamin, 243, 244
Contes à Ninon, 93, 94, 98
Coquiot, Gustave, 220
Corpus Christi, festival of, 41
Correspondance, 185
Coste, Numa, 44, 45, 50, 51, 75, 82, 89, 109, 118, 264, 268, 309, 310
Courbet, 84, 86, 87, 117, 139, 142, 145, 166, 193
Courrier de France, 154, 174
Cours Mirabeau, Le, 263
Courtauld Collection, 263
Cravache, Le, 232
CrimeanWar, 39
Curée, La, 141, 151

d'Arbaud, José, 265, 276, 277
Daubigny, 103, 104, 116, 117, 123, 139, 143, 144, 145, 157, 167
Daudet, Alphonse, 191
Daumier, 144, 231
Décanis, Mademoiselle E., 297
Degas, 114, 145, 151, 153, 154, 155, 173, 193, 241, 256, 259, 291, 294
Delacroix, 81, 82, 84, 86, 87, 89, 95, 165, 166, 194, 226, 284
Denis, Maurice, 238, 239, 291, 294, 296, 314
Deonoinville, Georges, 260
Dictionnaire Vèron, 200
Diderot, 203
Doria, Count Armand, 158, 233, 283
Dorival, Bernand, 229
Drawing School at Aix, 44, 50, 65, 132, 161, 185, 281
Dreyfus Affair, 279, 296, 298
Drouot Hôtel, 177, 244
Durance, river, 28
Durand-Ruel, 139, 141, 150, 169, 173, 255, 285
Duranty, 114, 167, 168, 172, 179, 194
Duret, Théodore, 114, 128, 145, 146, 164, 241

Emperaire, Achille, 69, 83, 111, 140, 141, 185, 257, 258, 279, 280
École des Beaux-Arts, 68, 78, 82, 83, 85, 87, 103, 142, 161, 193, 234, 256
École Polytechnique, 73
Édouard, Maison, 148, 149
Edouard Manet, 217
Elder, Marc, 115
Emile Zola, Notes d'un Ami, 198
En écoutant Cézanne, Degas, Renoir, 233, 234

Fanny, 211–213
Fantin-Latour, 114, 128
Farce ou Bohèmes en Villégiature, Une, 109
Faute de l'Abbé Mouret, La, 163

Fédération Artistique Belge, 235
Ferrier, Gabriel, 243
Ferry, Jules, 191
Figaro, Le, 117, 164, 169, 174, 261, 268
Fiquet, Marie-Hortense, (later Paul's wife), 126, 127, 129, 130, 132, 139, 140, 142, 147, 152, 159, 160, 161, 177, 178, 179, 180, 182, 184, 186, 192, 205, 206, 208, 212, 213, 215–217, 223, 226, 228, 235–237, 257, 269, 280, 294, 318
Flaubert, 188
Fontainebleau, 190, 257, 275
Fontenay-aux-Roses, 83
Forain, 255, 279
Fortunes des Rougon, La, 125, 126, 131, 134, 151
Fribourg, 236
Friends of the Arts, 263, 264

Gachet, Dr Paul-Ferdinand, 144–148, 168, 196
Galerie Georges Petit, 241, 284
Gambetta, 191
Gardanne, 42, 216, 217, 222, 223
Garde, Marquise de la, 19
Garde Mobiles, 133, 134, 139
Nationale, 132
Gasquet, Henri, 30, 92, 264
Joachim, 31, 38, 102, 122, 206, 245, 247, 265, 266, 267, 268, 273, 275–279, 287, 288, 291, 295, 299
Marie, 276
Gauguin, Paul, 168, 179, 197, 223, 225, 238, 241, 244, 246, 302
Gautier, Théophile, 157
Gazette de Hôtel Drouot, 297
Gazette des Beaux-Arts, 307
Geffroy, Gustave, 233, 241, 242, 245, 246, 247, 248, 249, 250, 259, 269
Geneva, 236
Gennevilliers, 240
Gêrome, 243, 244, 275, 289
Gervex, 256
Gibert, Honore, 127, 161, 183, 281
Joseph, 44, 47, 49, 50, 55, 58, 59, 69, 75, 82, 92, 112, 124
Gide, André, 290
Girard, Marie, 265
Giverny, 245, 246
Giverny, chez Claude Monet, A, 115
Glais-Bizoin, 133
Gleyre, 86, 95
Goncourt, Edmond de, 131, 191
Granet Prize, 103
Graphic Works of Mary Cassatt, The, 245
Guerbois, Café, 114, 115, 123, 127, 128, 139, 167, 220
Guigou, Paul, 205
Guillaume, Antoine, 184, 231, 249
Guillaumin, Armand, 89, 143, 147, 154, 167, 173, 177, 191, 223, 230, 244
Guillemet, Alphonsine, 112
Antoine, 70, 83, 85, 88, 96, 104, 105, 111, 112, 114, 117, 139, 144, 153, 187, 188, 192, 194, 196, 199, 208, 220
Gyp, 243

Hachette, Louis, 88, 94
Halévy, Ludovic, 100
Hamm, Henri, 308
Hattenville, 226
Hennique, 189
Hermann-Paul, 307
Hetzel et Lacroix, 90
Histoire de l'Impressionisme, 150, 157
Histoire des Croisades, 34
Hommes d'Aujourd'hui, 239
Houssaye, Arsène, 119
Humilis, Poete errent, 292
Hout, Joseph, 45, 50, 70, 75, 185
Huyghe, René, 229
Huysmans, 154, 189, 255, 232

'Impressionist Exhibition, The', 173, 174, 175, 192, 232, 306
Impressionists, 164, 171, 172, 174, 177, 178, 179, 181, 182, 187, 192, 193, 196, 200, 219, 234, 240, 241, 248, 259, 289
Infernets Gorge, 40
Ingres, 82

'J'accuse', 279, 294
Jacquet, 259
Jaloux, Édmond, 255, 276, 295
Jas de Bouffan, Le, 24, 52, 53, 55, 61, 64, 65, 75, 92, 112, 119, 120, 123, 124, 133, 134, 169, 180, 184, 203, 204, 206, 208, 211, 216, 222, 228, 232, 236, 237, 249, 250, 266, 268, 269, 280, 286
Jobbé-Duval, 149
Jourdain, Francis, 307, 308
Journal, 241, 259
Journal des Artistes, 242, 260
Justine, 53, 54

L'Art Français, 262
L'Art International, 262
L'Art Moderne, 154, 225
L'Artist, 119, 155
L'Assommoir, 171, 178, 190, 193, 194
L'Aurore, 279
L'Echo des Bouches-du-Rhône, 98, 110
L'Estaque, 92, 129, 130–134, 139, 170, 171, 178, 180, 183, 185, 198, 199, 206, 207, 208, 269, 303
L'Europe, 117
L'Événement, 100, 105, 107, 110, 268
L'Événement Illustré, 123
L'Impressionists, 174, 175, 297
L'Intransigeant, 299
L'Occident, 304
L'Oeuvre 102, 119, 121, 124, 125, 126, 158, 218–222, 226, 230, 232, 261, 268, 297
L'Oeuvre d'Art devant la Critique, 109
L'Univers, 306
Lacroix, Père, 146
Larguier, Léo, 168, 291–295
Lathuile, Père, 114
Lausanne, 236
Le Tholonet, 39, 46, 75, 258, 268, 287, 296
Leboeuf, Marshal, 129
Leroy, Louis, 155, 157
Leseaux, Gaston, 243
Leydet, Victor, 130, 309
Libre Esthétique, 289, 290
Lille, 144
Linz, 35
'Little Paul', 184, 186, 204, 222, 231. *See also* Young Paul
London, 139, 142
Louveciennes, 142
Louvre, the, 55, 58, 61, 68, 69, 89, 103, 107, 139, 172, 191, 197, 231, 247, 260, 282, 298
Luxembourg, 58, 68, 172, 241, 242, 243, 256, 275
Lycée Saint-Louis, 48, 49, 54
Lyons, 94, 134, 249

Madeleine Férat, 124
Madeleine Férat and *L'Oeuvre*, 115
Magallon, Xavier de, 265, 276, 277, 278
Magasin pittoresque, 30, 45
Manet Édouard, 68, 69, 85, 86, 87, 95, 96, 103, 104, 107, 108, 114, 115, 118, 121–123, 126–128, 139, 145, 150, 153, 157, 206, 219, 232, 241, 243, 255, 256
Mans, 134
Marguery, 41, 57, 92, 98, 99, 204
Mariage d'Amour, Un, 118, 121
Mariage de Chiffon, 243
Marines, 286
Marion, Fortuné, 92, 93, 99, 101, 110, 111, 112, 113, 119, 120, 121, 123, 124, 195, 218, 293
Marne, river, 231
Marlotti, 275
Marseilles, 20, 27, 35, 37, 54, 56, 99, 113, 120, 121, 124, 130, 132, 133, 179, 180, 182, 184, 185, 205, 206, 207, 218, 291, 292
Marseillaise, La, 131, 132
Martin, Coupin and Cézanne, 22, 27
Marx, Roger, 289, 307
Massenet, 191
Maupassant, Guy de, 189
Maurras, Charles, 265
  Joseph, 265

Maus, Octave, 234
Médan, 90, 188, 189, 192, 194, 197, 198, 203, 213, 214, 215, 232, 237, 261, 297
Meissonier, Colonel, 139, 231, 244
Meley, Gabrielle Éleonore Alexandrine (later Madame Zola), 90, 95, 109, 115, 116, 118, 125, 128, 131, 132
Melun, 188, 190, 191, 196
Mémorial d'Aix, Le, 98, 309
Mendès, Catulle, 171
Mennecy, 275
Mercure de France, 308, 309
Mes Haines, 109
Messager de Provençe, Le, 118, 131
Metz, 131
Millet, 84, 241
Minartz, Tony, 308
Mirbeau, Octave, 191, 244, 245, 246, 294
Moïse, 300
Mon Salon, 100, 108, 109, 117
Monde Illustré, Le, 306
Monet, Claude, 69, 87, 89, 90, 95, 96, 104, 108, 112, 115, 117, 122, 128, 139, 141, 145, 148, 150, 151, 154, 155, 163, 164, 166, 173, 192, 207, 219, 234, 241, 242, 244, 245, 246, 247, 249, 250, 256, 259, 283, 285, 291, 292, 294, 298
Mont du Cengle, 217
Mont Regaignas, 21
Mont Sainte-Victoire, 40, 42, 75, 124, 183, 204, 217, 218, 228, 258
Moniteur, Le, 84, 243
Monod, Lucien-Hector, 308
Montbriant, 228, 233, 251
Montgeroult, 284
Monticelli, Adolphe, 205, 206, 207, 223, 291
Montifaud, Marc de, 155
Moreau, Gustave, 273
Morisot, Berthe, 154, 164, 173
Morstatt, Heinrich, 99, 101, 110, 111, 120, 121, 124
Mortier, Arnold, 118
Mounet-Sully, 191
Mystères de Marseilles, Les, 118, 120, 121, 124

Nabis, the, 238
Nadar, 153, 154
Nana, 191, 193, 194
Napoleon, 39
Natanson, Thadée, 261
Neuchâtel, 235
Nietsche, 289
Nieuwerkerke, Comte de, 104–106, 123, 142
Noir, Victor, 129
Normandy, 95
Nouveau, Germain, 292
Nouveaux Contes à Ninon, 163
Nouy, Lecomte du, 243

O'Squarr, 154
Oiseaux s'envolent et les Fleurs tombent, Les, 152
Oller y Cestero, Francisco, 78, 83, 94, 248, 249, 250, 259
Ollivier, Émile, 129
Osthaus, Karl-Ernst, 307

Page d'Amour, 178
Pajot, Georges, 54
Palais de l'Industrie, 104, 127, 187
Paris, 21, 22, 29, 34, 41, 44, 46, 48–50, 53–61, 64–66, 70–78, 81, 86, 89, 91, 98, 103, 110, 113, 116, 119–121, 124, 131, 133, 134, 139, 141, 144, 146, 148, 152, 157, 160, 162, 165, 170, 179, 191, 194, 196, 199, 220, 223, 228, 230, 237, 240, 248, 250, 257, 274, 287, 292, 306, 263
Pastiche, 82
Pavillon des Lauves, 293, 303
Pays des Arts, Les, 194
Pellerin, Auguste, 262
Pelloquet, Théodore, 107
Petit Journal, Le, 94
Petit Parisien, Le, 175, 306
Peyron, Jules, 217, 222
Piet, Fernand, 308

Pissarro, Camille, 69, 70, 83–90, 95, 96, 104, 105, 108, 112, 114, 117, 120, 122, 128, 139, 141, 143, 144, 145–151, 153–155, 161, 166, 170–173, 175, 177, 179, 187, 196, 197, 223–225, 234, 241, 243, 244, 248–250, 256, 257, 259, 262, 284, 289, 294, 298, 302
Plédran, 148
Pontier, Henri-Modeste, 281
Pontoise, 142, 144, 145, 159, 173, 177, 196, 197, 198, 284
Portrait de Cézanne, Un, 211
Poussin, 277
Presse, La, 96
Prouvaire, Jean, 155
Provence, La, 57
Provence, Marcel, 263
Prussia, 129

Quintinie, L. de la, 308
Quost, 260

Raimbault, Maurice, 51
Rappel, the, 155
Redon, Odilon, 290
Rembrandt, 30, 51
Renoir, Auguste, 86, 87, 89, 90, 95, 96, 104, 117, 122, 128, 139, 145, 153–155, 163–166, 173, 175, 177, 187, 191, 192, 199, 200, 207, 213, 232, 233, 242, 246, 256, 259, 269, 291, 294
République français, La, 306
des Lettres, La, 171
Revue blanche, La, 261
bleue, La, 306
Rewald, John, 150, 157, 265, 314
Rimbaud, 292
Rivière, Georges, 174, 175, 176, 236, 307
Rochefort, Henri, 191, 297, 299
Rodert-Fleury, Tony, 243
Rodin, 245, 246
Roquefavour, 42, 52
Rouart, Henri, 153
Rougon-Macqart, 139, 151, 158, 214, 222
Roujon, Henri, 242, 256, 294
Roussel, K. X., 290, 314
Roux, Marius, 42, 93, 97, 98, 99, 108, 118, 120, 128, 131, 132, 133
Royal Museum of Modern Art, 234
Roybets, 255
Royère, Jean, 265, 276, 282
Rubens, 30
Ryssel Van. *See* Gachet

Saint-Joseph's School, 29, 30, 31, 38
Marc, 258
Quentin, 134
Victor, Paul de, 96
Zacharie, 31
Saligny, 126
Salon, the, 84, 85, 89, 90, 95, 96, 101, 103, 106, 107, 116, 122, 123, 124, 127, 140, 141, 150, 153, 154, 169, 171, 179, 182, 185, 187, 192, 195, 196, 197, 199, 208, 221, 281
Salon d'Automne, 305, 306
de 1868, Le, 123
de Bougereau, 246
des Refuses, 85, 101, 104, 106, 117, 142, 289
Salons, 123
Salut Public, Le, 94
Saporta, Gaston de, 93
Saisons Litteraires, 295
Schnerb, J. F., 307
Schuffenecker, Émile, 225, 238
Seine, river, 71, 230, 231
Serusier, Paul, 238, 290
Seurat, 244, 256
Seymard, 53, 54
Siècle, Le, 131, 134, 174
Signac, Paul, 225, 237, 249
Signoret, Emmanuel, 265
Sisley, Alfred, 87, 89, 95, 104, 117, 122, 128, 141, 150, 154, 164, 173, 187, 234, 241, 246, 256, 283, 294
Société des Artists Indépendants, 289
Nationale des Beaux-Arts, 290

Solari, Philippe, 28–30, 42, 44, 50, 75, 92, 103, 104, 108, 122, 123, 128, 139, 140, 141, 151, 220, 257, 264, 280, 293, 295, 296, 309
Émile, 257, 258
Son Excellence Eugene Rougon, 171
Souchon, Paul 265
Sportsman, Le, 174
Stock, Monsieur, 127
Suisse, Père, 61, 68
Switzerland, 235
Symbolists, 241, 242

Tabarant, 206, 256
Talloires, 274
Tanguy, Julian, 148, 149, 166, 167, 168, 181, 188, 191, 223–226, 232, 238, 239, 240, 244, 259, 290, 292, 300
Tempelaere, 255
Temps, Le, 261, 262, 275
Thiébault, Sisson, 261, 275
Travail, Le, 76
Tribune, La, 133
Trocadero, 282
Truphème, Auguste, 44, 50, 61, 81
François, 44

Valbrègue, Antony, 88, 90, 92, 94, 97, 101, 103, 108, 110, 112, 113, 114, 118, 119, 130, 131, 132, 133, 161, 207, 293
Vallier, 316
Valloton, Félix, 308
Van Dyck, 51
Van Gogh, Théo, 234
Vincent, 223, 226, 241, 244, 304
Vauxcelles, Louis, 255
Ventre de Paris, Le, 102, 151, 199
Vérane, Léon, 292
Verlaine, 292
Vernet, Paul, 308
Vernon, 214
Verrières, woods of, 83
Versailles, 68
Vevey, 236
Vichy, 274
Vie Artistique, La, 233
Vignon, Victor, 143
Vigny, Alfred de, 300
Villard, Nina de, 168
Villemessant, Hippolyte de, 100, 101, 105, 107
Villennes, 214
Villevieille, Joseph, 45, 50, 55, 57, 61, 71, 72, 74, 81, 82, 83, 180, 181, 183, 207, 263, 278
Vollard, Ambroise, 224, 233, 234, 239, 240, 255–257, 258, 260, 262 269, 273–275, 280–284, 290, 294, 296
Voltaire, Le, 190, 192
Vuillard, Édouard, 238

Wolff Albert, 164, 169, 172

'Young Paul', 235, 237, 257, 269, 294, 310, 316, 318

Ziems, 255
Zola, Émile, 32–42, 44–65, 67, 68, 70–77, 81, 83, 85, 87–90, 94–118, 120–126, 130, 132–134, 139, 141, 145, 151, 158, 163, 164, 171, 173, 178–182, 186, 188, 191–193, 197, 198, 203, 206, 214, 215, 218, 220, 221, 229, 235, 238, 257, 261, 262, 264, 268, 279, 294, 297, 298, 309
François, 19, 33, 35